COLONIAL GENO

INDIGENOUS NORTH AMERICA

COLONIAL GENOCIDE IN

INDIGENOUS NORTH AMERICA

ANDREW WOOLFORD, JEFF BENVENUTO,

and ALEXANDER LABAN HINTON, *editors*

Foreword by Theodore Fontaine

DUKE UNIVERSITY PRESS | DURHAM AND LONDON

2014

Designed by Barbara E. Williams
Typeset in Garamond Premier Pro and DIN Engschrift 1451 by BW&A Books, Inc.

Cover art: Daphne Odjig, *Genocide No. 1*, 1971. Permission of Stan Somerville.

Library of Congress Cataloging-in-Publication Data
Colonial genocide in indigenous North America / Andrew Woolford, Jeff Benvenuto,
and Alexander Laban Hinton, editors ; foreword by Theodore Fontaine.
pages cm
Includes bibliographical references and index.
ISBN 978-0-8223-5763-6 (cloth : alk. paper)
ISBN 978-0-8223-5779-7 (pbk. : alk. paper)
1. Indians of North America—Colonization.
2. Genocide—North America—History.
3. Off-reservation boarding schools—History.
I. Woolford, Andrew John, 1971–
II. Benvenuto, Jeff, 1984–
III. Hinton, Alexander Laban.
E77.C69 2014
970.004'97—dc23
2014020685

Duke University Press gratefully acknowledges the support of the Social Sciences
and Humanities Research Council of Canada, which provided funds toward the
publication of this book.

CONTENTS

FOREWORD

Theodore Fontaine

"Why can't Aboriginal people just get over Indian residential schools? Why can't they just get on with their lives?" These are two of the most common questions asked by Canada's non-Aboriginal peoples when confronted with the consequences of Indian residential schools as experienced through seven generations of Indigenous Nations in Canada and the United States.

These questions arise from societal denial of five centuries of colonization. History books and governments consistently portray the intent of colonization as the "discovery" of new lands, the establishment of agricultural economies, and the harvesting of natural resources to sustain westward immigration in the building of this "New World." Canadians therefore think of the Indian residential school policy as merely an isolated era of necessity to assist Indian people to adjust to a "better" (European) way of life and not as part of ongoing colonization efforts to rid the "New World" of Indian Nations, persistent barriers to lands and resources.

However, the consequences experienced by Indian residential school survivors and their descendants are a complex tangle of political, social, cultural, economic, mental, physical, emotional, and spiritual harms. The compounding burdens take an ever-increasing toll on the health, well-being, and very survival of Indigenous people.

I had just turned seven when I was taken to the Fort Alexander Indian Residential School, and later to the Assiniboia Indian Residential School. My life was not my own for the next twelve years. Although the Fort Alexander school was situated less than two miles from my home, I lost my family, my *mishoom* (grandfather) and *kookum* (grandmother), and my community, and I was lost to them.

Children taken to Indian residential schools were removed from their families either by force or by threat. We were locked up in these institutions behind barbed-wire fences, some of us close enough to see our own homes or our family members walking by on the road. Others were removed hundreds of miles from their community, not knowing if they would ever see their family again. We didn't know why we were locked up in these institutions or if we would ever get out. Those who died or were gravely ill or injured simply disappeared from our ranks; we were never told what happened to them.

Most attention has been given to the physical and sexual abuses that were common in the schools. Students were assaulted and maimed, resulting in lifelong deformities and social dysfunctions that often led to widespread criminalization and incarceration. Through these years of abuse and turmoil, I was filled with anger and imagined that when I was older I would be free to seek revenge. I had visions of dying alone, without ever seeing my mom and dad or grandparents again.

It was not until much later, in my intense discomfort with being an Indian, that I understood that the government and its agents, the churches, had in fact been intent on killing me as an Indian person. Their aim was to destroy the Indigenous Nations by taking away the children, using the tools of racism, indoctrination, removal, and institutionalization. We would no longer exist as Indigenous People or as Nations.

Despite what has already been written and published about the experiences of these child victims, less is understood about the spiritual and emotional abuses that were endured. Most survivors will not speak about their experiences because of shame and traumatization. Post-traumatic stress disorder is common among survivors. Untold numbers did not survive the schools or the devastating aftermath of their experiences.

The children lost their identity, name, home, family relationships, and sense of belonging. We lost our understanding of who we were, where we came from, and where we were going. Many never found their way home again. Many died trying.

The worst thing that was done to us was psychological manipulation. It was pounded into us repeatedly that Indians are no good, evil, savages, with heathen languages, no intelligence, no culture, no caring families, and no reason for existence. We were left, helpless and hopeless, to despise ourselves and our own people, with only anger, resentment, and deep sorrow over our abandonment and losses.

No mention of genocide was used by Canada in its reluctant message of apology to Indian residential school survivors. In response to legal action initiated by survivors, the government of Canada, very careful to exclude the term or even the insinuation of genocide, was court-ordered to enter into the Residential Schools Settlement Agreement with survivors.

The apology in the House of Commons became a feather in the hat of the government, distinctive in its attention to ceremonial detail yet almost self-congratulatory for its own perceived success in the removal of First Nations influence and participation in the development of the country.

Canada's government was confident that the apology would appear to be guided by its goodwill, as with all Indian treaties and countless agreements and commitments, while equally confident that it would control any and all ramifications. Aboriginal acceptance would be managed with short-term financial investment and limited, time-controlled programming.

Thus the term *genocide* was not applied to the deliberate, Parliament-sanctioned action to "kill the Indian in the child," and the Indian residential schools policy was portrayed as a well-intentioned though misguided, brief event in history, while also viewed darkly as a victory in the rape of the lands and natural resources of Turtle Island (aka North America).

Canada meanwhile lost forever the rich resource of generations of its First Peoples. The ingenuity and creativity of young minds were extinguished, the extreme amount of potential and talent were never nurtured or allowed to flourish, and the character and integrity of an Indigenous society founded on prized values and principles were almost destroyed.

Some individuals say that the term *genocide* is appropriate only to convey the complete destruction of a race. Ironically, given that we Indigenous Nations have inconveniently survived by the threads of our own spirituality, resilience, and courage, these same individuals use our survival to deny the truths of our history, whether or not it is called genocide.

There is only now a small, growing acknowledgment in Canada that everyone in Canada has been, is, and will be affected by the legacy of the Indian residential schools policy. For those who think of this as "ancient history," the last Indian residential school in Canada closed its doors only in 1996. The documentation and analysis in *Colonial Genocide in Indigenous North America* is thought-provoking and compelling. It reaches to the heart, mind, and spirit. From the voices of these scholars comes a call to every reader to examine our own awareness, depth of caring, and the integrity with which we apply our own thought processes and our voices to the lives and relationships we build, influence, protect, and empower.

In the end we must each make our own informed assessment about *colonial genocide* as a descriptor of the history of Indigenous North America and, more important, as a context for the future we must build together.

For myself, while in Indian residential schools I never did think that I would be killed there. I knew that my life as I knew it had ended and that I would never again experience the joy and freedom of my early years, the freedom of laughter, love, and security. They say that time heals all wounds, but that isn't true. The wounds just become part of you: the fear and frustration, tears and anguish, and the overwhelming feeling of futility.

At this point in my life I am coming to terms and dealing with what

Canada did to me and my people. As children, we were victims, helpless, unable to help ourselves or to change anything. I have reclaimed my language and my culture, family, and community and am working toward a higher degree of reconciliation. I am proud now to be an Anishinaabe, of the Ojibway Nation, one of Canada's First People.

Kitchi miigwech neechis. Thank you my friends, for building a platform for truth, reconciliation, restoration. This book has the power to lead us forward in building bridges of respect, caring, and change in the relationships between Indigenous and non-Indigenous peoples.

COLONIAL GENOCIDE IN INDIGENOUS NORTH AMERICA

Jeff Benvenuto, Andrew Woolford,
and Alexander Laban Hinton

That word is "genocide." That word, in fact, is what Aboriginal
people, elders, and Survivors generally [use to] talk about the fact
that, for many generations, they and their ancestors were subject to
significant oppression at the hands of the government, and the hands
of the Churches, and at the hands of society. And that oppression has
resulted in significant loss for them. And valuing that loss is very dif-
ficult, because that loss is often reflected in the loss of relationship, that
loss of identity . . . [and] that loss of a sense of direction.
— Justice Murray Sinclair, 2012

In the struggle to develop a larger social discourse on the ongoing legacy of colonial genocide in Indigenous North America, the current debate in Canada
over residential schools may provide a critical opening. Speaking to students,
scholars, and Survivors at the University of Manitoba in September 2012,
Justice Murray Sinclair, chair of the Truth and Reconciliation Commission of
Canada (TRC), delivered his keynote address on Canadian residential schools
and the question of genocide. The label of genocide in this context is contentious, evidenced by the fact that the word is not mentioned in the TRC's
mandate, the Canadian Indian Residential School Settlement Agreement
(2006), or the Canadian government's most recent apology to residential
school Survivors. Thus when Prime Minister Stephen Harper stood in front
of the House of Commons in June 2008, he apologized not for genocide per se
but rather for "this policy of assimilation" that removed an estimated 150,000
Canadian First Nations, Inuit, and Métis children from their families and
communities.

Clearly, just as in Australia, where there has been a similar debate over the "stolen generations" (Barta 2008), there is great reluctance on behalf of Canadian government officials and the broader public to acknowledge this shameful legacy as genocide. But the question of labels has inevitably arisen, and Justice Sinclair was forthright in unambiguously declaring his position on the issue. The intentions and administration of Canada's Indian residential school system, he stated, was an act of genocide. Building on Justice Sinclair's powerful charge, this volume begins with the specific legacy of Canadian residential schools in order to open up a larger discussion of colonial genocides in Indigenous North America.

Although the word *genocide* was introduced less than seventy years ago, it has garnered enormous rhetorical power that often overshadows its critical utility. There are semantic gaps not only between the colloquial understanding of genocide and its more nuanced conceptualizations in law and academia but even among scholars themselves (see Moshman 2001; Moses 2002; Jones 2010: 16–20). Seen through the lens of the Holocaust, the broader public and many academics consider genocide to be the most extreme form of violence imaginable. According to this widespread view, including other forms of destruction besides mass murder risks diluting the meaning of the term.

In confronting this definitional challenge in his 2012 address, Justice Sinclair pointed to the 1948 United Nations Convention on the Prevention and Punishment of the Crime of Genocide. The UN Genocide Convention, to which most nations are now signatories, defines genocide as:

> Acts committed with intent to destroy, in whole or in part, a national, ethnical, racial or religious group, as such, including the following:
> (a) Killing members of the group;
> (b) Causing serious bodily or mental harm to members of the group;
> (c) Deliberately inflicting on the group conditions of life calculated to bring about its physical destruction in whole or in part;
> (d) Imposing measures intended to prevent births within the group;
> (e) Forcibly transferring children of the group to another group.

This international legal statute clearly lists several indirectly lethal acts in its definition, including "causing serious bodily or mental harm" and "forcibly transferring children," all under the condition that these acts are committed with "intent to destroy." When thus measured against the stated intentions of residential school administrators—such as the Canadian deputy superintendent of the Department of Indian Affairs, Duncan Campbell Scott, who in 1920 proclaimed, "Our objective is . . . to get rid of the Indian problem" (quoted in Titley 1986: 50), or the American superintendent of the Carlisle

Indian Industrial School, Richard Henry Pratt ([1892] 1973: 261), who aimed to "kill the Indian in him, and save the man"—Justice Sinclair's charge of genocide appears justified.

But what is at stake in making this charge? Why does declaring the residential schools, or the broader history of North American colonialism, genocide matter? Considering the imperatives of Indigenous political theory, which aim to dismantle the structural realities of colonialism and work toward a not-yet-realized "postcolonial" situation (e.g., Alfred [1999] 2009; Tully 1995, 2008), what use is there in talking of genocide? Joseph P. Gone, a cultural clinical psychologist committed to addressing the contemporary life-and-death concerns and mental health outcomes of Native American individuals and communities, posed these questions to Justice Sinclair after his remarks. In this context, Gone asked, does the use of the word *genocide* have any practical value?[1] Might even the use of this powerful term foreclose any otherwise positive possibilities in dealing with the needs of Indigenous North Americans and moving toward reconciliation between Native and settler communities?[2]

Justice Sinclair responded that it is important to acknowledge the residential school legacy as genocide because, first and foremost, the Survivors have themselves raised the issue. For many of them, recognition of colonial malevolence is necessary for the process of reconciliation to move forward. Of course, as critical observers of an analogous discourse in Australia have noted, mere acknowledgments and apologies are insufficient when devoid of any meaningful policy changes (Short 2012). Ultimately the most crucial issue is to begin repairing the relationships damaged by these destructive realities, or, perhaps more accurately, forging new, nongenocidal relations in North America. Such transformation might take as many as seven generations, but acknowledgment of wrongdoing is only the first step in this process. As such it is important for the peoples of the United States and Canada to recognize their shared legacies of genocide, which have too often been hidden—ignored, forgotten, or outright denied. (On such "hidden genocides," see Hinton, LaPointe, and Irvin 2013.)

Genealogies of Genocide

How did we get to this point, where the inglorious legacies of North American Indigenous-settler relations are finally being exhumed? Is there now a chance for Indigenous and non-Indigenous North Americans to begin an unsettling dialogue and the arduous process of fashioning decolonizing forms of redress and reconciliation?

At the moment it may seem that this window of opportunity, however glimmering, is wider in Canada than in the United States. As suggested below, this may be because of a more concerted governmental effort to address these issues in Canada. Perhaps this reflects the different demographic positions of Indigenous peoples in either nation-state. While in absolute figures there are more people of Indigenous descent in the United States than in Canada—with 4.1 million in the former and 1.3 million in the latter—their proportional weight is markedly different. In Canada 4.5 percent of the total population claims Aboriginal ancestry, compared to 1.5 percent in the United States (Thornton 2008: 269; O'Donnell 2008: 286). Accordingly Indigenous peoples in Canada may be in a slightly better position to vocalize their concerns.

The somewhat greater window of opportunity to address colonial genocide in Canada compared to the United States may also reflect the different politics of self-determination in each country. The difficult federal acknowledgment process in the United States has often pitted Indigenous groups against one another, while simultaneously directing their attention to local nation-based rather than pan-Indigenous concerns (Cornell 1990), whereas First Nations in Canada are typically compelled to stand together to demand recognition of colonial harms, in part because they continue to experience shared injustices, such as the often restrictive policies of the all-encompassing Canadian Indian Act (Miller 2004: 4; Nichols 1998: 298).

That said, the Canadian Indian Act has often set First Nations, Métis, and Inuit peoples against one another, thus undermining a broader platform of solidarity among all Indigenous descendants in Canada. Regardless, considering that Canada may be in a relatively more advanced position to deal with colonial genocide, it was thus not coincidental that the workshop behind this edited volume was convened in Winnipeg, Manitoba, which is the home of the TRC, a body federally mandated to promote awareness and public education on the legacies of residential school experiences. Unfortunately no federal counterpart exists in the United States, where there seems to be even less public discourse on colonial genocides. Thus there are different things at stake in each country, and their divergent paths to the present should be clarified.

Yet one issue concerning both countries, especially for non-Indigenous citizens, is that their respective national identities may be fundamentally challenged by the charge of genocide. Popular historical narratives in Canada celebrate the myth of Canadians as peaceful colonizers. Such an image is rooted in the legacy of the French Canadian *coureurs des bois* who first settled this part of North America by establishing relatively harmonious relationships with Indigenous peoples. The very name *Canada*, derived from the Iroquoian word *Kanata*, meaning "village" or "settlement," reflects this heritage of mutual respect (Hall 2003: 82). Moreover Canada's constitutional traditions arguably provide space for Aboriginal rights (Borrows 2010). For instance, the Royal Proclamation of 1763, which remains a foundation of Canadian law, at least nominally acknowledges the prior settlement of Indigenous peoples. But like any nationalist myth, especially those of the settler colonial variety, these historical legacies typically silence and deny the tendency to eliminate the presence of First Nation, Métis, and Inuit peoples in Canada (Trigger 1985).

The Canadian myth of peaceful colonization has begun to crack in recent decades due in large part to Indigenous activism. When Minister of Indian Affairs Jean Chrétien released the 1969 White Paper, which ignored prior consultation with Indigenous groups and instead explicitly proposed a policy of assimilation through the elimination of the Department of Indian Affairs and the Indian Act, which, despite its many problems, offered protections for Aboriginal and treaty rights that remain essential to the preservation of Indigenous cultures, Indigenous peoples forcefully protested (Cardinal 1969; Turner 2006: 12–37). Soon afterward the National Indian Brotherhood, which has since been reformulated as the Assembly of First Nations, played a prominent role in the long process of constitutional reform that culminated in the 1982 Constitution Act, thereby ensuring the recognition and affirmation of the rights of Aboriginal peoples in Canada.

Their presence in the negotiations significantly raised the public profile of Indigenous peoples, both within Canada and abroad (Sanders 1983). The 1990 Oka Crisis, in which the Kanien'kehaka (Mohawk) people of Kanesatake, Quebec, stood against the Canadian government over a disputed piece of territory, likewise brought to the fore many unresolved issues in Indigenous–non-Indigenous relations in Canada. More recently the grassroots Idle No More movement, which began in late November 2012 in reaction to a slate of government bills that violate treaty rights, diminish the government's duty to consult Indigenous peoples, and encourage the privatization of reserve lands, has likewise pressured for a reexamination of the Canadian state's relationship with Indigenous communities.

Acknowledgment of residential school experiences became increasingly prominent just as such activism was enhancing the political stature of Aboriginal peoples in Canada. In the mid-1980s Survivors spoke out more frequently about their residential school experiences, and class action lawsuits were launched against the Canadian government and churches that ran many of the schools. By the late 1980s and 1990s the government and churches offered initial statements of regret for physical and sexual abuses within the schools, but these statements did not quell Indigenous demands for justice.

Indeed the class action lawsuits continued until the Indian Residential Schools Settlement Agreement (IRSSA) was signed in 2006 by the government, the churches, legal counsels of former students, the Assembly of First Nations, and other Aboriginal organizations. After its approval by the courts, the IRSSA mandated the administration of several measures to address the legacy of the schools. This included the Common Experience Payment, which provides lump-sum redress payments to eligible former students, and the Independent Assessment Process, which calculates compensation based on physical and sexual harms suffered within Canadian residential schools, as well as the funding of healing and commemorative measures such as the TRC.

It is in this context that the question of genocide in Canada is being raised once again. Until recently much of the scholarly discourse around this issue tended to be framed through the lens of the Holocaust (Annett 2001; Grant 1996; Neu and Therrien 2003). The sweeping claims made by such contributions have been criticized for problematically instrumentalizing the Holocaust as a rhetorical device (MacDonald 2007). As discussed below, this tendency is apparent in the broader field of genocide studies.

Apart from this deliberate framing, or perhaps because of it, there has been some reluctance to use the term *genocide* as an analytical concept in studies of Indigenous–non-Indigenous relations in Canada, especially those concerning the residential schools (Miller 1996; Milloy 1999). Such terminological hesitancy is further apparent in the nascent public discussions, where there has thus far been even greater reserve in expanding the discourse to consider the broader history of Canadian colonialism in terms of genocide. Much of this caution stems from a high degree of Holocaust consciousness among the Canadian public and the expectation that the destructiveness of Canadian colonialism should be analogous to that of Nazi death camps. Moreover matters such as the uneven spread of colonization across Canada, whereby different Indigenous groups experienced contact and colonization differently, as well as persistent beliefs that Canadian intentions were benevolent though misguided, continue to temper the use of the term *genocide* in Canadian discussions.

These issues came to a head in the summer of 2013, when a combination of events inspired discussion of genocide in Canada. The first was an article published by a postdoctoral researcher at Guelph University, Ian Mosby (2013), which detailed government-sponsored biomedical and nutritional experimentation on Indigenous children at six Canadian residential schools, as well as in northern Manitoban Indigenous communities. Soon after CBC radio reported on the story, debate about Canada's historic treatment of Indigenous peoples was reignited.

By this time the Truth and Reconciliation Commission of Canada had entered its final year of hearings after four years of recording Survivors' testimony about the violence, degradation, and suffering of Canadian Indian residential schools. But the thought of malnourished children used as test subjects for vitamin supplements and fortified flour that caused anemia struck a chord with the public. It is in this context that, alongside the revelation that the Canadian Museum for Human Rights will not refer to settler colonialism in Canada as genocide (although it does attempt to spark discussion about the applicability of this term), scholars and activists provoked a debate about genocide in Canada. This group included Phil Fontaine, former grand chief of the Assembly of First Nations, who with his coauthors called upon Ottawa to recognize Canada as the sixth official genocide, alongside the Holocaust, Srebrenica, the Armenian genocide, the Rwandan genocide, and the Holodomor (Fontaine, Dan, and Farber 2013).

However frustratingly slow and narrow the general conversations about colonial genocide might be in Canada, they arguably are even more so in the United States. As noted, in the United States there is no federally mandated counterpart to the Canadian TRC, despite the historical fact that off-reservation boarding schools for Native American children were just as prominent and officially sanctioned. There have at least been some efforts on a state level to begin acknowledging and redressing such issues, as with the Maine Wabanaki-State Child Welfare Truth and Reconciliation Commission, jointly convened in 2010 by the state of Maine and Wabanaki Confederacy (Attean and Williams 2011).

At the federal level Assistant Secretary of the Interior Kevin Gover (2000–2001: 161) formally apologized in September 2000 on behalf of the Bureau of Indian Affairs for its role in what he called "ethnic cleansing." While the apology was undoubtedly sincere, its immediate effects were hampered by silence and neglect. Gover, also a citizen of the Pawnee Nation, was unable to speak on behalf of the entire U.S. government, and although the Clinton administration did not oppose his apology, it did not publically endorse it either (Buck 2006; Tsosie 2006).

More recently, in 2009 the U.S. Congress passed a joint resolution that "apologizes . . . to all Native Peoples for the many instances of violence, maltreatment, and neglect inflicted on Native Peoples by citizens of the United States." Yet the resolution was mired in a series of legalistic disclaimers, thereby hindering whatever positive effects it may have. Moreover tucked away in a Defense Appropriations Bill (U.S. Congress 2009), the apology has been largely obscured and rejected by some as "too little, too late" (Rickert 2012). Accordingly these initiatives have yet to mobilize a broader public discourse or any governmental initiatives in the United States.

As in Canada, such inhibitions are largely due to predominant nationalist mythologies influencing nonacademic, scholarly, and policymaking discourses alike. The enduring beliefs in American exceptionalism and Manifest Destiny, both powerful themes in the collective identity of the United States, are formidable barriers that prevent any serious reckoning with the past and present, especially in terms of genocide (Kurtiş, Adams, and Yellow Bird 2010). Indeed there has long been a bardic tradition of historiography in the United States that glorifies the "peopling" of the "New World" at the expense of "feeble barbarians" (Bancroft 1834: 4) and "primitive tribes" (Schlesinger 1992: 22). According to this still prevalent view of history, genocide is antithetical to Americans' national character. In the words of the recent high-level report on genocide prevention coauthored by two former cabinet-level secretaries from the Clinton administration, genocide is supposedly "a crime that threatens not only our values, but our national interests" (Albright et al. 2008: ix).

Such hubristic myths have been critically challenged by Native American activists. Inspired by the civil rights movement of the 1960s and a wave of Indigenous revitalization, younger Native Americans spurned what they saw as more conciliatory bodies of Indigenous representatives, such as the National Congress of American Indians, in favor of more militant groups and actions. In 1973 a contingent of the American Indian Movement (AIM), which was founded five years earlier, occupied the town of Wounded Knee, South Dakota, on the Pine Ridge Indian Reservation. On the site of the infamous 1890 massacre of a Lakota camp of noncombatants, an inglorious episode that was then receiving renewed attention with Dee Brown's (1971) best-selling book, *Bury My Heart at Wounded Knee*, the AIM standoff with the U.S. government garnered some media coverage, much of it negative. Regardless, this intervention did expose long-standing but underrecognized transgressions against Indigenous peoples in the United States. More recent efforts have likewise called attention to the legitimate grievances of Native Americans.[3] It remains to be seen if such initiatives will foster greater public discussion and help crack the shell of the mythologized American identity.

Such activism has inspired positive scholarly developments, as with the emergence of "new Indian history" (Edmunds 1995; Fixico 1997), but much of the discourse regarding American genocides has been limited. A few publications emerged in the late-1970s and 1980s that focused on the legacies of racism and conquest in Native America, albeit not always through the critical lens of genocide (Dadrian 1976; Drinnon 1980; Todorov 1984; Thornton 1987). These works set the stage for the clamorous and very public commemorations of the 1992 Columbian quincentennial, which instantly became a lightning rod of the concurrent "culture wars" in the United States.

On one side were those who slighted any overt criticism of colonialism, with many conservatives continuing to celebrate the "myth of discovery," while those more liberally inclined opted for the sanitized "encounter/exchange" narrative that downplayed aspects of exploitation and domination (Bigelow 1992). On the other side were those ardent voices who unabashedly charged the entire Columbian legacy as one of genocide (Jaimes 1992; Stannard 1992; Churchill 1997). As passionate as these debates were, in the public forum they were ultimately short-lived, and dialogue about the past and present injustices in Native America quickly receded, leaving the question of colonial genocide to specialized corners of the academy.

While the reluctance in Canada and the United States to recognize Indigenous grievances has thus far been explained in ideational and cultural terms, there is a strong material basis for this collective denial as well. There is perhaps an unspoken fear that to acknowledge the destructive legacy of settler colonialism would undermine the perceived legitimacy of prevailing property regimes. After all, much of North America was swindled from Indigenous peoples through the mythical but still powerful Doctrine of Discovery, the perceived right of conquest, and deceitful treaties. Restitution for colonial genocide would thus entail returning stolen territories. The fear in settler society is that this would result in the abrogation of private property rights and create economic and political uncertainty for those who profit from the land, such as corporations in the areas of agriculture, logging, mining, and oil (Woolford 2005).

Yet Taiaiake Alfred (2005: 151–57) suggests that such restitution would not necessarily force non-Natives off the land; instead it would decolonize their relationships not only with the Indigenous peoples with whom they share the earth but with the land itself. Moreover Waziyatawin (2009) suggests that the hundreds of millions of acres of public land in Canada and the United States, territory that is not allotted as private property, should also be returned to their original inhabitants. Thus the fears of settler society over the status of their properties should not inhibit efforts to decolonize settler territorial relations.

Interestingly issues of territorial occupation and conquest were present in the very first formulation of genocide as provided by Raphael Lemkin. Lemkin (1944: 79), who coined the word *genocide* in his seminal study, *Axis*

Rule in Occupied Europe, wrote that genocide involves "two phases": first, the destruction of the targeted group's "national pattern" and second, "the imposition of the national pattern of the oppressor" on the territory of the former. This oft-quoted passage explicates that genocide may be deeply bound up with colonizing processes as a particular form of conquest and occupation (Curthoys and Docker 2008: 11; Docker 2008; Moses 2008: 9).

Moreover Lemkin's capacious definition of genocide, which included political, social, cultural, economic, biological, physical, religious, and moral components, provides a useful framework for understanding the multiple strands of the colonial assault on Indigenous peoples. For his tragically unfulfilled multivolume project, *History of Genocide*, Lemkin also researched dozens of historical case studies, including those in the Americas, clearly indicating that he thought his neologism was perfectly appropriate in this context (McDonnell and Moses 2005). His contributions have enjoyed a recent renewal of interest that has been concurrent with the increased attention paid to colonial genocides. But there has also developed a certain origin myth around Lemkin that overshadows conceptual weaknesses, particularly his static, rigid, and essentialized view of culture (Moses 2010b: 29–30; Hinton 2012: 5–6).[4]

Genocide studies lay dormant after Lemkin's death in 1959 for over a generation, until a coterie of mostly North American social scientists revived the field in the 1980s and 1990s. Many of these academics drew from Lemkin's origin myth, namely his scholarly activist bent and his passionate crusade for global justice (Totten and Jacobs 2002). However, they generally did not share Lemkin's broad conceptualization of genocide, which was primarily concerned with protecting the lives of groups, and instead offered truncated definitions that focused on the mass murder of individuals. Moreover, and again unlike Lemkin, this generation tended to implicitly adopt the Holocaust as a conceptual prototype for genocide studies.

Through this narrow frame of reference very little space was provided for discussion of colonial genocides in Indigenous North America (Chalk and Jonassohn 1990: 173–204; Fein 1990: 80–82). For the most part the alternative category of "ethnocide" or "cultural genocide" was used to label those cases that did not meet their reductive definitional standards of genocide, tacitly suggesting that these instances were less severe or important than the Holocaust and other major genocides of the twentieth century. The trend of conceptually splitting genocide from cultural genocide persists as a result of this generation of scholarship, inhibiting a full discussion of colonial genocides (Short 2010b).

Yet an even greater barrier to this discussion has been the identity politics that is seemingly intrinsic to the study of genocide. Associated with the same generation of genocide scholars of the 1980s and 1990s were proponents of the "uniqueness" thesis (Katz 1994; Bauer 2001). According to this view, the Holocaust was taken as the most important, if not the only, case of genocide.

This argument diminished the relevance of other peoples' traumatic pasts and provoked sharp responses from "rival" victim advocates. In particular David Stannard ([1995] 2001) and Ward Churchill (1997) advocated strongly for the study of colonial genocides in Indigenous North America. Although their critical responses are understandable, considering their righteous indignation against the rampant denial of Indigenous grievances in North America, the polemics produced by this debate often have produced far more heat than light, as scholar advocates of specific groups contested for the mantle of suffering through asymmetric comparisons with the Holocaust. Thankfully a new generation of genocide scholarship is moving beyond these timeworn and irreconcilable divisions (Moses 2010a: 7–9).

Much of this fresh work has emerged from Australia, where there has been a considerable degree of public discourse concerning the plights of Aboriginal peoples. Two significant political events—the 1992 Mabo decision by the Australian High Court, which rejected the doctrine of *terra nullius* and affirmed the existence of Native title in common law, and the 1997 publication of the *Bringing Them Home* report, which documented the forcible removal of Aboriginal and Torres Strait Islander children from their families and communities—precipitated an ongoing debate over the interpretation of Australian history (Veracini 2003; Brantlinger 2004). The visibility of this public discussion in Australia, the so-called History Wars, is much greater than in North America, and the government's role in initiating such dialogue is suggestive. This is especially so considering how the IRSSA and the TRC are functioning to promote a somewhat wider discourse in Canada compared to the United States, where the lack of any such national dialogue might be explained by the absence of comparable governmental initiatives.

In the context of this public discourse in Australia, the subfield of colonial genocide studies has flourished. Colin Tatz (1999), Tony Barta ([1987] 2000), Robert Manne (2001), and Henry Reynolds (2001) provided pathbreaking publications, followed by the substantial collection of essays compiled by Ann Curthoys and John Docker (2001). Likewise the work of Patrick Wolfe (2001, 2006) has been significant, especially in elucidating the links between Australian and American patterns of settler colonialism, a social formation that is distinct from other types of colonialism (see also Veracini 2010). In 2003 the historian Dirk Moses organized an important conference at the University of Sydney on genocide and colonialism and went on to edit a series of important volumes (Moses 2004, 2008; Moses and Stone 2007).

These contributions have focused on the multiple and interlinked ways through which group destruction might occur and the local and specific effects of these forces within Indigenous settings. They do not seek to show that colonialism in North America or Australia was identical to genocidal practices in Nazi Germany and instead demonstrate the destructiveness of colonial interventions in these regions on their own terms. In making this point, this literature returns to Lemkin's primary concern for the lives of groups rather than strictly for the lives of individual group members.

The last but not least important intellectual discourse that greatly informs the present discussion is the field of Indigenous studies. Beginning in the late 1960s North American universities began to institute programs that focused on the unique perspectives and histories of Indigenous peoples. More specifically this scholarship affirms that Indigenous peoples have the "intellectual sovereignty" to (re)produce their own epistemologies (Warrior 1994: 87; Mihesuah and Wilson 2004). In many ways this discourse resonates with subaltern studies and postcolonial theory (Memmi [1957] 1991; Said 1978; Spivak 1994), although many Indigenous scholars are rightly adamant that one cannot yet speak of a "postcolonial" era in the North American or Oceanic contexts, as colonialism persists in many guises (Smith 1999: 24; Cook-Lynn 2011).

And instead of taking for granted the essentialized label "Indian" within the reified category of the nation-state, these contributions encourage us to see North America from an Indigenist perspective that respects and promotes Indigenous peoples' diverse ways of being, doing, and knowing (Simpson 2004: 381–82). Otherwise known as Turtle Island, Indigenous North America comprises hundreds of unique groups, nations, and traditions that have existed since time immemorial. It is this cultural plurality that has been threatened by five centuries of colonization.

While this perspective is vitally important, some contemporary contributors of Indigenous histories have perhaps been reluctant to use the concept of genocide, as doing so might suggest a fatalistic passivity, an absence of Indigenous creativity and adaptability, and the irrevocability of death (Trevithick 1998; Gosden 2004: 25). As such it is important for genocide scholars to draw from Indigenous studies in order to stress what Gerald Vizenor (2008) has dubbed "survivance." Accordingly, in the face of enormous pressures for destruction and erasure, Indigenous peoples in North America rightly rejoice in their perseverance and revitalization (Alfred [1999] 2009: 57–58).

All of these various genealogical developments have converged to bring us to the present volume. Scholars of Indigenous North America are now ready to offer our own contributions to the field of genocide studies, thereby adding some analytical clarity to the growing scholarship and nascent public discussions concerning the legacy of Indigenous-settler relations. In particular many of the contributors to this volume are interested in unsettling and decolonizing genocide studies. This implies a critical stance toward the struggle of knowing genocide. In doing so it suggests that the very concept of genocide has been conventionally formulated and framed and generally understood through a Eurocentric lens and that its constitutive components (the idea of groups, intent, destruction, etc.) are all interpreted in ways that preclude and ultimately deny the ongoing domination, exploitation, and violence against Indigenous peoples (see Woolford 2009, 2011, 2013).

This orientation is less concerned with *decolonization* in the form of a noun, which implies a specific endpoint, than with *decolonizing* in the form of a verb, which is instead an open-ended process. As such this approach to the study of colonial genocide in Indigenous North America ultimately aims to contribute to broader social processes of acknowledgment, restitution, reconciliation, healing, and transformation. We believe the terminology of genocide has a role to play in such processes, and not merely as a means to adjudicate the past or to assign to it a dollar figure for purposes of compensation. Rather the concept of genocide offers an analytical device for evaluating destructive relations of domination and subordination so that such relations might be changed and ongoing patterns of colonial genocide in North America brought to a halt.

Intersections and Trajectories

The first section of this volume, "Intersections and Trajectories," features chapters that examine colonialism as a striated, multilevel, and uneven phenomenon across broad temporal frames and shifts. The complexity of this phenomenon challenges scholars of colonial genocide to fashion theoretical models and empirical approaches supple enough to capture the many forms taken by colonial relations in North America, without representing colonialism as an almost random and accidental set of processes. Thus in this section crooked pathways, unexpected convergences, and complex interactions are explored.

Andrew Woolford addresses colonial variations across space and time as they helped to shape specific residential school experiences (chapter 1). Woolford conceptualizes settler colonialism as a series of nets, or networks, formed by linkages between actors and institutions at macro, meso, and micro levels. When examined in sequence with one another, these nets form what Woolford refers to as the "colonial mesh," which stretches and retracts both historically and geographically, allowing the net to tighten around specific

Indigenous communities at particular times and in particular places. But the mesh is also prone to snags, especially at the lower meso and micro levels, where actors and institutions occasionally find the resources needed to resist capture and subvert colonial intentions. With this analytical tool in hand, Woolford looks at questions of discipline, desire, space, and territory as they relate to Indigenous boarding schools in the United States (New Mexico) and Canada (Manitoba), showing how such techniques and factors played different roles at different times in the histories of these schools.

Such complexity is not, however, simply an artifact of a more recent colonial era. As Robbie Ethridge demonstrates (chapter 2), colonizer-Indigenous relations from the sixteenth to the early eighteenth century in the North American Southeast do not fit any neat pattern of intention and destruction. Rather than limit herself to juridical terms such as *perpetrator*, *victim*, or even *genocide*, Ethridge advances the notion of the Mississippian "shatter zone," a term that implies the violence and destructiveness that results when multiple forces, such as slaving, global capital, and imperialism, come together and ignite patterns of destruction, loss, coalescence, and regeneration. Ethridge invites one to consider the roles played by substate actors but also world-system flows of trade and capital. Under these circumstances the collision between Indigenous peoples and colonizers played out in violent yet multifaceted ways, to some extent destroying the world that preceded European contact but also opening new possibilities for both Natives and newcomers.

Christopher Powell and Julia Peristerakis (chapter 3) argue that to understand genocide in Canada one must look beyond specific modalities of destruction such as residential schools, since they operate in relation with multiple colonial institutions and practices. However, in reviewing the many forms of potential destruction wrought by colonial powers in Canada, Powell and Peristerakis's goal is more than to offer a simple empirical accounting or fleshing out of colonial genocide. Their argument is that these intersecting avenues of colonial harm have accumulated in a manner that severely threatens the life of specific Indigenous groups. Such groups, which they understand as "figurations," comprise interrelated social institutions that enable the group to persist through practices of collective identity formation and material survival. In making this move, Powell and Peristerakis remind us that groups are dynamic entities that are often prone to degrees of change and that genocide marks the radical disruption of such group dynamics.

Erasure and Legibility

Part II explores genocide not only in terms of its violent consequences but also with respect to questions of "erasure and legibility." Indeed usually one of the key dynamics of genocides involves an erasure of local-level complexity that renders legible a stereotypic and reductive depiction of other groups. Thus in colonial North America Indigenous groups were collectively assigned a simplistic and devalued identity as "Indians," "redskins," or "savages."

Such processes of erasure and legibility have been ongoing in the colonial history of North America, as different strategies have been unfurled to remove or destroy Indigenous groups as perceived obstacles to land and resource acquisition as well as nation building. Moreover erasure and legibility continue to braid together in how we think about and represent this history, as colonial powers enlist nationalist forms of legibility to naturalize (Manifest Destiny) or minimize (peaceful expansion) destruction, removing the claims of the colonized from the historical record. Indigenous groups and their supporters have often sought to mobilize counternarratives of history to combat erasure and foment a decolonizing legibility, but even such efforts can be co-opted or corrupted, as they are translated by contemporary colonial powers into new discourses that continue to encourage Indigenous erasure.

In chapter 4 Benjamin Madley draws upon rare primary sources to narrate seven campaigns against the Modoc in California and Oregon between 1851 and 1873. Madley demonstrates how colonial genocidal actions are legitimated and mass murder erased from the historical record when Indigenous resistance is reframed as militaristic aggression. Although the Modoc experienced severe population decline (75–88 percent), scholars have largely ignored the attempted destruction during this period. In redressing this historical oversight, Madley draws upon the United Nations Genocide Convention to demonstrate its applicability to the Modoc and advises historians to avoid "sanitizing" genocide as war and to remain attuned to the fact that resistance is often present within genocide.

Gray Whaley also examines physical genocide against Indigenous peoples on the Pacific Coast (chapter 5). His chapter focuses on western Oregon Territory from 1846 to 1859, where regular army units and local militias engaged in extermination campaigns and then sought reimbursement from the federal government for their efforts. Here too portrayal of Indigenous groups as threats and their racialization by settlers made possible the mobilization of attempted physical erasure. Whaley locates these negotiations of racial and spatial "othering" within a broader political economic framework in which liberal notions of private property and the right of owners to protect their property lent further credence to the genocidal aims of colonizing settlers.

Shifting ahead to the present, Tricia Logan (chapter 6) addresses contemporary practices of erasure and legibility in Canada. Logan examines how the role of genocidal processes in the formation of Canada is removed from mythic national narratives. Her primary focus is on recent debates concerning two Canadian national museums: the Canadian Museum for Civilization (recently renamed the Canadian Museum of History) and the yet-to-open Canadian Museum for Human Rights. Logan argues that these public institutions, charged with the tasks of preserving Canadian memory, commemorating the past, and educating Canadians about their history, often instead contribute to the erasure of national history. Thus these institutions of public memory themselves become complicit in the creation of blind spots and "conceptual blockages" in the Canadian present, which not only prevent Canadians from adequately reckoning with historical colonial wrongs but also obstruct attention to ongoing colonial harms, such as the continuing high number of Indigenous children removed from their families by Canadian provincial governments.

In chapter 7 Jeremy Patzer analyzes in tandem the cultural erasure that occurred through residential schools and the quest to make Indigenous territory legible through colonial dispossession. He addresses these issues through consideration of the "therapeutic ethos" of the Indian Residential Schools Settlement Agreement (2006) and, in particular, the Truth and Reconciliation Commission of Canada. Following an overview of how the "Indian" was conceptualized as a "problem" amenable to high-modernist social engineering, Patzer critiques the Canadian TRC for "depoliticizing" colonialism, individualizing harms, and failing to adequately interrogate Indigenous-settler relations and persistent patterns of dispossession, disempowerment, and the loss of self-determination.

Transformations

Part III brings to the forefront the theme of "transformations." Colonial genocide itself is a radical form of imposed transformation, refiguring the Indigenous "Other" as a physical and cultural absence in the colonized terrain. But such refigurations are rarely final. Instead one genocidal moment leads to subsequent transformations and countertransformations, as targeted groups struggle to revive and reinvent Indigenous identities in the face of ongoing attempts to force them into the colonial political economic and symbolic orders. Genocide therefore cannot be understood simply as a process of destruction, since it is always accompanied by practices of regeneration, translation, and refiguration. Genocide, as a consequence of relations of power, is of necessity accompanied by both resistance, since power is not needed where resistance is absent, and production (rather than simply destruction), since genocidal power must constitute specific categories of knowledge (e.g., "the Indian") in order to lay waste targeted groups (Foucault 1980; see also Powell 2011).

In chapter 8 Margaret Jacobs shows how practices of refiguration can become habituated or patterned within colonial institutions, and even among Indigenous peoples themselves. Building upon Patrick Wolfe's (2006) notion of the "logic of elimination," Jacobs identifies a "habit of elimination" that is evident in Indigenous child removal practices in the nineteenth and twentieth centuries. Based on liberal presuppositions about what entails a "good" or "civilized" life, state officials in the nineteenth century naturalized child removal and reframed it as an act of benevolence that spared the child from a backward and destitute existence. This logic, however, is eventually absorbed into the bureaucratic workings of the state, and becomes an unthought reflex, as Indigenous child removals persist as the common sense of everyday child welfare practices.

Turning back to the early colonial era, Jeff Benvenuto (chapter 9) tackles the complex interplay of transformation, creation, and destruction in the ethnogenesis of the Choctaw in the early modern Atlantic world. He complicates taken-for-granted binaries of victimization versus agency, or cultural versus physical destruction, so as to open space for consideration of the often simultaneous processes of group destruction and group regeneration. Benvenuto puts forward the notion of "creative destruction" as a means for capturing the identity-forming agency of proto-Choctaw peoples, even as they wrestled with the destructive pressures of the Mississippian "shatter zone." In this manner Benvenuto advances our understanding of colonial genocide by demonstrating how, in a climate rife with physical threats, socioeconomic and political changes, enslavement, and disease, Indigenous practices of survivance continued. Thus Indigenous agency with respect to collective identity formation persists amid broader social transformations.

Connecting the historical origins of the Canadian state to today, Kiera Ladner (chapter 10) alerts us to how Indigenous institutions, and not just identities, were targeted for forced transformation in Canada. "Political genocide," she argues, has occurred in Canada through vehicles such as the Indian Act of 1876 and residential schools. Colonial interventions like these were intended to destroy Indigenous sovereignties, polities, and governance structures, thereby threatening the very viability of Indigenous nations. For example, traditional Indigenous governments and constitutional orders were replaced through the Indian Act by "band governments" that were meant to serve as a transitional form of governance on the pathway to "civilized" government. These band governments possessed only delegated powers and relied on federal government approval for even the most mundane of governmental activities, which severely hampered the ability of Indigenous peoples to govern themselves, and thereby survive, as nations.

Remaining in contemporary Canada, Colin Samson (chapter 11) turns our attention toward how allegedly reparative processes of land claims are still strongly infused with acts of colonial transformation and refiguration. Samson, who has long worked with the Innu in Labrador, critiques the ways the technical language of treaty making attempts to forge a new "us"—in the sense that land claims are essentially about finding a way to shape the Innu to dominant Canadian social and political realities. Rather than providing an opportunity to build mutually beneficial agreements, Samson argues, the Innu's social suffering and the continuing acquisitive pressures on their lands by outsiders place them in a position where there appears no alternative but to enter into treaty negotiations with the federal government. Under these conditions, in order to obtain a modicum of recognition and land restitution, the Innu must consent to a wide array of colonial desires, not the least of which is that the Innu provide the government with "certainty" by ceding all Aboriginal rights they may possess in exchange for those delineated in the treaty document. Likewise the treaty language opens multiple fissures through which Innu territories might be dispossessed, such as through federal claims to subsurface rights. Samson asks us to consider the implications of these sorts of "agreements" for the survival of Indigenous groups.

(Re)Imaginings

The final section of this volume provides insight into the ways we might (re)imagine the study of colonial genocide and decolonize Indigenous North America. On this score Joseph Gone (chapter 12) offers a difficult challenge for other authors in this volume. While most of the contributors accept, to varying degrees, the applicability of the label *genocide* to events, processes, or patterns in the history of North American settler-Indigenous relations, Gone advocates a more restrained usage of the term, respecting the deep tensions between its descriptive and evaluative functions.

As someone who works with Indigenous persons suffering various forms of mental health distress, Gone is all too familiar with the contemporary problems of Indigenous peoples. Thus his questioning of the language of genocide comes not from a place of historical denial but rather from both a definitional and a practical standpoint. First, he is particularly concerned with how advocates of the "historical trauma" (or "soul wound") approach to Native American psychology tend to make sweeping claims that paint the entire colonial process as genocidal. Such overgeneralizations, Gone argues, ignore the nuanced and multivalent patterns of colonialism in North America.

Moreover Gone states that definitional expansion of the genocide concept beyond mass murder, so as to include colonial interventions such as forced assimilation through residential schools, risks the creation of an unruly concept divorced from popular understandings of genocidal phenomena and deprived of its full moral impact. Finally, and perhaps most crucially, Gone questions the practicality of such sweeping claims of genocide for reimagining Indigenous-settler relations, since overly extended claims of genocide lock all into an us/them or victim/perpetrator binary based more on resentment than solidarity or hospitality.

In chapter 13 Tasha Hubbard takes an approach very different from that called for by Gone, reimagining colonial genocide in a manner that broadens rather than narrows its definition. In particular Hubbard pushes beyond human-centric notions of genocide to consider the place of the buffalo in discussions of colonial genocide. Drawing upon an Indigenous epistemological framework, she considers the buffalo as a "people" and demonstrates how the destruction of the buffalo fits prevalent definitions of genocide. She also demands that further consideration be given to the relationality between groups, species, and place, as too often in genocide studies groups are viewed as constituted in whole by their human members rather than their human members in relation with their territory and the other species that share the territory.

In chapter 14 David MacDonald addresses directly the question of how we might reimagine Canada by applying the term *genocide* to forced assimilation through residential schools. MacDonald rereads the UN Genocide Convention to show how its terms, in particular section II(e), capture the residential schooling experience in Canada. By paying specific attention to what it means to "forcibly transfer" children from one group to another, MacDonald clarifies some of the confusion that persists around what this clause actually means and to what situations it might apply. He then uses this clarification as a launching pad for reimagining what reconciliation might look like in Canada. In contrast to Gone, MacDonald sees in genocide recognition the basis for a decolonized form of Canadian biculturalism.

This volume does not aspire to serve as a comprehensive overview of all instances of colonial genocide in Indigenous North America. For reasons of space we were unable to cover all regions and periods in which colonial genocide can be argued to have occurred. However, in gathering together the authors presented in this volume, we have worked to bring a variety of Indigenous and non-Indigenous voices, as well as multiple disciplinary perspectives, to bear on this subject. We also sought out contributors who would not regularly locate themselves in the field of genocide studies, where the three editors of this volume sometimes make their home. The result is a set of original, provocative, and cutting-edge contributions to the growing research on colonial genocide.

Notes

1. The full exchange between Gone and Sinclair from the latter's keynote address on September 20, 2012, can be found as a podcast at http://itunes.rutgers.edu/.
2. For more on Gone's sobering caution against an overgeneralized application of the concept, particularly as it may stymie efforts to deal with vulnerabilities to mental health problems and reinforce dichotomous polarizations between Indigenes and settlers, see his chapter in this volume.
3. In the state of Minnesota the Dakota Wokiksuye Memorial Ride began in 2005 to commemorate the 1862 death marches, which ended the war between the United States and the Dakota Oyate ("people" or "nation"). Its participants and supporters have not hesitated to critically use the word *genocide* to describe this history (Faimon 2004; Wilson 2006; Waziyatawin 2008). And in April 2013 a group led by Lakota grandmothers traveled to United Nations headquarters in order to informally submit charges of an ongoing genocide by the United States and South Dakota governments against their nation (Armstrong 2013). At the same time, Indigenous groups and environmental activists on either side of the U.S.-Canadian border have critically used the term *genocide* to describe the destructive impacts of intensive resource exploitation (Huseman and Short 2012).
4. For an alternative and more positive reading of Lemkin's view of culture, see Short 2010a: 50–53.

References

Albright, Madeline K., et al. 2008. *Preventing Genocide: A Blueprint for U.S. Policymakers.* Washington, DC: United States Holocaust Memorial Museum, American Academy of Diplomacy, and Endowment of the United States Institute of Peace.

Alfred, Taiaiake. [1999] 2009. *Peace, Power, Righteousness: An Indigenous Manifesto.* 2nd ed. New York: Oxford University Press.

Alfred, Taiaiake. 2005. *Wasáse: Indigenous Pathways of Action and Freedom.* Orchard Park, NY: Broadview Press.

Annett, Kevin. 2001. *Hidden from History: The Canadian Holocaust.* Vancouver: Truth Commission into Genocide in Canada.

Armstrong, Jeff. 2013. "Lakota to File UN Charges against U.S., South Dakota." *CounterPunch*, May 29. Accessed August 7, 2013. http://www.counterpunch.org/2013/05/29/lakota-to-file-un-genocide-charges-against-us-south-dakota/.

Attean, Esther, and Jill Williams. 2011. "Homemade Justice." *Cultural Survival Quarterly* 34 (1): 36–41.

Bancroft, George. 1832. *A History of the United States: From the Discovery of the American Continent.* Vol. 1. Boston: Little, Brown.

Barta, Tony. [1987] 2000. "Relations of Genocide: Land and Lives in the Colonization of Australia." In *Genocide and the Modern Age: Etiology and Case Studies of Mass Death*, edited by Isidor Wallimann and Michael N. Dobkowski, 237–51. Revised ed. Syracuse, NY: Syracuse University Press.

Barta, Tony. 2008. "Sorry, and Not Sorry, in Australia: How the Apology to the Stolen Generations Buried a History of Genocide." *Journal of Genocide Research* 10 (2): 201–14.

Bauer, Yehuda. 2001. *Rethinking the Holocaust.* New Haven, CT: Yale University Press.

Bigelow, Bill. 1992. "Two Myths Are Not Better Than One." *Monthly Review* 44 (3): 28–48.

Borrows, John. 2010. *Canada's Indigenous Constitution.* Toronto: University of Toronto Press.

Brantlinger, Patrick. 2004. "'Black Armband' versus 'White Blindfold' History in Australia." *Victorian Studies* 46 (4): 655–74.

Brown, Dee. 1971. *Bury My Heart at Wounded Knee: An Indian History of the American West.* New York: Holt, Rinehart and Winston.

Buck, Christopher. 2006. "'Never Again': Kevin Gover's Apology for the Bureau of Indian Affairs." *Wicazo Sa Review* 21 (1): 97–126.

Cardinal, Harold. 1969. *The Unjust Society: The Tragedy of Canada's Indians.* Edmonton: Hurtig.

Chalk, Frank, and Kurt Jonassohn. 1990. *The History and Sociology of Genocide.* New Haven, CT: Yale University Press.

Churchill, Ward. 1997. *A Little Matter of Genocide: Holocaust and Denial in the Americas, 1492 to the Present.* San Francisco: City Lights.

Cook-Lynn, Elizabeth. 2011. *A Separate Country: Postcoloniality and American Indian Nations.* Lubbock: Texas Tech University Press.

Cornell, S. 1990. *Return of the Native: American Indian Political Resurgence.* New York: Oxford University Press.

Curthoys, Ann, and John Docker. 2001. "'Genocide'? Australian Aboriginal History in International Perspective." *Aboriginal History* 25: 1–172.

Curthoys, Ann, and John Docker. 2008. "Defining Genocide." In *The Historiography of Genocide*, edited by Dan Stone, 9–41. New York: Palgrave.

Dadrian, Vahakn N. 1976. "The Victimization of the American Indian." *Victimology: An International Journal* 1 (4): 517–37.

Docker, John. 2008. "Are Settler-Colonies Inherently Genocidal? Re-reading Lemkin." In *Colony, Empire, Genocide: Conquest, Occupation, and Subaltern Resistance in World History*, edited by A. Dirk Moses, 81–101. New York: Berghahn.

Drinnon, Richard. 1980. *Facing West: The Metaphysics of Indian-Hating and Empire-Building.* Minneapolis: University of Minnesota Press.

Edmunds, R. David. 1995. "Native Americans, New Voices: American Indian History, 1895–1995." *American Historical Review* 100 (3): 717–40.

Faimon, Mary Beth. 2004. "Ties That Bind: Remembering, Mourning, and Healing Historical Trauma." *American Indian Quarterly* 28 (1–2): 238–51.

Fein, Helen. 1990. "Genocide: A Sociological Perspective." *Current Sociology* 38 (1): 1–126.

Fixico, Donald L., ed. 1997. *Rethinking American Indian History*. Albuquerque: University of New Mexico Press.

Fontaine, Phil, Michael Dan, and Bernie Farber. 2013. "A Canadian Genocide in Search of a Name." *Toronto Star*, July 19.

Foucault, Michel. 1980. *Power/Knowledge: Selected Interviews and Other Writings, 1972–1977*. New York: Pantheon.

Gosden, Chris. 2004. *Archaeology and Colonialism: Cultural Contact from 5000 B.C. to the Present*. New York: Cambridge University Press.

Gover, Kevin. 2000–2001. "Remarks at the Ceremony Acknowledging the 175th Anniversary of the Establishment of the Bureau of Indian Affairs." *American Indian Law Review* 25: 161–63.

Grant, Agnes. 1996. *No End of Grief: Indian Residential Schools in Canada*. Winnipeg: Pemmican, 1996.

Hall, Anthony J. 2003. *The American Empire and the Fourth World*. Montreal: McGill-Queen's University Press.

Hinton, Alexander Laban. 2012. "Critical Genocide Studies." *Genocide Studies and Prevention* 7 (1): 4–15.

Hinton, Alexander Laban, Thomas La Pointe, and Douglas Irvin-Erickson. 2013. *Hidden Genocides: Power, Knowledge, Memory*. New Brunswick, NJ: Rutgers University Press.

Huseman, Jennifer, and Damien Short. 2012. "'A Slow Industrial Genocide': Tar Sands and the Indigenous Peoples of North America." *International Journal of Human Rights* 16 (1): 216–37.

Jaimes, M. Annette, ed. 1992. *The State of Native America: Genocide, Colonization, and Resistance*. Boston: South End Press.

Jones, Adam. [2005] 2010. *Genocide: A Comprehensive Introduction*. 2nd ed. New York: Routledge.

Katz, Steven T. 1994. *The Holocaust in Historical Context*. Vol. 1: *The Holocaust and Mass Death before the Modern Age*. New York: Oxford University Press.

Kurtiş, Tuğçe, Glenn Adams, and Michael Yellow Bird. 2010. "Generosity or Genocide? Identity Implications of Silence in American Thanksgiving Commemorations." *Memory* 18 (2): 208–24.

Lemkin, Raphael. 1944. *Axis Rule in Occupied Europe: Laws of Occupation, Analysis of Government, Proposals for Redress*. Washington, DC: Carnegie Endowment for International Peace.

MacDonald, David. 2007. "First Nations, Residential Schools, and the Americanization of the Holocaust: Rewriting Indigenous History in the United States and Canada." *Canadian Journal of Political Science* 40 (4): 995–1015.

Manne, Robert. 2001. *In Denial: The Stolen Generations and the Right*. Melbourne, Australia: Schwartz.

McDonnell, Michael A., and A. Dirk Moses. 2005. "Raphael Lemkin as Historian of Genocide in the Americas." *Journal of Genocide Research* 7 (4): 501–29.

Memmi, Albert. [1957] 1991. *The Colonizer and the Colonized*. Boston: Beacon Press.

Mihesuah, Devon A., and Angela Wilson, eds. 2004. *Indigenizing the Academy: Transforming Scholarship and Empowering Communities*. Lincoln: University of Nebraska Press.

Miller, J. R. 1996. *Shingwauk's Vision: A History of Native Residential Schools*. Toronto: University of Toronto Press.

Miller, Mark Edwin. 2004. *Forgotten Tribes: Unrecognized Indians and the Federal Acknowledgment Process*. Lincoln: University of Nebraska Press.

Milloy, John S. 1999. *A National Crime: The Canadian Government and the Residential School System, 1879 to 1986*. Winnipeg: University of Manitoba Press.

Mosby, Ian. 2013. "Administering Colonial Science: Nutrition Research and Human Biomedical Experimentation in Aboriginal Communities and Residential Schools, 1942–1952." *Histoire Sociale/Social History* 46 (91): 145–72.

Moses, A. Dirk. 2002. "Conceptual Blockages and Definitional Dilemmas in the 'Racial Century': Genocides of Indigenous Peoples and the Holocaust." *Patterns of Prejudice* 36 (4): 7–36.

Moses, A. Dirk, ed. 2004. *Genocide and Settler Society: Frontier Violence and Stolen Indigenous Children in Australian History*. New York: Berghahn.

Moses, A. Dirk, ed. 2008. *Colony, Empire, Genocide: Conquest, Occupation, and Subaltern Resistance in World History*. New York: Berghahn.

Moses, A. Dirk. 2010a. "The Field of Genocide Studies." In *Genocide: Critical Concepts in Historical Studies*. Vol. 1: *The Discipline of Genocide Studies*, edited by A. Dirk Moses, 1–23. New York: Routledge.

Moses, A. Dirk. 2010b. "Raphael Lemkin, Culture, and the Concept of Genocide." In *The Oxford Handbook of Genocide Studies*, edited by Donald Bloxham and A. Dirk Moses, 19–41. New York: Oxford University Press.

Moses, A. Dirk, and Dan Stone, eds. 2007. *Colonialism and Genocide*. New York: Routledge.

Moshman, David. 2001. "Conceptual Constraints on Thinking about Genocide." *Journal of Genocide Research* 3 (3): 431–50.

Neu, Dean, and Richard Therrien. 2003. *Accounting for Genocide: Canada's Bureaucratic Assault on Aboriginal People*. Black Point, Canada: Fernwood.

Nichols, Roger L. 1998. *Indians in the United States and Canada: A Comparative History*. Lincoln: University of Nebraska Press.

O'Donnell, C. Vivian. 2008. "Native Populations of Canada." In *Handbook of North American Indians*. Vol. 2: *Indians in Contemporary Society*, edited by Garrick A. Bailey, 285–93. Washington, DC: Smithsonian Institute.

Powell, Christopher. 2011. *Barbaric Civilization: A Critical Sociology of Genocide*. Montreal: McGill-Queen's University Press.

Pratt, Richard H. [1892] 1973. "The Advantages of Mingling Indians with Whites." In *Americanizing the American Indians: Writings by the "Friends of the Indian," 1880–1900*, edited by Francis Paul Prucha, 260–71. Cambridge, MA: Harvard University Press.

Reynolds, Henry. 2001. *An Indelible Stain? The Question of Genocide in Australia's History*. Ringwood, Australia: Viking.

Rickert, Levi. 2012. "Apology to American Indians Unacceptable." *Native News Net-*

work, December 20. Accessed December 21, 2012. http://adambeachfoundation. org/dec-20-apology-to-american-indians-unacceptable-too-little-too-late-nativenewsnetwork/.

Said, Edward. 1978. *Orientalism*. New York: Pantheon Books.

Sanders, Douglas E. 1983. "The Indian Lobby." In *And No One Cheered: Federalism, Democracy, and the Constitution Act*, edited by Keith Banting and Richard Simeon, 301–32. Toronto: Methuen.

Schlesinger, Arthur, Jr. 1992. "Was America a Mistake? Reflections on the Long History of Efforts to Debunk Columbus and His Discovery." *Atlantic* 270 (3): 16–30.

Short, Damien. 2010a. "Australia: A Continuing Genocide?" *Journal of Genocide Research* 12 (1–2): 45–68.

Short, Damien. 2010b. "Cultural Genocide and Indigenous Peoples: A Sociological Approach." *International Journal of Human Rights* 14 (6): 833–48.

Short, Damien. 2012. "When Sorry Isn't Good Enough: Official Remembrance and Reconciliation in Australia." *Memory Studies* 5 (3): 293–304.

Simpson, Leanne R. 2004. "Anticolonial Strategies for the Recovery and Maintenance of Indigenous Knowledge." *American Indian Quarterly* 28 (3–4): 373–84.

Sinclair, Murray. 2012. "Keynote Address: Residential Schools and the Question of Genocide." Colonial Genocide and Indigenous North America Workshop. University of Manitoba, Winnipeg, September 20.

Smith, Linda Thuiwai. 1999. *Decolonizing Methodologies: Research and Indigenous Peoples*. New York: Zed Books.

Spivak, Gayatri C. 1994. "Can the Subaltern Speak?" In *Colonial Discourse and Post-Colonial Theory: A Reader*, edited by Patrick Williams and Laura Chrisman, 66–111. New York: Columbia University Press.

Stannard, David E. 1992. *American Holocaust: Columbus and the Conquest of the New World*. New York: Oxford University Press.

Stannard, David E. [1995] 2001. "Uniqueness as Denial: The Politics of Genocide Scholarship." In *Is the Holocaust Unique? Perspectives on Comparative Genocide*, edited by A. S. Rosenbaum, 245–90. 2nd ed. Boulder, CO: Westview.

Tatz, Colin. 1999. "Genocide in Australia." *Journal of Genocide Research* 1 (3): 315–52.

Thornton, Russell. 1987. *American Indian Holocaust and Survival: A Population History since 1492*. Norman: University of Oklahoma Press.

Thornton, Russell. 2008. "United States Native Population." In *Handbook of North American Indians*. Vol. 2: *Indians in Contemporary Society*, edited by Garrick A. Bailey, 269–74. Washington, DC: Smithsonian Institute.

Titley, E. Brian. 1986. *A Narrow Vision: Duncan Campbell Scott and the Administration of Indian Affairs in Canada*. Vancouver: University of British Columbia Press.

Todorov, Tzvetan. 1984. *The Conquest of America: The Question of the Other*. Translated by Richard Howard. New York: Harper and Row.

Totten, Samuel, and Steven L. Jacobs, eds. 2002. *Pioneers of Genocide Studies: Confronting Mass Death in the Century of Genocide*. Westport, CT: Greenwood Press.

Trevithick, Scott. 1998. "Native Residential Schooling in Canada: A Review of Literature." *Canadian Journal of Native Studies* 18 (1): 49–86.

Trigger, Bruce. 1985. *Natives and Newcomers: Canada's "Heroic Age" Reconsidered*. Montreal: McGill-Queen's University Press.

Tsosie, Rebecca. 2006. "The BIA's Apology to Native Americans: An Essay on Collective Memory and Collective Conscience." In *Taking Wrongs Seriously: Apologies and Reconciliation*, edited by Elazar Barkan and Alexander Karn, 185–212. Palo Alto, CA: Stanford University Press.

Tully, James. 1995. *Strange Multiplicity: Constitutionalism in an Age of Diversity*. New York: Cambridge University Press.

Tully, James. 2008. *Public Philosophy in a New Key*. 2 vols. New York: Cambridge University Press.

Turner, Dale. 2006. *This Is Not a Peace Pipe: Towards a Critical Indigenous Philosophy*. Toronto: University of Toronto Press.

U.S. Congress. 2009. Section 8113, Public Law 111–118. *Making Appropriations for the Department of Defense for the Fiscal Year Ending September 30, 2010, and for Other Purposes*.

Veracini, Lorenzo. 2003. "Of a 'Contested Ground' and an 'Indelible Stain': A Difficult Reconciliation between Australia and Its Aboriginal History during the 1990s and 2000s." *Aboriginal History* 27: 224–39.

Veracini, Lorenzo. 2010. *Settler Colonialism: A Theoretical Overview*. New York: Palgrave Macmillan.

Vizenor, Gerald. 2008. *Survivance: Narratives of Native Presence*. Lincoln: University of Nebraska Press.

Warrior, Robert A. 1994. *Tribal Secrets: Recovering American Indian Intellectual Traditions*. Minneapolis: University of Minnesota Press.

Waziyatawin. 2008. *What Does Justice Look Like? The Struggle for Liberation in the Dakota Homeland*. St. Paul, MN: Living Justice Press.

Waziyatawin. 2009. "You Can't Un-ring a Bell: Demonstrating Contrition through Action." In *Response, Responsibility, and Renewal: Canada's Truth and Reconciliation Journey*, edited by Gregory Younging, Jonathan Dewar, and Mike DeGangé, 193–99. Ottawa: Aboriginal Healing Foundation.

Wilson, Waziyatawin Angela, ed. 2006. *In the Footsteps of Our Ancestors: The Dakota Commemorative Marches of the 21st Century*. St. Paul, MN: Living Justice Press.

Wolfe, Patrick. 2001. "Land, Labor, and Difference: Elementary Structures of Race." *American Historical Review* 106 (3): 866–905.

Wolfe, Patrick. 2006. "Settler Colonialism and the Elimination of the Native." *Journal of Genocide Research* 8 (4): 387–409.

Woolford, Andrew. 2005. *Between Justice and Certainty: Treaty-Making in British Columbia*. Vancouver: University of British Columbia Press.

Woolford, Andrew. 2009. "Ontological Destruction: Genocide and Aboriginal Peoples in Canada." *Genocide Studies and Prevention: An International Journal* 4 (1): 81–97.

Woolford, Andrew. 2011. "Genocide, Affirmative Repair, and the British Columbia Treaty Process." In *Transitional Justice: Global Mechanisms and Local Realities after Genocide and Mass Atrocity*, edited by Alexander L. Hinton, 137–56. New Brunswick, NJ: Rutgers University Press.

Woolford, Andrew. 2013. "Nodal Repair and Networks of Destruction: Residential Schools, Colonial Genocide and Redress in Canada." *Settler Colonial Studies* 3 (1): 61–77.

PART I

INTERSECTIONS AND TRAJECTORIES

CHAPTER 1

DISCIPLINE, TERRITORY,
AND THE COLONIAL MESH

Indigenous Boarding Schools
in the United States and Canada

Andrew Woolford

To date there has been very little comparative work on Indigenous boarding schools in the United States and Canada.[1] The extant literature tends to offer only general comparisons, as in Reyhner and Eder's (2004) *American Indian Education*, where a few key differences between Canadian and American boarding schools are noted amid a broader discussion of U.S. Indigenous education policy: Canadian residential schools lasted longer on average than U.S. schools; Canadian policies were unrelentingly assimilationist, since no reformist period occurred in Canada as it did in the United States in the 1930s; Indigenous parents in Canada had less say regarding to which schools their children were sent; and some Canadian religious denominations lobbied vigorously to prevent diminishment of their control over or the closing of boarding schools (Reyhner and Eder 2004). The cumulative effect of these differences is that Indigenous children in Canada typically entered boarding schools at an earlier age than their U.S. counterparts, and the Canadian system affected more generations of Indigenous children, in a more brutalizing form, than was true in most parts of the United States. However, one must also acknowledge that information about the schools has emerged from very different discursive contexts, since a public culture of traumatic memory and testimony has taken prominence through multiple class actions lawsuits and now the Truth and Reconciliation Commission of Canada (e.g., see Niezen 2013).

In the few comparative examinations of boarding schools in the United States and Canada, however, little attention is given to regional and temporal differences in the development, application, and experience of boarding school policy. Such is the case with Ward Churchill's (2004) *Kill the Indian, Save the Man*, which uses the term *genocide* to hammer all school experiences into a single block and thereby fails to capture the ebb and flow of colonial genocidal processes. Similarly, but in a wider comparison than that offered by Churchill, Andrea Smith (2009) writes about schooling and forced assimilation in the United States, Canada, Australia, and New Zealand, outlining their common assimilative purpose. In contrast to Churchill's and Smith's more critical perspectives, Charles Glenn's (2011) *American Indian/First Nations Schooling* offers a redemptive overview of Indigenous education, treating European schooling as a good that was simply mismanaged for Indigenous pupils. Glenn falls into the trap of accepting perpetrators' claims to humanitarianism as an alibi for their role in the attempted destruction of another group.

While comparative discussion of boarding schools is sparse and, where it exists, over-general, there is a wealth of detailed historical work on Indigenous boarding schools in each country. Some authors offer a broad overview of colonial schooling policy combined with illustrative examples of how it was enacted, in addition to how students adapted to, resisted, and suffered their time at the schools (e.g., Milloy 1999; Miller 1996; Grant 1996; Adams 1995; Szasz [1974] 1999; Reyhner and Eder 2004). But more recent historiography focuses on specific Indigenous boarding schools in an attempt to capture the local particularity of the schooling experience, as well as to offer a portrait of how Indigenous groups, rather than a homogeneous "Indian" people, lived their boarding school days (e.g., Lomawaima 1994; Ellis 1996; Child 1998; Trennert 1988). Most of these authors are critical of schooling policy, but they also seek to show its uneven application across time and space. It is within this unevenness that they locate examples of students who enjoyed aspects of their schooling experience, connected with certain teachers, or eventually used their education for positive purposes unexpected by policy makers, such as by reinforcing rather than shedding their Indigenous identities (McBeth 1983; Lomawaima 1994). Others go further to emphasize that Indigenous students, parents, and communities came to appropriate boarding schools for their own purposes (Gilbert 2010; Gram 2012).

By invoking the term *genocide* I do not ignore the historical nuance of such scholarship. However, my effort is to show how genocidal processes are themselves uneven and uncertain because the colonial networks that generate these processes manifest in unpredictable ways. Like all grandiose modernist projects of statecraft, boarding schools were prone to inconsistencies, variable applications, resistances, and subversions. Therefore, in this chapter genocide speaks more to the process of destruction than a foregone outcome. In short, this chapter looks at the negotiation of genocide—at how groups intending to destroy other groups seek to mobilize their destructive powers, face obstacles and resistances, enroll or combat other actors (including nonhuman actors), and either succeed (in whole or in part) or fail in their efforts.

Three Guidelines for Colonial Genocide Studies and Boarding Schools

To begin, three guidelines for examining colonial genocide in a settler context are in order. First, a multilevel analysis that integrates macro, meso, and micro factors into a processual account of forced assimilation through schooling is needed (Verdeja 2012). Second, a critical approach is required so that colonial regimes are held to account, even while acknowledging the diversity and unevenness of settler colonialism (e.g., see Moses 2000; Wolfe 1999; Veracini 2010). Third, study of colonial genocide should help decolonize genocide studies by challenging Eurocentric biases within the field (see also Logan in this volume).

A multilevel analysis has potential to overcome false dichotomies between agency and victimization in the historical literature on Indigenous boarding schools (Trevithick 1998; Davis 2001). Indeed the degree of structural victimization and the simultaneous possibilities of agency depend upon a multiplicity of factors and negotiations. To navigate this complex matrix, one can imagine colonialism as a series of nets that operate to constrain agency but are also prone to snags and openings that enable agentic resistance. The first net, the widest, traverses the entire social field and brings together dominant realms of social activity, such as economy, education, government, and religion.[2] It is at this broad level that dominant visions of the colonial order are negotiated, for example, the formulation of what was known as the "Indian problem" in both the United States and Canada. This vast net, however, can be effective only through the implementation of a group of increasingly smaller and more institutionally and regionally focused nets. At the upper meso level, within the bureaucratic field inhabited by government, one finds the institutional netting that brings together various state and state-sponsored agencies (see Wacquant 2009, 2010). Military, police, law, education, welfare, and health are a few examples of colonial institutions that are integral to the operation of settler colonialism. But each institution is itself the space for further levels of netting. Indeed at the lower meso or organizational level of the institution of education, a variety of schools (e.g., reservation and nonreservation, federal and mission, day and boarding) form a network of interactions, as they cooperate and compete with one another, depending on various circumstances. Finally, around a specific school we find the last layer of netting, which connects parents, children, teachers, principals, and communities in interactions defined by regionally adapted techniques of governance and control, and a local actor network that involves not just humans but also nonhuman interactants like disease, poverty, animals, and territory in the immediate experiences of assimilative schooling (Callon 1986; Latour 2005).

Together these layers of netting form a mesh, and understanding any particular experience of forced assimilative schooling in a local context requires a multilevel analysis of macro, meso, and micro networks so that one can identify when and where the mesh tightens or loosens in a manner that makes the genocidal project of settler colonialism more or less effective. The colonial mesh therefore must be examined processually, as it expands and contracts across time and differentially across space, with gaps in the mesh loosening in some regions while perhaps closing more tightly around Indigenous communities in others. As I discuss below, conceptualizations of the Indian problem, and the institutions coordinated to respond to this perceived problem—actions that occur at the macro and upper meso levels of this mesh—took distinct forms at specific schools, where superintendents and staff negotiated specific conditions and innovated techniques to try to address higher order concerns about the "Indian problem." These conditions included the resistances Indigenous groups mustered based on a balance of alliances.

This multilevel approach flows into the need for a critical colonial genocide studies (see Hinton 2012) by providing a framework that accounts for the varied and multidimensional nature of colonial destruction rather than basing genocide definitions on comparisons to a "core" of accepted genocide cases. Group destruction is an exceedingly complex undertaking, which requires those who have accepted a genocidal formulation (e.g., the "Indian problem") to enlist an array of institutions, organizations, and actors in the project. Under such conditions the destructive project of assimilation that seeks to resolve the Indian problem is negotiated, which means there is potential for snags in the colonial mesh. Schools adapt policy to local conditions, parents resist by removing and hiding their children within complicated geographies, and communities mobilize whatever power they possess to adjust the terms of forced assimilation. The mesh tightens or loosens, but the genocidal frame of reference remains, despite resistance or refusals of enrollment on the part of those targeted for destruction or the claims of benevolence on the part of its agents (see Jacobs in this volume). Because of this initial destructive framing, there can be no exculpatory or redemptive story of forced assimilation, even if some children enjoyed schools or some teachers showed kindness to children. Settler colonialism is a structure possessed by a "logic of elimination" that guides an imperfect network of institutions, organizations, and actors (Wolfe 2006; see also Barta 1987). Under policies of forced assimilation this logic of elimination takes on a genocidal air, since it is directed toward the purposive destruction of Indigenous groups as sui generis entities. As Jacobs (this volume) adds, this logic of elimination becomes entwined with the everyday practices that constitute a "habit of elimination" whereby destructive practices become taken for granted and their veneer of benevolence is seldom questioned.

To fully capture the meaning of group destruction one must begin to decolonize the Eurocentric assumptions of genocide studies. First, recognition of a multilevel colonial mesh comprising innumerable actors allows for the inclusion of those actors usually disregarded in genocide studies or viewed as external to human groups. For example, while one cannot impute agency to territory, territory is enrolled in either carrying out or resisting forced assimilation. The physical space of the campus imposes the alleged superiority of European "civilization," but proximate Indigenous space offers zones of escape from the designs of colonial destruction. Moreover such nonhuman actors are also potential participants in a group's identity formation and therefore, in some cases, inseparable from the group itself. (On this point as it relates to the buffalo, see also Hubbard in this volume.) For example, the role of story in many Indigenous cultures is to connect identity to territory (Cruikshank 1998) in a manner that makes any assault on the territory, or the stories that sustain the Indigenous group's connection to territory, an assault upon the group itself.

Second, the colonial mesh is not reducible to the plot of a single perpetrator or group of perpetrators. It is a collective rather than an individual endeavor. This means that we must move genocide studies past its individualism, as well as its focus on legalistic notions of specific intent, to try to understand how perpetrator collectivities come to problematize a target group and then to organize and undertake the attempted destruction of that group.

Finally, since colonial genocide studies helps us to understand that the group is more than just the sum of its individual members, it also pushes us to expand our notions of destruction. Genocide studies has often fixated on the physical destruction of groups (e.g., Chalk and Jonassohn 1990) rather than the collective interactions that allow the group to persist in the ongoing negotiation of its existence. The bonds of the group are more than the lives of group members, and any assessment of potential destruction requires some knowledge of how the group constitutes and reproduces itself rather than an oversimplified examination of the percentage of group members murdered by perpetrators (Woolford 2009).[3]

A full realization of these guidelines is not possible in this short chapter. But to illustrate their saliency I will offer a brief discussion of how the "Indian problem" was formulated in the United States and Canada, followed by meso- and micro-level examples of how discipline and desire operated as paired techniques of forced assimilation and how territory and space were enrolled in or used to resist the assimilative project.

Macro Level: The Indian Problem

Assimilative education is an example of "thinking like a state" to the extent that it represents an ambitious attempt at social engineering spawned by a specific governmental problematization that is perceived to be solvable through a strictly managed or scientifically guided intervention into the social world (see Scott 1998; Patzer in this volume). For boarding schools, it is the so-called Indian problem, a subject of much debate and discussion in the late nineteenth and early twentieth century, that provided the formulation of the problem to be solved. In the United States and Canada the settler population expanded and grew, expropriating Indigenous lands and resources by any means necessary. But settler violence failed to provide security on the frontier. Indeed the Indian Wars in the United States were an object lesson for governments in both the United States and Canada, as attempts to defeat Indigenous nations militarily proved an extremely costly approach to national consolidation (see Madley, Whaley in this volume). As Ben Madley (this volume) notes, the costs were more than monetary, as reports from the wars also impacted the nation's reputation, leaving it grasping for alternative solutions to the "Indian problem."

So if war and massacre were largely off the table, what was to be done with the "Indian"? By 1879 boarding schools began to win out as the primary answer to this question, although other institutional interventions into Indigenous lifeworlds would continue alongside and in combination with schools (see Powell and Peristerakis in this volume). But driving the establishment of the schools was the belief that Indigenous adults were too stubborn in their traditions for effective assimilation, making children the primary targets for a rapid transformation of Indigenous communities away from their cultural past and toward a Europeanized future (Szasz [1974] 1999; Miller 1996; Adams 1995). Debates persisted about the level of "civilization" possible for Indigenous peoples, with evolutionary and race science–based arguments that suggested only a limited or gradual uplift becoming prominent in the early twentieth century and to some degree supplanting ideas about Christian or liberal universalism, according to which all were "blank slates" upon which civilization could be writ. Despite such disagreements, general consensus was achieved on the necessity of schooling, and the language of "civilization" and (full or partial) "assimilation" served as a shorthand to draw together what might otherwise be disparate views, as well as a broad variety of policy interventions into Indigenous lives (Fear-Segal 2007; Hoxie 1983).

In the United States and Canada mission schools run by various religious groups preceded the creation of industrial-style or vocational boarding schools. These mission schools were sparsely sited, proselytizing institutions that were limited in their power to compel attendance. The birth of modern Indigenous boarding schools is thus often credited not to the missions but rather to Lt. Richard Pratt, who began his experiment in education in the late 1870s, working on seventy-two captured Indian warriors (thirty-four Cheyenne, two Arapaho, twenty-seven Kiowa, nine Comanche, and one Caddo) at the Fort Marion prison in Florida (Adams 1995). Rather than simply let prisoners sit in cells and perish, Pratt launched a school of "civilization." This education presented a welcome contrast to the brutal conditions of the prison, and many prisoners succumbed to Pratt, accepting his lessons and the improvements to prison life that came with them. Pratt, though, knew that his experiment would gain recognition only if it were visible, and thus he made sure to place his prisoners on regular public display. As public acclaim grew for his methods, Pratt pressed his superiors to allow him to release some of the younger prisoners to an institution where they could continue their education. After some searching, Pratt received word in 1878 that Samuel Chapman Armstrong—founder and principal of the Hampton Normal and Industrial Institute, a school that taught African American freedmen—would accept seventeen of Pratt's pupils (Adams 1995).

Then, in 1879, Pratt opened his own school in an abandoned army barracks in Carlisle, Pennsylvania. Pratt's vision of the nonreservation boarding school, which he enacted at Carlisle, became the model for the early U.S. federal boarding school system: Indigenous children were removed from their communities and habituated to the ways of European life in close proximity to white "civilization." As Pratt stated, "We make our greatest mistake in feeding our civilization to the Indians instead of feeding the Indians to our civilization" (quoted in Adams 1995: 53).

Around the time that Pratt was opening Carlisle, Nicholas Flood Davin was sent by John A. MacDonald's government in Canada to investigate Indian Education in the United States. Davin completed a short tour that included stops in Washington, where he met with chiefs from the "Five Civilized Tribes," and Minnesota, where he observed a mission-run contract boarding school. In his report Davin favorably cites U.S. efforts to have Indigenous peoples concentrated on reservations, possessing lands in severalty rather than in common, and prepared for citizenship through industrial education. Like others at the time, Davin (1879: 1) was unconvinced that day schools, where children returned to their home after a day's education, could work with Indigenous children to overcome the "influence of the wigwam." The industrial boarding school was therefore, in his view, the best option for Indians and half-breeds "to be merged and lost" within the idea of the nation (11). But Davin also felt that the migratory nature of Indigenous groups in the Northwest would make extensive establishment of industrial boarding schools expensive and inefficient; therefore it would be best for Canada to make use of the already existing network of denominational missions as a foundation for the residential schooling system. Soon several government-sponsored, mission-managed boarding schools were opened, including the Qu'Appelle and Battleford Industrial Schools in Saskatchewan. (For further discussion of Davin, see MacDonald in this volume.)

This cursory overview of the conceptualization of the "Indian problem" in the late nineteenth century and the development of a network of schools to attend to this problem gives some sense that a collective action frame was emerging to coordinate forced assimilation and "civilization." Such a frame is seldom entirely coherent or stable; it is subject to ongoing negotiations, influence from lower levels in the colonial mesh, and local applications, and therefore this level of the colonial netting tells us very little about the actual experiences of attempted group destruction. In contrast, looking at the colonial mesh at its meso and micro levels allows one to better understand the uneven spread of such an action frame. At the meso level institutional (upper) and organizational (lower) networks provided the foundation upon which individual schools negotiated their own particular approach to assimilative education. For example, schools were buttressed by other state institutions, such as the police, welfare services, or health provisions, drawing upon these resources to compel or entice parents to enroll their children. As well, suborganizational networks of schools promoted the circulation of techniques of school management and assimilation but also fostered competition among schools for students. At the micro level techniques and alliances multiply, making for complicated networks of action that impact the assimilative designs of specific schools. For the purposes of this chapter, I focus on one set of techniques, discipline and desire, and one form of alliance, territorial and spatial, to illustrate some ways that these two layers of the colonial mesh tighten or slacken, making it either more damaging to Indigenous groups or more open to resistance and subversion. For the micro-level analysis, examples will be drawn from the Albuquerque (AIS) and Santa Fe (SFIS) Indian

Schools in New Mexico and the Fort Alexander (FA) and Portage la Prairie (PlaP) Indian Residential Schools in Manitoba.

Discipline and Desire at the Meso and Micro Levels

In the boarding school literature the term *discipline* is often used to discuss corporal punishment. In contrast, I use it here to broadly capture the techniques and tactics employed within schools to shape student behavior. But it must also be recognized that such visions of order are pursued and achieved by means other than discipline. For this reason the concept of discipline is coupled with desire to capture how pleasure and excitement were enlisted and operated in conjunction with discipline within specific schools as a further technique to facilitate Indigenous assimilation.

Although deriving from a place of mutual influence, boarding schools in the United States and Canada were erected on somewhat different disciplinary models. Whereas Pratt's militarism influenced U.S. boarding schools in the late 1800s, only to be gradually replaced by a professionalized and expert-driven Indian civil service in the early decades of the twentieth century, monastic modes of discipline were more prominent and lasting within Canadian schools. These different disciplinary styles often resulted in similar treatment for students: loss of all emblems of cultural identity upon entry into the school, prohibitions against use of Indigenous languages, a regimented time table with days split between education and manual labor, and severe punishments for perceived indiscretions.

Differences can also be discerned, such as the more frequent use in the United States of military marching and parades and the organization of students within battalions or other military units. In general, Indigenous children were perceived to be lacking in discipline. According to Samuel Armstrong, military discipline was necessary because it "enforces promptness, accuracy and obedience and goes further than any other influence could do to instill in the minds of the students what both the Negro and Indian sadly lack, a knowledge of the value of time" (quoted in Coleman 1993: 42–43). Superintendent Cart at SFIS agreed about the need for military discipline. On May 27, 1891, he wrote to the commissioner of Indian Affairs for a copy of "The New Drill Regulations for the Army," commenting, "I consider any kind of military drill an aid in disciplining a school."[4] Cart also pushed to have all his students in military dress.

Yet the military model in U.S. boarding schools did not have the backing of an upper meso-level institutional matrix to support its continuation. Although several principals and school workers had military backgrounds and students often found success in the U.S. military, the military was not a primary actor in delivering education. Professional and managerial technologies of control thus came to replace militaristic forms, since the organizational logic of the civil service was much more entrenched within the American Indian bureaucracy. But the transition from military discipline to managerial governance happened more quickly at some schools than others. AIS abolished its military system in 1924, eight years prior to its being formally discontinued within the Indian Affairs system, replacing it with a model of student self-governance (Gram 2012). Ted Jojola, an Isleta Pueblo scholar, argues, "In Albuquerque, Pratt's approach was short-lived. Almost immediately, pueblo parents began keeping their children home. A lawsuit was filed on behalf of an Isleta boy who was prevented from leaving the school. The parents prevailed and the school quickly softened its militaristic tone" (quoted in Linthicum 2002).[5]

In contrast Christian denominations charged with the delivery of schooling in Canada formed an institutional structure with vested interests in the continuation of schooling and the delivery of religious education. Thus while military discipline largely disappeared from U.S. boarding schools by the late 1920s, monastic discipline would continue in evidence well into the 1950s in Canada. At the Oblate schools, for example, the strictures of the "Durieu system" were still felt. As Miller (1996: 91) describes it, "This regime, named after Oblate Paul Durieu, employed methods of total control over mission Indians for the purpose of effecting a permanent conversion to Christian religious values and practices. The Durieu system aimed at eradicating all unchristian behaviour by means of strict rules, stern punishments for transgressors, and use of Indian informers and watchmen as proctors to ensure conformity and inflict punishments as necessary."

In a Roman Catholic boarding school, such as Fort Alexander, prayer and confession were regular parts of the disciplinary regime. Reflecting on his time at FA in the 1930s, Joseph Boubard reports that he "didn't learn much at school. Lot of praying."[6] School inspector B. Warkentin noted the continuation of monastic discipline at the FA school in the early 1940s: "What has been wrong, if I may presume to criticize, is that church authorities have been and are concerned about saving the Indian's soul. . . . Instructors shall not destroy the excellence of the Indian character by ill-advised behavior or by the teaching of incomprehensible and disputed dogma. Our aim always should be to build on the existing foundation rather than to substitute a new basis."[7] At FA Roman Catholic control over the school, sustained by isolation from regular inspection and reinforcement from Catholic institutional networks, meant a longer experience of monastic discipline than was the case for militaristic discipline in New Mexico.

But discipline was complemented by a regulated desire. Tactile, social, aural, physical, and other pleasures were made available in limited quantities to seduce Indigenous students to the school environment. Superintendent of Indian Schools Estelle Reel, in her 1904 annual report, writes of the girls at AIS who were so desperate to weave that they converted chairs into looms. Rather than discourage such traditional practices, Reel argued that this knowledge of the pleasure Indian girls take in weaving could be used to foster their insertion into American life, namely by encouraging them to use traditional arts as a means to earn income. Reel (1904: 22) wrote, "The arts and crafts of the Indian have a far greater value than is generally known, and in many sections of the country they become efficient aids to him in earning a livelihood."

Jacqueline Fear-Segal (2007) is one of the few scholars to note the role desire, or seduction, played in Indian education. Drawing from Stephan Lukes, she notes that the subject of power can be seduced into cooperation in his or her own domination (Fear-Segal 2007: 20). Adams (1995) likewise sees the force of "ritual" within the schools as religious ceremonies and secular holidays implemented a new set of rituals to replace the ceremonials of traditional Indigenous life. Dances and socials were occasions when exhibition of a regulated desire was acceptable and students could "acquire habits of politeness, refinement, and self possession" (Indian Office quoted in Adams 1995: 177). Sports were another opportunity for simultaneous experiences of excitement and disciplinary training within the schools. As well, schools offered access to American cinema. An anonymous interviewee from Jemez Pueblo recalls the seduction of film and food at AIS: "I went voluntarily there, and they didn't force me to go and then the kids that were there told such exciting stories about movies every Saturday night and this government gravy and beans, you know, and how they drilled, and that there were many other Indians besides Jemez."[8]

The last part of this quotation reinforces that discipline and desire are linked rather than oppositional categories. Indeed discipline fulfills certain desires—for regularity, for order—and it offers attractions: the cohesion of marching, the power of the uniform. Many students interviewed after their time at schools spoke fondly of the discipline: "That school was just a strict school, it was like a military school. I like it that way because there is discipline. . . . We used to go out in the field in the morning before breakfast, rain or shine, we used to drill every morning, military training, like the soldiers do in actual combat zones and we knew how to handle guns."[9]

The role played by desire as an assimilative technique is more evident at SFIS and AIS than at FA or PlaP, although the latter schools did use ritual, sports, dances, and movies to draw students to Westernized lifestyles.

Nonetheless instances of these enjoyments are more frequently mentioned in U.S. boarding school testimony. In contrast students more often recall the drab, brutal, and repetitive nature of Canadian residential schools. When newly arrived as principal at PlaP, A. C. Huston wrote, "An observant visitor to certain of our Indian Residential schools would ask why we have deliberately set out to make our residences such dull and unattractive places. I must confess that it might easily appear that we had done so intentionally. Some schools are as void of light illuminative colors as a medieval dungeon. Where an attempt has been made to introduce color dark brown floors and battleship gray walls has been the answer. The whole appearance is in many cases depressing. Hades could not appear more colorless, drab or forlorn."[10]

In these brief examples a glimpse is available of how meso-level institutional forces could bolster disciplinary regimes or create spaces for the emergence of less restrictive and more autonomous systems of control. In New Mexico the shift toward managerial strategies of governance meant schools were not beholden to a strict disciplinary regime and had more room for innovation and for increased micro-level applications of techniques of desire and seduction to enlist students in the project of their assimilation. In contrast, in Manitoba meso-level institutional networks propped up regimes of monastic discipline, leaving less space for micro-level variations.

Territory and Space at the Meso and Micro Levels

Adrea Lawrence (2011: 18), in her study of the day school at the Santa Clara Pueblo, writes, "Land—the physical geography, the flora and the fauna of a place—is a full-fledged participant in the story of how Santa Clarans, Hispanos, and Anglos learned their positions, roles, and strategies in the colonization of the place called 'New Mexico.'" Indeed territory and space are at once the crucial stakes of settler colonialism, a basis for Indigenous collective identity and resistance, and actors enlisted to resolve the "Indian problem."

With respect to territory, at the meso level the location of U.S. federal boarding schools in urban centers placed them more within the observational sight lines of other institutional actors and the general public. In contrast the distance of a school like FA from centers of government meant that although policies continued to be developed by government and circulated among schools, inspections were rare. As the Truth and Reconciliation Commission of Canada (2012: 18) notes, "Indian Affairs regularly adopted various policies regarding health, discipline, and education, but these were not enforced consistently. At the outset, it had few school inspectors (and those it did have lacked educational qualifications). In later years, provincial school inspectors, who had no power to have their recommendations implemented, inspected the schools."

At the micro level territory and space could play numerous roles in the assimilative education. First, the buildings and grounds of the schools were themselves actors enrolled by governing authorities to transform Indigenous children, but also subverted for purposes of resistance. The buildings were typically larger than any the children had seen before and were meant to impart the superiority of European culture in both their grandness and style (de Leeuw 2007). Moreover space was used to separate children from opposite-sex siblings and to culturally disorient them, replacing the openness of Indigenous territory and structures with the regulated and compartmentalized space of the classrooms. Agricultural lands around the school communicated the taming of nature, and guardhouses, principals' offices, and the school cemetery were reminders of the destructive and punitive power of the white man (de Leeuw 2007; Fear-Segal 2007). But students also sought out and occupied the interstices of this regulated space—for example, hiding places where food could be stored, conversations could go unheard, plans could be made, love could blossom, or tears could be shed.

Second, space factored into how students and communities could avoid forced attendance at the schools or negotiate the terms under which they were instructed. At AIS Superintendent Bryan (1894–96) was persuaded that Indian students should be drawn from nearby communities rather than brought from long distances, and given opportunity to visit these communities on occasion, contrary to Pratt's vision of boarding schools. McKinney (1934) attributes this belief to Bryan's independence, but Gram (2012) more convincingly demonstrates that the Pueblo communities did much to influence Bryan on these matters, namely by using their proximity to monitor conditions at AIS and interschool competition to threaten to remove their children to mission schools unless AIS operated on terms more acceptable to the Pueblo. Under such pressure Bryan reformulated his compromise so that it was consistent with the goals of the Bureau of Indian Affairs: "The ultimate object of the Indian schools is, as I understand, not so much the improvement of individuals as the gradual uplifting of the race. To this end it is important to guard against the formation of a wide gulf between parent and child, and to prevent the child from acquiring notions inconsistent with proper filial respect and duty. . . . I would recommend that at this school, therefore, the term consist of nine months, giving the children three months at their homes" (quoted in McKinney 1934: 11). In this instance Bryan supported the government's objective of transforming Indigenous communities through their children but also suggested that the "Indian problem" was better addressed by keeping children in some provisional contact with their communities.

Complicating this picture, however, is the fact that there is no singular way in which territory factors into the boarding school experiences. For the Navajo (Diné), as for the Pueblo, territory is important, but its role is different. Removal from territory, in particular by the "Long Walk" (1864–69), served as a threat used to compel Navajo assimilation, but territory also intervened to obstruct this assimilation. The Navajo territory is vast, and, during the first half-century of assimilative schooling, the roads were poor to nonexistent. Because the U.S. government failed to provide the local schools promised under Article 6 of the Treaty of 1869, which returned the Navajo to their traditional territory after their forced removal to Fort Sumner during the time of the Long Walk, the Navajo were able to resist sending their children to boarding schools with the assistance of their territory. When trying to recruit Navajo for SFIS in 1891, Superintendent Cart noted, "At the Navajo Agency the prospect is not encouraging. The Indians are scattered over such a vast extend of rough country that at this time of the year, they are almost inaccessible."[11]

Students from Sagkeeng First Nation (formerly the Fort Alexander reserve) would, like the Pueblo, appear to be at an advantage in terms of their proximity to their boarding school. However, territorial proximity in and of itself was not sufficient for loosening the colonial mesh and creating opportunities for greater Indigenous control. As a Roman Catholic school in a relatively isolated region, FA was part of a Canadian colonial network that exhibited fewer policy fluctuations than the American network. The location of the school, which was difficult to reach by road, even though it was relatively close to towns like Lac du Bonnet and Pine Falls, also meant there was less opportunity for inspection and less opportunity for Indigenous leaders to speak to officials beyond the school to voice their concerns. Isolation and the power of the Indian agent helped ensure continued Indigenous enrollments without the Sagkeeng people, whose children were the majority at the school, increasing their negotiating power. But whereas FA was isolated, PlaP had more pressure to serve as a demonstration school, since visitors were more likely to come by: "I am particularly anxious that this school should always present a good appearance. It is in rather a public place and they always have a number of visitors, and people get a better impression [when] everything is up-to-date."[12] Under such circumstances accessibility of the school resulted in concerns about impression management that were not characteristic of all Canadian boarding schools.

Third, schools enlisted distance from territory to forge a radical break with

Indigenous communities. Child (1998: 27) argues, "Distance caused hardship, distress, and unimagined miseries but failed to extinguish the very real influence parents and family continued to exert over the lives of students. . . . The power of home was so intense and comforting that few students left that world behind." Child counters those who see distance as a pure break with the sociocultural world of the Indigenous community, but we must complicate her analysis and push it further to get to the variety of ways in which space, territory, time, and distance were enlisted by various actors in negotiating the boarding school experience. Distance could be catastrophic or overcome because it was always interacting with other factors, such as access for and the political power of the Indigenous group in question.

Child's insight speaks to another terrain of resistance: memory. Theodore Fontaine (2010: 11), who contributed the foreword to this volume, addresses this space in his memoir of FA when he writes, "Early on, I discovered that I could escape from the loneliness and sadness of my life at Indian residential school by recalling and reliving my joyous life as a boy at home before school. . . . The practice of retreating into my mind and my memories became a lifelong survival skill." And yet the disciplinary structure of the schools, and the disciplinary regimentation of time, meant it was often difficult for children to occupy this space of memory and to overcome the imposed distance. Later in his book Fontaine suggests that students regulated one another in a manner that made it difficult to inhabit the terrain of memory: "Memories of happy times surfaced a lot in my first year at school, particularly at night and in the dark. Eventually they came less and less often—perhaps mercifully, for whimpering and crying were reason for the older boys to belittle and abuse the younger ones—and later I thought perhaps they were only a dream" (91).

The proximity of a school like Fort Alexander to Sagkeeng First Nation did not automatically result in community empowerment, the retention of Indigenous traditions, or less loneliness for the children. Indeed looking outside to see a family member walking past the fence, yet with no ability to make contact with that person, could intensify longings for home and create resentments among those community members outside the schools who had failed to protect them from enrollment. One FA Survivor recalls, "When I was at the residential school there, my home was only about a quarter mile away. I can see my home from the boarding school, like, when you, you know, I was lonely, wondering why I can't go home, or why people can't come and visit me."[13] Reservation boarding schools could also taint the space of the reserve for Survivors. A child of Survivors tells of how her parents (Survivors of Portage la Prairie and Sandy Bay Residential Schools) moved away from their community to protect their children from attending such a school: "And so they raised us off reserve for one of those reasons, for that particular reason, so that none of us would ever have to go to residential school."[14]

In these examples one can see the regionally and temporally differentiated role played by territory and space within the project of assimilative schooling. Although the Indian problem was mapped over most of North America, its assimilative mesh was advanced or interrupted by the diverse alliances of key actors (schools, staff, families, communities, and students) formed with territory and space.

I have conceptualized a colonial mesh to understand the many layers of assimilative genocide in North America, as well as how this mesh tightens or loosens at different times and in different places. Although a comprehensive narrative of the processes by which this mesh tightens and loosens across time and space was not possible, illustrative examples were drawn from boarding schools in Manitoba and New Mexico to show how macro, meso, and micro levels of the colonial mesh interact with one another to create novel formations of assimilative schooling in specific locales. The destructive project of forced assimilation as conceptualized through the Indian problem therefore succeeds or fails depending on a set of institutional, organizational, and local conditions that are very complex and need to be carefully traced. In attempting to trace multilevel intersections of policy, institutions, organizations, and actors, this approach remains critically focused in that the collective framework of destruction envisioned at the higher levels of the colonial mesh is still held to account without sacrificing historical nuance. In addition this approach seeks to contribute to decolonizing of genocide studies by making space within it for participation by nonhuman actors, capturing nonindividualistic notions of destructive intentionality in the complex negotiation of the Indian problem, as well as the multipronged nature of government and school responses to this problem, and by leaving space for a deeper understanding of group life that acknowledges the importance of territory in both group self-definition and protection.

Notes

1. I use *boarding school* to refer, in general, to all forms of dormitory-based schooling for Indigenous children. This term therefore encompasses residential and federal boarding schools, industrial schools, mission schools, on- and off-reservation schools, and other variations. I use the term *Indigenous* to refer to both Canadian Aboriginal and American Indian peoples, although terms such as *Aboriginal* and *Indian* are used when appropriate to the historical or legal context of the discussion.

2. According to Bourdieu, a field is "a network, or a configuration, of objective relations between positions" (Bourdieu and Wacquant 1992: 97). Within such networks competition occurs for the symbolic power to determine the valuational standards of the field.

3. These three points are merely a preliminary contribution to the decolonization of genocide studies. More needs to be done in terms of conducting community-based participatory research, preventing epistemological violence, and recognizing the power of the researcher as he or she represents the experiences of members of targeted groups (e.g., see Smith 2012).

4. Letter from Superintendent Cart to Commissioner of Indian Affairs, May 27, 1891, RG 75.20.36, Reel M1473, Roll 1, vols. 1–2, Bureau of Indian Affairs (BIA) Records Created at the SFIS, Press Copies of Miscellaneous Letters Sent, SAL.

5. It is worth noting that Superintendent Reuben Perry transformed Sunday drills and parades into a health inspection exercise during which students would present their clothes and fingernails for inspection prior to marching to the athletic field for exercises.

6. Joseph Boubard, Sagkeeng Cultural Education Centre Oral History Project, August 5, 1987, C1623, AOM.

7. Letter from B. Warkentin to R. A. Hoey, Superintendent of Welfare and Training, Department of Indian Affairs, June 23, 1942, RG 10, vol. 8448, file 506/23-5-019, LAC.

8. Doris Duke American Indian Oral History Collection, 1968–72 (MSS 314 BC), Tape 446, interviewed December 4, 1970, CSWR.

9. Jerome Brody, Zia Pueblo, started at SFIS in 1916, Doris Duke American Indian Oral History Collection, 1968–72 (MSS 314 BC), Tape 24, interviewed April 5, 1968, CSWR.

10. Letter from A. C. Huston (Portage la Prairie Indian Residential School principal) to J. Waite, Indian Agent, February 4, 1946, RG 10, vol. 6274, file 583-5, part 8, LAC.

11. S. M. Cart to Commissioner of Indian Affairs, April 1, 1891, RG 75.20.36, Reel M1473, Roll 1, vols. 1–2, BIA Records Created at the SFIS, Press Copies of Miscellaneous Letters Sent, SAL.

12. Letter from W. M. Graham, Indian Commissioner, to D. C. Scott, Deputy Superintendent General, January 29, 1929, RG 10, vol. 6273, file 583-5, part 4, LAC.

13. File number 01-MB-26JY10-009, Long Plain, interviewed July 27, 2007, TRC.

14. File number 01-MB-26JY10-011, Long Plain First Nation, interviewed July 28, 2010, TRC.

References

PRIMARY SOURCES

Archives of Manitoba (AOM), Winnipeg, Sagkeeng Cultural Education Centre Oral History Project Records (1989).
Centre for Southwest Research (CSWR), University of New Mexico, Albuquerque, American Indian Oral History Collection, 1968–72.

Library Archives of Canada (LAC), Federal Archives Division, Ottawa, Ontario, RG-10, Records of the Department of Indian Affairs, Red Series, Black Series, and School Files.

Reel, Estelle. 1904. *Report of the Superintendent of Indian Schools.* Washington, DC: Government Printing Office.

State Archives and Library (SAL), Santa Fe, New Mexico, Santa Fe Indian School, Press Copies of Letters Sent and Received, Reel M1473 (SFIS).

Truth and Reconciliation Commission of Canada (TRC).

SECONDARY SOURCES

Adams, David Wallace. 1995. *Education for Extinction: American Indians and the Boarding School Experience, 1875–1928.* Lawrence: University Press of Kansas.

Barta, T. 1987. "Relations of Genocide: Land and Lives in the Colonization of Australia." In *Genocide and the Modern Age: Etiology and Case Studies of Mass Death*, edited by I. Wallimann and M. N. Dobkowski, 237–52. Syracuse, NY: Syracuse University Press.

Bourdieu, P., and L. Wacquant. 1992. *An Invitation to Reflexive Sociology.* Chicago: University of Chicago Press.

Callon, Michel. 1986. "Some Elements of a Sociology of Translation: Domestication of the Scallops and the Fishermen of St. Brieuc Bay." In *Power, Action and Belief: A New Sociology of Knowledge*, edited by John Law, 196–223. London: Routledge and Kegan Paul.

Chalk, Frank, and Kurt Jonassohn. 1990. *The History and Sociology of Genocide: Analyses and Case Studies.* New Haven, CT: Yale University Press.

Child, B. J. 1998. *Boarding School Seasons: American Indian Families, 1900–1940.* Lincoln: University of Nebraska Press.

Churchill, Ward. 2004. *Kill the Indian, Save the Man: The Genocidal Impact of American Indian Residential Schools.* San Francisco: City Lights.

Coleman, Michael C. 1993. *American Indian Children at School, 1850–1930.* Jackson: University Press of Mississippi.

Cruickshank, Julie. 1998. *The Social Life of Stories: Narratives and Knowledge in the Yukon Territory.* Lincoln: University of Nebraska Press.

Davin, Nicholas Flood. 1879. *Report on Industrial Schools for Indians and Half Breeds.* Ottawa, March 14.

Davis, Julie. 2001. "American Indian Boarding School Experiences: Recent Studies from Native Perspectives." *OAH Magazine of History* 15 (2): 20–22.

de Leeuw, Sarah. 2007. "Intimate Colonialisms: The Material and Experienced Places of British Columbia's Residential Schools." *Canadian Geographer* 51 (3): 339–59.

Ellis, Clyde. 1996. *To Change Them Forever: Indian Education at Rainy Mountain Boarding School, 1893–1920.* Norman: University of Oklahoma Press.

Fear-Segal, Jacqueline. 2007. *White Man's Club: Schools, Race, and the Struggle of Indian Acculturation.* Lincoln: University of Nebraska Press.

Fontaine, Theodore. 2010. *Broken Circle: The Dark Legacy of Indian Residential Schools, a Memoir.* Victoria: Heritage House.

Gilbert, Matthew Sakiestewa. 2010. *Education beyond the Mesas: Hopi Students at Sherman Institute, 1902–1929.* Lincoln: University of Nebraska Press.

Glenn, Charles, L. 2011. *American Indian/First Nations Schooling: From the Colonial Period to the Present*. New York: Palgrave.

Gram, John. 2012. "Education on the Edge of Empire: Pueblos and the Federal Boarding Schools, 1880–1930." Ph.D. dissertation, Southern Methodist University.

Grant, Agnes. 1996. *No End in Grief: Indian Residential Schools in Canada*. Winnipeg: Pemmican.

Hinton, Alexander L. 2012. "Critical Genocide Studies." *Genocide Studies and Prevention* 7 (1): 4–15.

Hoxie, Frederick. 1983. *The Final Promise: The Campaign to Assimilate the Indian, 1880–1920*. Lincoln: University of Nebraska Press.

Latour, Bruno. 2005. *Reassembling the Social: An Introduction to Actor-Network Theory*. Oxford: Oxford University Press.

Lawrence, Adrea. 2011. *Lessons from an Indian Day School: Negotiating Colonization in Northern New Mexico, 1902–1907*. Lawrence: University Press of Kansas.

Linthicum, Leslie. 2002. "Gone, but Not Forgotten: Memories and Photographs Are All That Remain of the Albuquerque Indian School." *ABQ Journal*, August 11.

Lomawaima, K. T. 1994. *They Called It Prairie Light: The Story of Chilocco Indian School*. Lincoln: University of Nebraska Press.

McBeth, Sally J. 1983. "Indian Boarding Schools and Ethnic Identity: An Example from the Southern Plains Tribes of Oklahoma." *Plains Anthropologist* 28 (100): 119–28.

McKinney, Lillie G. 1934. "History of the Albuquerque Indian School." Master's thesis, University of New Mexico.

Miller, J. R. 1996. *Shingwauk's Vision: A History of Native Residential Schools*. Toronto: University of Toronto Press.

Milloy, John S. 1999. *A National Crime: The Canadian Government and the Residential School System, 1879 to 1986*. Winnipeg: University of Manitoba Press.

Moses, A. Dirk. 2000. "An Antipodean Genocide? The Origins of the Genocidal Moment in the Colonization of Australia." *Journal of Genocide Research* 2 (1): 89–106.

Niezen, Ronald. 2013. *Truth and Indignation: Canada's Truth and Reconciliation Commission on Indian Residential Schools*. Toronto: University of Toronto Press.

Reyhner, Jon, and Jeanne Eder. 2004. *American Indian Education: A History*. Norman: University of Oklahoma Press.

Scott, James C. 1998. *Thinking Like a State: How Certain Schemes to Improve the Human Condition Have Failed*. New Haven, CT: Yale University Press.

Smith, Andrea. 2009. "Indigenous Peoples and Boarding Schools: A Comparative Study." Paper presented at Permanent Forum on Indigenous Issues, eighth session, New York, May 18–29.

Szasz, Margaret Connell. [1974] 1999. *Education and the American Indian: The Road to Self-Determination Since 1928*. Albuquerque: University of New Mexico Press.

Trennert, Robert A. 1988. *The Phoenix Indian School: Forced Assimilation in Arizona, 1891–1935*. Norman: University of Oklahoma Press.

Trevithick, Scott. 1998. "Native Residential Schooling in Canada: A Review of Literature." *Canadian Journal of Native Studies* 18 (1): 49–86.

Truth and Reconciliation Commission of Canada. 2012. *They Came for the Children: Canada, Aboriginal Peoples, and Residential Schools*. Winnipeg: Truth and Reconciliation Commission of Canada.

Veracini, Lorenzo. 2010. *Settler Colonialism: A Theoretical Overview*. Houndmills, England: Palgrave Macmillan.

Verdeja, Ernesto. 2012. "On Situating the Study of Genocide within Political Violence." *Genocide Studies and Prevention* 7 (1): 81–88.

Wacquant, L. 2009. *Punishing the Poor: The Neoliberal Government of Social Insecurity*. Durham, NC: Duke University Press.

Wacquant, L. 2010. "Crafting the Neoliberal State: Workfare, Prisonfare, and Social Insecurity." *Sociological Forum* 25: 197–220.

Wolfe, Patrick. 1999. *Settler Colonialism and the Transformation of Anthropology*. London: Continuum.

Wolfe, Patrick. 2006. "Settler Colonialism and the Elimination of the Native." *Journal of Genocide Research* 8 (4): 387–409.

Woolford, A. 2009. "Ontological Destruction: Genocide and Aboriginal Peoples in Canada." *Genocide Studies and Prevention: An International Journal* 4 (1): 81–97.

CHAPTER 2

GLOBAL CAPITAL, VIOLENCE, AND THE MAKING OF A COLONIAL SHATTER ZONE

Robbie Ethridge

Two hundred years after Europeans invaded what is now the American South, the precontact Mississippian world of the Native peoples was in collapse. This collapse was not sudden; it took almost two hundred years to run its course. This collapse was not caused by the mere exercise of European military might; indeed Natives participated in and, in some cases, precipitated it. Nor did the collapse extinguish Native peoples. Although thousands of Indians died and were enslaved, and virtually all Native polities were destroyed, there were survivors who regrouped and reformed new kinds of polities, and they reorganized and restructured their lives for living in the new geopolitical landscape that was securely in place by 1730.

To understand the scope and causes of these disruptions one needs a regional frame for integrating contact-era events and people from the Mississippi Valley to the Atlantic into a single interactive world. Scholars have begun to develop such a frame, called the "Mississippian shatter zone" (Ethridge 2006: 207–18; 2009a). The Mississippian shatter zone was a large region of instability in eastern North America that existed from the late sixteenth century through the early eighteenth century. It was created by the combined conditions of the inherent structural instabilities of the Mississippian chiefdoms; the introduction of Old World pathogens and the subsequent serial disease episodes and loss of life; the inauguration of a nascent capitalist economic system by Europeans through a commercial trade in Indian slaves, animal skins, and guns; and the intensification and spread of violence and warfare through the Indian slave trade and especially through the emergence of militaristic Native slaving societies that sought a larger share of the European trade (Ethridge 2006: 208–9; 2009a: 2).

My purpose in introducing the shatter zone concept here is that it may prove useful in understanding some of the root causes of colonial genocide. I come to the study of genocide not as a scholar of genocide but as a historical anthropologist interested in the effects of global capitalism on Indigenous peoples, and especially how the inauguration of Indigenous peoples into the modern world system in the sixteenth and early seventeenth century resulted in widespread disruptions and violence to Native life. I do not use the term *genocide* in examining this case study, although certainly the study I offer is commensurate with the larger colonial genocide theme of this volume (Benvenuto, Woolford, and Hinton in this volume). Rather my goal here is to contribute to the conversation on the root causes of modern genocide with my insights into a particular case study detailing how capitalism works to destabilize political and social systems in the periphery, in this case the American Indians of the sixteenth- and early seventeenth-century American South, resulting in widespread violence.[1]

Calling this destabilization genocide may not be entirely correct, despite the fact that it resulted in massive deaths and dislocations of Native peoples. The violence of this time period was a product of the intersection of global economic agendas and Western imperial aims and local Indian political aims and Indian economic agendas as they struggled to find a place in the new global economic system enveloping them. In such a complex colonial context it is difficult to identify a perpetrator and a specific intent to destroy a group, as is usual in genocide analysis. Hence the term *genocide* is probably not exact in describing the disruptions, violence, and instability that resulted from the Indian slave trade in the American South.

The Indians of the eighteenth-century American South are the ones familiar to most people and whose descendants are recognized today as the Creek, the Cherokee, the Chickasaw, the Choctaw, the Catawba, and so on. We now know that these societies formed out of the collapse of sixteenth-century polities such as Coosa, Mabila, Pacaha, Chicaza, Cofitachequi, and others as they broke apart in the late sixteenth and seventeenth century. We still do not have an adequate vocabulary to describe the Native societies of the eighteenth century. They have been called "confederacies," "tribes," "nations," and so on. We now generally call them "coalescent societies" because they were all, to varying degrees, coalescences of people from different societies, cultures, and languages who relocated and banded together after the fall of their polities (Hudson and Ethridge 1998).

The sixteenth-century ancestors of the southern coalescent societies were organized into what archaeologists call "chiefdoms." A chiefdom is a political and social group characterized by a ranked social order of ruling elite and nonelite lineages. Chiefdoms were the prevailing political unit in much of the South during the time known as the Mississippi Period (900 C.E. to 1700 C.E.). It was during the Mississippi Period that people of the chiefdoms built the flat-topped earthen temple mounds that one still finds throughout the American South. The chiefdoms in the South were tied together in myriad ways—ecologically, politically, socially, economically, and religiously. Although the exact nature of these ties has yet to be fully explained, they served to integrate these ancient chiefdoms into a single world, which has come to be known as the "Mississippian world" (see Knight 2010; King 2003; Pauketat 2009; Anderson 1994; Hally 2008; Ethridge 2010: 11–59).

The earliest Europeans to come to the American South, the Spanish explorers such as Hernando de Soto, Tristán de Luna, and Juan Pardo, encountered the Mississippian world. The presence of these Spaniards undoubtedly destabilized the Mississippian world through military encounters, the depletion of local food supplies, and Spanish interference in local political machinations and military exploits. Archaeological evidence points to the decline of some chiefdoms and a geopolitical reshuffling of others after the Spanish *entradas*. Still the Mississippian world did not fall after these first encounters, and in fact the evidence suggests that many of the polities that Soto and the other Spaniards saw were sustained into the seventeenth century (Ethridge 2010: 60–88).

Immediately after the early Spanish expeditions, the Spanish established the post of St. Augustine to patrol the Atlantic sea lanes and sent a handful of Catholic missionaries to convert the Indians in present-day Florida and south Georgia to the Catholic faith. Against all odds the friars succeeded in establishing a sprawling mission system. With these endeavors also came Spanish soldiers and settlers and a trade in European goods (Waselkov 1989; Smith 2000: 110–11; Hann 2006: 81, 83).

This early Spanish trade also served to inaugurate the European trade in deerskins, which would eventually become the economic mainstay of the South in the eighteenth century (Waselkov 1989). The Spaniards brought many things to Florida from the Old World other than trade items: domesticated animals, new plant species, and disease microbes. Current interpretations of the demographic consequences of the introduction of Old World diseases into the New World conclude that there was a 90 percent loss of Native life after contact, but this loss now appears to have occurred over about two hundred years (from roughly 1550 to 1750) in a gradual, not steep, demographic decline and only after sustained European contact. In addition scholars agree that disease was but one factor in the demographic decline, and they now point to contributing factors such as incorporation into the modern world economy, slaving, internecine warfare, dropping fertility rates, violent colonial strategies, and general cultural and social malaise from colonial oppression (Ethridge 2009a: 10–13).

Certainly the introduction of Old World disease epidemics and cultural exchanges with early Spaniards had profound effects on Native life. But these instabilities, epidemics, and exchanges in and of themselves were not transforming. The engagement of Native peoples in the world economy through contact with the English, French, and Dutch was the final hammer to complete the shatter zone, and Native polities across the South fell. But people adapted and survived by revamping their social, political, and economic orders.

During the seventeenth century England, France, and the Netherlands were knitting together a global economy by articulating economic circuits such as the Atlantic trade circuit with the Asian trade circuit. The North American overseas ventures were one set of commercial endeavors among a host of many others that crisscrossed the globe. And the North American settlements served mostly as extractive trade factories, at least in the first hundred or so years. These settlements may have been small and overwhelmed by Indian populations, but they were a conduit through which the economic power of the core countries flowed. Hence one should not look on the American colonies and colonists themselves as wielding extraordinary transforming power over Native life; rather it was the system in which they served that was so transformative. It was not Quebec, Albany, Plymouth, Jamestown, or Charles Town that created the Mississippian shatter zone; it was the global commercial power of the Netherlands, England, and France as funneled through these settlements (Ethridge 2009a: 16–19; 2010: 89–91; 2012: 295–303).

European colonial entrepreneurs engaged local Indians in trading beaver, deer, and other animal skins and furs. In addition early European traders kept up a brisk trade in Indian slaves. Slavery was not new to North American Indians at contact; most Native groups practiced an Indigenous form of slavery in which war captives sometimes were put into bondage. Large-scale captive taking, such as occurred during the seventeenth and early eighteenth century, however, was most likely not conducted during the precontact era but came about with the colonial commercial slave trade. As in precontact slavery, slaves sold on the commercial market were obtained in war through raiding and the capturing of prisoners. Male captives were usually killed, as in precontact days, but noncombatants were now spared and taken as war captives. The fate of war captives varied. Captors sometimes consigned them to forced labor with no social rights. In some cases captors adopted captives into a kin group, used them in prisoner exchanges with their foes, married them, gave them as gifts of alliance, obtained ransoms for them, or used them to forge trade alignments. By far, though, the vast majority of captives were sold to Europeans, who either kept them as slaves or sold them on the Atlantic slave market (Ethridge 2010: 91–93; Dye 1991; 2002: 137–38; Martin 1994: 308–10; Perdue 1979: 3–18; Snyder 2010; Rushforth 2012; Barr 2005; Usner 1989; Lauber [1913] 2002: 55–57, 82–86, 242–49; Gallay 2002: 288–314; Ramsey 2001: 168).

The commercial trade in Indian slaves provides a window on the transformative power of the modern world economy. In the slave trade Indian groups were responding to a powerful dynamic wherein Indian men incurred debts when they accepted guns, ammunition, metal tools, and other items from European traders. The European traders in turn requested that the debt be paid in slaves and skins. Armed with European-manufactured weapons, Indian groups raided rival groups for slaves. Members of the unarmed group would then have to acquire guns with which to defend themselves, and they in turn would become slave raiders. The result was a vicious cycle of slaving, trading, and weapons escalation (Ethridge 2010: 91–93).

The shatter zone, as the name implies, takes violence to be attendant to imperialism and the birth of the early modern world. It also takes violence to be part and parcel of capitalist incorporation, as theorized by Brian Ferguson and Neil Whitehead in *War in the Tribal Zone*. Ferguson and Whitehead ([1992] 1999) have begun to devise a theoretical framework for understanding the historical context of Indigenous violence. They argue that one general result of state expansion and capitalist incorporation is the militarization of Indigenous peoples through an increase, intensification, and transformation of Indigenous warfare on the edges of empire, or the "tribal zone." However, they do not understand Indigenous people to be victims of expanding states. They insist that in addition to the colonizers' violence, Indigenous people who lived and participated in the colonial world also contributed to and sometimes created colonial violence. They point out that this is especially true when Indigenous people became involved in commercial slave trading. Of all the types of colonial commerce, the commercial trade in slaves required a high level of force as a necessary accompaniment to trade. In other words, whereas trading in furs or skins did not necessarily involve warfare, trading in slaves did because it required force.

Ferguson and Whitehead ([1992] 1999) further argue that once Indigenous people became involved in European trade and colonial politics and military agendas, Indigenous warfare was directed by elements outside of a purely Native world. Access to European trade goods, control over the supply and distribution of Indian slaves and trade goods, the use of Indigenous mercenaries by the colonizers, as well as mutual military, political, and economic manipulation of each other by Europeans and Indigenous inhabitants, all began to figure into Indigenous motivations for and strategies of war. Certainly warfare penetrated Indian life throughout North America before contact, so much so that war, not peace, may have been the accepted state of affairs. Once Europeans arrived, however, Native war efforts became entwined with market interests and international commerce. As warfare became tied to commercial interests, Indigenous mechanisms for mitigating war and brokering peace broke down. In addition, in the American South Europeans exploited intra-Indian hostilities and fanned the flames of war in order to keep the trade flowing. In short, as Indian commercial interests in the colonial Indian trade intensified, so did warfare and the militarization of those Native groups who sought to control the trade (Ethridge 2006, 2009a, 2010).

The Indian slave trade, then, was primarily a commercial venture with violence and internecine warfare as part and parcel of the slaving business. In the shatter zone the commercial trade in Indian slaves was not a continuation and adaptation of preexisting captivity patterns; it was a new kind of slaving, requiring a new kind of occupation created on the edge of the modern world-system—that of organized militaristic slavers (Ethridge 2009a: 24–26; 2009b).

Militaristic Indian societies, created in the shatter zone, held control of the trade by annihilating their competitors. The Iroquois, who lived in present-day upstate New York, are perhaps the most famous example of a militaristic Indian slaving society. When the Dutch settled Albany, the Iroquois began a series of wars against any groups blocking their way to the European trade centers. The Mahican, Montagnais, Algonkin, Huron, Petun, Neutral, Wenro, and Erie broke apart. Iroquois warriors also dealt a severe blow to the Susquehannah and drove them into an alliance with the British in Maryland. By about 1660 Iroquois were moving into the South, where they began an intensive campaign against the Indians in the Appalachians and Piedmont (Edmunds, Hoxie, Salisbury 2007: 55–64; Starna and Watkins 1991: 41–46, 51–53; Richter 1992: 32–49, 51–62; Abler [1992] 1999: 158–60; Fox 2009: 65–66).

The repercussions of the turmoil in the Northeast reverberated across the eastern Woodlands to the Mississippi River. For one, as people fled the Iroquois assault, they moved north, west, and south, where they sometimes joined local populations and sometimes displaced local populations. In addition to Iroquois raiding, southern Indians came under attack in the mid-seventeenth century by two other militaristic slaving societies: the Westo

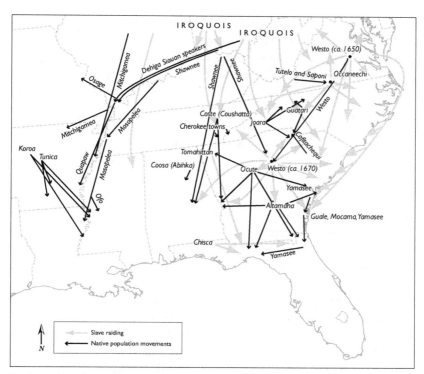

Map 2.1. Indian slaving and population movements, ca. 1650–1680.

and Occaneechi. The Westo were a group of Erie from present-day New York who had fled Iroquois raiding and relocated to Virginia. The Occaneechi were a relatively small Woodland group who lived in the lower Carolina piedmont. By around 1650 Virginia traders enlisted both as trade partners. Once Charles Town was established in 1670, the Westo switched partners from the Jamestown traders to a group of Charles Town slavers known as the Goose Creek men and moved to the Savannah River. Over the next thirty or so years gun-toting Occaneechi and Westo unleashed a reign of terror over much of the Southern Piedmont, Appalachians, and Atlantic seaboard as they raided their bow-and-arrow neighbors for slaves to sell to European buyers, precipitating the breaking apart of many of the Mississippian chiefdoms throughout this region, such as Cofitachequi, Joara, Guatari, Ocute, Mocama, and Guale (map 2.1; Woodward 1911: 133; Bland 1911: 16; Worth [1995] 2007: 9, 36, 40, 45; Rivers [1856] 1972: 388–89; Bowne 2005; Gallay 2002: 53–69; Ward and Davis 1993: 427–30; Ward and Davis 1999: 112–16, 258; Davis 2002: 139, 150–51).

The Westo and Occaneechi also effectively cut out any other Indian groups hoping to make trade alliances with the Europeans, thereby controlling the whole of the southern Indian trade. By 1680 the Goose Creek men and the Jamestown slavers, both wanting to open the slave and skin trade to interior groups, instigated conflicts that resulted in the annihilation of the Westo and the diminishment of the Occaneechi's trading power (Everett 2009; Ethridge 2010: 154–55; Cheves [1987] 2000: 388–89; Bowne 2005: 89–105; Gallay 2002: 53–69; Worth [1995] 2007: 9, 12–42, 45; 1998: 2:16–21; Woodward 1911; Rivers [1856] 1972: 388–89). With the Westo and Occaneechi neutralized, English traders freely courted the numerous other Indian polities forming throughout the South.

By the middle of the seventeenth century some of the interior polities had already begun a process of social and political transformations, and we see the emergence of the first coalescent societies. Recent archaeological research indicates that hereditary leadership of these chiefdoms did not suddenly collapse to be replaced by an egalitarian system of governance. Instead the evidence now suggests that hereditary leadership persisted, perhaps into the nineteenth century, except that it was being continually challenged, strained against, and thwarted by tendencies toward decentralization and a more democratic form of government that characterized the coalescent societies of the eighteenth- and nineteenth-century Native South. New trade opportunities intensified such strains and tensions to these old leadership patterns (Lapham 2005; Hall 2009: 12–54; Wesson 2008; Jenkins 2009; Ethridge 2010: 64–74, 82–87, 222–31; Waselkov 1989).

Before contact the elite controlled trade and access to exotic goods. European traders, however, were willing to trade with anyone, hence ambitious men and women could and did strike independent trade agreements, thus rising in status and challenging elite authorities. In time people quit building mounds and quit burying their elite dead with elaborate grave goods, signaling a severe disruption in Mississippian political and perhaps religious lives. In the place of temples on top of mounds, people constructed more democratic public spaces such as council houses adjacent to public plazas, where, rather than a small group of elites, all townspeople could gather to deliberate important decisions (Schroedl 2000: 208, 212–16; Marcoux 2010: 9–13; Rodning 2009; Jenkins 2009).

In addition survivors from fallen chiefdoms were seeking refuge with stable groups or banding together into new groups and seeking European alliances (map 2.2). For example, in present-day central Alabama and western Georgia four polities emerged from Mississippian chiefdoms: Abihka on the Coosa River, Tallapoosa on the Tallapoosa River, Alabama on the Alabama River, and Apalachicola on the Chattahoochee River. All would later form the Creek Confederacy. The functioning groups in central Alabama and Georgia were an especially attractive prospect to refugees, and many people joined their ranks. Elsewhere in the South similar processes of coalescence were occurring. By 1690 new groups such as the Esaw (later known as the Catawba), Yamasee, and Cherokee had emerged, all formed from fallen polities such as Cofitachequi, Ocute, Coste, and the numerous Cherokee-speaking simple chiefdoms in the southern Appalachians. In other cases, such as that of the Chickasaw, their Mississippian chiefdom declined sometime after encountering Soto, and the people began a long journey to the northwest, where they reformulated their towns near present-day Tupelo, Mississippi, and began taking in refugees. By this time, though, the Chickasaw political hierarchy was seriously diluted, and they only vaguely resembled the sixteenth-century Chicaza that Soto had fought in battle. The Choctaw, on the other hand, did not emerge from a precontact polity but formed as refugees from the Gulf Coast and Mississippi Valley began pouring into present-day central Mississippi. Other functioning polities such as the Tuscarora in eastern Carolina were also taking in refugees. All of these new polities were shedding their chiefly ways as they too, now armed with European guns, became militarized slavers. Carolina soon had agreements with all, and all began raiding throughout the Piedmont, Atlantic seaboard, present-day northern Florida, and along the Gulf Coast (Ethridge 2010: 149–93).

As the colonial competition over the American South intensified, virtually every Indian group became enveloped in the slave trade. By the late seventeenth century France was making inroads into the Mississippi Valley. England had taken notice and sent her scouts deep into the interior in the hopes of winning Native allies through an expanded trade system. In particular, Carolinians turned their trade attentions to the Chickasaw. Because of their geographic location on the Upper Trade Path and their willingness to engage with the English, the Chickasaw came to play a pivotal role in the slave trade, and so South Carolina had an unbroken chain of English-allied slaving partners across the entire extent of the Lower Trading Path from Charles Town to the Mississippi River. In addition a smallpox epidemic followed the slave traders, and disease swept through the Lower South in 1696, carrying off untold numbers of Indians (Ethridge 2010: 161–62; Kelton 2007: 152–54).

The documents generated by the early colonial efforts of the French on the Gulf Coast and lower Mississippi River Valley speak of a region in much turmoil. Everywhere the French explorers went, they saw evidence of disease, slaving, and severe disruptions to Indian life. The most vulnerable Indians were on the Gulf Coast, and they were abandoning their homelands and relocating farther away from the slave catchers. In the worst cases whole towns

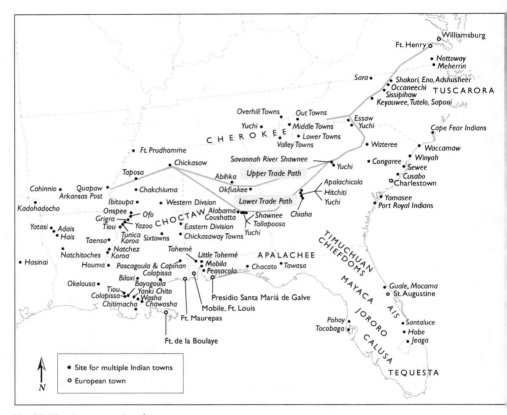

Map 2.2. The American South, ca. 1700.

were being destroyed, with survivors seeking solace elsewhere. All were fearful of English-armed slave raiders; in particular the Alabama, Tallapoosa, Apalachicola, Abihka, and Chickasaw were perpetrating much turmoil and unrest over the whole of the region (Iberville 1981: 4, 32–33, 37–38, 43–48, 63, 92, 135–36, 139–41, 168–70, 169; Pénicaut [1953] 1988: 5–8, 11, 18–20, 64, 81; Sauvole 1969: 28, 31, 33, 37; du Ru [1934] 1997: 58–62; Calderón 1936: 10; Boyd 1936: 12, 19; Knight and Adams 1981: 181–86, 189, 182; Rowland and Sanders 1927–32: 3:527–28, 535–37; La Harpe 1851: 20, 22–23; Tonti 1939: 224; Montigny [1935] 1967: 207–8, 220; Waselkov and Gums 2000: 7, 17, 22–26; Brain, Roth, and de Reuse 2004: 593, 596; Lankford 2004: 666; Usner 1998: 37–38, 44; Galloway 1995: 183–99, 246–49; Goddard et al. 2004: 175–76, 185, 189; Brightman 2004: 642–44).

Many of these Gulf Coast groups had deep precontact roots in the region; however, many had been pushed to the coast by forces of colonialism, particularly the commercial trade in Indian slaves. By the early eighteenth century along the Gulf Coast, numerous small Indian groups were clustered near the French colonies of Mobile, Biloxi, and New Orleans. They became collectively known as the *petites nations* (see map 2.2; Ethridge 2010: 245). These groups never coalesced but remained small, independent groups. Their eastern counterparts on the Atlantic Coast were known as the "settlement Indians." There is no doubt that the Gulf and Atlantic Coast Indians took the brunt of the Indian slave trade. One reason for this was the inability of these small nations to coalesce after the fall of their chiefdoms. In the interior, formidable Indian coalescent societies such as the Creek, Cherokee, Choctaw, and Chickasaw emerged out of precontact polities. Conducting successful slave raids against these coalescent societies would have been difficult at best, since all were also now armed with European weapons and engaged in the slave trade. Along the Gulf and Atlantic Coast, though, the groups did not coalesce and remained vulnerable to slavers. The petites nations and settlement Indians sought French and English protection from the slavers, but in both cases, in the end, the protection turned out to be very little (Ethridge 2011; 2010: 108–10, 168–93).

In its first decades the slave trade had been largely a commercial venture, controlled by Indian middle men and militarized slaving societies. And although frowned upon by colonial authorities, traders often instigated and fomented Indian wars in order to keep the supply of slaves flowing into Carolina. As the competition between France, England, and Spain for the American South escalated, this system of warfare and slaving became linked to the imperial aims of European rivals. In 1702 English hostilities against Spain and France erupted in a conflict known as Queen Anne's War. With the outbreak of war the imperial aims of England became strongly and inextricably tied to that of the commercial slave trade; the result was an intensification of and political and military purposefulness to slaving. In other words, the conflicts during Queen Anne's War were not simply military tactics; they were also brutal slaving expeditions, and Indian mercenaries and English slave traders stood to gain much economically while advancing the territorial boundaries of Carolina (Gallay 2002: 127–54; Ethridge 2010: 194–95).

The English took advantage of the outbreak of the war to attempt an aggressive assertion of English imperial aims in the South. The most blatant example of this occurred when Governor James Moore, a notorious slaver who had been appointed as interim governor in South Carolina, gathered Indian and English forces for an offensive to drive the Spanish out of Florida, thus making way for a push to the Mississippi River. This inaugurated a series of debilitating slave raids into Spanish Florida (Gallay 2002: 135–39, 144–45;

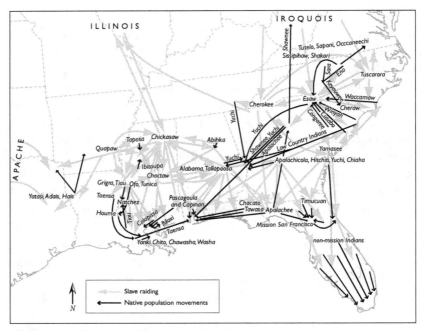

Map 2.3. Indian slave raids and population movements, ca. 1700–1715.

Crane [1929] 2004: 75–79, 86; Ethridge 2010: 206–10; Ashe 1911: 272; Hann 1988: 191, 234–35; 2006: 67; Worth 1998: 2:145; 2009: 302–3; Boyd, Smith, and Griffin, 1951; La Harpe 1851: 29).

At Ocmulgee in 1704 Moore assembled fifty Carolinians and a thousand Indian troops. The documentary evidence is somewhat garbled in its description of the Indian groups represented in this mission, but warriors from the Cherokee, Coweta, Tallapoosa, Abihka, Alabama, Apalachicola, Chisca, and Yamasee are usually identified as being in the force (Crane [1929] 2004: 78–79; Hann 1988: 191, 234–35; 2006: 67; Worth 1998: 2:145; 2009: 302–3; Gallay 2002: 144–45; La Harpe 1851: 29; Boyd, Smith, and Griffin 1951: 48–95). Within two years the Spanish missions and Native chiefdoms would lie in ruins, and most of the Native inhabitants of Florida were enslaved or had fled to French protection in Mobile (map 2.3). After the decimation in Spanish Florida, the only remaining Mississippian chiefdom in the entire South was the Natchez, on the lower Mississippi River.

After destroying the Spanish missions, Carolina now enlisted their Indian allies, the Yamasee, Cherokee, Catawba, Tallapoosa, Alabama, Abihka, and Chickasaw, to turn on any French-allied Indians. They also hoped to lure French allies, especially the Quapaw, Natchez, and Choctaw, into the

Carolina fold. The plan was to outfit English-allied interior groups and then pressure them into raiding and weakening any French Indian allies. Without Indian allies the French colony would then be left quite vulnerable. To achieve this the Carolina government spared no expense in securing Indian trade and military partnerships. The result, especially for the Gulf Coast Indians, was devastating. Scores of people were killed and enslaved, and dozens of towns were destroyed or severely diminished. By 1708 English-allied slave raiders forced the Gulf Coast Indians to contract their remaining towns toward Mobile and the protection of the French. The greatest toll from this slaving, however, was suffered by the Choctaw, as each raid resulted in massive losses for them (La Harpe 1851: 34–35; Crane [1929] 2004: 85–88; Pénicaut [1953] 1988: 98, 102–3; Rowland and Sanders 1927–32: 2:25, 3:26–27, 34; Gallay 2002: 137–40, 149–50, 151–53; Waselkov and Gums 2000: 26–27; Ethridge 2010: 210–22).

Queen Anne's War officially ended in 1713, but the conflagration had only whetted Carolina's appetite for westward expansion and helped to refine the strategy of bending intra-Indian conflicts to Carolinian goals. On the eve of the Indian and British conflict known as the Yamasee War, English traders could be found throughout Indian country and among the Chickasaw, Quapaw, Yazoo, Chakchiuma, Natchez, Siouan-speaking Piedmont groups, Cherokee, Catawba, Apalachicola, Tallapoosa, Alabama, Abihka, Savannah River Shawnee, Savannah River Apalachee, and Yamasee. The Choctaw too now accepted English offers and guns, and they too were now commercial slavers. All in all, Carolina counted over two hundred traders in Indian country. Given the penetration of the trade system throughout the South that came with Queen Anne's War, slaving campaigns became even more frequent, although Indian slavers had to go farther and farther afield to capture their human commodities. To make matters worse, the Iroquois began afresh their southern campaign. They especially harassed the Cherokee, Catawba, Tuscarora, and others (La Harpe 1851: 43; Pénicaut [1953] 1988: 159; Crane [1929] 2004: 102–3; Le Page du Pratz [1774] 1947: 57, 291, 297, 303–4; McDowell 1958: 32, 33, 77, 129, 168; Rowland and Sanders 1927–32: 2:39, 75, 185; Nairne 1988: 76–77; Oatis 2004: 60, 77, 122; Worth 2009; Merrell 2003: 118–24; Perdue 2003: 137–38; Boyce 2003: 153; Richter 1992: 237–38; Ethridge 2010: 232–36).

The whole of the American South was now a brutal network of slave raiders, slaving, warfare, and instability. We do not have a good reckoning of the number of southeastern peoples who were enslaved. The historian Alan Gallay recently calculated that between 1685 and 1715 the English enslaved twenty-four thousand to fifty-one thousand, although he thinks these numbers are low. The Canadians, English in New England, and Louisiana French were also engaged in the slave trade, but the number of southern Indians taken by these traders remains unknown. The exact number of Indians living in the South in 1685 also is not firmly known, but Peter Wood estimates there were around 199,400 people at that time. Thirty years later, in 1715, the population dropped to 90,100, a 54 percent loss of population (Gallay 2002: 298–99; Lauber [1913] 2002: 63–118; Alchon 2003: 138–39; Wood 1989: 38–39; Rushforth 2012: 163–64). Combining Wood's and Gallay's figures, slaving could account for as many as half of this population loss during these thirty years. Disease and deaths in warfare most likely account for most of the other half.

The first sign of Indian discontent with the British was the Tuscarora War of 1711, a limited engagement. The next outbreak of hostilities involved Indians from Carolina to the Mississippi River. This was the Yamasee War, named after the group that made the first strike. On April 15, 1715, Yamasee warriors killed the traders among them. Within the week the Apalachicola, Tallapoosa, Alabama, Abihka, Savannah River Shawnee, Savannah River Apalachee, Yuchi, Chickasaw, and Choctaw also killed their resident traders. Later estimates put the number at ninety traders killed in the first few days of the war. The involvement of the Chickasaw was most likely minimal and probably went no further than killing their resident traders. The Cherokee, Catawba, and Piedmont Siouans, somewhat reluctant to become involved, joined but only much later in the war (Oatis 2004: 127–28; Ramsey 2008).

The Yamasee War seriously threatened the colony of Carolina as warriors descended on the Carolina low country and came perilously close to sacking Charles Town. Although the Yamasee War was short lived, the magnitude of this conspiracy and inter-Indian alliance cannot be overstated; this was the first and only time the Indians of the American South acted in unison to defy the European and later American invasions into their lands. Not only did it force Carolina to reconsider its position in regard to Indian allies, but it also effectively ended the trade in Indian slaves. After the Yamasee War the focus of trade switched from slaves to deerskins, although Indian slaves continued to be bought and sold in small numbers into the nineteenth century and even later.

The Yamassee War also marked the emergence of the colonial South, a new South born out of the Mississippian shatter zone (Ethridge 2010: 243–54). In 1540 Indians lived in a purely Indian world; by 1715 they lived on the edge of an expanding and conflict-ridden European world and in a new social landscape that included not only Indians but also Europeans and Africans. The first two hundred years of European colonization of the American South, then, is a story about the collision of two worlds: the emerging modern world of Europe and its American colonies and the centuries-old Mississippian world. The meeting of these two worlds was not peaceful or orderly; it was marked by warfare, violence, struggle, disease, and hardship for all involved. The Mississippian chiefdoms, structured to rise and fall, fell spectacularly with European contact, and they failed to rise again because of the turmoil and wide regional instability created by the introduction of Old World diseases and the increased violence and disruptions from the commercial trade in Indian slaves. Faced with the collapse of their chiefdoms, people invented new ways of putting their social lives back together, ways that sought to adapt to a field of play with nation-states and a global capitalist economy.

The shatter zone concept is useful for understanding colonial genocide because it provides a frame for the larger historical and global context of colonial instabilities in the wake of capitalist penetration. The concept moves us away from causal explanations for colonial genocide such as racism, xenophobia, and cultural dominance and instead asks us to consider the intersection of both Indigenous and external forces at play in the creation of violence that is oftentimes a handmaiden to global capitalism.[2]

Notes

1. The shatter zone concept is more akin to Mark Levene's (2004a, 2004b) "post-genocide," concept, which suggests that the global political economy has been intrinsic to the causes of genocide since its emergence in the early sixteenth century.
2. Mark Levene's observation, although on twentieth-century genocide, applies to earlier centuries when he notes that "the micro-level of radicalized state violence cannot in the twentieth century be isolated from the macro-context in which it occurs any more than a perpetrator society's possibly historic hatred against a particular group or groups can be disentangled from hegemonic, globalizing pressures which may finally and fatally push it over the genocidal precipice." See Levene 2004a: 1, 162, 164n5.

References

Abler, Thomas S. [1992] 1999. "Beavers and Muskets: Iroquois Military Fortunes in the Face of European Colonization." In *War in the Tribal Zone: Expanding States and Indigenous Warfare*, edited by Brian R. Ferguson and Neil Whitehead, 158–68. 2nd ed. Santa Fe, NM: School of American Research.

Alchon, Suzanne Austin. 2003. *A Pest in the Land: New World Epidemics in a Global Perspective*. Albuquerque: University of New Mexico Press.

Anderson, David G. 1994. *Savannah River Chiefdoms: Political Change in the Late Prehistoric Southeast*. Tuscaloosa: University of Alabama Press.

Ashe, John. 1911. "The Present State of Affairs in Carolina, by John Ash, 1706." In *Narratives of Early Carolina, 1650–1708*, edited by Alexander S. Salley Jr., 135–60. New York: Charles Scribner's Sons.

Barr, Julianna. 2005. "From Captives to Slaves: Commodifying Indian Women in the Borderlands." *Journal of American History* 92 (1): 19–46.

Bland, John. 1911. "The Discovery of New Brittaine, 1650." In *Narratives of Early Carolina, 1650–1708*, edited by Alexander S. Salley Jr., 1–20. New York: Charles Scribner's Sons.

Bowne, Eric E. 2005. *The Westo Indians: Slave Traders of the Early Colonial South.* Tuscaloosa: University of Alabama Press.

Boyce, Douglas W. 2003. "'As the Wind Scatters the Smoke': The Tuscaroras in the Eighteenth Century." In *Beyond the Covenant Chain: The Iroquois and Their Neighbors in Indian North America, 1600–1800*, edited by Daniel K. Richter and James H. Merrell, 151–64. University Park: Pennsylvania State University Press.

Boyd, Mark F., ed. and trans. 1936. "The Expedition of Marcos Delgado from Apalachee to the Upper Creek Country in 1686." *Florida Historical Quarterly* 16: 1–32.

Boyd, Mark F., Hale G. Smith, and John W. Griffin. 1951. *Here They Once Stood: The Tragic End of the Apalachee Missions.* Gainesville: University Press of Florida.

Brain, Jeffrey P., George Roth, and Willem J. de Reuse. 2004. "Tunica, Biloxi, and Ofo." In *Handbook of North American Indians*, vol. 14, *Southeast*, general editor, William C. Sturtevant, volume editor, Raymond D. Fogelson, 568–97. Washington, DC: Smithsonian Institution.

Brightman, Robert A. 2004. "Chitimacha." In *Handbook of North American Indians*, vol. 14, *Southeast*, general editor, William C. Sturtevant, volume editor, Raymond D. Fogelson, 642–52. Washington, DC: Smithsonian Institution.

Calderon, Gabriel Díaz Vara. 1936. "A Seventeenth-Century Letter of Gabriel Díaz Vara Calderón, Bishop of Cuba, Describing the Indians and Indian Missions of Florida." Trans. Lucy L. Wenhold. Smithsonian Miscellaneous Collections 95, no. 16. Smithsonian Institution, Washington, DC.

Cheves, Langdon, ed. [1987] 2000. *The Shaftesbury Papers and Other Records Relating to Carolina and the First Settlement on the Ashley River Prior to the Year 1676.* Collections of the South Carolina Historical Society, no. 5, Charleston.

Crane, Verner W. [1929] 2004. *The Southern Frontier: 1670–1732.* Tuscaloosa: University of Alabama Press.

Davis, R. P. Stephen, Jr. 2002. "The Cultural Landscape of the North Carolina Piedmont at Contact." In *The Transformation of the Southeastern Indians, 1540–1760*, edited by Robbie Ethridge and Charles Hudson, 135–54. Jackson: University Press of Mississippi.

du Ru, Paul. [1934] 1997. *Journal of Paul du Ru February 1 to May 8, 1700: Missionary Priest to Louisiana*, translated by Ruth Lapham Butler. Fairfield, WA: Ye Galleon Press.

Dye, David H. 1991. "Warfare in the Sixteenth Century: The de Soto Expedition in the Interior." In *Columbian Consequences*, vol. 1, *Archaeological and Historical Perspectives on the Spanish Borderlands: West*, edited by David Hurst Thomas, 211–22. Washington, DC: Smithsonian Institution.

Dye, David H. 2002. "Warfare in the Protohistoric Southeast." In *Between Contact* and Colonies: Archaeological Perspectives on the Protohistoric Southeast, edited by Cameron Wesson and Mark Rees, 126–41. Tuscaloosa: University of Alabama Press.

Edmunds, R. David, Frederick E. Hoxie, and Neal Salisbury. 2007. *The People: A History of Native America*. New York: Houghton Mifflin.

Ethridge, Robbie. 2006. "Creating the Shatter Zone: The Indian Slave Trader and the Collapse of the Mississippian World." In *Light on the Path: The Anthropology and History of the Southeastern Indians*, edited by Thomas J. Pluckhahn and Robbie Ethridge, 207–18. Tuscaloosa: University of Alabama Press.

Ethridge, Robbie. 2009a. "Introduction: Mapping the Mississippian Shatter Zone." In *Mapping the Mississippian Shatter Zone: The Colonial Indian Slave Trade and Regional Instability in the American South*, edited by Robbie Ethridge and Sheri M. Shuck-Hall, 1–62. Lincoln: University of Nebraska Press.

Ethridge, Robbie. 2009b. "The Making of a Militaristic Slaving Society: The Chickasaws and the Colonial Indian Slave Trade." In *Indian Slavery in Colonial America*, edited by Alan Gallay, 251–76. Lincoln: University of Nebraska Press.

Ethridge, Robbie. 2010. *From Chicaza to Chickasaw: The European Invasion and the Transformation of the Mississippian World*. Chapel Hill: University of North Carolina Press.

Ethridge, Robbie. 2011. "A French Middle Ground in the Colonial South? The Colonial Indian Slave and the Formation of the Petites Nations." Paper presented at the annual meeting of the Southern Historical Association, October 27–30, Baltimore, Maryland.

Ethridge, Robbie. 2012. "Early Capitalist Inauguration and the Formation of a Colonial Shatter Zone." In *Routledge Handbook of World-Systems Analysis*, edited by Salvatore Babones, 295–303. Oxford: Routledge.

Everett, Christopher S. 2009. "'They Shalbe Slaves for Their Lives': Indian Slavery in Colonial Virginia." In *Indian Slavery in Colonial America*, edited by Alan Gallay, 67–108. Lincoln: University of Nebraska Press.

Ferguson, R. Brian, and Neil L. Whitehead. [1992] 1999. "The Violent Edge of Empire." In *War in the Tribal Zone: Expanding States and Indigenous Warfare*, edited by R. Brian Ferguson and Neil L. Whitehead, 1–30. 2nd ed. Santa Fe, NM: School of American Research.

Fox, William A. 2009. "Events as Seen from the North: The Iroquois and Colonial Slavery." In *Mapping the Mississippian Shatter Zone: The Colonial Indian Slave Trade and Regional Instability in the American South*, edited by Robbie Ethridge and Sheri M. Shuck-Hall, 63–80. Lincoln: University of Nebraska Press.

Gallay, Alan. 2002. *The Indian Slave Trade: The Rise of the English Empire in the American South, 1670–1717*. New Haven, CT: Yale University Press.

Galloway, Patricia. 1995. *Choctaw Genesis, 1500–1700*. Lincoln: University of Nebraska.

Goddard, Ives, Patricia Galloway, Marvin D. Jeter, Gregory A. Waselkov, and John E. Worth. 2004. "Small Tribes of the Western Southeast." In *Handbook of North American Indians*, vol. 14, *Southeast*, general editor, William C. Sturtevant, volume editor, Raymond D. Fogelson, 174–90. Washington, DC: Smithsonian Institution.

Hall, Joseph M. 2009. *Zamumo's Gift: Indian-European Exchange in the Colonial Southeast, 1400–1735*. Philadelphia: University of Pennsylvania Press.

Hally, David J. 2008. *King: The Social Archaeology of a Late Mississippian Town in North-western Georgia*. Tuscaloosa: University of Alabama Press.

Hann, John H. 1988. *Apalachee: The Land between the Rivers*. Gainesville: University Press of Florida.

Hann, John H. 2006. *The Native American World beyond Apalachee: West Florida, and the Chattahoochee Valley*. Gainesville: University Press of Florida.

Hudson, Charles, and Robbie Ethridge. 1998. "The Early Historic Transformation of the Southeastern Indians." In *Cultural Diversity in the U.S. South: Anthropological Contributions to a Region in Transition*, edited by Carole E. Hill and Patricia D. Beaver, 34–50. Athens: University of Georgia Press.

Iberville, Pierre Le Moyne, Sieur d.' 1981. *Iberville's Gulf Journals*, edited and translated by Richebourg Gaillard McWilliams. Tuscaloosa: University of Alabama Press.

Jenkins, Ned. 2009. "Tracing the Origins of the Early Creeks, 1050–1700 C.E." In *Mapping the Mississippian Shatter Zone: The Colonial Indian Slave Trade and Regional Instability in the American South*, edited by Robbie Ethridge and Sheri M. Shuck-Hall, 188–249. Lincoln: University of Nebraska Press.

Kelton, Paul. 2007. *Epidemics and Enslavement: Biological Catastrophe in the Native Southeast, 1492–1715*. Lincoln: University of Nebraska Press.

King, Adam. 2003. *Etowah: The Political History of a Chiefdom Capital*. Tuscaloosa: University of Alabama Press.

Knight, Vernon James, Jr. 2010. *Mound Excavations at Moundville: Architecture, Elites, and Social Order*. Tuscaloosa: University of Alabama Press.

Knight, Vernon J., Jr., and Sherée L. Adams, eds. 1981. "A Voyage to the Mobile and Tomeh in 1700, with Notes on the Interior of Alabama." *Ethnohistory* 28 (2): 179–94.

La Harpe, Sieur de Jean-Batiste Bénard. 1851. "The Historical Journal of the Establishment of the French in Louisiana." In *Historical Collections of Louisiana*, vol. 3, edited and translated by B. F. French, 9–118. New York: D. Appleton.

Lankford, George E. 2004. "Chacato, Pensacola, Tohomé, Naniaba, and Mobila." In *Handbook of North American Indians*, vol. 14, *Southeast*, general editor, William C. Sturtevant, volume editor, Raymond D. Fogelson, 664–68. Washington, DC: Smithsonian Institution.

Lapham, Heather. 2005. *Hunting for Hides: Deerskins, Status, and Cultural Change in the Protohistoric Appalachians*. Tuscaloosa: University of Alabama Press.

Lauber, Almon Wheeler. [1913] 2002. *Indian Slavery in Colonial Times within the Present Limits of the United States*. Honolulu: University Press of the Pacific.

Le Page du Pratz, Antoine Simon. [1774] 1947. *The History of Louisiana*. New Orleans: Pelican Press.

Levene, Mark. 2004a. "A Dissenting Voice: Or How Current Assumptions of Deterring and Preventing Genocide May Be Looking at the Problem through the Wrong End of the Telescope." Part 1. *Journal of Genocide Research* 6 (2): 153–66.

Levene, Mark. 2004b. "A Dissenting Voice." Part 2. *Journal of Genocide Research* 6 (3): 431–45.

Marcoux, Jon Bernard. 2010. *Pox, Empire, Shackles, and Hides: The Townsend Site, 1670–1715*. Tuscaloosa: University of Alabama Press.

Martin, Joel W. 1994. "Southeastern Indians and the English Trade in Skins and Slaves."

In *The Forgotten Centuries: Indians and Europeans in the American South 1521–1704*, edited by Charles Hudson and Carmen Chaves Tesser, 304–24. Athens: University of Georgia Press.

McDowell, William L., Jr., ed. 1958. *Journals of the Commissioners of the Indian Trade, 1710–1718*. Columbia: South Carolina Archives Department.

Merrell, James H. 2003. "'Their Very Bones Shall Fight': The Catawba-Iroquois Wars." In *Beyond the Covenant Chain: The Iroquois and Their Neighbors in Indian North America, 1600–1800*, edited by Daniel K. Richter and James H. Merrel, 115–33. University Park: Pennsylvania State University Press.

Montigny, François-Jolliett de. [1935] 1967. "François de Montigny, S.J. to the Comte de Pontchartrain, 1699." In *Colonial Captivities, Marches, and Journeys*, edited by Isabel M. Calder, 201–24. Port Washington, NY: Kennikat Press.

Nairne, Thomas. 1988. *Nairne's Muskhogean Journals: The 1708 Expedition to the Mississippi River*, edited by Alexander Moore. Jackson: University of Mississippi Press.

Oatis, Stephen. 2004. *A Colonial Complex: South Carolina's Frontiers in the Era of the Yamasee War, 1680–1730*. Lincoln: University of Nebraska Press.

Pauketat, Timothy R. 2009. *Cahokia: Ancient America's Great City on the Mississippi*. New York: Viking.

Pénicaut, André. [1953] 1988. *Fleur de Lys and Calumet: Being the Pénicaut Narrative of French Adventure in Louisiana*, edited and translated by Richebourg Gaillard McWilliams. Tuscaloosa: University of Alabama Press.

Perdue, Theda. 1979. *Slavery and the Evolution of Cherokee Society 1540–1866*. Knoxville: University of Tennessee Press.

Perdue, Theda. 2003. "Cherokee Relations with the Iroquois in the Eighteenth Century." In *Beyond the Covenant Chain: The Iroquois and Their Neighbors in Indian North America, 1600–1800*, edited by Daniel K. Richter and James H. Merrell, 135–50. University Park: Pennsylvania State University Press.

Ramsey, William L. 2001. "'All and Singular the Slaves': A Demographic Profile of Indian Slavery in Colonial South Carolina." In *Money, Trade, and Power: The Evolution of a Planter Society in Colonial South Carolina*, edited by Jack P. Greene, Rosemary Brana-Shute, and Randy Sparks, 166–86. Columbia: University of South Carolina Press.

Ramsey, William L. 2008. *The Yamasee War: A Study of Culture, Economy, and Conflict in the Colonial South*. Lincoln: University of Nebraska Press.

Richter, Daniel K. 1992. *The Ordeal of the Longhouse: The Peoples of the Iroquois League in the Era of European Colonization*. Chapel Hill: University of North Carolina Press.

Rivers, William J. [1856] 1972. *A Sketch of the History of South Carolina to the Close of the Proprietary Government by the Revolution of 1719*. Spartanburg, SC: Reprint Company.

Rodning, Christopher. 2009. "Mounds, Myths, and Cherokee Townhouses in Southwestern North Carolina." *American Antiquity* 74: 627–63.

Rowland, Dunbar, and Albert Sanders, eds. and trans. 1927–32. *Mississippi Provincial Archives: French Dominion*, vols. 1–3. Jackson, MS: Department of Archives and History.

Rushforth, Brett. 2012. *Bonds of Alliance: Indigenous and Atlantic Slaveries in New France*. Chapel Hill: University of North Carolina Press.

Sauvole, Sieur de. 1969. *The Journal of Sauvole*, edited by Prieur Jay Higgenbotham. Mobile, AL: Colonial Books.

Schroedl, Gerald F. 2000. "Cherokee Ethnohistory and Archaeology from 1540 to 1838." In *Indians of the Greater Southeast: Historical Archaeology and Ethnohistory*, edited by Bonnie G. McEwan, 204–41. Gainesville: University Press of Florida.

Smith, Mavin T. 2000. *Coosa: The Rise and Fall of a Mississippian Chiefdom*. Gainesville: University Press of Florida.

Snyder, Christina. 2010. *Slavery in Indian Country: The Changing Face of Captivity in Early America*. Cambridge, MA: Harvard University Press.

Starna, William A., and Ralph Watkins. 1991. "Northern Iroquoian Slavery." *Ethnohistory* 38 (1): 34–57.

Tonty, Henri. 1939. "Henri Tonty's Letters," ed. by John Delanglez. *Mid-America* 21: 209–38.

Usner, Daniel H., Jr. 1989. "American Indians in Colonial New Orleans." In *Powhatan's Mantle: Indians in the Colonial Southeast*, edited by Peter H. Wood, Gregory A. Waselkov, and M. Thomas Hatley, 102–27. Lincoln: University of Nebraska Press.

Usner, Daniel H., Jr. 1998. *American Indians in the Lower Mississippi Valley: Social and Economic Histories*. Lincoln: University of Nebraska Press.

Ward, H. Trawick, and R. P. Stephen Davis Jr. 1993. *Indian Communities on the North Carolina Piedmont A.D. 1000 to 1700*. Chapel Hill: University of North Carolina, Research Laboratories of Anthropology, Monograph no. 2.

Ward, H. Trawick, and R. P. Stephen Davis Jr. 1999. *Time before History: The Archaeology of North Carolina*. Chapel Hill: University of North Carolina Press.

Waselkov, Gregory A. 1989. "Seventeenth-Century Trade in the Colonial Southeast." *Southeastern Archaeology* 8: 117–33.

Waselkov, Gregory A., and Bonnie L. Gums. 2000. *Plantation Archeology at Rivière aux Chiens, ca. 1725–1848*. University of South Alabama Archeological Monograph 7. Report submitted to the Alabama Department of Transportation by the University of South Alabama, Center for Archaeological Studies, Mobile.

Wesson, Cameron. 2008. *Households and Hegemony: Early Creek Prestige Goods, Symbolic Capital, and Social Power*. Lincoln: University of Nebraska Press.

Wood, Peter. 1989. "The Changing Population of the Colonial South: An Overview by Race and Region." In *Powhatan's Mantle: Indians in the Colonial Southeast*, edited by Peter H. Wood, Gregory Waselkov, and M. Thomas Hatley, 35–103. Lincoln: University of Nebraska Press.

Woodward, Henry A. 1911. "A Faithfull Relation of My Westoe Voiage Was Written in December 1674." In *Narratives of Early Carolina, 1650–1708*, edited by Alexander S. Salley, 125–34. New York: Charles Scribner's Sons.

Worth, John E. [1995] 2007. *The Struggle for the Georgia Coast: An Eighteenth-Century Spanish Retrospective on Guale and Mocama*. Anthropological Papers of the American Museum of Natural History, no. 75. Tuscaloosa: University of Alabama Press.

Worth, John E. 1998. *The Timucuan Chiefdoms of Spanish Florida*, 2 vols. Gainesville: University Press of Florida.

Worth, John E. 2009. "Razing Florida: The Indian Slave Trade and the Devastation of Spanish Florida, 1659–1715." In *Mapping the Mississippian Shatter Zone: The Colonial Indian Slave Trade and Regional Instability in the American South*, edited by Robbie Ethridge and Sheri M. Shuck-Hall, 295–311. Lincoln: University of Nebraska Press.

CHAPTER 3

GENOCIDE IN CANADA

A Relational View

Christopher Powell and Julia Peristerakis

Our goal in this paper is to demonstrate how the experiences of Indigenous peoples in Canada can be understood as including genocide. To do this, we use a relational conception of genocide, which understands cultural collectivities as dynamic social networks or "figurations" and genocide as a process of figurational destruction. We define genocide as the violent erasure of a collective identity and understand genocide as a multidimensional process that works through the destruction of the social institutions that maintain collective identity as well as through the physical destruction of human individuals. The first part of this chapter explains this relational conception of genocide, and the second part illustrates the applicability of this concept to the colonization of Indigenous peoples in Canada,[1] focusing not only on the Indian residential school system but on the wider processes of destruction of Indigenous economic, political, religious, artistic, gender, and family institutions. Many of the components of this genocidal process would not qualify as genocide if taken in isolation. It is their combined and cumulative effect that renders them genocidal.

We are hardly the first authors to apply the term *genocide* to the Canadian context.[2] Despite a growing body of scholarly work, however, the application of the term to the Canadian context remains controversial, especially in public discourse. Importantly, we do not take it on ourselves to claim that genocide "is what happened" in Canada. Raphael Lemkin (1944, 1947) formulated the concept of genocide as a political tool for protecting the right to life of cultural collectivities (see also Moses 2008). In this sense the use of the word *genocide* is only one possible means to an end. Sometimes using the term *genocide* can distract from or impede the very struggles it is meant to assist because of the considerable historical baggage that it evokes (see, e.g., Gone's contribution in this volume). Therefore we feel that the decision of whether or not to use the word *genocide* to describe the experiences of Indigenous peoples in Canada is best left to those peoples themselves. Our goal is to show how the word is applicable according to a historically and theoretically informed understanding of its meaning.

A Relational Conception of Genocide

WHY IS GENOCIDE EVIL?

It may seem perverse to ask *why* genocide is wrong. But how we answer this question affects how we define what genocide is. For instance, there is no question that from an individualistic point of view genocide constitutes one of the most extreme violations of individual agency. In physical genocide people are targeted for murder not for what they have done but for who they are—or, worse, for what the perpetrator thinks they are. They are not even killed as individuals but as anonymous members of the group. According to this logic, genocide is evil because it negates human individuality as such, thereby violating the ontological basis of human rights. If this were our only concern, then defining genocide in terms of mass killing, as many authors do (e.g., Jones 2006: 16–20; Powell 2011: 312–19), would be entirely adequate. For although the forcible destruction of culture violates an individual's right to cultural self-determination, in principle a person left alive might find the means to regain that right, whereas death is irreversible.

However, this leaves us with the problem of Lemkin's writings, in which he persistently treats measures causing loss of life as only one of several dimensions of genocide (see Lemkin 1944: 79–80, 82–90; McDonnell and Moses 2005). Notably he writes:

> Generally speaking, genocide does not necessarily mean the immediate destruction of a nation, except when accomplished by mass killings of all members of a nation. It is intended rather to signify a coordinated plan of different actions aiming at the destruction of essential foundations of the life of national groups, with the aim of annihilating the groups themselves. The objectives of such a plan would be disintegration of the political and social institutions, of culture, language, national feelings, religion, and the economic existence of national groups, and the destruction of the personal security, liberty, health, dignity, and even the lives of the individuals belonging to such groups. (Lemkin 1944: 79)

One could interpret this and similar statements as implying that the destruction of social institutions serves as a precondition to the physical extermination of the group, but Lemkin goes on to write:

Genocide has two phases: one, destruction of the national pattern of the oppressed group; the other, the imposition of the national pattern of the oppressor. This imposition, in turn, may be made upon the oppressed population which is allowed to remain, or upon the territory alone, after removal of the population and the colonization of the area by the oppressor's own nationals. (79)

Here and elsewhere Lemkin assumes that genocide happens as part of a *colonial* process (Moses 2008). More to the point, however, Lemkin equates genocide not with physical extermination but with the destruction of the collective life, the "national pattern" of the group. This means that when he writes of the destruction of a group by genocide, he means the destruction of the sociocultural existence of the group, and not necessarily the physical destruction of its members. Lemkin saw cultural genocide not as a different and lesser offense compared to physical genocide, but he saw physical and cultural violence as differing paths to the same end.

Lemkin's position has its flaws. He assumes a primordialist view of nations, in which nations are naturally evolved organic wholes that serve as the natural unit of human cultural community (Powell 2007: 535, 541; 2011: 76, 180). This view does not cohere with contemporary views of nationalism, which treat nations as social constructions and which emphasize the agency of political actors contending for power in the construction of these "imagined communities." And, ironically, primordialist views of nationality serve all too often as parts of genocidal ideologies. However, Powell (2007, 2011) has argued that Lemkin's goals are worth recuperating even as we reject his primordialist assumptions. In *Axis Rule in Occupied Europe*, Lemkin (1944) explains why genocide is evil by making two important claims: first, that nations have a collective life of their own, analogous but irreducible to the lives of individuals; second, that this collective life is the source of the cultural achievements of the human species as a whole depend: "The world represents only so much culture and intellectual vigor as are created by its component national groups. . . . The destruction of a nation, therefore, results in the loss of its future contributions to the world. Moreover, such destruction offends our feelings of morality and justice in much the same way as does criminal killing of a human being: the crime in the one case as in the other is murder, though on a vastly greater scale" (91). Both of these points can be defended on nonessentialist grounds using a relational conception of social identity.

Whereas an individualist conception of social identity treats identity as arising primarily from within individuals, and a holist conception treats identity as inscribed upon individuals by the society they belong to, a relational conception treats identity as constructed through dynamic relationships among actors. Norbert Elias (1987: xii, xxxix, lxi, lxvi; 2001: 156, 196–205) proposed that each human being possesses both an "I-identity," a sense of self as an individual, and a "we-identity," a sense of self as belonging to a collectivity, both of which are integral to the subject's selfhood and both of which are constituted relationally. These relations are dynamic, and therefore identities are fluid over time. Richard Jenkins (2008) also views identity as relational and adds that collective identities depend on the symbolic construction of *sameness* or similarity among group members (Cohen 1985), shared *difference* between the group members and outsiders (Barth 1969), and the ongoing *institutionalization* of these relations of sameness and difference (Berger and Luckmann 1966). Integrating these ideas, we may understand ethnic groups as *figurations*. A figuration is a process of interrelationship among human beings that has a distinct pattern and that generates constraints and opportunities which may or may not be intended by any of the actors participating in them (Elias 2000: 403, 456–57, 482). An ethnic group is a figuration composed of multiple social institutions that combine to maintain a collective identity by establishing commonalties among members and differences between members and nonmembers. Ethnic figurations operate as engines of cultural production. In the process of maintaining relations of sameness and difference, cultural institutions enable the transmission and evolution of the distinctive cultural knowledges and practices of the group. The distinctive relations that constitute the group also engender the "ways of worldmaking" (Goodman 1978) through which people experience differing ways of relating to themselves and to reality. Thus different cultures enable not only different ways of doing things and different practical accomplishments but also different ways of experiencing existence and different ways of being human.

It follows from this conception that to destroy an ethnic group—and hence to commit genocide—one must destroy not just individual lives but the relationships that bind individuals into a collectivity. To do this it may suffice to disrupt the social institutions through which those relationships are produced and reproduced. In this way genocide disrupts a collective life that emerges from, but is distinct from, the lives of individuals. Genocide is evil partly because it negates individual agency but *also* because it destroys the shared life of a collectivity, which is the source of social identity for individuals and a crucial source of cultural achievements for the collective human heritage. Defining Indigenous experiences of colonization in Canada as genocidal goes beyond affirming the humanity of Indigenous persons as individuals, which could be accomplished by other concepts. Doing so affirms the worth of Indigenous cultures as such.

We understand genocide as a process of the violent destruction of sociocultural groups,[3] where a group is a figuration characterized by a collective social identity. Cultural figurations require an ensemble of interconnected social institutions in order to survive, materially and meaningfully. To destroy a group it is necessary to destroy these institutions. In principle this institutional destruction is also *sufficient* to destroy a group, for a collection of living individuals that no longer shares a collective identity is no longer a group.

One factor that complicates the analysis of cultural genocide is that a cultural group, like all figurations, is inherently dynamic and subject to change. Thus replacing the existing institutions of a cultural group with new ones does not amount to genocide, as long as collective identity can be redefined in a continuous way (see, e.g., Powell 2009: 16). Identities change. Whether or not imposed institutional change has a genocidal effect will depend on whether or not new processes of institutionalization can be articulated with the preexisting ones, so that the group can preserve, on changed terms, the coherence and distinctiveness of its collective identity. Whether or not this continuity amid change can be maintained will likely depend on the suddenness and severity of the change in question, the amount of control that group members have over the implementation of changes, and the extent of the prior cultural difference between colonized and colonizer. In the colonization of Canada imposed institutional change was often radical, sudden, and implemented in a way that gave Indigenous groups as little control as possible over the direction of their development.

Two further qualifications are worth mentioning briefly. First, genocide can occur alongside ethnogenesis, as collectivities struggle to redefine themselves or recombine across formerly salient boundaries (see the contribution by Benvenuto to this volume). Second, we focus on genocidal consequences of colonization and give much less attention to the complex question of intent.[4] Some consequences are clearly intended; there can be no doubt that the colonizers in Canada have intended to appropriate Indigenous lands, dismantle Indigenous governments, or forcibly assimilate Indigenous children, for instance. For some consequences, intent is more indirect; it seems unlikely that the Canadian state intends to produce high rates of substance abuse and suicide on reserves, but it has chosen not to invest in economic and social development policies that would ameliorate these pathologies. So a strong case can be made that the Canadian state has intentionally committed acts with demonstrable genocidal consequences. Whether or not this constitutes a genocidal intent per se depends on whether such intent requires that the perpetrators possess a subjective understanding of their actions as genocidal. This in turn depends on how genocide is conceptualized: whether it is defined in strictly individualist terms that reduce it to a form of collective murder, or whether it refers to the destruction of culture as such. That question, of course, is precisely one of the stakes of this chapter.

Empirical Examples of Genocidal Processes in Canada

Genocide in Canada is a complex, multidimensional process. Each Indigenous group has its own distinct experience of colonization, so that from a pan-Indigenous perspective there has not been one genocide in Canada, but many. The policies and actions of the Canadian state have varied across time and across regions, affected by continually shifting local balances of power and by major institutional factors such as the presence or absence of treaties. Moreover, as Woolford points out in his contribution to this volume, policies and practices have varied among and between local settings (e.g., individual residential schools or reservations), meso-level institutions (provincial governments, specific government agencies), and the macro level (the Canadian state apparatus as a whole). Furthermore the influence of nonstate actors such as the churches, private corporations, employers, and unaffiliated non-Indigenous Canadian subjects also varies considerably. The behavior of individual non-Indigenous Canadians, for instance, has varied from racist exclusion and violence to active support for Indigenous self-determination, with every shade of variation in between. However, despite the varying actions and motives of the many diverse actors involved in the colonization of Canada's Indigenous peoples, for us the ultimate test of the genocidal quality of that colonization is its effects on the survivability of the figurations that maintain Indigenous identities. It is important to note that these effects may be cumulative. *Specific measures or practices or forms of action that would not be genocidal on their own may combine with other processes, undertaken by other agents and for unrelated motives, to form a cumulatively genocidal process.*

In the discussion that follows we offer concrete examples that serve not as proof but as evidence that these effects have been genocidal. We have organized these examples into five institutional categories, loosely based on the categories employed by Lemkin in his analysis of genocide in eastern Europe. In *Axis Rule* Lemkin (1944: 82–90) discusses eight "fields" in which genocide is being carried out: political, social, cultural, economic, biological, physical, religious, and moral. However, over the course of his life work he adapted this schema to fit differing contexts (e.g., McDonnell and Moses 2005; Schaller 2005). Accordingly we have chosen five types of social institutions affected by genocidal processes: economic; political; spiritual, artistic, and linguistic ("culture" in the narrow sense of the term); gender and sexuality; and family. Our discussion of these five areas is followed by a brief examination of the ways that institutional destruction has been fatal for individual human lives. We conclude by touching on the vital (in every sense of the word) matter of Indigenous resistance to genocide and cultural revitalization.

It is important to acknowledge that our categories are Eurocentric: they reflect an understanding of social life grounded in Western scientific naturalism. Our aim has been to translate the historical record of Indigenous experiences under colonial occupation into terms that can circulate through the political discourse of settler society. Like all translations, this involves some distortion and loss of meaning. In particular we have not fully recaptured the extent to which economic and political institutions, thoroughly secularized in settler Canada, are infused with spiritual meanings in Indigenous societies. To a Western or Westernized observer this spiritual dimension can be understood as dissolving the distinction between those practices that are merely instrumental and those that are constitutive of the deepest elements of personal and collective selfhood.

DESTRUCTION OF ECONOMIC INSTITUTIONS

Economic dispossession is one of the constant themes of Indigenous experience under European and Canadian colonization. This is not surprising, given that economic gain is one of the primary motives for colonialism in the first place. The loss of access to land and control over its use experienced by all Indigenous groups in Canada has meant a loss of the carefully cultivated resource base upon which those groups had materially depended. It has also meant the loss of a spiritual relationship with the land integral to the social and personal identities of Indigenous peoples (see, e.g., Woolford 2009: 89). Immediate consequences of these losses have included starvation leading to malnutrition, causing illness and death (Paul 2006: 179) in the short term. In the long term this loss of economic bases has consigned many groups to economic dependence on the Canadian state accompanied by interminable poverty. Indigenous peoples in Canada entered the global capitalist economy on the most unfavorable terms possible: without accumulated wealth that could serve as capital, very often in debt to and dependent upon settler capital, and facing racist discrimination and exclusion (Bourgeault 1983). Added to this has been the insufficiency of public education provided on reserves (St. Germain and Dyck 2011) and, in at least some areas, government policies that have actively excluded Indigenous workers and entrepreneurs from the settler economy (Paul 2006: 179; Lutz 2008; Carter 1990).

Indigenous peoples today are the poorest in Canada. The United Nations' Human Development Index measures income, education, and life expectancy and ranks countries based on these variables; Canada often ranks in first place, but based on 1996 census information, registered Indians on reserves would rank sixty-second and registered Indians on and off reserve would rank forty-seventh (Ariss 2012: 14). Data from 1996 also show that Indigenous peoples living on reserve have half the average annual income of Canadians in general (Lutz 2008: 291). Indigenous peoples on or off reserve have more than two and a half times the unemployment rate of the average for all Canadians (292). Furthermore the income gap between Indigenous and non-Indigenous peoples in Canada is growing (292).

The forced relocation of the Innu provides a striking illustration of the broad social effects of loss of land. In 1948 the government relocated the Mushuau Innu to Nutak and then to Davis Inlet in 1967 (Steele 2011: 25–26). The resettlement resulted in "increased social problems, including violence, alcohol abuse, illness and premature death" (26). Peter Dawson (2001) has likewise argued that the forced relocation of the Cheslatta T'en of British Columbia in 1952 and of the Sayisi Dene of Manitoba between 1957 and 1967 caused enough institutional disruption to eradicate their distinct cultures. Under the auspices of the 1935 Prairie Farm Rehabilitation Act, the Métis inhabitants of St. Madeleine, Manitoba, were removed, many without compensation, and their former houses burned so that the land could be seeded as pasture as part of a soil retention strategy (Dussault et al. 1996: 450–52). This relocation caused the near-total dissolution of the community and the dispersal of its former inhabitants.

The Qikiqtani Inuit Association (2010) reports that the Inuit of the Baffin region were enticed and sometimes forced into year-round settlements from their small traditional groups beginning in the 1950s. Many families were coerced into moving, and those who resisted had their homes bulldozed and dogs slaughtered. The abrupt change to Inuit lifeways led to a high level of substance abuse within the settlements, and with that, addiction, physical and sexual abuse, neglect of children, poverty, and death became commonplace within the settlements.

The destruction of the bison had a devastating effect on the livelihood of Indigenous peoples of the prairies, especially the Métis, for whom it was the chief source of livelihood (Adams 1989: 60–61; Sawchuk 1978: 21, 31–32). Indeed this massive destruction might well meet established definitions of ecocide (see Gray 1995–96; Higgins 2010) in itself. Its economic significance for prairie First Nations and Métis was compounded with other measures by which Canadian development policies favored white settlers and excluded

Indigenous peoples from access to land (Sawchuk 1978: 28–30). Conveniently for federal policymakers, this economic exclusion undermined the basis for Métis political self-assertion and First Nations self-governance.

Destruction of Political Institutions

Indigenous political institutions were varied at the time of contact. Each nation had its own distinct institutions, which "were remarkably successful in keeping order, respecting individuals, and promoting social harmony" (McFarlane 1996: 117). There were some broad similarities: most societies had hereditary chiefs and had methods to ensure that power was not abused by those in leadership positions (118). "It was by the arrival of the European settlers and their governments, with their vast claims on First Nations territory, that traditional Native societies were most seriously undermined" (120).

McFarlane (1996) argues that the Canadian state took on individual leaders who fought for Indigenous sovereignty and undermined them through various political, legislative, and military actions. In these strategies the destruction of Indigenous economic supports facilitated the erasure of their political self-determination. In the territories of the Plains Cree, for instance, slaughter and near-extinction of the bison was used to force leaders like Big Bear to sign over land or else lose their people to starvation (123–25). This slaughter also had a direct cultural consequence: the bison were regarded as siblings, as part of the community, so that their slaughter was in itself a physical genocide (see Hubbard's contribution in this volume). Once treaties were signed, "Native leaders would no longer face the challenge of negotiating a fair deal with the settler government, but rather the more difficult task of freeing themselves from the sophisticated system of social and political control that the Canadian state gradually brought into force. Isolating and then undercutting the Native leadership would become a key element of Ottawa's strategy of overcoming Native resistance" (McFarlane 1996: 127).

The signing of treaties enabled the colonial state to subject Indigenous leaders to direct control by the federal Department of Indian Affairs (McFarlane 1996: 128). In 1868 the Canadian state gave itself power to decide who would and would not be recognized as chief. Indian Affairs could replace any chief and order government-sponsored elections and could also decide whether a candidate was "worthy" according to its own criteria of "competency" (128). Chiefly authority was reduced to the administration of municipal matters such as the maintenance of roads. Chiefs also lost symbolic influence within the community after 1880, when measures were introduced to suppress the potlatch, traditional dance ceremonies, and other important Native religious practices in which chiefs had played a central role. The federal government continued to replace most traditional chiefs with band council chiefs who were controlled and directed by Ottawa. Leaders were expected to serve the Crown rather than act as the representatives of self-governing bands.

Kiera Ladner, in her contribution to this volume, argues that these and related measures to extinguish Indigenous political self-determination constituted political genocide (see also Ladner 2003). Ladner notes that the goals of the Indian Act are the "Protection, Civilization and Assimilation of the Indian" and infers that assimilation means the incorporation of Indigenous persons *as individuals* into Canadian settler society while terminating the existence of Indigenous peoples *as collectivities.*

Bonita Lawrence's (2004) examination of the history of Indian status and its effects on the self-identity of "mixed-blood" and nonstatus urban Indigenous persons characterizes those effects as genocidal. For many decades Indian status was removed from women who married or became pregnant by non-(status-)Indian men and their children, a measure that contributed to the definition of Indigenous identity in both racist and patriarchal terms, while diminishing the numbers of persons legally recognized as Indigenous. Although reforms in 1985 enabled many persons affected by these provisions to regain their status, the social identity of urban mixed-blood Indigenous people remains fraught with tensions and contradictions, as individuals and communities struggle to define their individual and collective selfhood under the oppression of and in resistance to the colonizer's legal definitions.

SUPPRESSION OF INDIGENOUS SPIRITUALITY, ART, AND LANGUAGE

The Indian residential schools served as a major site for the suppression of institutionalized Indigenous cultural practices of all kinds (Chrisjohn, Young, and Maraun 2006; Churchill 2004; Dussault et al. 1996; Fontaine 2010; Knockwood 2001; Grant 1996; Partridge 2010; Rogers, DeGagné, and Dewar 2012; Truth and Reconciliation Commission of Canada 2012a, 2012b; Woolford 2009). Certainly children sent to those schools were cut off from the established political and economic institutions of their communities. But special policies at the schools actively suppressed those distinctive markers of Indigenous identities, the practical relations of identity, which physical separation alone was not sufficient to sever. At most Indian residential schools students were actively prohibited from speaking their native language, even momentarily; from practicing any aspect of their inherited spiritual traditions; and from engaging in any form of traditional dance, song, or artistic creation. Students commonly were required to adopt settler Canadian modes of dress, hairstyle, and general adornment immediately upon arriving at the schools.

The manifest purpose of these schools was to remove all vestigial elements of Indigenous cultures from the students, replacing them with the values and practices of Canadian settler society. In sociological terms each school (with some exceptions) functioned as a total institution (Goffman 1961: xiii), aimed at achieving an involuntary resocialization so complete as to effectively replace one social identity with another, "Indian" with "civilized." And the expected net effect of this resocialization of generations of children was to be the termination of Indigenous peoples as distinct social groups: the final abolition of the "Indian problem" so famously declared in the oft-quoted statement by Duncan Campbell Scott (see, e.g., Moore, Miller, and Lerchs 1978: 114).

The Indian residential school system on its own meets the definition of genocide specified in the 1948 United Nations Convention on the Prevention and Punishment of the Crime of Genocide. Article 2(e) defines "forcibly transferring children of the group to another group" as one of the acts that may, on its own, constitute genocide if carried out "with intent to destroy, in whole or in part, a national, ethnical, racial or religious group, as such" (United Nations 1997; see also MacDonald's contribution to this volume). This was the overt aim of the Indian residential school system. Its effects in this direction were substantial. Residential schools interrupted the intergenerational sharing of Indigenous culture, affecting "generations of lives by disrupting cultural patterns of parenting and cultural transmission" (Woolford 2009: 92). This was damaging for the culture not only of the children so effected but of their communities of origin, because "the economic and social survival of Indigenous societies depended on the transmission of a vast amount of spiritual and practical knowledge from elders to the young through an exclusively oral tradition" (Fournier and Crey 1997: 82).

Federal policies toward reserve Indians also suppressed religious and artistic practices. In 1884 the Canadian state prohibited the potlatch and the Tamanawas dance, practiced by West Coast First Nations. In 1895 it prohibited the Blackfoot Sundance and the Cree and Saulteax thirst dances (Ariss 2012: 11). By 1906 all types of dancing were banned (Dickason 1997: 288). These prohibitions remained in place until 1951. Prohibition of potlaches and dancing had wider ramifications, as these practices served as an "important expression of spiritual and cultural norms" (Royal Commission on Aboriginal Peoples, cited in Ariss 2012: 11). Potlatch rituals served as important occasions for the renewal and restructuring of social relations of kinship, economic interdependence, and political authority (Wheeler 1975). Dances likewise played an important part in ceremonies in which Indigenous groups institutionalized their cosmological and social ontologies, reestablishing relations within the community and between human and nonhuman actors and forces.

DISMANTLING AND EUROPEANIZATION OF GENDER AND SEXUALITY

Taken together the ensemble of practices designated by the terms *gender* and *sexuality* constitute one of the most fundamental and pervasive dimensions of social identity. On an individual level gender and sexuality inform nearly every aspect of a person's relationship to others. On a collective level gender and sexual norms permeate all other institutions in society and provide an important basis for the collective identification of group members; where they vary between groups they can constitute one of the most salient forms of difference by means of which members of one group differentiate themselves from outsiders. In the colonization of Canada, settlers whose gender and sexual institutions were decidedly patriarchal, heteronormative, and cissexist encountered Indigenous societies whose gender and sexual institutions had an altogether different history and took substantively different forms.

Kim Anderson (2001) has described the colonial encounter in terms of the systematic dismantling of gender equity. Joyce Green (2007) argues that Indigenous societies before colonization were characterized by a substantial degree of gender equality. This equality was apparent in economic production, political decision making, and spiritual matters. All of these institutionalized gynocentric or egalitarian practices were systematically dismantled by European colonizers, and gender relations were reconfigured along patriarchal lines. Aside from the sheer loss of culture intrinsic to this process, it has left Indigenous women among the most socially disenfranchised groups in Canada, vulnerable to poverty and to sexual and physical violence. Anderson and other writers (see, e.g., Brownlie and Korinek 2012; Green 2007; Suzack et al. 2011) identify the restoration of social esteem for women in Indigenous communities as crucial to the recovery of those communities from the ravages of colonialism.

Indigenous traditions recognizing two-spirited persons have also been damaged by the imposition of the settler society's heteronormativity (Deschamps 1998; Beaver 1991). *Two-spirited* is a generic term for a range of institutionalized third (and sometimes fourth) gender roles found in Indigenous societies, which recognize certain persons as having both masculine and feminine spirits within a single body. Although its specific forms have varied widely, two-spiritedness generally involves a special spiritual sanction authorizing behavior transgressive of gender dimorphism, including crafts and domestic work for men; warfare, hunting, and leadership for women; and cross-dressing and homosexuality or bisexuality for either (Roscoe 1998). As with the suppression of gender equality, the suppression of institutionalized recognition of two-spirited persons has involved a violent inscription of colonizer culture onto the collective and individual identities of Indigenous peoples and has exposed individual two-spirited people to social marginalization and violence.

DESTRUCTION OF FAMILIES

In addition to its effects on the transmission of cultural practices, the Indian residential school system had devastating effects on family relations. Children were separated from their family for years at a time with only occasional or minimal contact, and sometimes no contact at all. Students who graduated from the schools very often felt alienated from their parents and from their extended kinship networks (Dussault et al. 1996: 359–61). In addition many students raised in residential schools did not have the skills to raise their own children, having only harshly punitive examples of caregiver behavior to model themselves on (Grant 1996: 78). Survivors of these schools report negative effects on their parenting, including difficulty showing affection or forming close attachments with their children and a range of dysfunctional coping behaviors (Stout and Peters 2011). But rampant emotional, physical, and sexual abuse in the schools has also left an intergenerational legacy of abuse within Indigenous families (Dussault et al. 1996: 359–61).

As residential schools were being phased out in the last decades of the twentieth century, the child welfare system replaced them in the mass removal of Indigenous children from their communities and families of origin (Armitage 1993: 147; Bennett, Blackstock, and De La Ronde 2005: 19). From the early 1960s to the late 1980s thousands of Indigenous children were taken from their homes and placed in residential schools and non-Indigenous families, some of them out of province or out of country, many without being told about their true heritage, in what has been referred to as the "Sixties Scoop" (Johnson 1983: 23; Bennett, Blackstock, and De La Ronde 2005: 19; Trocme, Knocke, and Blackstock 2004: 579). Standard procedure was not to offer culturally meaningful support or to find alternatives to out-of-home care but rather to apprehend the children, sometimes en masse (Bennett, Blackstock, and De La Ronde 2005: 20; Fournier and Crey 1997: 87). Entire generations of children were lost from their communities this way.

Disproportionate removal of Indigenous children continues into the present. While Indigenous children make up 5 to 6 percent of the population in Canada, they presently account for 30 to 40 percent of the children living in out-of-home care (Blackstock et al. 2005: 115). The main reasons that Indigenous children experience neglect are poverty, poor housing, and caregiver substance misuse (Blackstock 2010: 187). However, there has also been little federal effort to address the drivers of child maltreatment on reserves, such as poverty, unemployment, and substandard housing conditions, or the lack of culturally based prevention services (Blackstock, Trocme, and Bennet 2004: 903). In its removal practices the child welfare system has "overlooked significant differences between the society where the system originated and the one on which it was imposed" (Armitage 1993: 151), including traditional Indigenous practices of communal responsibilities for raising children. The imposition of child welfare onto Indigenous communities has broken down cultural traditions of extended families and surrounding communities sharing responsibilities for raising children when their biological parents could not (Fournier and Crey 1997: 81). For many families, traditional Indigenous child care practices have thereby been interrupted and may take time to be reestablished (Hudson and McKenzie 1985: 132).

Indigenous families have also been subject to violence through the auspices of provincial eugenics programs (Grekul, Krahn, and Odynak 2004). In Alberta between 1929 and 1972, of the 4,739 peoples recommended to be sterilized by the Alberta Eugenics Board, 6 percent were Indigenous, double the proportion of the Alberta population, making Indigenous peoples the most overrepresented racial or ethnic group (Grekul, Krahn, and Odynak 2004: 375). The "mentally defective" diagnosis, which removed the necessity for consent, was applied in Indigenous cases half again as often as all cases taken together. In sum, it appears that Aboriginal peoples were "the most prominent victims of the board's attention" (Grekul, Krahn, and Odynak 2004: 375).

PHYSICAL CONSEQUENCES OF
INSTITUTIONAL DESTRUCTION

Our account so far has steered away entirely from what usually is the central focus of accounts of genocide: the physical destruction of human life. We have endeavored to show how the holistic destruction of Indigenous social institutions, taken on its own, warrants the label of genocide. With the exception of the Indian residential schools, each of the institutional processes we have examined would not amount to genocide if it had occurred in isolation. Together, however, they combine to form a genocidal figuration—that is, a figuration that proceeds toward the destruction of Indigenous groups as such.

Human beings depend on social relations both for constitution of their own subjectivities and for their physical well-being. It is not surprising therefore that the wholesale destruction of social institutions should have deeply pathological and often fatal consequences for individuals. This is evident in the documented effects of the Indian residential schools on their students both while in attendance and after leaving. According to a review by Duncan Campbell Scott in 1913, "fifty per cent of the children who passed through these schools did not live to benefit from the education which they had received therein" (quoted in Milloy 1999: 51). The documentary record makes it unclear how many children died in the schools; certainly hundreds, possibly thousands (77). The schools were poorly constructed, cheaply built, and unsanitary and had poor ventilation, which created an unhealthy and unsafe environment for the children, leading to some of the deaths (78–79). Overcrowding and malnutrition allowed tuberculosis to spread, which was the cause of the majority of deaths (83–84). However, not all deaths occurred from illness. There are reports of students being beaten to death (Grant 1996: 134–35). Fires and suicide claimed lives as well (137).

Anecdotal evidence reports students being injured or maimed while performing the vocational labor required in some schools (Knockwood 2001: 64–68). Ian Mosby (2013: 145) has recently documented that "some of Canada's leading nutritional experts, in cooperation with various federal departments," conducted nutritional experiments on Indigenous communities and residential school students, sometimes going so far as to conduct controlled experiments without the subjects' informed consent or knowledge. These experiments included the deliberate withholding of food to enable baseline measurements of the effects of malnutrition and the withholding of dental services to facilitate using gum health as a measure of nutritional deficiency. In addition a 1954 report by a school nurse, Kathleen Stewart, has recently surfaced which documents the experimental use of drugs on students at Cecilia Jeffrey Indian Residential School in Kenora, leading to loss of hearing in one ear for six students and in both ears for three (Porter 2013).

Among students who left the Indian residential schools, "survivors reported a legacy of alcohol and drug abuse problems, feelings of hopelessness, dependency, isolation, low self-esteem, suicide behaviors, prostitution, gambling, homelessness, sexual abuse, and violence" (Elias et al. 2012: 1561). Women survivors have been at greater risk than men. Research shows that "manifestations of such cumulative emotional and psychological wounding over generations have included high rates of suicide and the major correlates of suicide—abuse, poor social support and difficulty forming and maintaining relationships" (Braveheart, cited in Elias et al. 2012: 1561). Chief Councilor Charlie Cootes, speaking before the Royal Commission on Aboriginal Peoples (1992: 19), claimed, "Two thirds of that last generation to attend residential schools has not survived. It is no coincidence that so many fell victim to violence, accidents, addictions and suicide. Today the children and grandchildren of those who went to residential schools also live with the same legacy of broken families, broken culture and broken spirit." These deaths and broken lives result from the damaged relationship of many residential school survivors to their own selves. In sociological terms, shame operates through the adoption toward one's own self of attitudes of contempt and hatred first performed by others (Powell 2011: 152). The most extreme form of shame is abjection, a complete negation of the worth of the subject; relations of abjection are common to other encounters between colonizers and indigenous peoples (187, 216–19). We suggest that in this context abjection occurs as a transmutation of the colonizer's violence toward the colonized into a violence within the colonized subjects themselves, a violence that impels subjects to destroy themselves.

The dissolution of relatively egalitarian Indigenous gender relations has also had destructive or fatal consequences for many individuals. Aboriginal women in Canada are overrepresented as victims of violence. Young Aboriginal women in Canada experience 3.5 times more sexual and physical violence than non-Aboriginal women and are five times more likely to die from violence (Amnesty International 2009: 1). In the 1984–2004 period alone, more than five hundred Aboriginal women and girls in Canada had been murdered or gone missing in circumstances that suggest violence (Amnesty International 2004: 27). For these women, the loss of dignified gender roles has synergized with the loss of Indigenous economic and political independence and the racist and sexist marginalization of Indigenous women in settler society to create a perfect storm of vulnerability to predatory violence.

The history of deliberate massacre in Canada is far smaller than it is in, for instance, the United States, but it is not altogether absent. During the Cypress Hills massacre of 1873, wolfers and traders in the Cypress Hills of southwestern Saskatchewan attacked a camp of Assiniboine, killing twenty (Allen 1983: 235; Hildebrandt and Hubner 1994: 68). Much earlier, in 1749, a proclamation in Nova Scotia promised "a reward of ten Guineas for every Indian Micmac taken or killed, to be paid upon producing such savage taken or his scalp if killed" (Paul 2006: 116).[5] Also in the eighteenth century, clashes between the Beothuk and settler fisheries along the Newfoundland coast resulted in the prolonged persecution of the Beothuk and several small massacres (Marshall 2001: 12; Rowe 1977: 1). In the latter case physical violence gave way to economic violence, which was ultimately more fatal. Small-scale massacres served mainly to deprive the Beothuk "of the free use of the Shores and the Rivers" (Marshall 2001: 41–46), driving them into the interior of Newfoundland, where, deprived of an adequate resource base, they succumbed to starvation and disease (Dickason 1997: 74).

The long-term collapse of Indigenous economies continues to have physically damaging effects on individuals today. In 2000 the life expectancy of First Nations men was seven years less than that of non–First Nations men and five years less for First Nations women compared to non–First Nations women (Waldram, Herring, and Young 2006: 76). Suicide rates are five to seven times higher among Aboriginal youth than non-Aboriginal youth in Canada (Health Canada 2006). Some have argued that this continued high rate of suicide among Indigenous persons too young to have attended residential schools is a manifestation of the cumulative destruction of Indigenous societies and Indigenous collective identities (Cassidy 2002). If this argument is correct, then Richard Pratt's (1973) adage "Kill the Indian, save the man" turns out to contain a fallacy. A person is his or her identity. To destroy a person's identity is, all too often, to destroy the person, even if the final turn of the knife comes from his or her own hand.

Summary: Resistance and Renaissance

The story does not end there, however. Genocide in Canada, if that is what we choose to call it, has not entirely succeeded. It is owing to decades of persistent community revitalization, political organization and activism, and journalistic and scholarly writing by Indigenous people themselves that we as settler Canadians are able even to think about, let alone write and publish on, the idea of genocide in Canada. The ultimate validation of this concept, beyond its theoretical coherence and applicability to the empirical facts, is its effectiveness as a tool for facilitating what is already an ongoing process of collective revitalization. This revitalization depends on reconstruction in multiple institutional dimensions of social life, including economics, politics, ceremony, art, gender, sexuality, and the family, as well as the many other formal and informal processes by which people strengthen their social relations with each other. Such rebuilding involves the innovation of new cultural practices as much as the remobilization of old ones. What matters is not the content of the practices themselves, but their effect in producing and reproducing, in an endlessly changing way, the relations of commonality that join groups together and the relations of differentiation that distinguish them from those around them.

If the concept of genocide can serve this end, then it serves a grand purpose that goes even beyond the protection of individual human rights. For as the formerly separate societies of the human species become increasingly interconnected, interdependent, and intimately crowded together by the ensemble of processes glibly called "globalization," a global human society is emerging. Since 1492 the processes that have fed this human globality have put severe pressure on the survivability of different cultures, threatening to drastically reduce the ethnodiversity of the world and, with it, the range of human cultural knowledge, the range of ways in which people have discovered how to live in the world. If this tendency is not to reach its logical culmination in global cultural homogeneity, then vulnerable cultural groups must be allowed to find the means to restore their own inner life.

Notes

1. We will use the name Canada to refer not only to the sovereign state of Canada but also to the entire geographical territory presently governed by that state, even when referring to historical periods prior to the Confederation of 1867.
2. See, for instance, Davis and Zannis (1973) on land appropriation; Manitoba (1985) on Canada's child welfare system; Robinson and Quinney (1985) on Canada's constitutional process; Cardinal (1969) on the 1969 White Paper; Roseau River Anishnabe First Nation Government (1997) and Neu and Therrien (2003) on welfare and development policies toward First Nations reserves; Cassidy (2002) on suicide; Dawson (2001) on forced relocations; Lawrence (2004) on blood quantum rules; Chrisjohn, Young, and Maraun (2006), Churchill (2004), and Grant (1996) on the Indian residential school system; and Woolford (2009, 2010) on cultural destruction and on treaties.
3. We use the term *culture* in the strong sense referring to the totality of human phenomena that are produced through social interaction, including not only high culture but folkways, and not only aesthetic practices but all forms of social institutions and relations.
4. For a distillation of the ongoing debates about genocidal intent, see Lewy 2007; Barta 2008; Finzsch 2008; Stannard 2008. Our position in this chapter is based on Powell 2011: 58–84, 221–26.
5. Daniel Paul (2006: 177) reports that in 1763 General Jeffery Amherst, the commander-in-chief of British forces in North America, sent a memo to Colonel Henry Bouquet, a Huguenot in the service of England, asking, "Could it not be contrived to send the Smallpox among the disaffected Tribes of Indians," to which Bouquet responded, "I will try to inoculate the Indians by means of blankets." However, Paul's account does not indicate whether this plan was actually carried out.

References

Adams, Howard. 1989. *Prison of Grass: Canada from a Native Point of View.* Rev. ed. Saskatoon, Canada: Fifth House.
Allen, Robert S. 1983. "A Witness to Murder: The Cypress Hills Massacre and the

Conflict of Attitudes towards the Native People of the Canadian-American West during the 1870s." In *As Long as the Sun Shines and Water Flows: A Reader in Canadian Native Studies*, edited by I. L. Getty, 229–46. Vancouver: UBC Press.

Amnesty International. 2004. *Stolen Sisters: A Human Rights Response to Discrimination and Violence against Indigenous Women in Canada*. Ottawa: Amnesty International.

Amnesty International. 2009. *No More Stolen Sisters: The Need for a Comprehensive Response to Discrimination and Violence against Indigenous Women in Canada*. Ottawa: Amnesty International.

Anderson, Kim. 2001. *A Recognition of Being: Reconstructing Native Womanhood*. Toronto: Sumach Press.

Ariss, Rachel. 2012. *Keeping the Land: Kitchenuhmaykoosib Inninuwug, Reconciliation and Canadian Law*. Halifax: Fernwood.

Armitage, Andrew. 1993. "Family and Child Welfare in First Nations Communities." In *Rethinking Child Welfare in Canada*, edited by B. Wharf, 131–71. Toronto: McClelland and Stewart.

Barta, Tony. 2008. "With Intent to Deny: On Colonial Intentions and Genocide Denial." *Journal of Genocide Research* 10 (1): 111–19.

Barth, Fredrik, ed. 1969. *Ethnic Groups and Boundaries: The Social Organisation of Culture Difference*. Oslo: Universitetsforlaget.

Beaver, Susan. 1991. "Gays and Lesbians of the First Nations." In *Piece of My Heart: A Lesbian of Colour Anthology*, edited by M. Silvera, 197–98. Toronto: Sister Vision Press.

Bennett, Marlyn, Cindy Blackstock, and Richard De La Ronde. 2005. *A Literature Review and Annotated Bibliography on Aspects of Aboriginal Child Welfare in Canada*. 2nd ed. Winnipeg: First Nations Child and Family Caring Society of Canada.

Berger, Peter, and Thomas Luckmann. 1966. *The Social Construction of Reality: A Treatise in the Sociology of Knowledge*. London: Penguin Books.

Blackstock, Cindy. 2010. "The Canadian Human Rights Tribunal on First Nations Child Welfare: Why If Canada Wins, Equality and Justice Lose." *Children and Youth Services Review* 33 (1): 187–94.

Blackstock, Cindy, John Loxley, Tara Prakash, and Fred Wien. 2005. *Wen:de: We Are Coming to the Light of Day*. Ottawa: First Nations Child and Family Caring Society of Canada.

Blackstock, Cindy, Nico Trocme, and Marlyn Bennet. 2004. "Child Maltreatment Investigations among Aboriginal and Non-Aboriginal Families in Canada." *Violence against Women* 10 (8): 901–16.

Bourgeault, Ron G. 1983. "The Indians, the Metis and the Fur Trade: Class, Sexism and Racism in the Transition from 'Communism' to Capitalism." *Studies in Political Economy* 12: 45–80.

Brownlie, Robin Jarvis, and Valerie J. Korinek. 2012. *Finding a Way to the Heart: Feminist Writings on Aboriginal and Women's History in Canada*. Winnipeg: University of Manitoba Press.

Calvino, Italo. 1974. *Invisible Cities*. London: Picador Books.

Cardinal, Harold. 1969. *The Unjust Society: The Tragedy of Canada's Indians*. Edmonton: M. G. Hurtig.

Carter, Sarah. 1990. *Lost Harvests: Prairie Indian Reserve Farmers and Government Policy*. Montreal: McGill-Queen's University Press.

Cassidy, Barbara. 2002. "Getting Rid of the Indian Problem: Aboriginal Suicide as a Manifestation of Genocide." Environmental Studies, York University, Toronto.

Chrisjohn, Roland, Sherri Young, and Michael Maraun. 2006. *The Circle Game: Shadows and Substance in the Indian Residential School Experience in Canada*. Rev. ed. Penticton, Canada: Theytus Books.

Churchill, Ward. 2004. *Kill the Indian, Save the Man: The Genocidal Impact of American Indian Residential Schools*. San Francisco: City Lights.

Cohen, Anthony Paul. 1985. *The Symbolic Construction of Community*. London: Tavistock.

Davis, Robert, and Mark Zannis. 1973. *The Genocide Machine in Canada: The Pacification of the North*. Montreal: Black Rose Books.

Dawson, Peter E. 2001. "The Relocation of Aboriginal People in Canada, 1952 to 1967: A United Nations Human Rights Analysis from a Cultural Perspective." Cultural Genocide, Sociology, York University, Toronto.

Deschamps, Gilbert. 1998. *We Are Part of a Tradition: A Guide on Two-Spirited People for First Nations Communities*. Toronto: 2-Spirited People of the 1st Nations.

Dickason, Olive. 1997. *Canada's First Nations: A History of Founding Peoples from Earliest Times*. 2nd ed. Toronto: Oxford University Press.

Doubt, Keith. 2006. *Understanding Evil: Lessons from Bosnia*. New York: Fordham University Press.

Dussault, René, Georges Erasmus, Paul I. A. H. Chartrand, J. Peter Meekison, Viola Rosbinson, Mary Sillett, and Bertha Wilson. 1996. *Royal Commission Report on Aboriginal Peoples*. Government of Canada.

Elias, Brenda, Javier Mignone, Madelyn Hall, Say P. Hong, Lyna Hart, and Jitender Sareen. 2012. "Trauma and Suicide Behaviour Histories among a Canadian Indigenous Population: An Empirical Exploration of the Potential Role of Canada's Residential School System." *Social Science and Medicine* 74 (10): 1560–69.

Elias, Norbert. 1987. *Involvement and Detachment*. Oxford: Basil Blackwell.

Elias, Norbert. 2000. *The Civilizing Process: The History of Manners and State Formation and Civilization*. Translated by E. Jephcott. Rev. ed. Oxford: Blackwell.

Elias, Norbert. 2001. *The Society of Individuals*. New York: Continuum.

Finzsch, Norbert. 2008. "If It Looks Like a Duck, If It Walks Like a Duck, If It Quacks Like a Duck." *Journal of Genocide Research* 10 (1): 119–26.

Fontaine, Theodore. 2010. *Broken Circle: The Dark Legacy of Indian Residential Schools, a Memoir*. Victoria: Heritage House.

Fournier, Suzanne, and Ernie Crey. 1997. *Stolen from Our Embrace*. Vancouver: Douglas and McIntyre.

Goffman, Erving. 1961. *Asylums: Essays on the Social Situation of Mental Patients and Other Inmates*. Garden City, NY: Anchor Books.

Goodman, Nelson. 1978. *Ways of Worldmaking*. Indianapolis: Hackett.

Grant, Agnes. 1996. *No End of Grief: Indian Residential Schools in Canada*. Winnipeg: Pemmican.

Gray, Mark Allan. 1995–96. "The International Crime of Ecocide." *California Western International Law Journal* 26: 215–71.

Green, Joyce, ed. 2007. *Making Space for Indigenous Feminism*. Black Point, Canada: Fernwood.

Grekul, Jana, Harvey Krahn, and Dave Odynak. 2004. "Sterilizing the 'Feeble-Minded': Eugenics in Alberta, Canada, 1929–1972." *Journal of Historical Sociology* 17 (4): 358–84.

Health Canada. 2006. *First Nations and Inuit Health: Mental Health and Wellness.* Accessed November 30, 2012. http://www.hc-sc.gc.ca/fniah-spnia/promotion/mental/index-eng.php.

Higgins, Polly. 2010. *Eradicating Ecocide: Laws and Governance to Stop the Destruction of the Planet.* London: Shepheard-Walwyn.

Hildebrandt, Walter, and Brian Hubner. 1994. *The Cypress Hills: The Land and Its People.* Saskatoon: Purich.

Hudson, Pete, and Brad McKenzie. 1985. "Native Children, Child Welfare and the Colonization of Native People." In *The Challenge of Child Welfare,* edited by K. Levitt and B. Wharff, 125–41. Vancouver: UBC Press.

Jenkins, Richard. 2008. *Social Identity.* 3rd ed. London: Routledge.

Johnson, Patrick. 1983. *Native Children and the Child Welfare System.* Toronto: Canadian Council on Social Development with James Lormier.

Jones, Adam. 2006. *Genocide: A Comprehensive Introduction.* 2nd ed. London: Routledge.

Knockwood, Isabelle. 2001. *Out of the Depths: The Experiences of Mi'kmaw Children at the Indian Residential School at Schubenacadie, Nova Scotia.* 2nd ed. Lockeport, Canada: Roseway.

Ladner, Kiera. 2003. "Rethinking Aboriginal Governance." In *Reinventing Canada: Politics of the 21st Century,* edited by J. Brodie and L. Trimble, 43–60. Toronto: Pearson Education Canada.

Lawrence, Bonita. 2004. *"Real" Indians and Others: Mixed-Blood Urban Native Peoples and Indigenous Nationhood.* Vancouver: UBC Press.

Lemkin, Raphael. 1944. *Axis Rule in Occupied Europe: Laws of Occupation, Analysis of Government, Proposals for Redress.* Washington, DC: Carnegie Endowment for International Peace, Division of International Law.

Lemkin, Raphael. 1947. "Genocide as a Crime under International Law." *American Journal of International Law* 41: 145–51.

Lewy, Günter. 2007. "Can There Be Genocide without the Intent to Commit Genocide?" *Journal of Genocide Research* 9 (4): 661–74.

Lutz, John Sutton. 2008. *Makúk: A New History of Aboriginal-White Relations.* Vancouver: UBC Press.

Manitoba, Review Committee on Indian and Metis Adoptions and Placements. 1985. *No Quiet Place: Final Report to the Honourable Muriel Smith, Minister of Community Services,* edited by M. C. Services. Winnipeg.

Marshall, Ingeborg. 2001. *The Beothuk.* St. John's: Newfoundland Historical Society.

McDonnell, Michael A., and A. Dirk Moses. 2005. "Raphael Lemkin as Historian of Genocide in the Americas." *Journal of Genocide Research* 7 (4): 501–29.

McFarlane, Peter. 1996. "Aboriginal Leadership." In *Visions of the Heart: Canadian Aboriginal Issues,* edited by D. A. Long and O. P. Dickason, 117–45. Toronto: Harcourt Brace Canada.

Milloy, John S. 1999. *A National Crime: The Canadian Government and the Residential School System, 1879 to 1986.* Winnipeg: University of Manitoba Press.

Moore, Robert, Kahn-Tineta Miller, and George Lerchs. 1978. *The Historical Development of the Indian Act.* 2nd ed. Ottawa: Treaties and Historical Research Centre, P.R.E. Group, Indian and Northern Affairs.

Mosby, Ian. 2013. "Administering Colonial Science: Nutrition Research and Human Biomedical Experimentation in Aboriginal Communities and Residential Schools, 1942–1952." *Histoire sociale/Social History* 46 (91): 145–72.

Moses, A. Dirk. 2008. "Empire, Colony, Genocide: Keywords and the Philosophy of History." In *Empire, Colony, Genocide: Conquest, Occupation, and Subaltern Resistance in World History*, edited by A. D. Moses, 3–54. New York: Berghahn Books.

Neu, Dean, and Richard Therrien. 2003. *Accounting for Genocide: Canada's Bureaucratic Assault on Aboriginal People.* Winnipeg: Fernwood.

Partridge, Cheryle. 2010. "Residential Schools: The Intergenerational Impacts on Aboriginal Peoples." *Native Social Work Journal* 7: 33–62.

Paul, Daniel N. 2006. *We Were Not the Savages: Collision between European and Native American Civilizations.* 3rd ed. Halifax: Fernwood.

Porter, Jody. 2013. "Ear Experiments Done on Kids at Kenora Residential School." Canadian Broadcasting Corporation, August 8, 2013. Accessed September 20, 2013. http://www.cbc.ca/news/canada/thunder-bay/ear-experiments-done-on-kids-at-kenora-residential-school-1.1343992.

Powell, Christopher. 2007. "What Do Genocides Kill? A Relational Conception of Genocide." *Journal of Genocide Research* 9 (4): 527–47.

Powell, Christopher. 2009. "The Wound at the Heart of the World." In *Evoking Genocide: Scholars and Activists Describe the Works That Shaped Their Lives*, edited by A. Jones, 11–17. Toronto: Key.

Powell, Christopher. 2011. *Barbaric Civilization: A Critical Sociology of Genocide.* Montreal: McGill-Queen's University Press.

Pratt, Richard H. 1973. "The Advantages of Mingling Indians with Whites." In *Americanizing the American Indians: Writings by the "Friends of the Indian" 1880–1900*, edited by F. P. Prucha, 260–71. Cambridge, MA: Harvard University Press.

Qikiqtani Inuit Association. 2010. *QTC Final Report: Achieving Saimaqatigiingniq.* Qikiqtani Truth Commission.

Robinson, Eric, and Henry Bird Quinney. 1985. *The Infested Blanket: Canada's Constitution—Genocide of Indian Nations.* Winnipeg: Queenston House.

Rogers, Shelagh, Mike DeGagné, and Jonathan Dewar, eds. 2012. *Speaking My Truth: Reflections on Reconciliation and Residential School.* Ottawa: Aboriginal Healing Foundation.

Roscoe, William. 1998. *Changing Ones: Third and Fourth Genders in Native America.* New York: St. Martin's Press.

Roseau River Anishnabe First Nation Government. 1997. *Genocide in Canada.* Roseau River Anishnabe First Nation.

Rowe, Frederick W. 1977. *Extinction: The Beothuks of Newfoundland.* Toronto: McGraw-Hill Ryerson.

Royal Commission on Aboriginal Peoples. 1992. *Public Hearings: Overview of the First Round.* Indian and Northern Affairs Canada. Accessed September 19, 2013. http://www.publicsafety.gc.ca/lbrr/archives/e%2098.c87%20b33%201992-eng.pdf.

Sawchuk, Joe. 1978. *The Metis of Manitoba: Reformulation of an Ethnic Identity*. Toronto: Peter Martin.

Schaller, Dominik J. 2005. "Raphael Lemkin's View of European Colonial Rule in Africa: Between Condemnation and Admiration." *Journal of Genocide Research* 7 (4): 531–38.

St. Germain, Gerry, and Lillian Eva Dyck. 2011. *Reforming First Nations Education: From Crisis to Hope*, edited by Standing Senate Committee on Aboriginal Peoples. Ottawa: Senate of Canada.

Stannard, David E. 2008. "Déjà vu All Over Again." *Journal of Genocide Research* 10 (1): 127–33.

Steele, Gerry. 2011. *Bathtubs but No Water: A Tribute to the Mushuau Innu*. Halifax: Fernwood.

Stout, Roberta, and Sheryl Peters. 2011. *Kiskinohamâtôtâpânâsk: Inter-generational Effects on Professional First Nations Women Whose Mothers Are Residential School Survivors*. Winnipeg: Prairie Women's Health Centre for Excellence.

Suzack, Cheryl, Shari M. Huhndorf, Jeanne Perreault, and Jean Barman, eds. 2011. *Indigenous Women and Feminism: Politics, Activism, Culture*. Vancouver: UBC Press.

Trocme, Nico, Della Knocke, and Cindy Blackstock. 2004. "Pathways to the Overrepresentation of Aboriginal Children in Canada's Child Welfare System." *Social Services Review* 78: 577–600.

Truth and Reconciliation Commission of Canada. 2012a. *They Came for the Children: Canada, Aboriginal Peoples, and Residential Schools*. Winnipeg.

Truth and Reconciliation Commission of Canada. 2012b. *Truth and Reconciliation Commission of Canada Interim Report*. Winnipeg.

United Nations. 1948. *Convention on the Prevention and Punishment of the Crime of Genocide*. Accessed November 29, 2012. http://www.hrweb.org/legal/genocide.html.

Waldram, James B., D. Ann Herring, and T. Kue Young. 2006. *Aboriginal Health in Canada: Historical, Cultural and Epidemiological Perspectives*. 2nd ed. Toronto: University of Toronto Press.

Wheeler, Dennis. 1975. *Potlatch: A Strict Law Bids Us Dance*. Moving Images Distribution.

Woolford, Andrew. 2009. "Ontological Destruction: Genocide and Canadian Aboriginal Peoples." *Genocide Studies and Prevention* 4 (1): 81–97.

Woolford, Andrew. 2010. "Genocide, Affirmative Repair, and the British Columbia Treaty Process." In *Transitional Justice: Global Mechanisms and Local Realities after Genocide and Mass Atrocity*, edited by A. L. Hinton, 137–56. New Brunswick, NJ: Rutgers University Press.

Woolford, Andrew, and Jasmine Thomas. 2010. "Genocide and Aboriginal Peoples in Canada: A Dialogue in Waiting." In *Genocide of Indigenous Peoples: A Critical Bibliographic Review*, edited by S. Totten and R. K. Hitchcock, 61–86. Edison, NJ: Transaction.

PART II

ERASURE AND LEGIBILITY

CHAPTER 4

CALIFORNIA AND OREGON'S MODOC INDIANS

How Indigenous Resistance Camouflages

Genocide in Colonial Histories

Benjamin Madley

On Good Friday 1873, the Modoc leader Kintpuash—or Captain Jack—stood up in the lava beds of northeastern California and shot General E. R. S. Canby in the face. It was the first and last time a Native American ever killed a regularly commissioned United States Army general. In conjunction with the Modoc killing of two other men that day, this violence provoked the final phase of the 1872–73 Modoc War. Yet little is known of the genocide that precipitated these acts.

Between 1851 and 1873, whites launched seven campaigns against the Modocs that, along with disease, displacement, and less organized violence, reduced the Modoc population from one thousand to two thousand people or more, to some 250, a decline of roughly 75 to 88 percent.[1] Despite the many books about the 1872–73 Modoc War—during which a handful of Modocs held off the U.S. Army and state militiamen—scholars have written little about these prior anti-Modoc campaigns, and no author has addressed the 1851–73 campaigns as genocide.[2] While exploring the broader occurrence of genocide in California for a book on that topic, the fact that the Modoc case merited further detailed study became clear (Madley: forthcoming). Using varied sources, including some new to Modoc studies, this chapter will narrate the seven anti-Modoc campaigns, explain how they constituted genocide, and explore how indigenous resistance can camouflage genocide in colonial histories before suggesting ways to overcome such misunderstandings.

The Modocs apparently suffered their first massacre at white hands in 1840. According to an early twentieth-century Achumawi Indian chief who lived south of the Modoc, "About the year 1840 the first white men, a party of about forty trappers came from the north and stopped among the Modoc at

Tule lake." The trappers invited the Modocs to a feast: "The food was spread in a long line on the ground, and the Indians sat down; but Captain Jack's father and another man stood apart." This saved their lives. "At one end of the line was a small cannon, the use of which the Indians of course did not understand." Then, "While they were eating, the cannon was fired, and a large number of the feasters fell dead" ("Chief of the Fall River band" quoted in Curtis 1924: 132). This unprovoked and now all but forgotten atrocity primed the Modoc people to resist incursions. Their resistance then became notorious, so well remembered that it camouflaged the genocide they endured.

Before contact, Modocs called themselves *Maklaks*, or "People," and inhabited an area about the size of Connecticut (Johansen and Pritzker 2008: 1142; James 2008: 19; see map 4.1). On their lake-studded plateau between the snowcapped Cascades and the arid Great Basin they built semi-subterranean lodges, fished from dugout pine canoes on several major lakes, hunted waterfowl and game, and harvested seeds, fruits, berries, pine nuts, and tubers (Stern 1998: 448–49, 452). As an observer wrote in 1873, "Their country was rich in everything necessary to sustain aboriginal life."[3] Their hills, grasslands, lakes, and lava beds constituted a delicate, semi-arid ecosystem. It had sustained the Modocs since perhaps 5000 B.C.E. or, as some believe, "since time immemorial" (Stern 1998: 446; Allison 1994: 39). The early nineteenth-century introduction of horses and guns revolutionized their world, intensifying trade and hostilities with neighboring tribes (Stern 1998: 460). Mass migration brought yet far more dramatic changes (see figure 4.1).

In 1846, the Applegate Trail ripped through Modoc lands, damaging the Modocs' ecosystem. Immigrants passing through scared off and killed game while their livestock devoured the grasses and plants upon which Modoc people depended. Unsurprisingly, Modocs resisted the trespassers. The first recorded killing was "in the fall of 1846," when an "immigrant was killed on the southern Oregon immigrant road, near Lost river, by Modoc Indians."[4] Migrants also brought disease, likely reinforcing Modocs' will to resist. According to the nineteenth-century ethnographer Stephen Powers, "In 1847, the small-pox destroyed about 150 of the tribe."[5] Far worse was yet to come.

The First Vigilante Campaign, 1851

In January 1851, California's first civilian U.S. governor, Peter Burnett, defined the new state's Indian policies by declaring "that a war of extermination will continue to be waged . . . until the Indian race becomes extinct." He added, "the inevitable destiny of the race is beyond the power or wisdom of man to avert."[6] State legislators then endorsed Burnett's declaration. One

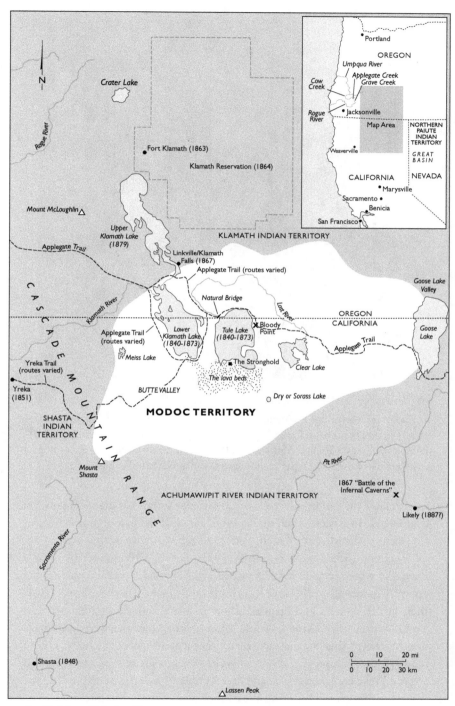

Map 4.1. Map of Modoc Territory.

4.1. Eadweard Muybridge, "Winema or Tobey Riddle, a Modoc, standing between an agent and her husband Frank (*on her left*), with four Modoc women in front." Photograph, 1873. National Archives and Records Administration, Record Group 165: Records of the War Department General and Special Staffs, 1860–1952.

month later they appropriated $500,000 to pay for anti-Indian state militia campaigns.[7] Prospectors and others soon launched the first organized operation against the Modocs, which, until now, scholars have overlooked.[8]

A veteran Indian hunter, John Ross, recollected arriving in Yreka, California, in what seems to have been April or May 1851. Several days after his arrival, Modocs allegedly "stole forty mules and horses" at or near Yreka.[9] Ross then led "20 men . . . and surprised them in Butte Valley 60 miles east from Yreka," killing fifteen Modocs while "three or four white men were wounded," one mortally.[10] This 1851 massacre established a pattern of "retaliatory" killing repeated throughout the 1850s: when livestock went missing, men in and around Yreka launched search and destroy operations against distant Modoc communities, generally killing any Modoc people they encountered.

The posse then initiated a ghoulish local tradition: "seven scalps were brought in." Arriving in Yreka, Ross displayed a "chief's scalp," and Ben Wright "pitched his tent with a long pole to the top of which some one fastened an Indian scalp." An interpreter—possibly Modoc—saw one of the scalps, "ran, and . . . was shot to death."[11] The campaign soon continued with a second expedition.

Late that summer, unidentified rustlers stole "forty-six fine mules and horses" near "Butteville." Modocs may have taken them, or it may have been white rustlers then active in the area (Wells 1881: 123). Either way, Yrekans organized and sent for Ben Wright, a Quaker turned Indian hunter (William Fanning in Wells 1881: 123; see figure 4.2). Meanwhile, rustling continued. Posse member William Kershaw later explained that when the squad finally set out that autumn, they were "in pursuit of some two hundred head of stock."[12] "About twenty men," with Wright as "scout and guide," traced some animals to a Lost River Modoc village, about "one hundred miles from Yreka" just inside Oregon.[13]

Posse member William Fanning reported that Wright instructed the group to pass the village in full sight of its inhabitants, who made no hostile gestures. The posse then returned and attacked at dawn. "The Indians came rushing out of their wickiups in confusion, and fought desperately for a while, having nothing but bows and arrows and protecting themselves with shields made of tule rushes, old tin pans, etc." The Modocs then retreated. Eventually, according to Fanning, "we found some sixteen dead Indians" but "captured [only] several . . . horses."[14] Exactly how many Modocs died in the massacre may never be known, but it is certain that no whites perished.

Modocs now counterattacked the posse at Willow Creek, catalyzing an extended killing campaign. Fanning wrote, "We came to the conclusion that they needed a better drubbing than we had given them, and four of us started to Yreka for provisions for a new campaign." Meanwhile, other posse members killed "a number of Indians" in a "running fight" before attacking another village at dawn "near the mouth of Lost river." There they captured about thirty Modoc people and chased others "who plunged into the icy water . . . and hid in the grass. . . . We spent the entire day in hunting them, and killed fifteen or twenty." The posse then murdered a prisoner before riding south through November snows to the rugged lava beds south of Tule Lake. There they "killed several" more Modocs.[15] When the expedition ended at least thirty-eight Modoc people, and perhaps many more, were dead. Only two of Wright's men sustained wounds; both recovered.[16]

The 1851 Modoc-hunting operations killed at least fifty-five Modoc people but were hardly anomalous. By early 1852 California legislators needed more money to fund ongoing anti-Indian state militia campaigns. Thus, in May 1852, they raised an additional $600,000 for Indian-hunting operations.[17] That summer, Yrekans launched the first state militia campaign against the Modocs.

The Siskiyou Volunteer Rangers Expedition, 1852

Cognizant of California's Indian policies and the possibility of collecting substantial sums as volunteer state militiamen, on July 12 fifty-nine Yrekans petitioned Burnett's successor, Governor John Bigler, for help against Shasta Indians west of Yreka, whose "conduct has been generally insulting and overbearing and marked by several acts of Robery [sic]."[18] Ten days later five leading Yrekans requested forty to fifty rifles and pay in order to muster a volunteer state militia unit into service against Indians.[19]

In response, Governor Bigler met with U.S. Army General Ethan Hitchcock, and on July 27 Hitchcock ordered 1st Dragoons Brevet Major E. H. Fitzgerald to take two companies and ride north from Benicia, in the San Francisco Bay Area, to Fort Reading, Yreka, and beyond to "prevent a war."[20] However, in the months before their arrival an inferno of killing engulfed the Modocs.

Resistance triggered the conflagration when Modocs attacked "a small [wagon] train" in Modoc territory. Siskiyou County Sheriff Charles McDermitt reported that on August 6, "forty packers arrived" in Yreka and urged him to send "assistance and protection" to "some three or four families" at Tule Lake who would otherwise "undoubtedly be all murdered by the Indians."[21] McDermitt wasted no time. Having raised "volunteers and gold dust," on August 7 he led twelve men east through the high grasses and lava boulders to Tule Lake.[22] He arrived too late. The emigrants were "all murdered by the Indians," although one packer apparently escaped.[23] Then, on August 30, McDermitt lost three men to a Modoc attack.[24]

Meanwhile, Wright—later described as "a genuine Indian-killer"—organized twenty-one volunteers who rode east from Yreka on August 29 to reinforce McDermitt.[25] According to an 1884 history, this was "an expedition to annihilate utterly and without remorse" the Modocs who had attacked McDermitt (Walling 1884: 205). En route, Wright's men "killed several Indians [almost certainly women] digging camas," or edible plant bulbs.[26] Arriving at Tule Lake on August 31, and finding circled wagons besieged by Modocs, Wright attacked. According to him, Modoc people—including women and children—"broke for the [shoreline] Tulies [sic].... We followed them about an hour and a half firing whenever we could get a sight of the Red Devils,

4.2. Captain Ben Wright. Photograph, undated. Courtesy of the Oregon Historical Society, Portland, OrHi 1711.

about sixty shots were fired by our company and ten or twelve Indians killed, [plus] a number of women and children [who] must have been drowned."[27] Another attacker later recollected sixty-four Modoc people killed.[28] Finally, another eyewitness wrote that after the massacre a male prisoner "was . . . shot and scalped."[29]

Death toll estimates for this encounter range from fifteen to sixty-four, probably because some Modoc bodies slipped below Tule Lake's surface or were lost in its bulrush-choked shores. Moreover, white (and perhaps some Modoc) accounts tended to count only Modoc men killed in attacks on Modoc settlements.[30] No matter how many Modocs died, the killing was one-sided. Kershaw later testified, "Our company sustained no loss whatever."[31] Wright's volunteers soon found new motives for additional atrocities.

Wright's men discovered eighteen immigrant bodies near Bloody Point, according to John Ross—now an Oregon territorial militia officer—who, with twenty-two Oregon volunteers, had joined Wright's operation that September after reportedly finding fourteen other immigrant corpses at Lost River.[32] Decades later, one source suggested that Modocs killed as many as "seventy-five white persons in 1852."[33] Although this estimate, made in the emotional aftermath of the 1872–73 Modoc War, smacks of exaggeration, in 1873 the Modoc chief Old Sc[h]onchin did recollect that the Modoc "made legitimate war ... the whites had imposed upon them in the beginning, and they undertook to kill them off."[34] The Modocs were, after all, a people resisting invasion and repeated massacres.

Having discovered the immigrant bodies on September 2, Wright requested supplies and additional volunteers.[35] Five days later, fifty-five Yrekans petitioned Governor Bigler for help and authority to enroll a state militia company, enclosing Wright's report and the proceedings of a public meeting.[36] Genocidal rhetoric now began to suffuse anti-Modoc operations. That same day one Yrekan, H. S. Lewis, wrote to Bigler asking him to assign authority "to enlist men here and procure the necessary supplies for a company to go against these Indians and subdue or exterminate them."[37]

General Hitchcock, meanwhile, hardened army objectives. No longer interested in deploying dragoons as peacekeepers, on September 15 he reported to Bigler, "Major Fitzgerald has about Eighty mounted men with him and I cannot doubt he will be successful in punishing the Indians."[38] Wright's reported discovery of "the bodies of three men, one woman, and two children ... butchered by the Indians" east of Yreka probably informed Hitchcock's intentions.[39]

The dragoons now arrived in Modoc territory (Wells 1881: 131). Fitzgerald's company gave Wright a boat and by "scouting along the shores" of Tule Lake forced "all of the hostiles to seek refuge on [an] island."[40] Meanwhile, Fitzgerald's dragoons "burned fourteen Indian rancherias [villages]" and "Somebody killed an Indian" (Strobridge 1994: 45). Additional violence probably accompanied the systematic village burnings, but by early November Fitzgerald's cavalcade was in Yreka en route to "winter quarters at Scott's Valley," well beyond Modoc territory.[41] Wright, meanwhile, relieved McDermitt and continued "hunting Indians" until November 24 with a command that grew to thirty-six men.[42]

William Barry participated in an 1852 Wright action that may have been an additional massacre by Wright's men. Barry, an Englishman who subsequently moved to Australia, wrote in 1878 that, after receiving news of immigrants killed by Modocs, some eight hundred whites had "set out to exact a severe retaliation." Probably exaggerating, given that no other sources reported an 1852 anti-Modoc operation of this scale, Barry recalled that after locating some six hundred Modocs at "a small lake," Wright's men charged as "darkness set in" but could not locate their quarry. However, at "daylight, when the Indians showed in a body. ... We immediately charged them, shooting down men, women, squaws, and papooses indiscriminately." Barry continued, "The slaughter—for it could hardly be called a fight—was over in half an hour, and we reckoned that scarcely fifty out of the mob escaped; the rest were despatched [sic] to the 'happy hunting-grounds' without the slightest show of mercy."[43] If Barry meant to report that Wright's men killed some 550 Modocs, and if that is accurate—even by half—the atrocity represents one of the largest massacres in U.S. history, rivaling the 260 to 300 Miniconjou Lakota massacred in 1890 at Wounded Knee, South Dakota (Jensen 1990: 198; Ostler 2004: 345). Barry, shot in the leg during the attack, recollected, "The loss on our side was trifling, ten killed and twenty wounded, the onslaught being so sudden that the foe could not make any stand at all."[44] Following his Bloody Point Massacre, Wright found engaging the Modocs difficult. Kershaw recollected, "We had only light and occasional skirmishes with the Indians after we relieved the train at 'Bloody Point.'"[45] Finally, Wright captured a Modoc woman whom he released with an invitation to attend a diplomatic conference.[46] Thus "on the north bank of Lost River, a few hundred yards from the Natural Bridge," Modocs "attended, and, as agreed upon by both parties, no weapons were brought."[47] Yet Wright's intentions were not peaceful.

On the morning of November 8, Wright's men armed themselves, surrounded the Modoc peace delegates, and opened fire. On November 21 one Yrekan explained that "thirty-one Indians had been killed, and two of our citizens wounded."[48] In December, McDermitt reported to the governor, "Wright's Company have had another battle with the Lake Indians, and succeeded in killing forty-three."[49] This was, of course, no battle. Such martial language was camouflage. Indeed, based on information from participants, Hitchcock confirmed the surprise attack on the negotiators: "Upon a signal indicated by Captain Wright, they suddenly fired upon the Indians and succeeded in killing about thirty-eight."[50] Still camouflaging language persisted. Four years later Kershaw reported that it was "a smart engagement, in which we killed about forty."[51] However, in 1873 Kintpuash recollected, "when I was a little boy, Ben. Wright murdered my father and forty-three others who went into his camp to make peace."[52] That same year an anonymous correspondent echoed Kintpuash's estimate, and William Turner wrote that Wright had killed all but two of the fifty-one Modoc peace delegates.[53] Then, in 1881 and 1884, Wells reported forty-seven men and "a few squaws" massacred.[54] Finally, Frank Riddle, who was married to the Modoc woman Wi-me-ma and was also "one of Ben Wright's men," asserted that about ninety Modocs had been murdered in the trap (Thompson 1912: 80; Riddle in Thompson 1912: 83). In 1914 his son Jeff explained why his father's estimate was higher than other reports: "about half of the killed . . . had sunk to the bottom of the river" and could not be recovered (Riddle 1914: 31). So complete was the surprise and the Modocs' disarmament that none of Wright's men were killed and only two were injured.[55]

Wright's volunteers returned to Yreka some time before November 29, with "Indian scalps dangling from their rifles, hats, and the heads of their horses. Scores of scalps were thus flaunted." Then "the enthusiastic crowd lifted them from their horses and bore them in triumph to . . . the saloons, and a grand scene of revelry commenced."[56]

California's Senate Committee on Indian Affairs later asserted that Wright's "Mounted Rangers" had killed "in all, seventy-three of the enemy."[57] This was probably the minimum figure from two incidents. The death toll was almost certainly much higher, possibly 159 or more, according to other sources. There may also have been additional killings, as Barry's account suggests. In 1873 Chief Sc[h]onch[in], presumably well acquainted with Modoc casualties, estimated that Wright's 1852 "Summer campaign" killed half of all Modoc warriors and "nearly 200" Modoc people in all.[58] By contrast, Wright reportedly lost only two or three men killed and three wounded.[59]

The violence of 1852 marked a turning point. As the historian Erwin Thompson observed, it "left a heritage of bitterness on both sides." More important, "The prevailing attitude among whites that all Indians should be exterminated was greatly reinforced" (Thompson 1971: xvii). State and federal policymakers soon fortified that "prevailing attitude." Meanwhile, the Modocs would not forget the Lost River massacre.

California legislators emphatically approved Wright's campaign, while Oregon's Indian Affairs superintendent and federal decision makers did so indirectly. Despite evidence of premeditated massacre, on April 16, 1853, California legislators passed an act providing $23,000 to reimburse the "Volunteer Rangers under Captain B[en] Wright and Charles McDermitt."[60] State legislators thus sanctioned Wright's killings after the fact. The following year, Oregon's Indian Affairs superintendent rewarded him with the position of "special sub-Indian agent" in southwestern Oregon (Douthit 1999, 410). On August 5, 1854, U.S. congressmen voted to pay some or all of the $924,259.65 California had spent on Indian-hunting militia expeditions from 1850 through 1853, which included Wright and McDermitt's 1852 Siskiyou Volunteer Rangers Expedition.[61]

Cosby's Vigilante Campaign, 1853

Meanwhile, the Rogue River War, between southern Oregon Indians and immigrants, inspired calls for the total annihilation of all northern California Indians. On August 7, 1853, the *Yreka Mountain Herald* roared, "Now that general Indian hostilities have commenced, we hope that the Government will render such aid as will enable the citizens of the North to carry on a war of extermination until the last red skin of these tribes has been killed." The author added, "Extermination is no longer even a question of time—the time has already arrived, the work has been commenced, and let the first white man who says treaty or peace be regarded as a traitor and coward." Imagining a vast alliance joining California and Oregon Indians, the *Herald* saw enemies everywhere: "the Rogue River, Cow Creek, Grave Creek, Applegate Creek, Umpqua, Shasta, and Klamath Indians, and probably the Pitt River's, and also the Indians about the Klamath and other Lakes [the Modocs] have united and declared an open and general war against the whites."[62] On August 6, "twenty or thirty volunteers and fifteen soldiers left Yreka" for the Rogue Valley, and the *Herald* soon bellowed, "Let extermination be our motto!"[63]

In this atmosphere, Yreka-area men apparently launched a third killing campaign in Modoc territory. In 1914 Jeff Riddle, born in 1863 to Frank and Wi-me-ma Riddle, wrote that "about the year 1853" sixty-five vigilantes under "Jim Crosby [almost certainly Cosby]" were returning to Yreka from an expedition against Achumawi Indians, south of Modoc territory, when Achumawis attacked them at night on "the east side of Tule Lake," in Modoc territory (Riddle 1914: 15–17). In response, Crosby initiated a brief but lethal campaign against the Modocs.

According to Jeff Riddle, "Capt. Crosby and his men left their camp early that morning. They had not gone far when they saw a few Modoc men and squaws. The Indians were preparing their morning meal. Crosby ordered his men to fire on the Indians, which they did. Only three Indians made their escape out of fourteen." Next, near Oklahoma, California, Crosby's men encountered "some Hot Creek Modocs" who "came right up with their wives and children and said, 'How do!' The answer was a volley from the white man's deadly guns. Only a few made their escape. Several women and children were murdered in cold blood, as well as men." Riddle concluded that when Crosby reached Yreka, "The men had quite a few scalps to show their friends, but they did not say that some of the scalps they carried were off poor old, innocent squaws and little children" (Riddle 1914: 17).

In what might have been a report on one of these massacres—or the participation of Yrekans in Oregon's Rogue River War—on August 11, 1853, the Marysville *Daily Evening Herald* announced, "The citizens of Yreka have recently killed twenty-five out of a band of thirty thieving Indians."[64] Finally, on October 1 the *Yreka Herald* reported, "peace with the Indians of that country is now obtained."[65] The pattern of exterminatory attacks was becoming clear. According to Jeff Riddle, "about five or six months after the Modoc Indians had been killed by Crosby's men . . . Captain Jack's father" announced at a council that, "God put our fathers and mothers here. We have lived here in peace [but] we cannot get along with the white people. They come along and kill my people for nothing. Not only my men, but they kill our wives and children." He added, "They will hunt us like we hunt the deer and the antelope," and he called on Indians to resist (Riddle 1914: 19). Modocs did defend themselves—rather effectively, considering the odds—but lost men, women, children, and entire villages in resisting each killing campaign. Now, a severely weakened Modoc people faced a fourth campaign sent against them, this time from Oregon.

Walker's Oregon Militia Campaign, 1854

On July 7, 1854, five men at Jacksonville, in southern Oregon Territory, petitioned the territorial governor, John Davis, to call out volunteers to protect Applegate Trail emigrants. It was to be a preemptive campaign: the petitioners, who included John Ross and Oregon's militia quartermaster general, cited no recent Indian aggression. Instead, they mentioned the opposite: the killing of two Indians who might have been Modocs and a consequent concern that other Modocs might seek "redress for real or imaginary wrongs from any or all citizens who may fall within their grasp." As a more concrete justification for attacking Indians, they cited California state militia units organized to fight them. The petitioners, well aware that their campaign could be lucrative, offered to help obtain federal funding "by way of memorializing Congress to defray the expenses."[66]

Governor Davis agreed. Ten days later he authorized Colonel John Ross of the Oregon Militia to "enlist a company of volunteers" to "proceed out upon what is known as the southern route to Oregon for the protection of the coming immigration against hostile Indians."[67] Sixty or seventy men joined up, and on August 8 Ross ordered their commander, Captain Jesse Walker, to establish a base in Modoc territory, granting him carte blanche in dealings with Indians: "Your treatment of the Indians must in a great measure be left to your own judgment and discretion. If possible, however, cultivate their friendship; but if necessary for the safety of the lives and property of the immigration, whip and drive them from the road."[68] Walker would exercise both options.

Walker reported reaching Lost River on August 18, 1854, where he met thirteen Yreka men who claimed to have been fired upon—but uninjured—by "not less than 150 or 200 [Modoc] warriors . . . on the north side of Tulé lake, at the sink of Lost river." Eschewing diplomacy, Walker immediately assaulted a nearby Tule Lake village. He reported that surprised Modocs "fled in great confusion to their boats and canoes." Like previous anti-Modoc campaigners, Walker burned "the ranches." He did not state the Modoc death toll there, but did report that between August 18 and September 4, "we had several skirmishes with these Indians, killing several and taking a few prisoners" and that "In all of these skirmishes the Indians would (when hard pushed by us) retreat to their boats." Walker's men tried to kill retreating Modoc people, but even "wading in water up to our armpits . . . it was impossible to follow them." However, Walker did deploy "small boats . . . to attack the enemy successfully." Finally, on September 4, some Modocs "being entirely out of provisions, were compelled to beg for quarters, which were granted them upon their faithfully promising to be friendly and never to kill or rob another white person."[69] This informal 1854 treaty would provide Modocs with frail protection.

On October 1, Walker moved east to Goose Lake, which separates traditional Modoc and Northern Paiute territory. "In Goose Lake valley" his men "surprised an Indian ranche [perhaps Modoc and] killed two Indians and took one prisoner." Northeast of Goose Lake, they killed at least sixteen to eighteen other Indians, whom Walker identified as Paiutes.[70] Oregon legislators later estimated that Walker's volunteers had killed "some thirty or forty" "Modocs and Piutes [sic]," noting that "not a single" militiaman or white immigrant was killed during Walker's ninety-six days in the field.[71] Killing Modoc women apparently bothered some militiamen. A Captain Judy, for example, explained how "a few squaws were killed by accident!" with the inconsistent and improbable claim that an all-female Modoc war party had led an attack on his unit.[72] Despite such reports, Oregon politicians began lobbying Congress to pay for this campaign, in which from perhaps five to thirty-eight or more Modocs were killed.[73]

By the fall of 1855 some Siskiyou County Californians were openly advocating the total annihilation of the Modoc people.[74] As one Yrekan reported, "The citizens of Siskiyou, are exasperated to the highest pitch. They desire no interference on the part of the agents of the General Government to procure a peace. They are determined to leave not a vestage [sic] of the savage race alive." Winter weather delayed the continuation of this "war of extermination," but not for long.[75]

The Modoc Expedition, 1856

In the early summer of 1856, California state senator and militia general J. D. Cosby began orchestrating a fifth campaign in Yreka (see figure 4.3). On June 12, he reported, "isolated parties of miners and herdsmen . . . murdered

4.3. C. C. Kuchel, "Yreka, Siskiyou County, Ca, 1856." Lithograph, 1856. Courtesy of the Bancroft Library, University of California at Berkeley.

and robbed," probably by "the 'Modock' [*sic*] and 'Klamath Lake' tribes . . . and the Klamath River and Applegate tribes on the north." That day he also dispatched "thirty mounted men to ascertain the position and strength of the enemy, and for the immediate protection of the threatened country."[76] Thus, under flimsy pretexts and the camouflage of martial rhetoric, Cosby launched what was probably the largest operation yet hurled at the Modocs: a campaign that would last for months, deploy over 230 militiamen, and kill scores of Modoc people. The informal 1854 Modoc treaty was now conveniently forgotten in favor of another potentially lucrative state militia campaign.

Between July 17 and 23, "three companies of mounted volunteers raised by Gen. Cosby, by authority of [California] Gov. [J. Neeley] Johnson," mustered in and rode east "for the Modoc country."[77] Yreka newspapers described their campaign in glowing terms: "The ball opened at Tule Lake" on July 29 or 30. "Capt. Martin's company made a descent upon a rancheria, leaving it desolate. The village was burned to the ground and one Indian killed," a militiaman mortally wounded, and another Modoc warrior killed elsewhere. Several days later Lieutenant H. H. Warman "attacked a large body of warriors near Tule Lake" and Bloody Point. "After four hours' hard fighting, in which Lieut. Warman was killed and two of his men wounded, the volunteers were compelled to retire, leaving the Indians master of the field." Such was the tenacity and skill of Modoc resistance. Yet with eight Modocs dead, it was a pyrrhic victory. The tribe, worn down by four prior killing campaigns, could ill afford such losses. That same day, Cosby chased another Modoc group, "killing three" more.[78]

Unaware of these attacks, on August 4 Governor Johnson urged Cosby "to take such measures and employ all the power you may possess, as the Major General commanding the 6th Division Cal. militia under the laws of this State, which may be absolutely necessary for the protection from Indian hostilities of the persons and property of the people within your command."[79] The state militia's supreme commander thus granted Cosby power to do as he saw fit. Cosby now went on a murderous rampage.

After killing ten or eleven more Indians—probably not Modoc people—in the Pit River region, on August 17 or 18 Cosby's men detected Modocs on an island near Bloody Point. They "waded through the water and tules" to attack, "but the Indians had left in their canoes and nearly all escaped." The militiamen did kill "two or three Indians. . . . There was a squaw shot some five or six times whilst in the water, and after being brought to the shore it was impossible to do anything for her. She was left on the island."[80] Another source reported that after the two men and a woman in a boat fought back, all three were killed. A correspondent in the militia camp ominously concluded that remaining Modoc warriors "need a good cleaning out [of] the worst kind," presumably meaning extermination.[81]

Cosby's men now visited Goose Lake, Russian Springs, and Klamath Lake. Some time between August 21 and September 4, they surprised "a large ranch of Indians," killing at least four men—who may or may not have been Modocs—on "Great Klamath Lake." They also killed an Indian man near "the base of the Sierra Nevada."[82] On September 20, they "had a skirmish . . . on Clear Lake, in which eight or ten Indians were killed without having an opportunity to fire a shot or an arrow." The day after this massacre, reported as a "skirmish," militiamen killed "two men and one squaw" in "another fight."[83]

To the west, Cosby's men prepared to continue hunting Modoc people, now with a deadly new asset: a "fleet of eight boats."[84] As one Yrekan later explained, "boats were made here [Yreka], and hauled out over the mountains . . . and then the hostile Indians were hunted in their former inaccessible marshes and islands in the large Klamath lakes, which before had been impregnable to their enemies."[85] Once sanctuaries, these watery refuges now became killing fields.

On or just before October 3, deploying three boats on Tule Lake, Cosby's men "[ran] down a lot of Indians in the tule; twenty-six are killed, and but four made their escape."[86] Cosby's officers then located a Modoc village on a

Lower Klamath Lake peninsula. Attacking at daylight on October 9, militiamen killed "several" Modocs on land. Militiamen waiting in boats then sank three fleeing Modoc canoes while the land-based militiamen "destroy[ed] their ranches, *muk-a-muk, ic ters, etc.*" and captured "several children." In total, militiamen counted five Indians killed; many others likely disappeared in the lake.[87] Modoc Expedition members now began mustering out.[88]

With his 237 militiamen, Cosby reported killing some 185 Indians in this campaign, most or all of them presumably Modoc.[89] In several months, the Modocs had lost perhaps 10 percent of their 1851 population. The operation was thus a devastating blow to the already reeling Modoc people.

As before, state and federal lawmakers subsequently sanctioned the campaign. California legislators retrospectively approved paying participants and their suppliers over $188,000 (California State Military Museum 2002). In 1861, Congress allocated $400,000 "to defray the expenses incurred" by California militia operations, including the Modoc Expedition.[90] The U.S. Treasury then gave California over $80,000 to help pay for the expedition (California State Military Museum 2002). State and federal authorities thus sanctioned the killing ex post facto.

A period of relative calm ensued while federal officials sought to control and contain surviving Modocs. In 1862, Superintendent of Oregon Indian Affairs William Rector called for them to "be subjugated and governed like a colony," and in 1864 federal agents began laying the groundwork for a treaty.[91] Meanwhile, Yreka lawyer Elijah Steele initiated his own negotiations. Although no longer Indian Agent for Northern California Indian Affairs— Steele had left that post in 1863—he signed an 1864 treaty with the Modocs that implied their right to remain on their lands (Stern 1998: 460).[92]

Federal officials, however, insisted on a new agreement. Still recovering from the five killing campaigns of 1851–56, Modocs complied. On October 15, 1864, Modoc leaders signed the Klamath Lake Treaty, ceding their homeland for payments, education, other benefits, and a shared reservation along the Klamath lakes in the territory of Oregon's Klamath Indians.[93] That year Chief Sc[h]onchin summarized his people's devastation at white hands and their commitment to peace: "Once my people were like the sand along yon shore. Now I call to them, and only the wind answers. Four hundred strong young men went with me to war with the Whites; only eighty are left. We will be good, if the White man will let us, and be friends forever."[94] That autumn, Oregon's Indian Affairs superintendent counted just 339 surviving Modoc people at Fort Klamath, Oregon.[95]

Crook's Army Expedition, 1867

Some Modocs refused to live on the reservation, and in 1867 the U.S. Army launched a brief campaign that killed an unknown number of them. On September 22, General George Crook led several hundred soldiers and Indian auxiliaries from Oregon into California and south through Modoc territory west of Goose Lake, as part of the so-called Snake War. The Modoc people were not fighting in this conflict, but in four days Crook's men killed perhaps a dozen unidentified Indians, and took at least one scalp.[96] Crook's men then surrounded "about seventy-five Paiutes and thirty [Achumawi], plus a few Modocs," in a lava field near what is today Likely, California.[97] Crook's intent was clear: "the General said the siege should be continued . . . until the red devils were all killed or starved to death."[98] Crook himself recollected, "I never wanted dynamite so bad."[99] How many died during the three-day-long Battle of the Infernal Caverns may never be known. However, soldiers found at least eight Indian bodies, and contemporary sources estimated fifteen to twenty Indians killed before survivors escaped (Indian survivor in Minchno 2007: 264; Minchno 2007: 265).[100] How many were Modoc people remains unknown, but seven of Crook's men died in the attack.[101]

Relative peace followed after several Modoc bands left the Klamath Reservation for their homelands, to which they believed they still held legal title through their 1864 treaty with Elijah Steele (Stern 1998: 460). Their return, in 1870, initially caused no upheaval. However, on July 6, 1872, U.S. Indian Affairs Commissioner F. A. Walker ordered Oregon's Indian Affairs superintendent "to remove [the Modocs] to the Klamath reservation—peaceably, if you possibly can; but forcibly, if you must."[102] Commissioner Walker thus precipitated the final campaign against the Modoc people.

The Modoc War, 1872–1873

Although Modoc bands had been living peacefully in their homeland for over two years, the U.S. Cavalry and local auxiliaries used deadly force in their November 29, 1872 attempt to force these bands back to the reservation. Shots were exchanged, and Captain James Jackson reported that at Lost River, "I poured in volley after volley among their worst men [while losing] one man killed and seven wounded."[103] As Modoc people fled, cavalrymen torched the village (Murray 1959: 89). At least one Modoc warrior, named Watchman, was killed, and a sick Modoc woman was burned to death.[104] Meanwhile, local men opened fire in another Modoc village across Lost River, killing, according to U.S. Special Commissioner to the Modocs Alfred Meacham, "an

4.4. "The Modoc War—Captain Jack's Cave in the Lava Beds." *Harper's Weekly Journal of Civilization*, June 28, 1873.

infant in its mother's arms." Meacham wrote that in these two engagements, attackers killed two Modoc infants, a girl, and one or two women.[105] Resisting these assaults, Modocs killed one civilian attacker and another mistaken for an attacker (Murray 1959: 88–89). Furious renegade Modoc warriors then killed twelve local white men, while sparing white women.[106] Thus began the infamous 1872–73 Modoc War.

Retreating, Kintpuash led his people into the lava beds—a "Hell with the fires gone out"—and to what became known as Captain Jack's Stronghold, a natural rock fortress reinforced by the Modocs (Jesse Applegate quoted in Dillon 1973: 160; see figures 4.4 and 4.5).[107] The U.S. Army, California Volunteers, and Oregon militiamen soon besieged them, but could not break in despite a major assault on January 17, 1873, that left twelve attackers and two Modocs dead (Thompson 1971: 43, 169).[108] On March 13 the head of the U.S. Army, General William Sherman, told General E. R. S. Canby that if the Modocs failed to cooperate: "I trust you will make such use of the

4.5. [Louis Heller], "Captain Jack (Kintpuash), A Modoc subchief; executed October 3, 1873; bust-length, full face." Photograph, 1873. National Archives and Records Administration, Record Group 165: Records of the War Department General and Special Staffs, 1860–1952.

military force that no other Indian tribe will imitate their example, and that no other reservation for them will be necessary except graves among their chosen lava-beds."[109] This was precisely what the Modocs—who had suffered repeated surprise attacks and massacres at white hands—feared. They did not know of Sherman's order, but they were now wary to the point of planning their own preemptive strike.

Negotiations continued until April 11, 1873. That day, A. B. Meacham, the Reverend Eleasar Thomas, L. S. Dyar, their translators, and the chief negotiator, General Canby, rode into that black sea of jagged rock. The Modoc negotiators greeted them, but this latest round of peace talks soon ran into familiar roadblocks. General Canby demanded that the Modocs surrender as prisoners of war and submit to U.S. authority. The Modocs continued to insist that Canby withdraw his soldiers, as a demonstration of good faith, and promise them some small portion of their homeland instead of deporting them from it. Finally, the Modoc negotiator John Schonchin exclaimed, "Take away the soldiers, and give us Hot Creek, or stop talking." Then, before Schonchin's statement could be fully translated, Kintpuash stood and gave the signal, "Ot we kantux-e"—"*all ready.*"[110]

Perhaps with the 1852 Lost River Massacre in mind, Kintpuash had planned an ambush. He immediately shot Canby in the face.[111] A moment later, the Modoc warrior Boston Charley shot the Reverend Thomas. The Modocs quickly killed and stripped both men. Meacham ran, was shot repeatedly, and eventually fell, but not before shooting Schonchin.[112] Both men survived. Meanwhile, on the east side of the lava beds, Curley Headed Jack and other Modoc men initiated impromptu negotiations with the U.S. infantry officers Lieutenant William Sherwood and Lieutenant W. H. Boyle. As the officers turned away, the Modocs opened fire, mortally wounding Sherwood.[113]

The killings of Sherwood, Thomas, and especially Canby created an uproar in white America and orders sanctioning a final, extermination war. Upon receiving news of Canby's assassination and the two other killings, General Sherman telegraphed the new commander, Brevet Major General Alvan Gillem, via his commanding officer, "the President . . . authorizes me to instruct you to make the attack so strong and persistent that their fate may be commensurate with their crime. You will be fully justified in their utter extermination."[114] In keeping with the Modoc killing campaigns of the 1850s, the army's highest-ranking general considered "utter extermination"—what we would today call total genocide—a legitimate strategy that he could recommend while passing on President Ulysses Grant's instructions. Gillem's commanding officer, General J. M. Schofield, forwarded this message with an endorsement note of his own: "Let your work be done thoroughly."[115] On April 14, General Schofield added, "Nothing short of their prompt and sure destruction will satisfy the ends of justice or meet the expectations of the Government."[116]

Gillem agreed that extermination was a legitimate path to victory. Artillery began shelling the Stronghold, and on April 14 hundreds of troops closed the noose (see figure 4.6).[117] Fighting a skillful rearguard action, Kintpuash's fifty-five to seventy warriors slowly retreated closer and closer to the Stronghold (Thompson 1971: 168). On the third morning of the attack Gillem made his intentions clear: "We will endeavor to end the Modoc War today. . . . Let us exterminate the tribe."[118] That was easier said than done. When soldiers finally entered the Stronghold's caves they found them almost abandoned. Kintpuash and his people had slipped away on the night of April 16, having inflicted twenty-three casualties. In total, the Modocs lost between three and sixteen killed in the battle and its immediate aftermath (Thompson 1971: 74–76, 168, 170).[119] Inside the Stronghold, soldiers apparently shot an old woman, murdered and scalped a wounded elderly man, and kicked a severed Modoc head (Quinn 1997: 143). Such actions were unsurprising given commanders' previous orders and persisting attitudes. That very day Sherman wrote of Kintpuash's Modocs, "the order to attack is against the whole, and if all be swept from the face of the earth, they themselves have invited it."[120] On the spot, Gillem reported, "I have dislodged the Modocs from their stronghold. . . . No effort will be spared to exterminate them."[121]

4.6. "The Modoc Indians in the Lava Beds." *Illustrated London News*, June 7, 1873.

Gillem would never carry out this intent. Following an April 26 battle in which Modoc marksmen killed twenty-three of Gillem's men and wounded nineteen while losing perhaps one warrior, Sherman replaced Gillem with Colonel Jefferson Davis (Thompson 1971: 82, 92; Murray 1959: 236). Meanwhile, in the barren lava beds Kintpuash's approximately 165 people became desperate for supplies. On May 10, Kintpuash and some warriors attacked soldiers at Dry or Sorass Lake, southeast of the lava fields. Only one Modoc, Ellen's Man George, was killed, but the soldiers and their Paiute auxiliaries routed Kintpuash and his men. More important, by capturing their horses, powder, and ammunition, they broke the back of Modoc resistance (Murray 1959: 243, 246–51). Now in need of food and water, the fragmenting, exhausted, and poorly supplied Modocs became easier to kill. They avoided troops, but on May 18 cavalrymen killed two men and three women (H. C. Hasbrouck in Brady 1907: 324). Understanding their weakness and fearing annihilation, survivors began surrendering. Others were captured. From this point on, most of the direct, state-sponsored killing ceased.

Why? The army had become more careful, in large part, because the eyes of America were now on this last California Indian war. Reporters from New York, Portland, Sacramento, and San Francisco were on site. Indian

4.7. Modoc prisoners of war. Photograph, 1873. Courtesy of the Oregon Historical Society, Portland, #bb008056.

advocates like the Quaker Lucretia Mott and Philadelphia's Radical Club were pressuring President Grant, Interior Secretary Columbus Delano, and Indian Affairs Commissioner Edward Smith not to allow the army to exterminate the Modocs.[122] In addition, General Davis was sensitive to charges of misconduct given that, during the Civil War, he had abandoned ex-slaves as Confederate cavalrymen advanced, thus leading to civilian deaths and the loss of his command (Glatthaar 1985: 64; Murray 1959: 204). Finally, the fact that in January 1873 California Indians had at last become eligible to serve as witnesses in California criminal trials may also have curbed the killing.[123]

Still, there were those who wanted to kill Modoc people even after they had surrendered or been captured. On June 8, two horsemen—probably Oregon militiamen serving under John Miller or John Ross—accosted a wagonload of Modoc prisoners and at point blank range shot four men dead, "Little John, Tehee Jack, Poney [and] Moocha," and wounded Little John's wife.[124] Sherman also wanted some killed. He ordered General Schofield, Davis's commander, to have "some" Modocs "tried by court martial and shot."[125] However, when Davis tried in June to summarily hang "8 or 10 ringleaders," Schofield stopped him, in order to allow the U.S. attorney general to decide whether to try the defendants in a civil or military court.[126] Even after a farcical kangaroo court-martial—in which the six Modoc defendants served as their own lawyers, their translators testified against them, and they were judged by the men they had just fought—Lucretia Mott "burst in upon [an] elegant dinner party" and all but forced President Grant to commute

Table 4.1 Modoc Population Decline, 1851–1873

Year	Estimated Total Modoc Population
1846–51	1,000–2,000+
1864 (Huntington)	339+
1870 (Nourse) [1]	350–360
1873 (Powers)	~250
1881 (Office of Indian Affairs)	249

[1] "Geo. Nourse, sutler at Fort Klamath," in *Yreka Weekly Union*, September 28, 1870. See also endnote 1.

the sentences of the two youngest Modoc defendants, Barncho and Slolux (Murray 1959: 285–86, 297; Quinn 1997: 180). Still, at 10:20 A.M. on October 3, 1873, Kintpuash, John Schonchin, Boston Charley, and Black Jim were hanged at Fort Klamath and decapitated, their heads sent to the Army Medical College in Washington, D.C. (Thompson 1971: 124–25, 126). The curtain thus closed on the final act of the last Modoc killing campaign, which had taken the lives of at least twenty-four Modoc people and perhaps thirty-nine or more.[127] The number of Modoc survivors in 1873 was less than one-quarter of the 1851 Modoc population.

Federal officials now deported 153 Modoc survivors to Oklahoma's Quapaw Agency (see figure 4.7).[128] As a result more than a third died from poor conditions and disease exacerbated by corruption (Hurtado 1981: 86–107). By 1881, despite intervening births, the Indian Affairs Office reported just ninety-eight Modoc at the Quapaw Agency and 151 at Oregon's Klamath Agency (see table 4.1).[129]

Modoc people remain today because their ancestors resisted the seven campaigns sent against them between 1851 and 1873. In the 2010 census, over 2,100 U.S. citizens self-identified as Modoc or part-Modoc.[130] Many of them generously shared information for this chapter and are enrolled members of Oregon's Klamath Tribes or the Modoc Tribe of Oklahoma. They are the descendents of genocide survivors, although historians have described their ancestors as belligerents in a series of wars.

Genocide and Resistance

The killing campaigns launched against the Modocs clearly fit the 1948 United Nations Genocide Convention definition. First, perpetrators articulated, in both word and deed, their "intent to destroy, in whole or in part, a national, ethnical, racial [or] religious group, as such." Second, the "Killing" was highly organized. The state tolerated or sanctioned and financed seven anti-Modoc campaigns, all of which emphasized the massacre of civilians. Militiamen and soldiers also committed another genocidal crime that likely contributed to Modoc deaths by exposure, malnutrition, decreased fecundity, fetal death, and increased mortality rates. By deliberately destroying at least seventeen Modoc villages and their food supplies, militiamen and U.S. soldiers seem to have been "deliberately inflicting on the group conditions of life calculated to bring about its physical destruction in whole or in part" (United Nations 1948: 78:1021, 280).

Interpreting the Modoc ordeal as genocide is complicated by two major factors: disease and resistance. Disease is widely considered the leading cause of California Indian population decline under nineteenth-century U.S. rule (Cook 1978: 92; Hurtado 1988: 1). Yet apart from Powers's reference to 150 Modoc deaths from smallpox in 1847—representing not more than 15 percent of the 1851 Modoc population—extant primary sources provide little evidence of Old World epidemics among the Modocs before their 1873 relocation and incarceration.

Modoc resistance poses a larger challenge to an interpretation of genocide because many scholars define genocide as one-sided.[131] Was this not simply a series of wars in which both sides killed civilians but one side had overwhelming firepower? Modoc warriors did kill civilians, notably in 1852 and 1872. Yet these killings were unusual, while from at least 1851 whites waged seven campaigns against the Modocs in which civilian massacres were commonplace.

Comparing casualties helps clarify the fact that while Modocs resisted, they also suffered genocide. Whites killed at the very least 231 to 1,106 Modoc people between 1851 and 1873, including many women and children. These estimates are built on specific reported killings and do not include nonspecific or undated reports of Modoc killings, even when found in nineteenth-century sources.[132] For example, Chief Schonchin reported 320 young Modoc men killed by 1864. In contrast, primary sources suggest that Modocs killed 119 to 149 non-Modocs, sixty-eight of them soldiers, state militiamen, and auxiliaries during the 1872–73 war launched by the United States (see table 4.2).[133]

The Modoc genocide is hardly the only genocide against indigenous people that has been sanitized as "war." For example, some characterize the early nineteenth-century genocide of Tasmanian Aborigines as a "war" or a "clash" (Bonwick 1870; Plomley 1992).[134] Likewise, some California legislators described the state's mid-nineteenth-century genocide of Yuki Indians as a "war."[135] Many Germans also initially referred to their early twentieth-century

Table 4.2 Comparative Reported Death Tolls, 1851–1873

Year	Reported number of white civilians killed by Modocs	Reported number of vigilantes, militiamen, and soldiers killed by Modocs	Reported number of Modocs killed (civilians and warriors) by whites and their allies
1851	0	1	55–61+
1852	30–42 (Meacham estimated a total of 75 whites killed in 1852)	3–10	74–709
1853	?	?	17–42+
1854	0	0	5–38+
1856	0–4+?	2	56–185(?)
From "war with the Whites" to 1864			320 young warriors (not counting women, children or the elderly)
1867	0	7 (?)	0–32 (it is possible that none of these victims were Modocs)
1872–73	15	68	24–39+
TOTALS	45–61	74–88	231–1,106

genocide of the Herero and Nama peoples, in what is today Namibia, as "wars" or "fights."[136] Genocide and war are not mutually exclusive. Indeed, they often coexist.[137] Moreover, the 1948 United Nations Genocide Convention designates genocide a crime "whether committed in time of peace or in time of war" (United Nations 1948: 280). We must not let war camouflage genocide.

Groups targeted for annihilation usually resist, often violently. Armenians fought against their World War I genocide at Ottoman hands with extensive irregular warfare (Dasnabedian 1990: 110–23). During World War II, Jews likewise resisted the Holocaust in ghettos, camps, and beyond. The 1943 Warsaw Ghetto and Treblinka uprisings, the Sobibór revolt that led to its destruction that year, and the 1944 Auschwitz uprising are well known, and tens of thousands of Jews also fought as partisans (Bauer 1982: 254–74). During the second half of the twentieth-century, as the historian Ben Kiernan has observed, Cambodia's Eastern Zone uprising against Pol Pot's regime led to Vietnam's 1979 invasion and the end of the Khmer Rouge genocide. Finally, as Kiernan also observed, "In Rwanda in 1994, it was left to an externally-trained but indigenous, predominately Tutsi insurgent army, the Rwandan Patriotic Front, to overthrow the Hutu Power regime and halt its genocide of Tutsis."[138] Like Armenians, Jews, Cambodians, and Tutsis, Modocs violently resisted genocide.

Variations of the Modoc ordeal occurred elsewhere during the conquest and colonization of Africa, Asia, Australia, and North and South America. Indigenous civilizations repeatedly resisted invaders seeking to physically annihilate them in whole or in part. Many of these catastrophes are known as wars. Yet by carefully examining the intentions and actions of colonizers and their advocates it is possible to reinterpret some of these cataclysms as both genocides and wars of resistance. The Modoc case is one of them.

Notes

The author thanks Tom Ball, Peter Carini, Torina Case, Taylor David, Don Gentry, John Faragher, Bill Follis, Cheewa James, Ben Kiernan, Patty Limerick, Timothy Macholz, Preston McBride, George Miles, Susan Madley, Bill Nelson, Jesse Philips, Robin Philips, Samuel Redman, Jack Shadwick, Susan Snyder, the Bancroft and Rauner Library staffs, the Klamath Tribes, and the Modoc Tribe of Oklahoma for their help.

1. Working from post-1851 documents, which indicate that hundreds of Modoc people were killed between 1851 and 1873 while at least 250 survived, it is clear that there were at least one thousand Modocs in 1851, if not two thousand or more. For estimates of the population in 1851 and earlier, see Turner 1873: 22; Kroeber 1925: 320; A. L. Kroeber in Cook 1976: 45; Mooney 1928: 18; Cook 1976: 4, 6; Malinowski et al. 1998: 3:444; James 2008: 20. For the 1873 population, see Powers 1873: 536.

2. Examples include Odeneal 1873; Riddle 1914; Murray 1959; Sproull 1969; Thompson 1971; Dillon 1973; Reed 1991; Quinn 1997; Hathaway 1995; James 2008.

3. Turner 1873: 21.

4. Nathaniel Todd, February 3, 1858, in U.S. House of Representatives 1859, 57 (hereafter H. Mis. Doc. 47).

5. Powers 1873: 536.

6. Quoted in California 1851a: 15.

7. California 1851b: 520–21.

8. According to the recollection of a person who was in the area at the time, in 1851, "some reckless Oregonians had ruthlessly killed two Indians, and provoked by this means the massacre of unoffending travelers" in Modoc territory (Special Correspondent's letter, May 7, 1873, in *New York Times*, May 24, 1873).

9. Ross 1878: 1.

10. Ross 1878: 1, 22–23. Ross also recollected bringing in "5 or 6 female. . . . Modocs" (24).

11. Ross 1878: 23, 24.

12. Statement of W. T. Kershaw, November 21, 1857, in H. Mis. Doc. 47, 41 (hereafter Kershaw statement).

13. Fanning quoted in Wells 1881: 123; Kershaw statement, 41.

14. Harry Wells thought fifteen were killed in the attack at the Lost River's mouth (Wells 1884a: 133). Fanning in Wells 1881: 123–24.

15. Fanning in Wells 1881: 124–25. According to Wells, at least three were killed in the lava beds (Wells 1884a: 133).

16. Kershaw statement, 41.

17. California 1852: 59.

18. Fifty-nine petitioners to Gov. Bigler, July 12, 1852, in California Adjutant General's Office 1850–80 (hereafter IWP), F3753:197.

19. W. A. Robertson, John [illegible], J. D. Cooke, Daniel Frauer, and Elijah Steele to John Bigler, July 22, 1852, IWP, F3753:198.

20. John Bigler to Thos. Couts and fifty-eight other citizens of Siskiyou County, July 24, 1852, IWP, F3753:200; Assistant Adjutant General, Pacific Division to E. H. Fitzgerald, July 27, 1852, IWP, F3753:202.

21. Chas. McDermitt to John Bigler, December 19, 1852, in California 1853a, Document 21, 2.

22. Wells 1884b: 317; McDermitt to Bigler, December 19, 1852, Document 21, 3.

23. McDermitt to Bigler, December 19, 1852, Document 21, 2; Wells 1884b: 317.

24. Benj Wright to Gentlemen, September 2, 1852, IWP, F3753:203. See also McDermitt to Bigler, December 19, 1852, in California 1853a, Document 21, 2–3.

25. Special Correspondent's letter, May 7, 1873, in New York Times, May 24, 1873; Report of the Committee on Indian Affairs in California 1853a, Document 33, 4; Kershaw statement, 41.

26. Special Correspondent's letter, May 7, 1873, in New York Times, May 24, 1873.

27. Wright to Gentlemen, September 2, 1852, IWP, F3753:203.

28. J. C. Burgess summarized in Klamath Agency Correspondent, July 1, 1873, in New York Times, July 17, 1873.

29. Bradford n.d.: 39.

30. For death toll estimates, see H. S. Lewis to Bigler, September 7, 1852, IWP, F3753:211; McDermitt to Bigler, December 19, 1852, in California 1853a, Document 21, 3; Kershaw statement 42; Burgess summarized in New York Times, July 17, 1873; Wells 1881: 131; Walling 1884: 205; Wells 1884b: 318.

31. Kershaw statement, 42.

32. John Ross to Geo. Curry, November 10, 1854, in H. Mis. Doc. 47, 15. Kershaw reported twenty-two bodies (Kershaw statement, 42). Nathaniel Todd later reported thirty-six "murdered by the Modoc Indians on the southern Oregon emigrant road" in August 1852 (in H. Mis. Doc. 47, 57). In 1857 former Oregon Indian Affairs Superintendent Joel Palmer reported that Wright found eighteen to twenty bodies, while Ross's party found about a dozen (Joel Palmer to B. F.

Dowell, December 17, 1857, in H. Mis. Doc. 47, 54–56). Wells also wrote of thirty-six bodies (Wells 1884b: 318).

33. A. B. Meacham, "Report of A. B. Meacham, Special Commissioner to the Modocs, Upon the Late Modoc War," October 5, 1872, in U.S. Office of Indian Affairs 1874: 79.

34. Old Sc[h]onchin summarized in Special Correspondent's letter, May 7, 1873, in *New York Times,* May 24, 1873.

35. Wright to Gentlemen, September 2, 1852, *IWP,* F3753:203.

36. Fifty-five petitioners to John Bigler, September 7, 1852, *IWP,* F3753:204. This petition specified that the meeting occurred on September 6, 1852.

37. H. S. Lewis to Bigler, September 7, 1852, *IWP,* F3753:211.

38. E. A. Hitchcock to John Bigler, September 15, 1852, in U.S. War Department 1821–1920, M2114, Roll 1, Frame 392.

39. Jas. Strawbridge to Rains, September 28, 1852, in *Sacramento Daily Union,* October 4, 1852.

40. Walling 1884: 206; Wells 1884b: 318.

41. [Shasta?] *Courier* in *Daily Alta California,* November 8, 1852.

42. Committee on Indian Affairs, on the Claims of Wright and McDermitt's Command, in California 1853a: Document 33, 4; [Shasta?] *Courier* in *Daily Alta California,* November 8, 1852.

43. Barry 1879: 123, 124.

44. Barry 1879: 124.

45. Kershaw statement, 42.

46. E. A. Hitchcock to S. Cooper, March 31, 1853, in U.S. House of Representatives 1857 (hereafter H. Ex. Doc. 76): 78.

47. Turner 1873: 23.

48. Yreka Correspondent to *Shasta Courier,* November 21, 1852, in *Daily Alta California,* December 2, 1852.

49. McDermitt to Bigler, December 19, 1852, in California 1853a: Document 21, 3.

50. Hitchcock to Cooper, March 31, 1853, 78.

51. Kershaw statement, 42.

52. Captain Jack in Special Correspondent's letter, May 7, 1873, in *New York Times,* May 24, 1873.

53. Special Correspondent's letter, May 7, 1873, in *New York Times,* May 24, 1873; Turner 1873: 23.

54. Wells 1881: 133; Wells 1884b: 320.

55. Kershaw statement, 42.

56. Kershaw statement, 42–43. For quotations see Wells 1881: 133. Hitchcock, Barry, and Jeff Riddle reported similar details: Hitchcock to Cooper, March 31, 1853, 78; Barry 1879: 124, 125; Riddle 1914: 32.

57. Committee on Indian Affairs, on the Claims of Wright and McDermitt's Command, in California 1853a: Document 33, 4.

58. Chief Sc[h]onch[in] in *New York Times,* July 17, 1873.

59. McDermitt to Bigler, December 19, 1852, in California 1853a, Document 21, 3; Committee on Indian Affairs, on the Claims of Wright and McDermitt's Command, in California 1853a, Document 33, 4.

60. California 1853b: 95–96.

61. Minot 1855: 582–88.

62. *Yreka Mountain Herald*, "Extra!," August 7, 1853. George Miles kindly provided this source from Yale University's Beinecke Library.

63. *Mountain Herald* in *Daily Alta California*, August 15, 1853; *Mountain Herald* in *Shasta Courier*, August 27, 1853.

64. Marysville *Daily Evening Herald*, August 11, 1853, 2.

65. *Yreka Herald*, October 1, 1853, in Marysville *Daily Evening Herald*, October 10, 1853, 2.

66. C. S. Drew, E. H. Cleavland, Alex. McIntyre, O. B. McFadden, John Ross to Jno. Davis, July 7, 1854, in H. Mis. Doc. 47, 3–5.

67. John Davis to John Ross, July 17, 1854 in H. Mis. Doc. 47, 6–7. The governor simultaneously sent a similar letter to the quartermaster general authorizing the campaign (Jno. Davis to C. S. Drew, July 17, 1854, in H. Mis. Doc. 47, 5–6).

68. Walling 1884: 235; John Ross to Walker, August 8, 1854, in H. Mis. Doc. 47, 8.

69. Jesse Walker to John Ross, November 6, 1854, in H. Mis. Doc. 47, 12–13.

70. Jesse Walker to John Ross, November 6, 1854, in H. Mis. Doc. 47, 13–14.

71. Delazon Smith and A. P. Dennison, January 31, 1856, in H. Mis. Doc. 47, 29; L. F. Grover and James Kelly, January 13, 1857, in H. Mis. Doc. 47, 31.

72. Alvy Boles quoting Captain Judy in Powers 1873: 539.

73. Geo. Curry to Joseph Lane, September 20, 1854, in H. Mis. Doc. 47, 9–10; Joint Resolution of the legislative assembly of Oregon . . . adopted January 15, 1855, in H. Misc. Doc. 47, 26.

74. In 1858, Nathaniel Todd reported a person killed by Modocs on September 2, 1855 (in H. Mis. Doc. 47, 58).

75. Yreka correspondent in *Marysville Daily Herald*, November 18, 1855.

76. J. D. Cosby to J. Johnson, June 12, 1856, *IWP*, F3753:293; Comptroller of the State of California 1850–59, Modoc Expedition: 14.

77. Comptroller of the State of California 1850–59, Modoc Expedition: 9, 10, 12; *Yreka Union* in *Sacramento Daily Union*, August 5, 1856.

78. *Yreka Chronicle*, August 7, 1856, in *Sacramento Daily Union*, August 11, 1856; *Yreka Union*, August 7, 1856, in Wells 1881: 142. Army Captain H. M. Judah, stationed at Fort Jones, denied the accuracy of these reports (Judah in Wells 1881: 143).

79. J. Johnson to John Cosby, August 4, 1856, *IWP*, F3753:296.

80. Letter dated Clear Lake, August 19, 1856, in *Siskiyou Chronicle*, August 28, 1856, in *Sacramento Daily Union*, September 2, 1856; *Shasta Republican*, August 30, 1856.

81. August 19 letter to *Yreka Union* in *Shasta Republican*, August 30, 1856.

82. Jargon at Clear Lake to Editors Yreka Union, September 4, in *Yreka Union*, September 11, 1856, in *Sacramento Daily Union*, September 17, 1856.

83. *Sacramento Daily Union*, October 8, 1856.

84. "A correspondent, writing from head quarters, Clear Lake, September 29th," in *Yreka Union*, October 9, 1856, in *Sacramento Daily Union*, October 17, 1856.

85. Geo. Furber in Yreka *Siskiyou Chronicle*, July 9, 1859.

86. Correspondent, October 3, 1856, in *Yreka Union*, October 9, 1856, in *Sacramento Daily Union*, October 17, 1856.

87. Correspondent in *Yreka Union*, October 16, 1856, in *Sacramento Daily Union*, October 21, 1856, emphasis original.

88. Comptroller of the State of California 1850–59, Modoc Expedition: 9–12, 22.

89. Comptroller of the State of California 1850–59, Modoc Expedition: A6; Cosby in Wells 1881: 143.

90. "An Act for the Payment of Expenses Incurred in the Suppression of Indian Hostilities in the State of California," in Sanger 1863: 12:199–200.

91. Wm. Rector to Wm. Dole, September 2, 1862, in U.S. Office of Indian Affairs 1863: 262.

92. For the treaty text, see *Yreka Union*, July 19, 1873.

93. "Brief of treaty with Klamath and Modoc Indians of Southern Oregon of October 15, 1864," in U.S. Office of Indian Affairs 1865: 104–5.

94. Old Sc[h]onchin quoted in Turner 1873: 23.

95. J. W. Huntington to Wm. Dole, December 10, 1864, in U.S. Office of Indian Affairs 1865: 101–2. Huntington suggested that he might not have counted every Modoc. Nor were all Modoc survivors then at the reservation. Thus, the total Modoc population in October 1873 was likely considerably higher.

96. Robinson 2001: 96; Bourke 1891: 645; Joe in *The Owyhee Avalanche*, November 2, 1867.

97. Crook 1946: 155n3.

98. Joe in *Owyhee Avalanche*, November 2, 1867.

99. Crook 1946: 154.

100. J. M. Bassett, October 28, 1867, in *Yreka Weekly Union*, November 2, 1867.

101. Crook 1946: 155n3.

102. F. A. Walker to T. B. Odeneal, July 6, 1872, in U.S. House of Representatives 1873: 3:263.

103. James Jackson to John Green, December 2, 1872, in U.S. House of Representatives 1874 (hereafter H. Ex. Doc. 122): 42–43.

104. Meacham 1876: 81; Murray 1959: 88–89.

105. Meacham 1876: 80–81.

106. James Jackson to John Green, December 2, 1872.

107. These lava fields are today in Lava Beds National Monument.

108. The Modoc Greasy Boots was killed and Shacknasty Frank was wounded and died in the Lava Beds (Thompson 1971: 169).

109. W. T. Sherman to E. R. S. Canby, March 13, 1873, in H. Ex. Doc. 122, 70–71.

110. Schonchin and Kintpuash in A. B. Meacham to Commissioner of Indian Affairs, October 5, 1872, in U.S. Office of Indian Affairs 1874: 78, italics original.

111. Meacham 1875: 492; Murray 1959: 189.

112. Meacham 1875: 492–97.

113. Boyle n.d.: 55–57. See also Murray 1959: 192–93.

114. W. T. Sherman to Schofield, April 12, 1873, in *Daily Alta California*, April 14, 1873.

115. J. M. Schofield to Gillem, April 13, 1873, in *Daily Alta California*, April 14, 1873.

116. John M. Schofield to Gillem, April 14, 1873, in *Army and Navy Journal,* 10:57 (1873), 585.

117. Meacham 1875: 522–23.

118. Gillem to Mason, April 16, 1873, in Hagen 1865–78: 2:1061.

119. The Modocs Old Tales and Ike were killed in the battle (Thompson 1971: 170).

120. Sherman to Dear Sir, April 17, 1873, in *Army and Navy Journal* 10:57 (1873), 586–87.

121. A. C. Gillem to Schofield, April 17, in *Daily Alta California*, April 19, 1873.

122. Lucretia Mott, Elizabeth Bladen, and E. M. Davis to Ulysses Grant, Columbus Delano, E. P. Smith, and others, April 19, 1873, in Hagen 1865–78: 1:885–86.

123. California 1874: 455; *People v. McGuire* 1872.

124. *Daily Alta California*, June 10, 1873.

125. W. T. Sherman to J. M. Schofield, June 3, 1873, in H. Ex. Doc. 122, 86.

126. Jeff Davis to Assist. Adjut. General, June 5, 1873, in Hagen 1865–78: 2:1028; Thompson 1971: 120–21.

127. Thompson listed sixteen warriors who died during the war (1971: 168–70).

128. H. C. Hasbrouck to Samuel Breck, November 5, 1873, in H. Ex. Doc. 122, 102. Two of the original 155 prisoners were sent to the prison on Alcatraz Island in San Francisco Bay (Murray 1959: 297).

129. U.S. Office of Indian Affairs 1881: 278, 284.

130. U.S. Census Bureau 2010, "Modoc alone or in any combination" (accessed July 5, 2013).

131. For 1959–2009 academic definitions of genocide, see Jones 2011: 16–20.

132. In 1877, Stephen Powers wrote, in a chapter on the Modocs, "I have more than once ... listened to old Oregonians telling with laughter how when out hunting deer they had shot down a 'buck' or a squaw at sight, and merely for amusement, although the tribe to which they belonged were profoundly at peace with the Americans!" (Powers 1877: 254).

133. For soldiers, militiamen, and auxiliaries killed in the 1872–73 Modoc War, see Thompson 1971: 171.

134. For scholarship on the Tasmanian genocide, see Madley 2008a. See also Ryan 2012.

135. California 1860. For scholarship on the Yuki genocide, see Carranco and Beard 1981; Madley 2008b.

136. Rust 1905; Salzmann 1905; Bayer 1906; Kriegsgeschichtlichen Abteilung I des Großen Generalstabes 1906, 1907. For summaries of the German South West African genocide and an annotated bibliography, see Madley 2005; Schaller 2011.

137. Martin Shaw has argued that, "instances of genocide—not only the Holocaust, but also Armenia and Rwanda—have been clearly connected with war contexts, and this is an overwhelming empirical trend" (2007: 43).

138. Kiernan 2008: 3, 7–58.

References

PRIMARY SOURCES

Army and Navy Journal
Barry, William J. 1879. *Up and Down California, or, Fifty years' colonial experiences in Australia, California, New Zealand, India, China, and the south Pacific: being the life history of Capt. W. J. Barry.* London: S. Low, Marston, Searle and Rivington.

Bayer, Maximilian. 1906. *Der Krieg in Südwestafrika und seine Bedeutung für die Entwickelung der Kolonie Vortrag gehalten in 35 deutschen Städten.* Leipzig: Engelmann.

Boyle, W. H. n.d. "Personal Observations On the Conduct of the Modoc War." BANC MSS P-A 96. Bancroft Library, University of California at Berkeley.

Bradford, Ward. n.d. *Biographical Sketches of the Life of Major Ward containing a graphic description of the manners and life of early times; vivid incidents in Indian wars, and wilds of the mountains; life in the gold regions of Nevada; perils by land and sea. Together with reliable statements concerning the products and resources of many lands and many climes.* Self-published.

California. 1851a. *Journals of the Legislature of the State of California at its Second Session held at the city of San José, commencing on the sixth day of January, and ending on the first day of May, 1851.* San José, CA: Eugene Casserly.

California. 1851b. *The Statutes of California, Passed at the second session of the legislature, begun on the sixth day of January, 1851, and ended on the first day of May, 1851, at the city of San José.* San José, CA: Eugene Casserly.

California. 1852. *The Statutes of California passed at The Third Session of the Legislature, begun on the fifth day of January, 1852, and ended on the fourth day of May, 1852, at the cities of Vallejo and Sacramento.* San Francisco: G. K. Fitch.

California. 1853a. *Journals of the Fourth Session of the Legislature of the State of California, begun on the third day of January, 1853, and ended on the nineteenth day of May, 1853, at the Cities of Vallejo and Benicia.* San Francisco: George Kerr.

California. 1853b. *The Statutes of California passed at The Fourth Session of the Legislature, begun on the 3rd day of January, 1853, and ended on the 19th day of May, 1853, at the cities of Vallejo and Benicia.* San Francisco: George Kerr.

California. 1860. *Majority and Minority Reports of the Special Joint Committee on the Mendocino War.* Sacramento: C. T. Botts.

California. 1874. *The Penal Code of the State of California*, edited by Creed Haymond and John C. Burch. San Francisco: A. L. Bancroft.

California Adjutant General's Office. 1850–80. *Military Department, Adjutant General, Indian War Papers* (F3753). California State Archives, Sacramento.

Comptroller of the State of California. 1850–59. "Expenditures for Military Expeditions Against the Indians During the Years 1850–1859." Modoc Expedition. California State Archives, Sacramento.

Crook, George. 1946. *General George Crook: His Autobiography*, edited by Martin Schmitt. Norman: University of Oklahoma Press.

Hagen, Olaf T., ed. 1865–78. Modoc War and Lava Beds National Monument, correspondence and documents. 2 vols. BANC MSS C-A 232. Bancroft Library, University of California at Berkeley.

Harper's Weekly Journal of Civilization

The Illustrated London News

Kriegsgeschichtlichen Abteilung I des Großen Generalstabes, ed. 1906. *Die Kämpfe der deutschen Truppen in Südwestafrika.* Vol. 1. 2 vols. Berlin: Ernst Siegfried Mittler und Sohn.

Kriegsgeschichtlichen Abteilung I des Großen Generalstabes, ed. 1907. *Die Kämpfe der deutschen Truppen in Südwestafrika.* Vol. 2. 2 vols. Berlin: Ernst Siegfried Mittler und Sohn.

[Marysville] *Daily Evening Herald*

Marysville Daily Herald

Meacham, A. B. 1875. *Wigwam and War-Path; or, the Royal Chief in Chains*. Boston: John P. Dale.

Meacham, A. B. 1876. *Wi-ne-ma (The Woman-Chief) and Her People*. Hartford, CT: American.

Minot, George, ed. 1855. *The Statutes at Large and Treaties of the United States of America*. Vol. 10. Boston: C. C. Little and J. Brown.

New York Times

Odeneal, Thomas B. 1873. *The Modoc War: Statement of Its Origins and Causes*. Portland, OR: "Bulletin" Steam Book and Job Printing Office.

The Owyhee Avalanche

Powers, Stephen. 1873. "The California Indians, No. VIII—The Modocs." *Overland Monthly and Out West Magazine* 10 (6): 535–45.

Ross, John. 1878. "Narrative of an Indian Fighter." BANC MSS P-A 63. Bancroft Library, University of California at Berkeley.

Rust, Conrad. 1905. *Krieg und Frieden im Hererolande: Aufzeichnungen aus dem Kriegsjahre 1904*. Berlin: Förster.

Sacramento Daily Union

[San Francisco] *Daily Alta California*

Salzmann, Erich von. 1905. *Im Kampfe gegen die Herero*. Berlin: Dietrich Reimer (Ernst Vohsen).

Sanger, George P. 1863. *The Statutes at Large, Treaties, and Proclamations, of the United States of America*. Vol. 12. 18 vols. Boston: Little, Brown.

Thompson, William. 1912. *Reminiscences of a Pioneer*. San Francisco: n.p.

Shasta Courier

Shasta Republican

Turner, William M. 1873. "Scraps of Modoc History." *Overland Monthly and Out West Magazine* 11 (1): 21–25.

United Nations. 1948. *Convention on the Prevention and Punishment of the Crime of Genocide. Adopted by the General Assembly of the United Nations on 9 December 1948*. In *Treaty Series*, vol. 78.

U.S. Census Bureau. 2010. "American Fact Finder." http://factfinder2.census.gov/faces/nav/jsf/pages/index.xhtml.

U.S. House of Representatives. 1857. *Indian Affairs on the Pacific* (H. Exec. Doc. 76). 34th Congress, 3rd Session. Washington, DC: Government Printing Office (*Serial Set* 906).

U.S. House of Representatives. 1859. *Protection Afforded by Volunteers of Oregon and Washington Territories to Overland Immigrants in 1854* (H. Mis. Doc. 47). 35th Congress, 2nd Session. Washington, DC: Government Printing Office (*Serial Set* 1016).

U.S. House of Representatives. 1873. *Reports of Committees of the House of Representatives for the Third Session of the Forty-Second Congress*. Vol. 3. 3 vols. Washington, DC: Government Printing Office.

U.S. House of Representatives. 1874. *Modoc War* (H. Exec. Doc. 122). 43rd Congress, 1st Session. Washington, DC: Government Printing Office (*Serial Set* 1607).

U.S. Office of Indian Affairs. 1863. *Report of the Commissioner of Indian Affairs for the Year 1862.* Washington, DC: Government Printing Office.

U.S. Office of Indian Affairs. 1865. *Report of the Commissioner of Indian Affairs for the Year 1865.* Washington, DC: Government Printing Office.

U.S. Office of Indian Affairs. 1874. *Annual Report of the Commissioner of Indian Affairs to the Secretary of the Interior for the Year 1873.* Washington, DC: Government Printing Office.

U.S. Office of Indian Affairs. 1881. *Annual Report of the Commissioner of Indian Affairs to the Secretary of the Interior for the Year 1881.* Washington, DC: Government Printing Office.

U.S. War Department. 1821–1920. *War Department Records of the Division and Department of the Pacific, 1847–1873.* National Archives and Records Administration. Records of U.S. Army Continental Commands, Record Group 393. Microfilm Publication M2114.

Yreka Chronicle

Yreka Herald

Yreka Mountain Herald

[Yreka] *Siskiyou Chronicle*

Yreka Union

Yreka Weekly Union

Wells, Harry. 1884a. "The Modocs in 1851." *West Shore* 10 (5): 132–34.

Wells, Harry. 1884b. "The Ben Wright Massacre." *West Shore* 10 (10): 314–20.

SECONDARY SOURCES

Allison, John. 1994. *The Cultural Landscape of the Klamath, Modoc and Yahooskin Peoples: Spirit, Nature, History.* Chiloquin, OR: Klamath Tribes.

Bauer, Yehuda. 1982. *A History of the Holocaust.* New York: F. Watts.

Bonwick, James. 1870. *The Last of the Tasmanians; or, The Black War of Van Diemen's Land.* London: Sampson Low, Son, and Marston.

Bourke, John G. 1891. "General Crook in the Indian Country." *Century Magazine* 41 (5): 643–60.

Brady, Cyrus T. 1907. *Northwestern Fights and Fighters.* New York: McClure.

California State Military Museum. 2002. "California and the Indian Wars: The California Militia and the 'Expeditions Against the Indians,' 1850–1859." www.militarymuseum.org/Militiasandindians.html.

Carranco, Lynwood, and Estle Beard. 1981. *Genocide and Vendetta: The Round Valley Wars of Northern California.* Norman: University of Oklahoma Press.

Cook, Sherburne F. 1976. *The Population of the California Indians, 1790–1970.* Berkeley: University of California Press.

Cook, Sherburne F. 1978. "Historical Demography." In *Handbook of North American Indians,* Vol. 8: *California,* edited by William Sturtevant and Robert Heizer, 91–98. 20 vols. Washington, DC: Government Printing Office.

Curtis, Edward. 1924. *The North American Indian: Being a Series of Volumes Picturing and Describing the Indians of the United States, the Dominion of Canada, and Alaska,* edited by Frederick W. Hodge. Vol. 13. 20 vols. Norwood, MA: Plimpton.

Dasnabedian, Hratch. 1990. *History of the Armenian Revolutionary Federation, Dash-naktsutiun, 1890/1924*. Milan: Oemme Edizioni.

Dillon, Richard H. 1973. *Burnt Out Fires: California's Modoc Indian War*. Englewood Cliffs, NJ: Prentice-Hall.

Douthit, Nathan. 1999. "Between Indian and White Worlds on the Oregon-California Border, 1851–1857: Benjamin Wright and Enos." *Oregon Historical Quarterly* 100 (4): 402–33.

Glatthaar, Joseph T. 1985. *The March to the Sea and Beyond: Sherman's Troops and the Savannah and Carolinas Campaigns*. New York: NYU Press.

Hathaway, Edward E. 1995. *The War Nobody Won: The Modoc War from the Army's Point of View*. Show Low, AZ: American Eagle.

Hurtado, Albert L. 1981. "The Modocs and the Jones Family Indian Ring: Quaker Administration of the Quapaw Agency, 1873–1879." In *Oklahoma's Forgotten Indians*, edited by Robert Smith, 86–107. Oklahoma City: Oklahoma Historical Society.

Hurtado, Albert L. 1988. *Indian Survival on the California Frontier*. New Haven, CT: Yale University Press.

James, Cheewa. 2008. *Modoc: The Tribe That Wouldn't Die*. Happy Camp, CA: Naturegraph.

Jensen, Richard. 1990. "Big Foot's Followers at Wounded Knee." *Nebraska History* 71 (4): 194–212.

Johansen, Bruce, and Barry M. Pritzker, eds. 2008. *Encyclopedia of American Indian History*. Vol. 4. 4 vols. Santa Barbara, CA: ABC-CLIO.

Jones, Adam. 2011. *Genocide: A Comprehensive Introduction*. New York: Routledge.

Kiernan, Ben. 2008. *Genocide and Resistance in Southeast Asia: Documentation, Denial & Justice in Cambodia & East Timor*. New Brunswick, NJ: Transaction.

Kroeber, A. L. 1925. *Handbook of the Indians of California*. Washington, DC: Government Printing Office.

Madley, Benjamin. 2005. "From Africa to Auschwitz: How German South West Africa Incubated Ideas and Methods Adopted and Developed by the Nazis in Eastern Europe." *European History Quarterly* 35 (3): 429–64.

Madley, Benjamin. 2008a. "From Terror to Genocide: Britain's Tasmanian Penal Colony and Australia's History Wars." *Journal of British Studies* 47 (1): 77–106.

Madley, Benjamin. 2008b. "California's Yuki Indians: Defining Genocide in Native American History." *Western Historical Quarterly* 39 (3): 303–32.

Madley, Benjamin. Forthcoming. *An American Genocide: The California Indian Catastrophe, 1846–1873*. New Haven, CT: Yale University Press.

Malinowski, Sharon, Anna Sheets, Jeffrey Lehman, and Melissa Doig, eds. 1998. *The Gale Encyclopedia of Native American Tribes*. Vol. 3. 4 vols. Detroit: Gale.

Minchno, Gregory. 2007. *The Deadliest Indian War in the West: The Snake Conflict, 1864–1868*. Caldwell, ID: Caxton.

Mooney, James. 1928. *The Aboriginal Population of America North of Mexico*. Washington, DC: Smithsonian Institution.

Murray, Keith A. 1959. *The Modocs and Their War*. Norman: University of Oklahoma Press.

Ostler, Jeffrey. 2004. *The Plains Sioux and U.S. Colonialism from Lewis and Clark to Wounded Knee*. Cambridge: Cambridge University Press.

Plomley, N. J. B. 1992. *The Aboriginal/Settler Clash in Van Diemen's Land: 1803–1831*. Hobart, Australia: Queen Victoria Museum and Art Gallery.

Powers, Stephen. 1877. *Tribes of California*. Washington, DC: Government Printing Office.

Quinn, Arthur. 1997. *Hell with the Fire Out: A History of the Modoc War*. Boston: Faber and Faber.

Reed, Gregory A. 1991. *An Historical Geography Analysis of the Modoc Indian War*. Chico, CA: ANCRR.

Riddle, Jeff C. 1914. *The Indian History of the Modoc War and the Causes That Led to It*. San Francisco: Marnell.

Robinson, Charles M. 2001. *General Crook and the Western Frontier*. Norman: University of Oklahoma Press.

Ryan, Lyndall. 2012. *Tasmanian Aborigines: A History since 1803*. Sydney, Australia: Allen and Unwin.

Schaller, Dominik J. 2011. "Genocide in Colonial South-West Africa: The German War against the Herero and Nama, 1904–1907." In *Genocide of Indigenous Peoples*, edited by Samuel Totten and Robert K. Hitchcock, 37–60. New Brunswick, NJ: Transaction.

Shaw, Martin. 2007. *What Is Genocide?* Cambridge, MA: Polity.

Sproull, Harry V. 1969. *Modoc Indian War*. Klamath Falls, OR: Craft Printers.

Stern, Theodore. 1998. "Klamath and Modoc." In *Handbook of North American Indians*, Vol. 12: *Plateau*, edited by William Sturtevant and Deward Walker Jr., 446–66. 20 vols. Washington, DC: Government Printing Office.

Strobridge, William F. 1994. *Regulars in the Redwoods: The U.S. Army in Northern California, 1852–1861*. Spokane, WA: Arthur H. Clark.

Thompson, Erwin N. 1971. *Modoc War: Its Military History and Topography*. Sacramento: Argus Books.

Walling, Albert G. 1884. *Illustrated History of Lane County, Oregon*. Portland, OR: A. G. Walling.

Wells, H. L. 1881. *History of Siskiyou County, California: Illustrated with views of residences, business buildings and natural scenery, and containing portraits and biographies of its leading citizens and pioneers*. Oakland, CA: D. J. Stewart.

CHAPTER 5

AMERICAN FOLK IMPERIALISM
AND NATIVE GENOCIDE IN
SOUTHWEST OREGON, 1851–1859

Gray H. Whaley

By the 1850s many American colonials believed that their constitutionally
enshrined citizenship legitimated the extermination of fully dehumanized
Indians perceived to be a threat to the public welfare. Southwestern Oregon,
the focus of this chapter, saw infrequent colonial-indigenous contact before
the California Gold Rush, and thus no stable means of communication and
conflict resolution developed. Indeed even if they had, failure was likely when
the demand for aboriginal land and resources was so absolute. As A. Dirk
Moses (2000: 192) explains regarding similar conditions in Tasmania and
Queensland, Australia, "The place to look for genocidal intentions [is] . . . in
the gradual evolution of European attitudes and policies as they were pushed
in an exterminatory direction by the confluence of their underlying assumptions, the demands of the colonial and international economy, their plans for
the land, and the resistance to these plans by the indigenous Australians."
Importantly, before the U.S. Civil War, imperial authority was weak in the
Far West, with only a token force of federal officers and regular troops to
maintain order. As in Australia, the line between a genocidal state and a
genocidal society can be difficult to establish in the colonial history of the
American West (Chalk 1994: 55; Barta 1987: 60, 238). The vague sense of benevolent assimilation offered by imperial apologists had little practical meaning in southern Oregon in the 1850s. Instead American citizens established
a system of folk imperialism in which supporters of colonization, including
the potential for genocide, created the necessary institutions to carry it out,
regardless of national support.

Like Norbert Finzsch, I find the explanatory power of settler colonialism to be limited. Developing Carl Degler's work, Finzsch (2004: 255–56)

conceptualized settler imperialism rather than colonialism to capture the interdependent roles of coastal elites and settlers in both the United States and post-1860 Australia. While his paradigm suggests a united American elite, which did not exist before the Civil War destroyed the rival capitalism of slavery, politicians and investors did facilitate the overall expansionist colonial project, albeit haltingly and acrimoniously. Sectional tensions ensured that a weak federal government generally followed the lead of citizens, particularly those who moved west, created boundary disputes with indigenous and imperial claimants, and fashioned U.S.-style but not U.S.-administered regimes. In the West Americans openly expressed disdain for assimiliationist sentiment popular in the East, and, as David Svaldi (1989) and others have explained, extermination rhetoric was more widely accepted. Still rhetoric did not necessarily equal actions, which relied on institutional support that had to be built.

In Oregon colonials established their own provisional government, complete with a land office and military, while petitioning the United States for the legitimacy of territorial status. Even after Congress established Oregon Territory in 1848, locals fought federal administration and East Coast economic control, attempting to make occupation the only acceptable form of speculation. They lobbied for treaties that met their interests and undermined those that did not. They successfully lobbied for donation land laws, though their dissatisfaction with the legislation and subsequent surveying methods demonstrates the limits of the periphery's ability to influence the metropol. Nowhere was the colonial-imperial dispute more starkly realized than the genocidal militia campaigns against the Native population of southwest Oregon in the 1850s. Oregon folk imperialism featured some of the most obvious and blatant extermination attempts in the American West. The potential for genocide grew quickly between 1851 and 1855, as the underlying exterminatory logic of folk imperialism gained local support.

In particular the colonial fear of an intertribal confederacy from northernmost California to British Columbia fed popular hysteria about the "Indian threat" and contributed to the virulence and pervasiveness of the calls for extermination. Indeed some evidence points to interethnic unity among Native bands of southwestern Oregon, the Columbia Plateau, and Puget Sound. However, outside the local regions the supposed confederacy never extended beyond sharing of a dystopian prophecy about miserable conditions on reservations and establishing some unprecedentedly long-distance kin relations. Many contemporary officials noted the limitations of Indian political unity, and the pan-Indian threat was simply an excuse for genocide.

The many instances of mass murder from antiquity to the modern day present numerous challenges to those who have followed in the footsteps of Raphael Lemkin (Moses 2004). Criteria, causality, typology, intentionality, prevention, and justice continue to complicate a unified paradigm (Hinton 2002: 48). Indeed history is implicated both as a philosophical narrative tradition descended from the Ancient West and as a modern discipline that self-consciously takes slowly to theories and paradigms. Victors tell the story, and the vanquished (if any survived) have often been able only to pass along their stories to disempowered descendants who lack the legitimacy of nation-states to counter the written record and the law. Moreover historians have drawn the ire of modern Native peoples for not generalizing the role of genocide in the colonization of North America to the satisfaction of some indigenous scholars and activists (White 1998: 234–37). I argue that there is good reason not to apply the term *genocide* too broadly. Although folk imperialism included the potential for genocide, the action did not always occur. As Joseph Gone argues in this volume, historical specificity is crucial, and contextualizing all of Native North American history as genocidal is misleading and counterproductive. This chapter explains genocide within the ideological and practical framework of Oregon folk imperialism. As Moses explained with regard to Australia, genocide evolved from a possibility inherent in the ethnocidal premise of benevolent assimilation in British imperialism into exterminatory action in the particular circumstances of Tasmania and Queensland. Similarly studying Native genocide in Oregon does not evidence continental North American genocide but instead sheds light on the conditions that produced this shift from assimilation to extermination when the colonial population came to believe that extermination was possible, necessary, and justified in a particular time and place. Federal officials worked to shift the focus back to assimilation or ethnocide.

The Limits of Conflict Resolution in Southwest Oregon

From the outset of settler imperialism in southwest Oregon, Americans knew that extreme violence was probable if not likely. In 1851 a failed gold seeker named Thomas Smith, who had come west with an emigrant train called The Company of Equal Rights, arrived in the domain of the Bear Creek Shastas and their headman Tipsu Tyee ("Bearded Chief" in Chinook Jargon). Smith sought a place to grow crops for sale to miners. Tipsu Tyee assented in exchange for Smith's pledge not to steal horses or women, activities in which some miners and Indian people engaged. After some months Smith blamed Tipsu Tyee for a personal property theft and threatened to summon a volunteer militia from Yreka, California, to "kill all your men and burn your stick houses and destroy all your people." Only the intervention of Tipsu Tyee's wife in the form of a thirty-minute monologue calmed her band and affected a settlement instead of Smith's immediate death (Smith n.d.: 3–15). A party of miners from the Oregon settlements had already established precedence for massive retaliation, massacring sixty people near the Coloma goldfields in 1849 and leaving the indigenous population divided over how to protect themselves (Ross 1878: 13–17). The situation became all too common (Cook 1976; Rawls 1984; Hurtado 1988; Trafzer and Hyer 1999). A Modoc raid on an emigrant train in 1852 left several newcomers dead but did not halt their flow and only brought more violent deaths to Indian Country.[1] By 1853 the situation had become exceedingly perilous as local resources strained under the weight of an exploding emigrant population and the environmental effects of agriculture and mining. Colonials renewed pressure on the federal government for action.

A year of intermittent, brutal violence helped Euro-Americans secure a successful round of treaties with several bands and tribes of western Oregon. The treaties signed between 1853 and 1855 retroactively legalized ten years of intensive colonization and land speculations in the Willamette and Columbia valleys and led to removals to reservations. Similarly in the south the United States secured the first treaties with the Takelmas of the Rogue River Valley and the Cow Creek Band of Umpqua and established reservations at Table Rock and Council Creek, respectively. The U.S. Army also built four forts—Fort Lane in the Rogue Valley, Fort Orford on Oregon's south coast, and Forts Reading and Jones across the pass in northern California—and maintained small garrisons to keep the peace. Despite local pressures, Captain Andrew Jackson Smith of Fort Lane saw little need for a fort on the Klamath Basin or for policing the Indians too closely in the Siskiyous and adjacent valleys. Indeed, with volunteer militias calling themselves "Squaw Hunters" and the "Exterminators" roaming the region at the first hint of violence, Smith and other federal officials tended to view Indians as the people needing protection.[2] Moreover a politically divided federal government proved incapable of sufficiently supporting the new Pacific Division of the Army.[3] Commanding General John Wool had too few resources for his charge of policing the major harbors of California, Oregon, and Washington, the outlying settlements from the Pacific Coast to Utah Territory, and the overland emigration routes from the new border with Mexico north to British Canada.[4] Wool distrusted civilians and their colonial pursuits and saw independent militias such as those of Oregon as an affront to his authority.[5] Captain Smith (1859: 68) represented his commander well and clashed several times over his refusal to attack Native bands suspected of theft or violence.[6]

Thus colonials could invite federal power but they could not direct it for their own purposes.

In response to the inaction of the "brass buttons" of the regular army, Charles S. Drew petitioned Oregon Territorial Governor John Davis for permission to organize a volunteer militia to patrol the western stretch of the southern emigrant road in 1854 (Riddle 1973: 22). Superintendent Palmer had visited the Klamath Basin and accepted pledges from Klamath and Modoc leaders that they would not attack emigrants again.[7] Two Native historical accounts support the federal officers' claims that emigrants no longer had anything to fear on the Klamath Basin (Riddle 1973: 27; Stern 1966: 38–39). A temporary federal appointee with relatively little authority, Governor Davis gave Ross approval for the Klamath campaign only "if it should be considered necessary." He also advised Ross, "You will be compelled to rely upon the liberality and patriotism of our fellow citizens, who in turn will be compelled to rely upon the justness of the General Government for their compensation."[8] In other words, although the treasury had recently disbursed remuneration funds for the Cayuse War of 1848 (six years after congressional approval), the citizenry should not hold its breath for similar compensation anytime soon, if at all.

The regular army continued to offer little assistance to Ross's southern militia or the Willamette Valley's retributive campaign to the Snake River. General Wool acted under a different set of prerogatives than the territorial militias and had no manpower and resources to spare. Moreover the army was not officially caught up in the profitability of colonizing Oregon, though the many desertions by soldiers to the gold fields might suggest otherwise. On the other side, volunteers from the Willamette and Rogue valleys acted similarly in their respective actions in the Snake River and Klamath Basin campaigns. Each claimed to be a security force for emigrants but was also demonstrably vengeful. Despite the pleadings of Superintendent Palmer to temper militia violence, Modoc and Northern Paiute were hunted and starved into submission.[9] Moreover Palmer's instructions to his subagent charged with representing federal authority to spare women and children "if possible," and a de facto instruction to kill the men, was not far removed from those like Charles Drew who called for outright extermination.[10]

Colonial Genocide Efforts

These official, territorial campaigns were in addition to the continued private militancy of the citizenry. After the death of a miner in August 1853, Benjamin Dowell, a Jacksonville lawyer and merchant, wrote that the "citizens mostly composed of miners . . . passed resolutions demanding the *Extermination of the Indian race.*" Dowell also recounted hangings, including that of an eight- to ten-year-old Indian boy "not for any alledged crime, but for the purpose of exterminating the indian race."[11] A few weeks later an association of speculators claimed land on the lower Chetco River. Athapaskan villagers on either side of the river mouth grudgingly acquiesced to the homesteads but refused to surrender their successful ferry business, by which they too profited from the Gold Rush. The Chetco also refused to allow the speculators' leader, a man named Miller, to live in their village on the south bank. Indeed Miller's proposed town site claim encompassed that entire village. On February 15, 1854, Miller and some hirelings from nearby Crescent City, California (veterans of an 1853 massacre of Athapaskan Tolowa), slaughtered fifteen Chetco and burned their villages. At a perfunctory hearing at Port Orford, Oregon, Miller offered no defense for his actions, and the surviving Chetco villagers could not legally testify because of their "race." Cleared for lack of evidence, Miller then took possession of his lower Chetco claim.[12] Desperate, some Chetco raided settlements during the winter to survive. Though they did not kill any Euro-Americans, eleven more Chetco men and women were killed by early May 1854.

Euro-Americans derided the Chetco and other south coast victims as savage renegades, ignoring the manner in which the Athapaskan villagers had become homeless and desperate. Forty more "renegades" of the south coast bands were killed in a militia raid during the Rogue River War in the spring of 1856 (Sutton and Sutton 1969: 258). Expeditions in 1856, 1857, and 1858 killed many more Native people of the Chetco and Pistol River bands near Port Orford during postwar efforts to "bring in" the Indians.[13] Locally contracted citizens continued to pursue extermination, though the federal commission allowed for removal only (ARCIA 1857: 324). Regular army officers refused to assist, but they did nothing to protect Native people either (Tichenor n.d.: 25, 27).

Most Native bands were small, and the massacre of one or two dozen people effectively exterminated some "tribes." On January 28, 1854, a few weeks before Miller's initial massacre of Chetco and a short distance to the north, Euro-Americans staged a predawn surprise attack simultaneously on the three Nasomah (Miluk-Kusan–speaking) villages on the lower Coquille River, shooting eighteen people indiscriminately as they fled their torched homes. The colonists claimed legitimate retribution for a damaged rope, a ricocheted shot meant for a duck but that passed near a ferry house, and a Nasomah man who reportedly uttered, "God-damned Americans." When an Indian agent reached the area some months later he indicated that two of the Nasomah villages were emptied and only John's band (though probably a composite of survivors) of thirty-eight adults and twenty-one children occupied the third (U.S. Senate 1854: 476–95). As a distinct people, the Nasomah never recovered from the massacre, and dispossession soon to follow as they *had* recovered from successive disease epidemics since 1800 (Hall and Hall 1991: 107).

Whereas colonials on the lower Coquille River prepared a formal list of grievances before the massacre, many attacks on Indians lacked any legal pretense (U.S. Senate 1854: 480–81). On the California side of the Siskiyous on May 24, 1854, colonists ambushed a band of Shasta from the Shasta Valley who had just come from a meeting with regular army captains of Forts Lane and Jones in which they had been assured of their continued friendship and safety.[14] The excuse for the militia's attack on them was that a Shasta man, "Indian Joe," allegedly tried to rape a white woman. That the accused man was not present and was from a different band did not matter, nor did a history of attempts by the assailed band to maintain amicable relations with colonists. The headman "Bill" had already killed his fellow Shasta headman Tipsu Tyee of the Rogue Valley, whose dwindling band was blamed for the alleged assault. Bill knew that colonial militias were not terribly discriminating in seeking revenge against Indians, and thus he killed Tipsu Tyee and his son in order to keep the peace with Euro-Americans. Still Bill was among the victims on May 24. A confused and despondent Shasta elder who witnessed the massacre inquired why, if rape was such a horrific crime to Euro-Americans, the colonists "constantly [ran] down, sometimes by men on horse," and raped Native women. There is no record of how or if Captain J. C. Bonnycastle or any members of the Yreka militia—the self-ascribed "Squaw Hunters"—replied (U.S. Senate 1855: 78).

Militias did not always find support for extermination among their fellow colonists. Captain Smith reported that, on February 3, 1854, nineteen miners attacked a village on southwestern Oregon's Illinois River "in which there were but seven squaws, one boy, and two children, with the avowed intention of killing them all." After firing nine shots into a pregnant woman, killing her, the miners found themselves routed by three other women and a boy. When the miners attempted to recruit "an increased force . . . to wipe out the Indians . . . the better portion of the community interfered and delayed" them until the Indian agent arrived (U.S. Senate 1855: 14–15). Still, by 1855 the ranks of the extermination-minded colonists swelled, counterdiscourse waned, and no colonist could probably do much to prevent the massacres of Native people.

In the summer of 1855, on the eve of the final Rogue River War, a group of Josephine County petitioners argued that they would lose "all invested here and if forced to leave by the hostility of the indians [would] be pecuniarly ruined and a mining locality capable of furnishing remunerative labor for thousands of men for years be again abandoned to be in unproductive idleness." They requested Governor George Curry "to expel from our midst these hostile indians and give us that security of our lives and property which is the birthright of all American citizens."[15] Calls for the formation of militia companies came from all over southwestern Oregon beginning in the early summer and continuing through autumn of 1855.[16] As John Ross put it to Governor Curry, the citizens of southern Oregon required his "aid in defending the inalienable rights of the people."[17]

The militia proponents used American settler colonial discourse—the racialized republican language of citizenship—almost exclusively in their appeals for support and in defense of their actions. In their public appeals for funding they consistently refer to themselves as "citizens" and the protection of their profitable pursuits as the "public welfare."[18] There were several reasons for such discourse: among them were attempts to legitimize extermination, to protect illicit land claims in Indian Country, and to receive federal remuneration for their militia activities. In the process they voiced the underlying racialized notion of American citizenship as white and closed, and they openly advocated extermination (Beeson 1857). In October 1855 a local farmer and territorial representative named James Lupton hatched a scheme to avenge the deaths of two packers on the Siskiyou Pass and to instigate a final solution to the Indian problem. He formed a militia in a Jacksonville tavern, and in the predawn light of October 8, 1855, they assailed "Old Jake's" Quachis band of Shasta on Little Butte Creek in the shadows of Fort Lane and the Table Rock Reservation. The militia had "the avowed purpose of killing every Indian in the [Rogue River] valley, regardless of age or sex."[19] Colonial trackers had previously determined, at least to their satisfaction, the band's guilt in waylaying and killing the two packers. The accompanying regular army officer disagreed with their assessment of the trail, particularly their conclusion that it led to Butte Creek and the reservation (Smith 1859: 73). A justifiably doubtful Captain Smith had refused to allow a vengeful militia access to the reservation to search for the suspects and ordered his federal troops to shoot the militiamen if they trespassed. Still, within days Lupton's locals slaughtered dozens of Shasta men, women, and children in the attack and hunted down others as they tried to reach the protection of Fort Lane. According to General Wool, militias killed eighty "friendly Indians" to ignite the warfare; others put the figure at 106. One volunteer stated that, although extermination made him feel bad, "the understanding was that [the Indians] were all to be killed. So we did the work" (U.S. House of Representatives 1859b: 44–46).[20]

Territorial militias wanted extermination, not treaty settlements.[21] Within weeks of the Little Butte Creek Massacre, General Wool reported to his superiors, "In Rogue River valley the threats of the whites to commence a war of extermination against the friendly Indians on the reserve, and in the vicinity of Fort Lane, have been put into execution, despite the efforts of the officers of that post to prevent it."[22] On October 9, 1855, the day after the initial massacre, many of the Indian people remaining on the reservation fled to the protection of the rugged canyon country of the Coast Range Mountains. Agent Samuel Culver had earlier permitted some bands to leave the disease-ridden and poorly supplied reservation because the death rate had soared to 20 percent in the first year (U.S. Senate 1854: 463).

In a self-fulfilling prophecy the colonists had finally pushed the Native peoples into the extremely violent, widespread "race war" that they had forecast for years.[23] Subsequent massacres drove neutral bands into the conflict. At an Umpqua camp on the Arrington Ranch, ten Euro-Americans annihilated a camp of "old men, women, and children" while the men were hunting in the nearby Olalla hills. The band had previously maintained amicable relations with the colonists; some Umpqua labored on local farms, regularly hung about the hotel, and some intermarriages occurred. The hunters, apprised of the Olalla Massacre by a boy who escaped, subsequently joined the warring bands along the lower Rogue River.[24] Such examples of Native peoples' traveling to assist in the fight against the colonials added fuel to the speculations regarding a pan-Indian threat.

Indeed a principal justification for the war by the colonists was defense against a perceived pan-Indian confederacy, which threatened extermination of the whites. Thus the colonialists' genocidal efforts supposedly mirrored Native intent and were thus morally defensible (Victor 1894: 423). Not all whites were of a common mind regarding the pan-Indian threat. George Roberts, an Englishman and administrator of the Hudson's Bay Company's Puget Sound Agricultural Association, gruffly dismissed the popular beliefs of a pan-Indian threat as so much "public clamour." Roberts insisted that the notion of an inevitable race war was part of what he called an "earth hunger" that was born of an ignorant, nationalist belief in Manifest Destiny that was being carried out by "ruffians," "squatters," and the "vilest of the vile ... hardy pioneers." He was equally critical of the leadership among the Americans. He expressed his astonishment upon hearing Joseph Lane, Oregon's preeminent early politician, "remark 'damn them [Indians], it would do my soul good to be after them.'"[25] The contrast between Anglo and American interpretations of Indian behavior and intent had been obvious since the early 1840s. Henry Perkins of the Dalles Mission had been convinced as early as 1843 that the Wascopam "Indians are endeavoring to form a general coalition for the purpose of destroying all the Boston people: that it is not good to kill a part of them, and leave the rest, but that every one of them must be destroyed" (quoted in Hines 1851: 143–44). Roberts and other Hudson's Bay Company officials regularly discounted such beliefs, leading some American officials by the 1850s to portray the British as being part of the Indian conspiracy.[26] The British officials were actually more akin with General Wool and the U.S. Army; they were imperial agents whose assimilative interests ran counter to the exterminatory interests of American colonials.

Federal Authority and Reversion to Assimilation

In the early spring of 1856 the regular army intervened and eventually ended the conflict, and again the joint action by Oregon Territory and the United States produced considerable acrimony between federals and colonials. By early February 1856 it was obvious that the Oregon militias could not finish what they had begun, and even Charles Drew, a principal architect of the colonial militia and Indian extermination efforts, was among eighty-one Jacksonville signatories to petition for General Wool's intervention. They of course blamed the "Barbarous Indians" who "murdered whole families," "pillaged and burned," and kept the people from trading, mining, and tilling. The volunteers were "wholly inadequate . . . [poorly] organized, and though brave, [were] undisciplined."[27] Wool blamed the colonists for the widespread bloodshed (hostilities also broke out in Washington Territory in the fall of 1855) but promised troops to end them after the winter, and he made his stance against extermination clear: "Whilst I was in Oregon, it was reported to me, that many citizens, with a due proportion of volunteers, and two newspapers, advocated the extermination of the Indians. . . . This principle has been acted on in several instances without discriminating between enemies and friends, which has been the cause, in Southern Oregon, of sacrificing many innocent and worthy citizens." Still he pledged federal forces to end the conflict. Similarly Wool advised Governor Isaac Stevens of Washington Territory that he would end the war on the Columbia Plateau after the winter, "provided the extermination of the Indians, which I do not approve, is not determined on, and private war prevented, and the volunteers withdraw."[28] Stevens was of a different mind and called for Wool's dismissal (*Standard*, October 16, 1856).

The Oregon press lashed out, condemning the regular army and echoing calls for extermination (*Oregonian—Extra*, March 28, 1856). The Oregon legislature censured General Wool and, like the Washington governor, called upon President Franklin Pierce to replace Wool.[29]

Wool instructed his regulars to bring in the Indians, protect them from the colonists, and remove them to the new Coast and Grand Ronde reservations. His plan was to use three forces to converge on the lower Rogue River, where most Indians had fled, "ferreting out . . . hostile bands" and establishing a peace council with the regions' headmen at Oak Flat.[30] This effort was mostly successful. In March 1856 Colonel Robert Buchanon led a small regular army force to reinforce Smith's sole company of fifty dragoons and several dozen infantry, and with the help of the militias and "friendly Indians" (those who fought colonialism with diplomacy and accommodation) convinced most of the Native bands to surrender by early summer 1856. The militias' continued brutality infuriated Colonel Buchanon for undermining the army's efforts.[31] However, although the regular army intended a forced removal strategy rather than one of extermination, green recruits became enraged by a "treacherous attack" against Captain Smith's unit, and retributive massacres resulted.[32] The behavior of these regular units suggests that the citizen militias' attitudes and behavior were hardly aberrant for Americans. Indeed, after the Civil War the regular army secured a near monopoly on anti-Indian violence. In the initial wave of U.S. settler colonialism, however, the citizenry paved the way.

Through the late spring and early summer of 1856 the temporary camps grew daily with despondent Native refugees, and the regular army was careful to place its own troops as guards.[33] The army had to arrange a defensive march to the reservations to prevent colonials from making good on promises to kill Native survivors. Such threats continued through the early years of reservation confinement on the lower Umpqua, Siletz, and Grand Ronde.[34] Militias also continued "round-ups" and slaughters of bands that had avoided the removals of 1856 (ARCIA 1857: Doc. 149, 361–62).

An investigation by the U.S. Treasury Department in 1857 determined that remuneration speculations did not cause the war. Instead the investigator J. Ross Browne faulted the discrepancies between imperial policies and colonial behavior and the role of violent racialism. In particular he cited confusion over jurisdiction caused by the ill-considered donation land laws, the failure to extinguish Indian title, and the "natural" results of a "superior race" coming into contact with an "inferior" one (U.S. Senate 1858: 4). Browne's conclusions are revealing: to comprehend the "Indian wars" of 1855–56, one must place them within the larger context of white supremacy and Euro-American

settler colonialism in western Oregon. The donation land laws (1850–54) created a sovereignty swamp: as a territory, Oregon should have been legally
Indian Country (until ceded by treaty), but the colonists acquired title pre-
emption to aboriginal lands without ratified treaties. Similarly mining claims
were completely unregulated, and Indians had no recourse from miners' in-
trusions and the ecological devastation caused by their endeavors. Thus it was
"Indian Country and it [was] not," as one befuddled Indian agent put it.[35] The
result, in the words of a contemporary critic, was "the mischief-making policy
of Squatter Sovereignty . . . and violence and outrage" against the Indians.[36]
Investigator Browne concluded, "That [the confusion regarding sovereignty]
has been a fruitful source of difficulty there can be no doubt. It was unwise
and impolitic to encourage settlers to take away the lands of the Indians." He
noted that Indians "could never be taught to comprehend that subtle species
of argument by which another race could come among them, put them aside,
ignore their claims, and assume possession, on the ground of being a superior
people" (U.S. Senate 1858: 4). The supposed racial superiority represented
popular folk beliefs linking whiteness, citizenship, and the rights of property
that undergirded this murderous example of Native dispossession (Smedley
1999; Harris 1998: 103–18). Attributing the brutal slaughter of Native peoples,
the open calls for their extermination, and the seizure of their lands solely to
the speculative machinations of a handful of greedy men such as John Ross,
James Lupton, and Charles Drew in 1855 misses the forest for the trees and
takes at face value accusations leveled by self-interested political factions.[37]

Summary

Euro-American colonialists wanted to possess Oregon—more, to create
Oregon according to a vision that left little or no room for the aboriginal
inhabitants of Illahee. As the postcolonial theorist Patrick Wolfe (1999: 1–2)
explains, "Settler colonies . . . are premised on displacing indigenes from
(replacing them on) the land." Indeed they are "premised on the elimination of native societies." Beginning in the mid-1840s, attempts at physical
extermination by colonial militias occurred when Native bands contested
colonization with "annoyances" and raids on mining camps, settlements, and
emigrant parties and when so-called Indian wars erupted intermittently from
1847 to 1856. Ending perceived and real threats to the "public welfare" by eradicating feared bands of Indians—particularly the men, as women could still
be useful for gaining larger land claims (320 acres for single men and 640 for
married men) as well as domestic, agricultural, and sexual labors.[38] The extermination of the Native peoples of southwestern Oregon, defined as "rogues,"

constituted an important part of colonization as conceived and effected by Euro-Americans who were convinced that profitable exploitation of Oregon was their birthright as U.S. citizens. Nineteenth-century Euro-Americans understood extermination to be a component of conquest and colonization, even a requisite of Christian civilization. Not all colonials favored extermination, nor did all militia members participate in massacres, but support for extermination was high and remained so for years after the war.

Euro-American colonists reserved for themselves settlement and economic speculation of southwestern Oregon's resources and ensured that "birthright" through extermination efforts. The discourse of American folk imperialism rationalized these endeavors as promoting the public welfare of the republican citizenry. Although they failed to either exterminate all the Indians or officially enlist the U.S. Army in their effort, the colonial actions did effect the forced removal of the Native population; that is, the fewer than two thousand survivors of an estimated 1851 population of 11,500 were removed to the Coast Reservation in 1856 (Beckham 1971: 9; Schwartz 1997: 149).[39] The fact that Euro-Americans attempted genocide as a central component of settler colonialism makes it a crucial topic for historical analysis. The case of Oregon also suggests that even a system premised on the natural rights of man could foster genocide when "the people" wield democratic values against those defined as outside the protection of those rights. Extermination in the American West was not simply rhetoric. In some cases, including southwest Oregon and neighboring California, American political rhetoric served to promote genocide, and citizens established mechanisms to carry it out. While American Empire certainly negated the continued existence of American Indians as culturally distinct peoples, the principal focus was ethnocidal: assimilation. However, under the absolutist conditions fashioned by Oregon folk imperialists, the local citizenry temporarily altered the course of colonization to genocide.

Notes

1. The massacre of the Modoc generated some controversy; see Meacham 1875: 677–78, and for a Native account see Albert Samuel Gatschet, *The Klamath Indians of Southwestern Oregon* (Washington, DC: Government Printing Office, 1890), 13.
2. U.S. Senate, *Message of the President of the United States, communicating . . . the Instructions and Correspondence between the government and Major General Wool* (33rd Congress, 2nd Session, Exec. Doc. 16, Serial 751: 1855), 15, 18–19; B. F. Dowell, MS P-A 133. The Bancroft Library, University of California, Berkeley, 5–6.
3. Davis to Wool, December 13, 1854, in U.S. Senate 1855: 125–27.
4. Wool to Major General Winfield Scott, February 28, 1854, in U.S. Senate 1855: 11.

5. Frustrated with the volunteer militias authorized by territorial governors, Wool claimed the sole right to call for militias and that he "should have all the staff departments within his command under his immediate and direct control." Wool to Jefferson Davis, January 7, 1854, in U.S. Senate 1855: 5–6. Wool blamed the Oregon volunteers, "mustered into service, by the authority of the governor," for speculating supply funds; Wool to L. Thomas, Headquarters of the Army, New York, September 14, 1854, in U.S. Senate 1855: 103–4.

6. Section 15 of the 1854 territorial militia law; see Drew to Davis, July 7, 1854, in U.S. House of Representatives 1859a: 3–5.

7. U.S. Senate, *Report of the Secretary of the Interior, 1854* (33rd Congress, 2nd Session, Exec. Doc. #, Serial 746: 1854), 470.

8. Drew to Davis, July 7, 1854; Davis to Ross, July 17, 1854; Ross to Davis, August 5, 1854; and Ross to Curry, November 10, 1854, in B. F. Dowell, MS P-A 133. The Bancroft Library, University of California, Berkeley, folder 4.

9. Walker to Ross, November 11, 1854, in Dowell n.d.: MS P-A 133, folder 4.

10. Palmer letter appointing a subagent for eastern Oregon, September 28, 1854, in Folder 47, Box 1/4 "1851–1855," in "Cayuse, Yakima, and Rogue River Wars Papers (1847–1858)," MS 72-322, Box 47. The Knight Library, University of Oregon.

11. Dowell n.d.: MS P-A 133, folder 5.

12. U.S. Senate 1854: 465–67.

13. William Tichenor, "Among the Oregon Indians," MS P-A 84. The Bancroft Library, University of California, Berkeley, 25–31, 82–85, 105–6; U.S. Senate, *Annual Report of the Commissioner of Indian Affairs, 1857* (35th Congress, 1st Session, Exec. Doc. 2, Serial 919: 1858b), 324; A. Z. Hedges to Commissioner George Manypenny, November 19, 1856, *Oregon Superintendent* n.d.: roll 609, frame 244.

14. Bonnycastle to Wool, May 28, 1854, in U.S. Senate 1855: 80–83.

15. *Cayuse Papers*, 1847–58, Folder 1, Box 6, "Undated; fragments," a petition from Josephine County residents to Curry, probably summer of 1855 given reference to an early July event and Curry's position.

16. B. F. Dowell, MS P-A 137. The Bancroft Library, University of California, Berkeley, 31, 102, 136, 152, 160, 164, 180, 230.

17. Dowell n.d.: MS P-A 137, 230.

18. For numerous examples of such discourse, see Dowell n.d.: MS P-A 133, 137. Dowell was an attorney for numerous federal remuneration claims on behalf of Oregon citizens, seeking to recover costs and damages from fighting Indians. His scrapbooks are replete with relevant testimony, editorials, and personal correspondence, much of which predates the remuneration attempts but served subsequently as evidence.

19. Beeson in *Oregon Superintendent* n.d.: roll 609, frame 19.

20. For a recent discussion of the Lupton Massacre, see Schwartz 1997: 85–86. For volunteer's quote, see Beeson 1957: 54–55; Schwartz 1997: 86.

21. Dowell n.d.: MS P-A 137, 172.

22. Wool to Thomas, November 3, 1855, in B. F Dowell, MS P-A 138. The Bancroft Library, University of California, Berkeley, 131.

23. An anonymous letter (probably Charles Drew) to the editor proclaimed that "the predictions... have been more than realized." *Oregonian*, October 12, 1855.
24. For the Olalla massacre, see *Reminiscences of Southern Oregon Pioneers* n.d.: Virginia McKay, 5–6.
25. George B. Roberts, "Recollections of George B. Roberts," MS P-A 83. The Bancroft Library, University of California, Berkeley, 20, 32, 34, 39, 41, 77, 90, 94.
26. Isaac Stevens address to "Fellow Citizens of Portland and Oregon Territory," *Standard*, October 16, 1856, in Dowell n.d.: MS P-A 134, 100.
27. Petition of citizens of Jacksonville to Wool, February 2, 1856, in Dowell n.d.: MS P-A 138, 40–45.
28. Wool quotes appear in an untitled newspaper clipping from February 12, 1856, in Dowell n.d.: MS P-A 134.
29. U.S. House of Representatives 1859b: 104–5.
30. For Wool's strategy, see U.S. House of Representatives 1859b: 48–49.
31. Edward Ortho Cresap Ord, "Edward Ortho Cresap Ord Papers," MSS C-B 479, Box 7. The Bancroft Library, University of California, Berkeley, May 6, 1856.
32. U.S. House of Representatives 1859b: 51–53. It remains unclear whether the "Battle of Big Meadows" was a failed truce attempt resulting from poor communication or a sneak attack by Tecumtum and his people, as charged by Euro-Americans. *Edward Ortho Cresap Ord Papers* n.d.: diary entry, June 6, 1856.
33. *Edward Ortho Cresap Ord Papers* n.d.: diary entry, June 17, 1856.
34. U.S. House of Representatives 1859b: 46; Sutton and Sutton 1969: 216; E. P. Drew Umpqua agency to Nesmith, June 30, 1858, in ARCIA 1858: Doc. 1, 254–57. Drew had allowed "a party of Indians to return to Kowes river and Ten-mile creek for the purpose of subsisting themselves for a time, and also to procure salmon for their winter's use." However, "the residents of Empire City... urgently petitioned this office to recall them, stating, in their petition, that the prevailing opinion in that vicinity was to the effect 'that any Indian found off the reserve could at once be shot, and no law or justice reach the offender.'"
35. Agent M. T. Simmons to Nesmith, June 30, 1858, in ARCIA 1858: 225. Although Simmons was describing his district of the Puget Sound, the same conditions had existed in western Oregon.
36. Editorial from southwestern Oregon settler John Beeson to the *True Californian* in *Oregon Superintendent: Letters Received, 1824–1881*, n.d.: roll 609, frame 20.
37. The political explanation can be found most recently in Schwartz 1997, which, while containing commendable research, nevertheless reinforces the "naturalness" of extermination by not critically examining it.
38. White men vastly outnumbered white women, 5,268 to 1,428, or approximately 3.7 to 1, in the six counties of southwestern Oregon (Coos, Curry, Douglas, Jackson, Josephine, and Umpqua). Still in 1860, after Indian removal, there were only thirty-two intermarriages on record in the six counties (U.S. Census 1860). Reminiscence accounts consistently cite land claims for the few intermarriages; see, e.g., *Reminiscences of Southern Oregon Pioneers* n.d.: Virginia Estes Applegate, 5; "Stonewall" Jackson Chenoweth, 2–3; and Virginia McKay, 3. Unofficial relations

certainly occurred as well, though it would be misleading to regard them as necessarily long lasting. In the words of Lottie Evanoff, a Coos woman, "The early whites here were just like Coyote—they would make a baby & just keep on going" (Harrington 1981: roll 24, frame 694).

39. As Schwartz 1997 notes, the 1857 census figure of 1,943 did not include the few individuals, mostly women, who had avoided removal.

References

PRIMARY SOURCES

Annual Report of the Commissioner of Indian Affairs (ARCIA) 1854, 1857, 1858. Washington, DC: Government Printing Office.

Beeson, John. 1857. *A Plea for the Indians; with facts and features of the late war in Oregon.* New York: John Beeson.

Cayuse, Yakima, and Rogue River Wars Papers (1847–1858). 1847–58. MS 72–322. Knight Library, University of Oregon.

Dowell, B. F. n.d. MS P-A 133, 134, 137, 138. Bancroft Library, University of California, Berkeley.

Edward Ortho Cresap Ord Papers. n.d. MSS C-B 479. Bancroft Library, University of California, Berkeley.

Harrington, John Peabody. 1981. *The Papers of John Peabody Harrington in the Smithsonian Collection, 1907–1957.* Millwood, NY: Kraus International.

Hines, Gustavus. 1851. *Life on the Plains of the Pacific.* Buffalo, NY: George H. Derby.

Meacham, A. B. 1875. *Wigwam and Warpath; or the Royal Chief in Chains.* Boston: John P. Dale.

Oregon Superintendent: Letters Received, 1824–1881. n.d. M234, no. 607-30. NARA.

Recollections of George B. Roberts. n.d. MS P-A 83. Bancroft Library, University of California, Berkeley.

Reminiscences of Southern Oregon Pioneers. n.d. MS CB H629. Knight Library, University of Oregon.

Ross, John E. 1878. *Narrative of an Indian Fighter.* MS P-A 63. Bancroft Library, University of California, Berkeley.

Smith, Thomas. n.d. *Account of the Rogue River Indian Wars of 1853 and 1855.* MS P-A 94. Bancroft Library, University of California, Berkeley.

Tichenor, William. n.d. *Among the Oregon Indians.* MS P-A 84. Bancroft Library, University of California, Berkeley.

U.S. Census. 1860. *Manuscripts, 1860.*

U.S. House of Representatives. 1859a. *Papers Transmitted by the Secretary of Oregon Territory, Relative to the Protection Afforded by the Volunteers of Oregon and Washington Territories to Overland Immigrants in 1854.* 35th Congress, 2nd Session, 1859, Misc. Doc. 47, Serial 1016.

U.S. House of Representatives. 1859b. *The Topographical Memoir and Report of Captain T. J. Cram, Relative to the Territories of Oregon and Washington, in the Military Department of the Pacific,* 35th Congress, 2nd Session, 1859, Exec. Doc. 114, Serial 1014.

U.S. Senate. 1854. *Report of the Secretary of the Interior, 1854.* 33rd Congress, 2nd Session, 1854, Exec. Docs., Serial 746.

U.S. Senate. 1855. *Message of the President of the United States, communicating . . . the Instructions and Correspondence between the government and Major General Wool.* 33rd Congress, 2nd Session, Exec. Doc. 16, Serial 751.

U.S. Senate. 1858. *Report of J. Ross Browne on Indian Affairs in the Territories of Oregon and Washington, 1857.* Special Agent of the Treasury Department J. Ross Browne, 35th Congress, 1st Session, 1858, Exec. Doc. 38, Serial 955.

SECONDARY SOURCES

Barta, Tony. 1987. "Relations of Genocide: Land and Lives in the Colonization of Australia." In *Genocide and the Modern Age,* edited by Isidor Wallimann and Michael Dobkowski, 237–51. New York: Greenwood Press.

Beckham, Stephen Dow. [1971] 1996. *Requiem for a People: The Rogue Indians and the Frontiersmen.* Northwest Reprints. Corvallis: Oregon State University Press.

Chalk, Frank. 1994. "Redefining Genocide." In *Genocide: Conceptual and Historical Dimensions,* edited by George J. Andreopoulos, 47–63. Philadelphia: University of Pennsylvania Press.

Cook, Sherburne F. 1976. *The Conflict between the California Indian and White Civilization.* Berkeley: University of California Press.

Finzsch, Norbert. 2004. "'The Aborigines . . . Were Never Annihilated, and Still They Are Becoming Extinct': Settler Imperialism and Genocide in Nineteenth Century American and Australia." In *Empire, Colony, Genocide: Conquest, Occupation and Subaltern Resistance in World History,* edited by A. Dirk Moses, 271–95. New York: Berghahn.

Gatschet, Albert Samuel. 1890. *The Klamath Indians of Southwestern Oregon.* Washington, DC: Government Printing Office.

Hall, Roberta L., and Don Alan Hall. 1991. "The Village at the Mouth of the Coquille River: Historical Questions of Who, When, and Where." *Pacific Northwest Quarterly* 82 (3): 101–8.

Harris, Cheryl. 1998. "Whiteness as Property." In *Black on White,* edited by David R. Roediger, 103–18. New York: Schocken Books.

Hinton, Alexander Laban. 2002. "Genocide: Its Political Use in the Twentieth Century." In *Genocide: An Anthropological Reader,* edited by Alexander Laban Hinton, 48–73. Malden, MA: Blackwell.

Hurtado, Albert. 1988. *Indian Survival on the California Frontier.* New Haven, CT: Yale University Press.

Moses, A. Dirk. 2000. "An Antipodean Genocide? The Origins of the Genocidal Moment in the Colonization of Australia." *Journal of Genocide Research* 2: 89–106.

Moses, A. Dirk. 2004. "Empire, Colony, Genocide: Keywords and the Philosophy of History." In *Empire, Colony, Genocide: Conquest, Occupation and Subaltern Resistance in World History,* edited by A. Dirk Moses, 3–24. New York: Berghahn.

Rawls, James. 1984. *Indians of California: The Changing Image.* Norman: University of Oklahoma Press.

Riddle, Jeff C. 1973. *The Indian History of the Modoc War and the Causes That Led to It.* Medford, OR: Pine Cone.

Schwartz, E. A. 1997. *The Rogue River Indian War and Its Aftermath, 1850–1980.* Norman: University of Oklahoma Press.

Smedley, Audrey. 1999. *Race in North America: Origin and Evolution of a Worldview.* 2nd ed. San Francisco: Westview.

Stern, Theodore. 1966. *The Klamath Tribe: A People and Their Reservation.* Seattle: University of Washington Press.

Sutton, Dorothy, and Jack Sutton, eds. 1969. *Indian Wars of the Rogue River.* Grants Pass, OR: Josephine County Historical Society.

Svaldi, David. 1989. *Sand Creek and the Rhetoric of Extermination: A Case Study in Indian-White Relations.* New York: University Press of America.

Trafzer, Clifford E., and Joel R. Hyer, eds. 1999. *Exterminate Them! Written Accounts of the Murder, Rape, and Enslavement of Native Americans during the California Gold Rush.* East Lansing: Eastern Michigan State University Press.

Victor, Frances Fuller. 1894. *The Early Indian Wars of Oregon, Compiled from the Oregon Archives and Other Original Sources with Muster Rolls.* Salem, OR: Frank C. Baker, State Printer.

White, Richard. 1998. "Using the Past: History and Native American Studies." In *Studying Native America: Problems and Prospects*, edited by Russell Thornton, 217–43. Madison: University of Wisconsin Press.

Wolfe, Patrick. 1999. *Settler Colonialism and the Transformation of Anthropology: The Politics and Poetics of an Ethnographic Event.* New York: Cassell.

CHAPTER 6

MEMORY, ERASURE, AND NATIONAL MYTH

Tricia E. Logan

*We have come to the day of audit. Annihilation is not a cheerful word,
but it is coined from the alphabet of Indian life and heralds the infinite
pathos of a vanishing race. We are at the end of historical origins.*
—J. K. Dixon, *The Vanishing Race*

Erasure is an elegant method of revising history. Erasure, omission, or willful blindness pervasively and sometimes insidiously overlooks portions of a historical narrative in favor of a dominant narrative. Often hidden in plain sight, the missing voices of a historical narrative can reveal as much as what is visible. Omissions in national history become omissions in national identity, which itself is formed from national memory (Simon 2005: 101). History, legacy, agency, and voice propel a group to a dominant space in a nation-state. There is a struggle to determine who and what is worth remembering. Canada, a country with oft-recounted histories of Indigenous origins and colonial legacies, still maintains a memory block in terms of the atrocities it committed in order to build the Canadian state.

There is nothing more comforting in a colonial history of nation building than an erasure or denial of the true costs of colonial gains. The comforting narrative becomes the dominant and publicly consumed narrative (MacKenzie 2010: 266). Memory production in national institutions promotes, confronts, or conflicts with national narratives. Inclusion and exclusion in public memory institutions, written histories, and curricula are both influenced by and have influence over national identities. How society perceives power relations between sociocultural and political economic groups translates into memory formation and vice versa. There is no doubt that power relations influence memory production (Lee and Thomas 2012: 15). In Canada the state influence over public history determines the public messaging for the narrative of Indigenous history. This includes whether or not Canada allows public institutions a capacity to apply the term *genocide* to atrocities and crimes it has committed.

Memory, remembering, forgetting, and denial are inseparable and critical junctures in the study and examination of genocide (Guerin and Hallas 2007: 10). Absence or suppression of memories is not merely a lack of acknowledgment of individual or collective experiences but can also be considered denial of a genocidal crime (Jones 2007: 352–54). Once memory suppression becomes a function of a state or a state-sponsored institution, it is a direct action to exclude public memory or recognition of a genocidal crime. States gain notoriety for perpetuating genocidal crimes by continuing to deny or suppress evidence of genocide committed by their states either in the past or the present (Jones 2007: 113–14).

For example, it is well known that Turkish authorities continue to deny the Armenian genocide (1915–23). Intergenerational Survivors of the Armenian genocide feel a great deal of the historical trauma, and the burden they carry is closely associated with the ongoing denial of the genocide perpetrated against them (Miller and Miller 1993: 5). Turkish denial of the Armenian genocide remains a *classic* example of the role of political influence that is lost or gained with denying a state's crimes. In 2005 Turkey escalated control over scholarly and journalistic reporting of the genocide in Article 301 of the Turkish Criminal Code (Powell 2011: 263). The Code prohibits "publicly denigrating Turkishness" and gives the state significant legal recourse to punish citizens for presenting histories or reports that denigrate the public image of Turkey (Algan 2008: 2238). This classic example of state control over memory and messaging acknowledges the role that states feel they have in preserving political leverage through their legislation of public memory.

This classic example of genocide denial shows how state control of memory removes agency and voice from survivors and witnesses (Dickenson, Blair, and Ott 2010: 9). States can control the version of memory and history that the bystander or unaffected public receives about genocidal crimes. This function also controls what the public or the bystander population may know about ongoing violations against the victim group. Yet while the state plays a dominant role in memory production, the roles of survivor or victim and the public still exist. Indeed the strongest influence arguably comes from the agency of the survivors and witnesses. There is a certain timelessness and power that survivor and witness testimony has that fuel advocacy and lobbying for memory and remembrance, in any form that it takes. Whether survivors of genocide choose to remember or to forget does not need to be state-sanctioned or vetted by the dominant society.

The role of public memory can thus be proactive and contribute to advocacy. In *Public Memory, Public Media and the Politics of Justice*, Phillip Lee and Pradip Thomas (2012) examine "the right to memory." They note that, while there is not an internationally entrenched declaration or convention on the right to memory, many of the internationally recognized human rights instruments implicitly rely on such a notion (11). Using the example of the 1948 United Nations Convention on the Prevention and Punishment of Genocide, the authors argue, "It seems obvious that 'mental harm' would include the 'repressive erasure' of the socio-cultural memories that bind a group together" (11).

Lee and Thomas (2012) cite both the stolen generations in Australia and residential schools in Canada when they refer to the "mental harm" element of the Genocide Convention and the essential nature of memory in the interpretation of international human rights instruments. They identify the right to memory in the Declaration on the Rights of Indigenous Peoples. Article 11 of the Declaration states, "Indigenous peoples have the right to practice and revitalize their cultural traditions and customs. This includes the right to maintain, protect and develop the past, present and future manifestations of their cultures such as archaeological and historical sites, artefacts, designs, ceremonies, technologies and visual performing arts" (United Nations General Assembly, 2007).

Lee and Thomas (2012) acknowledge that this human right to memory is related to both justice and sociocultural rights. Moreover, and at least theoretically, public memory of atrocity or genocide could have an influence over the state of current or ongoing atrocities or genocides. Allowing agency for civil society may allow individuals to gain a level of control over how their lives and rights are represented in mainstream or public memory. The onus on the state to record events and histories in a national historic narrative remains. This is never a neutral role and is always influenced by both the public and policymakers (15). Thus when the state fails to do so, Lee and Thomas call on civil society to take a role in constructing or preserving memory. They acknowledge the reign of "enforced amnesia" over Indigenous memory in particular and describe the struggle for memory between civil society and those who control the medium of memory. When events are "consigned to oblivion," it is inherently unjust and becomes part of a larger human rights–driven movement (15).

Realistically, though, a nation-creating narrative in Canada is simply incomplete without the narrative of colonial genocide. Land and resources were not accumulated for new Canadians from *terra nullius*, or the principle that the land belonged to no one, and Euro-Canadian governance did not originate in a vacuum. Massive removal and dispossession in every segment of Indigenous lives took place in order to create a nation (Dickason 1992: 420).

Integrating colonial genocide into revised histories of Canadian nation-building narratives has the potential to generate a new understanding of genocide in Canada and move away from inherited colonial mythologies (Moses 2012: 218). An alternative national historical narrative rooted in Aboriginal history has thus emerged over recent decades. Decolonization of Canadian history continues, and a space for Indigenous voices and Indigenous epistemologies is being made. There are clearly differences, though, in how a history is *included* and how a history is *integrated*. Indeed there is a problematic way that these moves toward decolonization of a national historic narrative create a new orthodoxy within Canadian historiography. Compliance with Indigenous methodologies has, in some spaces, translated to obligatory reference to Aboriginal origin stories in some Canadian histories. This sort of acknowledgment can sometimes be seen as nothing more than a rubber stamp. Somewhere along the line in Canadian historiography, Aboriginal history became an obligation or a hurdle to a contested history.

The public narrative that occupies not only written academic histories but the institutional histories of museums and Canadian curricula has thus been revised in accordance with such obligatory yet perhaps superficial treatments. At the same time, however, this emerging dominant narrative still holds firm to its comforting essence. Rarely do the histories of "Canada as safe haven" and of immigrant homesteading become fairly aligned with the parallel histories of Aboriginal eliminationism and massive dispossession.

Even though calls for fair treatment of Aboriginal history have become part of a decolonized methodology in Canadian history, there are still "conceptual blockages" to the methodologies (Moses 2002). There are definitional debates and levels of public acceptability that often *block* members of the Canadian public from being able to conceive of genocidal crimes occurring in Canada. Conceptual blockages and a perceived deficit in colonial genocide scholarship inform Canadian historians and historical institutions (Flanagan 2000).[1] Advances in genocide scholarship and colonial genocide writing have not been adequately integrated into Canadian history. The histories of colonial genocide quickly become relegated to "Aboriginal peoples' histories" on the periphery and are not integrated into the center or the dominant history.

In terms of interpretation of national origin and colonial genocide, there are two major conceptual blockages in Canadian history (Moses 2002: 7). First, the concept of colonial genocide is blocked by the tendency to frame such experiences primarily through the lens of American or Australian colonialisms (Levene 2005: 69). Examinations of settler colonial genocides have emerged as a growing sector of genocide studies. As an emerging field, it is often used as an analytical pivot point to change thinking over an often Holocaust-centered field. Volumes like A. Dirk Moses's *Empire, Colony and Genocide: Conquest, Occupation and Subaltern Resistance in World History* (2008) and Mark Levene's *The Rise of the West and the Coming of Genocide* (2005) are representative in this regard. However, there is still a tendency of blockage even within this growing body of settler colonial genocide scholarship (Levene 2005: 69). For example, Levene presents a formidable volume on the role genocide plays in the rise of the West, including a comprehensive survey of colonial genocide in America. In his examination he evaluates the role of British colonialism and its genocidal impact in the Americas. Yet in his entire 450-page volume, of which one-third is devoted to settler colonial genocides, he relegates the Canadian experience of genocide to a mere qualifier in a single sentence, effectively omitting Canada from consideration: "Having been evicted from their North American possessions, *bar Canada*, in the American War of Independence of 1775–83, much of the British direct settlement effort turned to the more temperate regions of the southern hemisphere, particularly the antipodes" (69, emphasis added). In this omission a certain type of conceptual blockage is apparent, insofar as the emergent conventional approach to settler colonial genocide studies is primarily oriented toward the histories of the United States and Australia.

In fairness to genocide scholars who are preoccupied with American and Australian examples, their writing depends on an inclusive narrative of Canadian history. Revising Canadian history so that it includes genocide as a process that occurred in Canada could modify descriptors used by genocide scholars and begin to include Canada in a broader genocide historiography. Canadian historical narrative typically conceptually blocks the term *genocide*. Crimes committed by the Canadian state, churches, and corporations are rarely referred to or considered genocide. Historic narrative in Canada has often come to the conclusion that the nation was built in amiable partnership with First Peoples rather than their eliminationist removal. Conceptually the use of the term *genocide* faces decades of national history and a national identity built on the memory of peaceful relations with First Peoples (Miller 2004: 25).

The second source of conceptual blockages of genocide in Canada is perhaps more familiar, insofar as it was the primary concern of Moses's 2002 article that introduced the very idea of conceptual blockages. The prevailing assumption that the Holocaust is *the* example of genocide still blinds many observers to the fact that genocide occurred outside of Europe prior to the twentieth century. This second form of conceptual blockage is presently playing out in Canada, where memory battles are being waged over the remembrance of various genocides. Remembrance of the Holocaust has prompted other diaspora groups in Canada to come forward to lobby for memory of their atrocities. Over time the fight between the Holocaust and other genocides over space and recognition in the public memory becomes the conceptual blockage that eclipses settler colonial genocides. In his article "The Canadian Museum for Human Rights and the 'Uniqueness of the Holocaust' and the Question of Genocide," Moses (2012: 217–18) conveys how this museum, as an emerging institution for memory in Canada, has ignited a competitive battle between various diaspora population groups in Canada over public memory. This contest, primarily between members of the Jewish and Ukrainian communities, is overwhelming, insofar as it further marginalizes the place of Indigenous peoples in the arena of public memory. Public debate over representation of genocide at the Canadian Museum for Human Rights (CMHR) has a place in the current lobbying efforts for public claims to museum floor space. However, the debate builds a screen over settler colonial genocide committed inside Canada.

It is important to note the contemporary implications of this trend of "competitive memory battles." For the degree of media attention that these battles have gained, there is a critical disparity between the amount of attention those stories receive in the media and the amount of attention given to the current human rights violations against Indigenous peoples in Canada. Curiously Canadians may soon notice this discrepancy. There may be a strong influence over representations of the past and of memory on current or ongoing human rights violations in Canada. Does acknowledging their pasts mean they will be addressed in the present?

Memory and Erasure

The attempted elimination of First Nations, Métis, and Inuit in Canada has been driven by a colonial desire for land, resources, and the perpetrator's motivation to dominate and subsume the oppressed. The origins of the language of genocide can come only from the system that was imposed upon Indigenous peoples. Genocide as total destruction of biological, physical, and cultural spheres of life, destruction of the religious order, obliteration of language, the mass murder of all people, and destruction of the land is conceived from an Indigenous community's perspective because of what was imposed upon them. Theoretical understandings and ontological underpinnings originate from a destructive imposition of colonial mechanisms perpetuated to eliminate Indigenous presence from the Americas and elsewhere (Woolford 2009).

A significant part of decolonizing genocide studies should entail following an Indigenous approach to memory. Integrating an Indigenous perspective on orality, use of oral history, and an Indigenous concept of intangible memory systems will reveal a narrative of genocide history that will not come from an entirely Western perspective.

Considering both the aforementioned relationship between memory and genocide, as well as the need to decolonize genocide studies, how do Indigenous community epistemologies apply to memory? First Nations, Métis, and Inuit communities in Canada rely on collective knowledge and memories passed on orally and through the use of tradition and stories. Entrenching stories, histories, and knowledge within written works, memory institutions, and colonially controlled media conflicts with an Indigenous perspective on memory. Integrating Indigenous memories of genocide into colonial or Western institutions or pedagogical frames may always meet such challenges. Aside from the misaligned theoretical structure of Indigenous knowledge inside Western institutions, there is the more pragmatic motivation for decolonizing colonial treatment of Indigenous memory ways: trust. Stories are sacred and are powerful agents of memory. Accounts of settler colonial genocide are also traumatic accounts and sacred accounts. First Nations, Métis, and Inuit communities in Canada hesitate to transfer knowledge and stories to colonially controlled histories and institutions. Cognizant of the power-knowledge-memory nexus, Indigenous communities wisely fight to retain control over their own stories and histories. When asked to share their accounts of genocide with the state, how could any Survivor not consider: What are you going to do with this story?

Canadian Mythologies and National Historical Narratives

One form of history and remembering has been favored over another one. A narrower, politically sanctioned celebration of public history receives public funds and attention while Library and Archives Canada, home to Canada's national archives in the nation's capital, loses the ability to retain records. The political climate for public history is grim in Canada right now. There is increased federal influence over which segments of Canadian history will be promoted for popular consumption. Building a national historical narrative is clearly not entirely an exercise in reflexivity, pondered by historians and delivered by mainstream media. As such, governments are taking direct and decisive action on what Canadians are permitted to remember. Presentations and interpretations of Canadian histories are accordingly situated in political and economic contexts. Consider the recent federal financial capital funneled into public history events related to the War of 1812 (Government of Canada 2012). To observe the two-hundredth anniversary of the war, the government of Canada ramped up interest in preconfederation colonial history. Within weeks of cutting thousands of federal jobs and projects, $28 million was allocated to commemorate the war, which was designed to bolster a strong nation-building narrative. Cited as a "seminal event in the creation of Canada," the War of 1812 draws what many consider an unwarranted amount of government funds and attention (Government of Canada 2012). Nearly simultaneously institutions central to procurement of Canadian history, like Library and Archives Canada, faced crippling cutbacks (CBC News 2012c). Funding for Library and Archives Canada and many critical sites belonging to Parks Canada was slashed by government cuts. Currently Library and Archives Canada is facing reduced ability to serve the public, critical changes to operations that lead to threats to the quality of storage and records, reduced numbers of archivists available to researchers, decentralization of records management, third-party control of records, and serious implications for both acquisitions and record-sharing abilities of Canada's national archive (CBC News 2012d). Parks Canada also saw massive job cuts during this period. Closure or reduced services at national historic sites and cuts to archaeological work, conservators, archivists, and hundreds of heritage jobs followed this trend. Canada's "living" history and heritage was going to be determined by a very narrow allocation of government-controlled funds (Galloway 2012).

In October 2012 the federal government of Canada followed massive cuts to Library Archives Canada and Parks Canada with a rebranding of the Canadian Museum of Civilization (CMC). The Department of Heritage announced that the CMC would be renamed the Canadian Museum of History. Accused of creating a government "spin machine" or "propaganda arm" in this rebranding, Heritage Minister James Moore stated, "Canadians deserve a national museum that tells our stories and presents our country's treasures to the world" (CBC News 2012a). Tracing the cuts and the changes the federal government has made over 2012, one can probably presume which version of history and Canadian memory the Department of Heritage has in mind.

A new role for institutional history in Canada will be absorbed by the CMHR in Winnipeg. As the first national museum to be built from scratch since 1967, the Museum is poised to either challenge, confront, or comply with the national historical narrative(s) in Canada. Public knowledge and interest in the Museum has been driven by media attention of the debates over the presence of exhibit and gallery content on the Holocaust and the Holodomor, the Ukrainian famine of 1932–33 perpetrated by the Stalinist regime (Moses 2012). When it opens in 2014, visitors and critics will see that it is just the start of Canada's human rights commentary and debate. Political and donor influences are undoubtedly shaping memory in gallery and exhibit design. As Moses notes, "professionalization" at the museum could prevail if academic rigor and a human rights approach to design take precedence over donor and political influence (232). However, like other segments of Canadian public history, political and financial influence still draws certain dominant narratives into the center and relegates the rest to the periphery.

The CMHR is promoting a "renewed version" of Canadian history and human rights history in Canada. There are two prevailing messages currently promoted by the Museum with a level of corporate certainty about its public voice. Official messages about the Museum have repeatedly stated that this is not a memorial museum, there are no permanent galleries, and all of the content is changeable. In other words, the content of the CMHR will not be permanent but rather open, fluid, and subject to change.

The Museum will not open with "completed" exhibits until 2014 or 2015. At this time I can only presume how the historical narratives will be perceived in a "completed" museum. As the curator of all Indigenous content at the museum, I see the impermanence of the content and the messaging differently from those at the core of the institution. I personally think that there is something speaking much louder than the static images, texts, and exhibits. Since I started working at the museum, I have maintained the position that *how* the exhibits are built and *what* they are saying are interconnected. The type of wood that is used matters; the view or vista from a window matters; light matters; concrete under your feet matters; sound matters. How the exhibits and the Museum are built ultimately factors into what it is saying about human rights and, in this case, Indigenous peoples in Canada.

In a theoretically impermanent institution, how do you reconcile the need for a permanent, prominent statement about the respected rights won and violated on the very piece of land on which the museum stands? Indeed a permanent statement is being made by the geographical presence of the institution. The Museum physically sits at the forks of the Red and Assiniboine rivers, which remains a deeply sacred space for First Nations and Métis peoples in Canada. As such, I believe there is museum content that is not at all "changeable" or fluid, insofar as the Museum is situated in a space that is rooted in Indigenous histories. These stories tell a narrative of rights that does not get changed out with curatorial or interpretive museum practice. The physical presence on this particular geographical site, then, will absolutely be a permanent statement on the relationship between this institution and the rights of Indigenous peoples. This is a connection that cannot be erased or removed. Interpretation may be lost in exhibit content, but it will never be lost at large, in the sheer presence of the institution in the center of Indigenous lives and territory.

The CMHR maintains that, because it is not a memorial and its content is changeable over time, it does not have to engage in "competitive suffering." Yet whatever intentions the CMHR may have, it will ultimately be perceived in different ways. In *Places of Public Memory: The Rhetoric of Museums and Memorials*, Jeffrey Olick considers the role of public memory and the influence of all social actors on the interpretation of public history in a memory institution: "Memory makers don't always succeed in creating the images they want and in having them understood in the ways they intended. Social actors are often caught in webs of meaning they themselves participate in creating though not in ways they necessarily have predicted" (Dickenson, Blair, and Ott 2010: 14). Assuming the role of Canadian memory makers, the CMHR has officially stated leading up to its inaugural opening that it is not going to memorialize genocide. Thus visitors to the museum will embody "social actors" and the "webs of meaning." Visitors will likely come to a conclusion that differs from the government-prescribed formula for memory. Whether or not visitors feel the selection, interpretation, and placement of images, text, artifacts, and oral histories in a federal memory institution serve as memory or memorial may be a decision left up to them. This Canadian institution may choose to remember or to forget portions of public history and Canada's human rights narrative. More actors are at play, and not knowing the responses of visitors makes it difficult to offer projections on how human rights advocacy will meet with memory production. Shock, apathy, exhaustion, guilt, or anger may trigger the Canadian conscience when accounts of settler colonial genocide in Canada enter or do not enter a public memory institution. A rupture between the margins and center of Canadian historic narrative may do more than revise history—it may start to revise Canadian identity.

For the sake of argument, though, we could consider that the CMHR position is valid, that it is not at all a memorial, according to the state or to the public. We could hypothetically consider that the public will perceive it in the way that it is intended, namely as an "ideas museum" and a space for dialogue on human rights in Canada. If that is the case, then what is the dialogue? In the range of human rights stories, the museum builds a narrative about genocide and what it means for Canada. A 4,500-square-foot gallery on the Holocaust, placed at the heart of a human rights journey through the Museum, makes a significant statement in this "ongoing dialogue," insofar as it suggests Canada's primary connection to genocide is via the Holocaust. The Museum will also feature seven distinct exhibit elements on the Holodomor (Werth 2010: 414–15). Exhibit content on the Holodomor has been enhanced in the CMHR after an almost decade-long battle for representation. Public pressure and lobbying has played a definitive role in public memory and the way that human rights stories are curated in the CMHR (Moses 2012: 217–18). Human rights advocacy inevitably includes a level of advocacy for acknowledgment and a "right to memory."

In Canada, First Nations, Métis, and Inuit advocates are leading a number of human rights advocacy campaigns. Indigenous rights movements require resources and funding that often run thin. These advocates have pressing concerns needing to be fought for, such as the right to have access to clean water in their communities, adequate schools in their communities, access to health care, and advocacy for the over one thousand missing and murdered Aboriginal women in Canada. There is a call for memory and public acknowledgment of rights victories and struggles by Indigenous communities in Canada. When the inaugural exhibits are open to the public in 2014, the implied partnership between public memory and public advocacy will take a new role for community stakeholders that have invested interests in the CMHR. If we presume that there is a right to memory, and that memory in public institutions aids advocacy and human rights movements, perhaps the role of the Museum and selection stories past the inaugural opening could include a level of advocacy rather than solely public interest. In turn, ongoing violations of Indigenous rights, or what many consider continued settler colonial genocide, may be placed in check against a reflection of social conscience and memory.

The Canadian Museum for Human Rights firmly maintains that it will not establish or engage in a hierarchy of suffering. However, with the changes to the Canadian Museum of Civilization, Library and Archives Canada, and the current direction of the CMHR, will there be a hierarchy of memory? As a microcosm of society, the public institution may only really reflect a socio-economic reality in contemporary Canada.

First Nations, Métis, and Inuit in Canada are not without voice and agency. Even though they occupy the socioeconomic margins and their memories may be relegated to the periphery of the mainstream, they are still actors in this memory game. During the time that the residential schools were open, the forced secrecy and active cover-ups of what was occurring at the schools could be considered complacent denial (Milloy 1999: 296–97). Now that evidence is gradually surfacing of the "colonially endorsed" accounts of what occurred at residential schools for over a century, there is still a mode of denial in the public discourse of truth and reconciliation. While survivors come forward by the thousands to share their stories and truths, a mainstream history is maintained as a suppressed portion of Canadian history. In the case of residential school accounts from survivors, they are a history from the periphery being injected into the Canadian public center.

Are the fragments in the debate over the use of the term *genocide* reliant solely on the ongoing debate among genocide scholars? Are the fragmented debates originating from the same public policy machine that influences Canadian memory? Is the dialogue on residential schools as genocide, through findings of the Truth and Reconciliation Commission (TRC) or otherwise, at a stage of robust debate? Are the discussions preemptive and part of a wider scheme to prevent the TRC from entering the debate at all? In other words, what role does the federally funded TRC have in controlling memory and erasure of what the public interprets out of their publicly accessible records? Records handed over to the TRC in the form of Survivor statements, church records, and government records will likely record a different narrative from the dominant historical memory than will be extrapolated by independent historians.

Oral histories, recorded accounts, and formal reports on abuse that originate from Survivors and intergenerational Survivors of residential schools have existed since the schools opened. Almost a century passed before these oral histories and accounts were considered "valid" in Western institutional settings. They are still considered by the colonial-minded governmental mandates on residential schools as supplementary to written and archival evidence (Bombay et al. 2010). Would a different narrative emerge if there was a revised respect for Indigenous knowledge in Canada?

First Nations, Métis, and Inuit communities in Canada hold centuries of records in their respective bodies of knowledge and memory systems. Oral histories have been transferred to subsequent generations. These histories, stories, and embedded memories hold an understanding and a narrative about the generations who faced colonial eliminationism. Canadian historians and national institutions are guilty of claiming inaccessibility or an invisibility of Indigenous history (Miller 2004: 13–14). In turn Indigenous scholars charge Canadian historians with a lack of reflexivity or creativity and an overall inability to engage with Indigenous histories and the transfer of Indigenous knowledge (Baker 2009: 497–506).

Erasure of historical memory and modification of historical narrative influence the perception of genocide. If it is possible to avoid conceptually blocking colonial genocides for a moment, we can consider denial in a colonial context. Perpetrators initiate and perpetuate denial (Jones 2010: 518). Questioning the number of dead or discounting the evidence of genocide becomes part of a mythology. Settler colonial genocide is subjected to comparative scrutiny and is steadily held against the measuring tape of Holocaust scholarship.

In the case of residential schools in Canada, the evidence from the missing children's project research and work to identify mass graves at the sites of residential schools is still ongoing (Truth and Reconciliation Commission 2012). Only broad estimates are available to those who want to integrate quantifiable evidence into the Survivor testimonies of mass graves and student deaths. Those in the mainstream who are likewise concerned with the question of genocide in the TRC rely on this information. Certainly any evidence that the TRC presents via reporting or the accumulated collection at the National Research Centre will inform definitions of genocide in Canada. Historiographical examination of statements and records will consider the "transfer of children from one group to another," the cultural obliteration via extinguishment of languages and cultural heritage, and the pivotal question of *intent*.

The work of the missing children research group has been chronically delayed throughout the proceedings of the TRC, and it has continually indicated that there may be government or church information worth concealing or denying. The final report of the TRC will be completed in 2014, and entry of the results into public memory institutions remains a question. The Commission will include a summary report on use of the term *genocide* in the final report.

Integration of TRC findings into the national historic narrative has started but will continue into 2014 with the establishment of a National Research Centre on residential schools in Canada. It remains to be seen how these institutional developments will influence the national historical narrative of Canada. It seems that two streams of memory will emerge as Indigenous Canada and non-Indigenous Canada formulate divergent definitions of genocide from these recent revisions to Canadian historical memory. On the one hand, the Legacy of Hope Foundation and various other community-run initiatives continue to advocate for public education and memory of residential schools. Yet on the other hand, non-Indigenous Canadians may continue to gravitate toward either a comforting version of colonial history or a seemingly obligatory account of Aboriginal history. Guilt, apathy, and exhaustion plague Canadians and influence absorption into a Canadian identity (Starzyk, Blatz, and Ross 2007).

Writing on memory and genocide, David Moshman (2010: 71–92) states, "Diverse conceptions of genocide generate divergent perceptions of history." The reverse may also be true, that divergent perceptions of history generate diverse concepts of genocide. Colonial genocide definitional debates incur a dominant set of examples, namely, the United States and Australia. Canada often appears as a subheading or footnote of those dominant examples

(Levene 2005: 69). This applies to the work of genocide scholars and Canadian historians and arguably public history in Canada. Mainstream and Indigenous historical narratives diverge on matters of interpretation of national origin and national myth. The result is discrepancies in definitions of settler colonial genocide in Canada.

Absence of any acknowledgment of genocide or genocidal processes in Canadian history allows some genocidal processes to continue. This is one of the most ardent responses to the establishment of the TRC. Survivors are left questioning, "If we learn about destruction at residential schools, what is the assurance that something will change?" (Blackstock 2008). If we rip open the new or old wounds of a collective in search of truth, what promises are made to end the legacy of elimination and marginalization? In good faith Survivors and intergenerational Survivors share their accounts, with government-sanctioned promises and apologies that promise their voices will be heard and that Canada will respond to them. Public or historical acknowledgment of perpetrator actions against First Nations, Métis, and Inuit in Canada could potentially force Canada or Canadians to address current and ongoing violations. However, in addition to a comforting national historic narrative, the role of denying genocide in Canada could also be motivated by an unwillingness for Canada and Canadians to address trends that still exist. Children are still removed from their homes, and many of their basic human rights are not protected under a systematic, destructive child welfare system in Canada. Sexual violence continues to circulate in Aboriginal communities in Canada as a descendant from the residential school legacy. Environmental degradation and climate change erodes lives, homes, and land bases in Canada to a point where the health of Aboriginal people is at risk of corporate or government control. The number of murdered and missing women and girls grows in Canada.

Denying genocides in Canadian history creates blind spots in Canada's present. Of course these blind spots, or conceptual blockages, derive from the debate over how to define genocide. Moreover these blind spots are created by the question of the role of the CMHR, that is, whether or not it should be a memorial or a site of commemoration. If the Museum asserts that it is not a memorial or a space for memorialization of the Holocaust and other genocides, then what kind of museum institution will it be when it opens in 2014? Furthermore if public memory and history in Canada have a role in defining settler genocide in Canada, how will the recent influx of state control over public history alter the results?

Notes

1. Consider objections and assumptions about the absence of credibility in Aboriginal oral histories from Flanagan (2000: 4): "What I call the aboriginal orthodoxy is an emergent consensus on fundamental issues. It is widely shared among aboriginal leaders, government officials and academic experts. It weaves together threads from historical revisionism, critical legal studies, and the aboriginal political activism of the last thirty years. Although its ideas are expressed in many books, it has no Marx and Engels, that is, no canonical writers to authoritatively define the ideology."

References

Algan, Bülent. 2008. "The Brand New Version of Article 301 of Turkish Penal Code and the Future of Freedom of Expression Cases in Turkey." *German Law Journal* 9 (12): 2237–52.

Baker, Emerance. 2009. "Locating Ourselves in the Place of Creation: The Academy as Kitsu'lt melkiko'tin." In *First Voices: An Aboriginal Women's Reader*, edited by Patricia Monture and Patricia McGuire. Toronto: Inanna.

Blackstock, Cindy. 2008. "Reconciliation Means Not Saying Sorry Twice: Lessons from Child Welfare in Canada." In *From Truth to Reconciliation: Transforming the Legacy of Residential Schools*, edited by Marlene Brant Castellano, Linda Archibald, and Mike Degagne. Ottawa: Aboriginal Healing Foundation.

Bombay, A., L. Ellsworth, S. Fryer, T. Logan, and G. Reimer. 2010. *Common Experience Payment: Impacts on Survivors' Healing Journeys*. Ottawa: Aboriginal Healing Foundation.

CBC News. 2012a. "Civilization Museum's $25M Rebranding to Focus on History." October 16. http://www.cbc.ca/news/technology/story/2012/10/16/ottawa-canadian-museum-civilization-becomes-canadian-museum-history.html.

CBC News. 2012b. "Conservatives Draw Fire for War of 1812 Spending." June 15. http://www.cbc.ca/news/politics/story/2012/06/14/pol-war-of-1812-bicentennial-federal-events.html.

CBC News. 2012c. "Federal Libraries, Archives Shutting Down." May 28. http://www.cbc.ca/news/canada/ottawa/story/2012/05/02/ottawa-libraries-archives-closing-budget-cuts.html.

CBC. 2012d. "Library and Archives Interlibrary Loans Soon Eliminated." November 7. http://www.cbc.ca/news/canada/ottawa/story/2012/11/06/ottawa-library-and-archives-canada-interlibrary-loans-cancelled.html.

Dickason, Olive. 1992. *Canada's First Nations: A History of Founding Peoples from Earliest Times*. Norman: University of Oklahoma Press.

Dickason, Olive, and David McNab. 2009. *Canada's First Nations*. 4th ed. Don Mills, Canada: Oxford University Press.

Dickenson, Greg, Carole Blair, and Brian L. Ott. 2010. *Places of Public Memory: The Rhetoric of Museums and Memorials*. Tuscaloosa: University of Alabama Press.

Dixon, J. K. 1913. *The Vanishing Race: The Last Great Indian Council*. New York: Doubleday.

Flanagan, T. 2000. *First Nations? Second Thoughts*. Montreal: McGill-Queens University Press.

Galloway, Gloria. 2012. "Budget Cuts Imperil Canada's National Parks." *Globe and Mail*, July 12. http://www.theglobeandmail.com/news/national/budget-cuts-imperil-canadas-national-parks/article4409268/.

Government of Canada. 2012. Official website for Bicentennial of the War of 1812. http://1812.gc.ca/eng/1305743548294/1305743621243.

Guerin, Frances, and Roger Hallas, eds. 2007. *The Image and the Witness: Trauma, Memory and Visual Culture*. London: Wallflower Press.

Jones, Adam. 2007. *Genocide: A Comprehensive Introduction*. New York: Routledge.

Jones, Adam. 2010. *Genocide: A Comprehensive Introduction, Second Edition*. New York: Routledge.

Lee, Philip, and Pradip Ninan Thomas, eds. 2012. *Public Memory, Public Media and the Politics of Justice*. New York: Palgrave Macmillan.

Levene, Mark. 2005. *The Rise of the West and the Coming of Genocide: Genocide in the Age of the Nation State*. Vol. 2. London: I. B. Tauris.

MacKenzie, John M. 2010. *Museums and Empire: Natural History, Human Cultures and Colonial Identities*. Manchester, UK: Manchester University Press.

Miller, Donald, and Lorna Miller. 1993. *Survivors: An Oral History of the Armenian Genocide*. Berkeley: University of California Press.

Miller, J. R. 2004. *Reflections on Native-Newcomer Relations: Selected Essays*. Toronto: University of Toronto Press.

Milloy, J. S. 1999. *A National Crime*. Winnipeg: University of Manitoba Press.

Moses, A. Dirk. 2002. "Conceptual Blockages and Definitional Dilemmas in the 'Racial Century': Genocides of Indigenous Peoples and the Holocaust." *Patterns of Prejudice* 36 (4): 7–36.

Moses, A. Dirk. 2008. *Empire, Colony and Genocide: Conquest, Occupation and Subaltern Resistance in World History*. New York: Berghahn.

Moses, A. Dirk. 2012. "The Canadian Museum for Human Rights and the 'Uniqueness of the Holocaust' and the Question of Genocide." *Journal of Genocide Research* 14 (2): 214–38.

Moshman, David. 2010. "Conceptions of Genocide and Perceptions of History." In *The Historiography of Genocide*, edited by Dan Stone. London: Palgrave Macmillan.

Powell, Christopher. 2011. *Barbaric Civilization: A Critical Sociology of Genocide*. Montreal: McGill-Queens University Press.

Simon, Roger I. 2005. "The Touch of the Past: The Pedagogical Significance of a Transactional Sphere of Public Memory." In *The Touch of the Past: Remembrance, Learning and Ethics*, edited by Roger I. Simon. New York: Palgrave Macmillan.

Starzyk, Katherine B., Craig W. Blatz, and Michael Ross. 2007. "Addressing and Acknowledging Historical Injustices." In *Social and Psychological Bases of Ideology and System Justification*, edited by J. T. Jost, A. C. Kay, and H. Thorisdottir. Boston: Blackwell.

Truth and Reconciliation Commission of Canada. 2012. *Interim Report*. http://www

.attendancemarketing.com/~attmk/TRC_jd/Interim%20report%20English%20 electronic%20copy.pdf.

United Nations General Assembly. 2007. *United Nations Declaration on the Rights of Indigenous Peoples: Resolution/adopted by the General Assembly.* October 2. A/ RES/61/295. http://www.unhcr.org/refworld/docid/471355a82.html.

Vesely, Carolin. 2012. "Ukrainian Experts to Speak on Holodomor." *Winnipeg Free Press*, November 16. http://www.winnipegfreepress.com/local/ukrainian-experts-to-speak-on-holodomor-179620841.html.

Werth, Nicolas. 2010. "The Crimes of the Stalinist Regime." In *The Historiography of Genocide*, edited by Dan Stone. Basingstoke, UK: Palgrave Macmillan.

Woolford, Andrew. 2009. "Ontological Destruction: Genocide and Canadian Aboriginal Peoples." *Genocide Studies and Prevention* 4 (1): 81–97.

CHAPTER 7

RESIDENTIAL SCHOOL HARM
AND COLONIAL DISPOSSESSION

What's the Connection?

Jeremy Patzer

The condemnation of the history of residential schooling in Canada is becoming well rehearsed—and rightly so. In the late nineteenth century many Aboriginal leaders were initially in favor of schooling for their children, although with varying stances on possible religious components. This willingness was often due to a mixture of pragmatic reasoning: desire for their children to have a life as advantageous as European settlers had, recognition that their way of life was disappearing, and sensitivity to the fact that American policy had often demonstrated a much more violent alternative to mere schooling (Miller 1996). In all seven treaties signed across western Canada in the 1870s, Aboriginal leaders stipulated that the government provide *day schools* on reserves so long as the band wanted them (Miller 1996; Milloy 1999).

Simultaneous to signing these agreements, however, the government and missionaries were hardening on the perceived need to isolate and control Aboriginal students for a more effective civilizational conversion. In 1879 the Canadian government sent Nicholas Flood Davin to the United States to investigate the American experience with industrial boarding schools—some of which were administered by churches under contract—under the aegis of President Ulysses S. Grant's "aggressive civilization" policy. Davin saw the American system as a success, and his report was very positive concerning the idea of church involvement in First Nations and Métis education in Canada. His argument was that something would be required to replace "simple Indian mythology" on the Indians' journey to civilization and that capitalizing on the schools already established by missionaries, as well as on their evangelical enthusiasm, would ultimately make the venture more cost effective (Miller 1996: 102; Titley 2011: 75–77). In 1883 Canada began funding a handful of new residential industrial schools to be run by various church denominations, while preexisting schools, including residential boarding institutions, gained government support. The larger institutions with the "industrial" designation were generally placed far from reserves in order to better isolate students from the influence of family and cultural community, while the smaller day and residential boarding schools were more often on or near reserves and housed younger students.

Many schools encountered Aboriginal resistance to the prolonged removal of children, however, and controversies quickly arose around inadequate clothing, inadequate nutrition, and widespread disease. With students' days divided between education and vocational work, questions of exploitation also shadowed these schools since their early history. To this controversial history one can add severe discipline, punishment, and cultural degradation, as well as a startling number of sexual and physical abuse allegations. It is estimated that more than 150,000 Aboriginal children were taken to residential schools; seventy thousand to eighty thousand First Nations, Inuit, and Métis survivors were still alive as of 2009 (Walker 2009). While the system was officially ended in 1969, several government-run schools continued on into the 1990s.

It would seem eminently sensible, then, that such a history would require some sort of reckoning or process of reconciliation. Spurred on by the legal actions of thousands of former students, the 2006 Indian Residential Schools Settlement Agreement (IRSSA) became the largest class action settlement in Canada's history. Under the auspices of the agreement came the Indian Residential Schools Truth and Reconciliation Commission of Canada (TRC). A number of critics suggest, however, that the IRSSA and the TRC are oriented toward promoting preemptive reconciliation while eliding underlying issues, the greatest of which is colonial dispossession and the struggle for decolonization and self-determination (Alfred 2009; Corntassel, Chaw-win-is, and T'lakwadzi 2009; Corntassel and Holder 2008; Green 2012; Henderson and Wakeham 2009; Jung 2011). This raises the question of the connection between the very real issue of harm caused by residential schooling and the historical political issues of dispossession and the denial of self-determination. Is there a connection, or should land and self-determination form the crux of another argument at another time?

My argument is that there is a connection. Although the history is complex and varies by region, changes in circumstances underlying the colonization of what is now Canada saw Aboriginal peoples increasingly cast as a *problem* to be solved. In effect less European interest in trade and alliance with Aboriginal peoples and a greater desire for the very land upon which they lived underwrote the advent of the "Indian problem." One relation to be drawn between dispossession, the dismantling of traditional Aboriginal governance structures, and residential schooling is thus through their role as solutions to historical facets of the Indian problem. For a nascent, expansionist Canada, the elimination of Aboriginal possession of land to make way for settlement was a first order of business. Then, for a country that actually saw Aboriginal nations, Indian status, and the federal Indian department as temporary necessities on the road to complete assimilation, the subsequent policies demonstrated the rising tenor of solutions to a problem cast in increasingly social and cultural terms: the undermining and elimination of traditional Aboriginal governance structures and, in a *high modernist* historical moment, residential schooling.

Residential schooling for Aboriginal peoples is particularly remarkable in that it represented a rationally planned form of social engineering that envisaged the elimination of *Aboriginal difference* itself. It is the insidiousness and multigenerational harm caused by such a highly interventionist "solution" that invites contemporary suggestions of genocide—especially those forms of it married to ethnic and cultural qualifiers. Yet I would also suggest that dispossession, the removal of self-determination, and residential schooling—more than simply being of like category or three facets of the Indian problem—should also be connected by the issue of causability. In effect the depredations of colonization—the despoilment of land and the means of survival on it, as well as the assumption of a plenary political bureaucratic control over First Nations—create the very conditions of possibility for tragedies such as Canada's history of residential schooling, such that any full reckoning with the latter cannot be dissociated from the former.[1]

The Several Historical Facets of the "Indian Problem"

The first volume of the *Final Report of the Royal Commission on Aboriginal Peoples* (Royal Commission on Aboriginal Peoples [RCAP] 1996), commissioned by the federal government in reaction to the Oka Crisis of 1990, invests a considerable amount of energy outlining and examining how European-Aboriginal relations in what is now Canada transitioned from an era of *contact and cooperation* to one of *displacement and assimilation*. Indeed the question is so fundamental that it should be a primary area of historical interest for all Canadians. While this chapter is not intended to give an exhaustive account of five hundred years of history, understanding the changing circumstances underlying the relationship will go some way toward establishing a context for the declining sense of moral obligation that the Crown felt toward

Aboriginal peoples in Canada, ultimately identifying indigeneity itself as a problem to be solved.

Initially First Nations were of far greater number than the arriving Europeans, and they possessed knowledge and skills critically useful to the latter. Relations were thus established "in a context in which Aboriginal peoples initially had the upper hand in population and in terms of their knowledge of the land and how to survive in it" (RCAP 1996: 100). The postcontact spread of disease was devastating for many Aboriginal populations, however. And while the alliances, competition, and hostilities between various European and Aboriginal groups during the fur trade era were not without grave consequences for many First Nations in North America—the chapters in this collection authored by Joseph Gone, Robbie Ethridge, and Jeff Benvenuto offer some striking examples from the United States, not shying away from outlining Aboriginal participation in such calamities—the role of Aboriginal peoples in the fur trade nevertheless made it in the best interests of the European powers to have many of them actually remain in possession of much of their lands. More important, such intersocietal commercial links "did not interfere in a major way with long-standing Aboriginal patterns of pursuing their livelihood and actually tended to build on Aboriginal strengths" (RCAP 1996: 101). In addition Aboriginal interests benefited for an extended period of time from a balance of power between two European nations that was not too much askew. According to Leonard Rotman (1996: 36), they knew "full well that they were the catalysts in the European struggle in North America" and "that their precarious interests were best served by maintaining the delicate balance of power between the two European nations."

These factors would change with time, however, and all with grave strategic consequences for Aboriginal peoples. The 1763 Treaty of Paris ended the Seven Years' War. Great Britain made significant gains as the French ceded the vast majority of its North American territory. General Thomas Gage encapsulated the significance of this to First Nations with his observation, "All North America in the hands of a single power robs them of their Consequence, presents, & pay" (cited in White 2011: 256). Yet if this was true after the Seven Years' War, it became all the more the case after the War of 1812, which was followed by a period of relative peace that eliminated Britain's need for military alliances with Aboriginal peoples (RCAP 1996: 138; Llewellyn 2002: 256). And while Aboriginal populations had been decimated by disease, the non-Aboriginal population would see dramatic increases, especially after the American Revolution and the arrival of United Empire Loyalists (RCAP 1996: 137). The fur trade, for its part, would rise and fall in different regions of the continent at different times, but its inevitable decline created a situation in which the economies of the two peoples were increasingly incompatible. More and more, non-Aboriginal immigrants were interested in establishing permanent settlements on the land, clearing it for agricultural purposes, and taking advantage of the timber, fish and other resources to meet their own needs or to supply markets elsewhere. . . . In something of a return to earlier notions of the "civilized" and "savage" uses of land, Aboriginal people came to be regarded as impediments to productive development. Moreover, as Aboriginal economies declined because of the loss of the land, the scarcity of game and the continuing ravages of disease, relief payments to alleviate the threat of starvation became a regular feature of colonial financial administration. In short order, formerly autonomous Aboriginal nations came to be viewed, by prosperous and expanding Crown colonies, as little more than an unproductive drain on the public purse. (RCAP 1996: 138)

In what is now Canada, early treaties between European and Aboriginal peoples were treaties of alliance, peace, and friendship, involving no purported "cession" or "surrender" of territory. Many of these took place around the St. Lawrence Valley and the Atlantic region in the eighteenth century (Sprague 1995: 341). The end of the Seven Years' War and the Treaty of Paris were followed by the Royal Proclamation of 1763, which, among other things, stated that the acquisition of lands was under the sole purview of the Crown and would be done in public meetings with representatives from Aboriginal groups arranged for that purpose.[2] This paved the way for treaties that envisaged the procurement of land for European settlement. The specific format of these later treaties evolved over time, but even the broad strokes concerning the fate of Aboriginal groups and their relationship with the Crown remain contentious issues in Crown-Aboriginal relations to this day.

In effect the report of the Royal Commission on Aboriginal Peoples (1996) states that it is unlikely, in many cases concerning the postconfederation numbered treaties,[3] that the participating First Nations knew of the significant discrepancies between the oral agreements they concluded and the corresponding written texts they signed. It characterizes the possibility that the parties acting on behalf of the Crown took advantage of the Aboriginal representatives' inability to read the written texts and their lack of understanding of the legal implications as "disturbing" (174). Terms such as "cede, surrender, extinguish, yield and forever give up all rights and titles appear in the written text of the treaties, but discussion of the meaning of these concepts is not found anywhere in the records of treaty negotiations" (175). The treaties are also replete with the language of subjection, referring to the Aboriginal peoples as subjects of the Crown and the Crown as having dominion over the territories concerned, but the Commission's finding is that the patterning of First Nations' relationships along kinship lines means that they would have understood the relationship as something "more akin to 'brothers' or 'partners' of the Crown" and, since they were being asked for the land, "that they were the ones giving the land to the Crown and that they were the owners of the land" (175).

As for preconfederation treaties, such as many of the peace and friendship treaties around the Atlantic Coast, William Wicken (1994) recognizes that their present-day evaluation is complicated by the dearth of records detailing anything concerning the treaty negotiations themselves. Nonetheless he finds it unlikely that the Mi'kmaq and Wuastukwiuk (Maliseet) representatives would have willingly recognized the British Crown's "dominion" over their territories, or themselves as its subjects in their eighteenth-century treaties (250). There are records of Mi'kmaq leaders' expressions to the contrary, and the British had little military influence in the region until late in the eighteenth century (Wicken 1994). In addition Wicken looks to contemporaneous treaties that the British signed with the Penobscot people and the Abenaki people in the same region. Concerning the former, Loron, the speaker of the Penobscot, sent a letter to the lieutenant-governor of Massachusetts after the fact, stating, "Having hear'd the Acts read which you have given me I have found the Articles entirely differing from what we have said in presence of one another, 'tis therefore to disown them that I write this letter unto you" (cited in Wicken 1994: 251). Similarly French speakers present at the signing of the Abenaki treaty at Casco Bay wrote that the articles read to the Indians had not included references to submitting to the king, accepting responsibility for beginning hostilities with the English, or submitting to English law—despite the inclusion of these in the written text of the treaty (Wicken 1994).[4]

This aspect of the history is significant because "First Nations were assured orally that their way of life would not change unless they wished it to. They understood that their governing structures and authorities would continue undisturbed by the treaty relationship" (RCAP 1996: 174). From the perspective of First Nations, there was nothing in the formation of the nation-to-nation relations or in the promises made in treaty negotiations that would envisage or legitimate the invasive, assimilative, and paternalistic approach of nineteenth- and twentieth-century Indian policy. It represents such a comprehensive incursion into Aboriginal self-determination that Kiera Ladner (see her chapter in this collection) advocates the use of the term *political genocide* to refer to policies and practices designed to eliminate Aboriginal sovereignty and governments. And it was a body of policy whose statutes would encompass even those First Nations with whom the Crown did not bother signing treaties—largely in the north and the west of Canada—and those whose older treaties of peace, friendship, and alliance had clearly not arranged for the cession of territory.

The Gradual Enfranchisement Act, enacted two years after confederation, permitted interference with tribal self-government, which was seen as a main impediment to the formal goal of assimilation.[5] The original Indian Act of 1876 coalesced and retained much of the assimilative policies that had been enacted until that point, and future amendments only continued further in the same direction with, among other things, the forcible enfranchisement of certain categories of Indian, prohibitions on certain cultural practices, artifacts, and dress, and the prohibition of raising funds to pursue issues of rights and title in the courts. In arguing in favor of Bill 14 in 1920, which would allow the forcible enfranchisement of any status Indian should an appointed civil servant recommend it, Duncan Campbell Scott said, "I want to get rid of the Indian problem. I do not think as a matter of fact, that this country ought to continuously protect a class of people who are able to stand alone. That is my whole point. Our objective is to continue until there is not a single Indian in Canada that has not been absorbed into the body politic, and there is no Indian question, and no Indian Department and that is the whole object of this Bill" (cited in Neu and Graham 2004: 590). For an extended period of time, then, Indian policy had a certain provisional character underlying it. It was very much focused on the future, but it was a future with no distinct Aboriginal peoples, no Indian status, and therefore no Indian Department. More than just a manifestation of the European desire for Aboriginal lands, the Indian problem was now a question of the total assimilation of a people that remained intransigently *different*.

High Modernity and the Suppression of Aboriginal Difference

Duncan Campbell Scott's goal of eliminating the Indian question itself was the mark of a young, ambitiously expansionist nation-state, but also of what Zygmunt Bauman (1991: 37) would term the *modern spirit*, an Enlightenment-inspired hubris with a "vision of society as pliable raw material to be moulded and brought into proper shape by architects armed with a proper design." Yet while Bauman suggests that most genocidal campaigns against Aboriginal peoples were characteristically *premodern* in their simple motivations of hatred, heterophobia, or competitive gain, it is striking the extent to which the aspirations of Scott and the policies typical of his era mirror Bauman's (1989: 91, emphasis in original) notion of *modern genocide*: "The *end itself is a grand vision of a better, and radically different, society.* Modern genocide is an element of social engineering."

While Bauman does not elaborate much on his categorization of colonial genocide as generally premodern, his brief sketch of it does seem inspired by a view of colonial violence that is largely familiar with certain aspects of American colonial history—namely, overt physical violence and extermination in the pursuit of Aboriginal lands. Tellingly, around the same time the once "quasi-diplomatic" responsibility of Indian affairs in Upper and Lower Canada was transferred from military to civil authorities (RCAP 1996: 138), the United States transferred that responsibility to its War Department (Miller 2000). When Canada was seeking to expand westward in the late nineteenth century, the Plains peoples of western Canada came into the treaty-making process weakened by disease, intertribal warfare, and the disappearance of the bison. They were also cognizant of the fact that, just to the south, the American cavalry was "inflicting enormous damage on any nations that resisted the assertion of American authority. In 1871, just as Canada was about to begin negotiating a series of western treaties, the United States turned its back on treaty making and began to use force to control Native Americans in the West" (Miller 2007: 22).

At the negotiations for Treaty Six, which was to span the mid-latitudes of Saskatchewan and Alberta, Cree leaders held a meeting among themselves in which senior chiefs such as Mistawasis, Ahtahkakoop, and Sweetgrass attempted to convince their younger colleagues, such as Poundmaker and the Badger, of the pragmatic need to sign a treaty with the British Crown. Mistawasis underscored their dire circumstances and, referring to the American cavalry with their long bayonets, told his fellow Cree to "look to the great Indian nations in the Long Knives' country who have been fighting since the memory of their oldest men. They are being vanquished and swept into the most useless parts of their country. Their days are numbered like those of the buffalo. There is no law or justice for the Indians in the Long Knives' country" (quoted in Miller 2007: 26). Yet if Canada can boast a lesser degree of physical destruction of Aboriginal peoples than that which occurred in the United States—be it by virtue of contentious treaties or the simple settlement of regions without treaty[6]—then it seems just as certain that, as a settler state that would inherit a significant internal minority of Aboriginal peoples, it would readily edge into the period, the spirit, and the perceived functional need for some form of what Bauman calls a modern genocide of social engineering. In short, doing away with the Indian problem would be about a *remaking* rather than a *removal*, and high modernity would be up to the task.

Thus from the advent of the Indian problem—that is, the moment when the colonizers had no more use for Indians as *Indians*—the evolving practices and policies exacted against Aboriginal peoples in Canada can be understood as historical facets of the Crown's solution for it. The Crown has sought the elimination of Aboriginal possession of land for the sake of an expansionist Canada, as well as the elimination of traditional governance structures and Aboriginal self-determination, which it identified as a key impediment to achieving its assimilationist policy goals (RCAP 1996: 275). Residential schooling was the continuance of this process of attempting to solve the Indian problem, as Canada, like so many other nations in the nineteenth and twentieth century, sunk deeper into what James C. Scott (1998) terms "high-modernist ideology." Concomitant with the birth of the social sciences and their sometimes dangerously ambitious naïveté, high modernist ideology saw "an enlightenment belief in the self-improvement of man" become, "by degrees, a belief in the perfectibility of social order" (92–93). Stated otherwise, "industrial-strength social engineering was born" (91).[7] (In their respective chapters on Indian residential schools in this collection, both Andrew Woolford and David MacDonald touch upon this nineteenth- and early twentieth-century zeitgeist.) Although Scott mainly sees his work as useful for examining the histories of countries in Eastern Europe and the developing world, Western countries were by no means immune from the high modernist spirit. His observations on the authoritarian nature of high modernist ideology can easily be accommodated by the acutely asymmetrical relations that evolved between the colonizers and the colonized in nineteenth- and early twentieth-century Canada. Upon the assumption of sovereignty over Aboriginal territory, the federal government instituted in statute a plenary power for itself and its Indian agents over the lives, rights, and identities of First Nations peoples. As Kiera Ladner notes in her chapter, the Indian Act can affect every aspect of an Aboriginal person's life from conception to death. Scott's concern for how marginalized subpopulations "might be made the objects of the most intensive social engineering" is particularly fitting (92). This was, after all, the ideology of bureaucratic intelligentsia and planners such as Duncan Campbell Scott:

> The position accorded to them is not just one of rule and privilege but also one of responsibility for the great works of nation building and social transformation. Where this intelligentsia conceives of its mission as the dragging of a technically backward, unschooled, subsistence-oriented population into the twentieth century, its self-assigned cultural role as educator of its people becomes doubly grandiose.... One might in fact speculate that the more intractable and resistant the real world faced by the planner, the greater the

need for utopian plans to fill, as it were, the void that would otherwise invite despair. The elites who elaborate such plans implicitly represent themselves as exemplars of the learning and progressive views to which their compatriots might aspire. (Scott 1998: 96)

Similarly Bauman (1989: 70) claims that "from the Enlightenment on, the modern world was distinguished by its activist, engineering attitude toward nature and toward itself." Attentive to the modern state's preoccupation with rationally designing society, Bauman employed the metaphor of the garden. The envisioned design "supplied the criteria to evaluate present-day reality. These criteria split the population into useful plants to be encouraged and tenderly propagated, and weeds—to be removed or rooted out" (1991: 20). The modern state, simply put, "was a gardening state" (20). While Bauman's interests bring him to consider the rational planning behind the Holocaust and the Iron Curtain, he lucidly observes that "there were also plants which turned into weeds simply because a superior reason required that the land they occupied should be transformed into someone else's garden" (29).

Thus if previous practices and policies of the Crown saw the solution to the ongoing Indian problem in the elimination of Aboriginal lands and then the elimination of Aboriginal self-determination, residential schooling itself was a solution to the problem that envisaged the elimination of *Aboriginal difference itself*. It was among the most grandiose of Canada's social engineering projects, with a clear view to what was, for these planners, an ideal, "civilized" society. As stated in the *Annual Report of the Department of Indian Affairs* for 1895, "If it were possible to gather in all the Indian children and retain them for a certain period, there would be produced a generation of English-speaking Indians, accustomed to the ways of civilized life, which might then be the dominant body among themselves, capable of holding its own with its white neighbours, and thus would be brought about rapidly decreasing expenditure until the same should forever cease, and the Indian problem would have been solved" (quoted in Llewellyn 2002: 257). Indian residential schooling therefore *does* need to be understood within the larger context of dispossession and the coercive removal of the capacity for self-determination. However, this must go a step further than the simple recognition of residential schooling as one of several "solutions," or of its place as a modernist high-water mark in the attempts to eliminate the Indian problem. A full evaluation of the lessons learned and of the efforts at reconciliation in the wake of residential schooling needs to recognize that dispossession and subjugation were necessary in order to create the very conditions of possibility for something so acutely interventionist and misguided as the residential schooling debacle.

Initially the federal government used its vast resources to defend itself vigorously against contemporary legal claims launched by residential school survivors. While it was named in the actions, this was not always the case for the four most common church denominations—Roman Catholic, Anglican, Presbyterian, and Methodist, with many congregations of the latter two integrating into the amalgamated United Church in 1925—that helped to operate the residential schools. In the interests of reducing its potential liability, the government pursued a strategy of putting forth third-party claims against the church organizations in order to include them in the suits, claiming that they were in fact liable or, at the very least, that they shared liability and should be included in any findings of fault for damages.[8]

The *Final Report of the Royal Commission on Aboriginal Peoples* had recommended a full public inquiry into residential schooling, but in 1998, two years after the commencement of the first residential schools class action lawsuit of *Blackwater v. Plint*,[9] the federal government unveiled *Gathering Strength: Canada's Aboriginal Action Plan*, which put $350 million toward the establishment of the Aboriginal Healing Foundation. Jane Stewart, then minister of Indian and Northern Affairs, also read a "Statement of Reconciliation" to indigenous leaders and civil servants "at a lunchtime ceremony held in a government meeting room in Ottawa" (Corntassel and Holder 2008: 473). The statement was carefully worded so as to express that the federal government was "deeply sorry" to those individuals who suffered physical and sexual abuse at the schools, thereby circumventing any engagement with the issues of assimilation, cultural loss, and systemic harm caused by residential schooling as a whole. This did not stem the flow of lawsuits.

By the time the *Baxter* class action was being settled in 2006—the settlement that ultimately became the Indian Residential Schools Settlement Agreement—residential schools were the subject of around fifteen thousand ongoing claims in Canadian courts,[10] and many religious bodies had long been expressing fears of insolvency. Interestingly enough the sheer number of court claims related to specific instances of sexual and physical abuse may have ultimately paved the way, through the IRSSA, for *all* former students of federally funded residential schools who were alive as of May 30, 2005, to receive compensation in the form of a "common experience payment."[11] The prospect of a settlement that somewhat universalizes the denunciation of the residential school experience must have seemed to the government a more favorable option than contesting fifteen thousand court claims, despite the fact that, in its 2005 decision on the *Blackwater* class action, the Supreme

Court of Canada signaled its reticence to consider the larger issues of cultural and community harm as legally actionable wrongs:

> A more general issue lurks beneath the surface of a number of the specific legal issues. It concerns how claims such as this, which reach back many years, should be proved, and the role of historic and social science evidence in proving issues of liability and damages. For example, to what extent is evidence of generalized policies toward Aboriginal children relevant? Can such evidence lighten the burden of proving specific fault and damage in individual cases? I conclude that general policies and practices may provide relevant context for assessing claims for damages in cases such as this. However, government policy by itself does not create a legally actionable wrong. For that, the law requires specific wrongful acts causally connected to damage suffered. This appeal must be decided on the evidence adduced at trial and considered by the Court of Appeal.[12]

In the IRSSA the Independent Assessment Process has been designed—by itemizing and quantifying harm and, consequently, pecuniary liability through a points system—to respond to the cases of those students who can claim damages for the "legally actionable wrong" of abuse. In spite of the Supreme Court's prior inclination, it is the common experience payment for which all former students are eligible and the TRC that have helped push the common discourse in Canada further toward the wholesale acceptance of residential schooling as a *wrongful act*. But the TRC, while sealed off from the legalism of fault, liability, and the courts in its mandate, is an enclosure of legalistic negative space that is simultaneously constituted by it and through it. This is the exchange implicit in a TRC mandated by an out-of-court settlement: a space in which victims' voices are given free rein but with all legal risk defined out. Hence Canada's development of a TRC with a profoundly victim-centered, therapeutic ethos.

INDIVIDUALIZATION: THE THERAPEUTIC ETHOS

The nature of the TRC's mandate is indicative of the unique position of Canada's TRC as being the first truth commission to flow from an out-of-court settlement of civil litigation. As Jula Hughes (2012: 109–10) states, such settlements "are protected by a host of legal privileges, all of which operate to protect the integrity of the settlement process by excluding the prying eyes of the public. Secrecy and confidentiality are said to encourage settlement." In the section of the TRC's mandate entitled "Establishment, Powers, Duties and Procedures of the Commission," it is stated that participation in the Commission's activities is entirely voluntary and the commissioners "are authorized to receive statements and documents from former students, their families, community," and, vaguely, "*all other interested participants*" (IRSSA 2006, emphasis mine). In addition the commission is neither a formal hearing nor a public inquiry nor a formal legal process. It shall therefore not name names, make any findings regarding the misconduct of any person, or make any reference "to the possible civil or criminal liability of any person or organization, unless such findings or information about the individual or institution has already been established through legal proceedings" (IRSSA 2006). It seems a safe assumption, then, that perpetrators of violence and abuse or those who had a hand in creating and running the schools will not be presenting before the TRC in large numbers—largely limiting purported processes of truth and reconciliation to victims alone.

Employing a therapeutic ethos is not new to the practice of transitional justice. With former students likely forming the vast majority of participants, however, Canada's current TRC is *particularly* reliant on mobilizing the trope of healing. In this way it is also able to have its work seen to coincide with traditional Aboriginal notions of healing, the implication being that it is more culturally appropriate and more restorative. Similarly Archbishop Desmond Tutu, chair of the South African TRC, repeatedly invoked the traditional southern African form of justice known as *ubuntu*, suggesting it "was profoundly anti-retributive and simultaneously pro-healing" (Moon 2009: 81).

Nevertheless the imprint of Aboriginal agency cannot be completely erased from this history. Robyn Green (2012) thus expresses misgivings about dismissing Canada's reconciliation process as a purely mechanistic form of domination, given that the IRSSA was negotiated with the churches and the government by Aboriginal organizations and residential school survivors themselves. In fact the broad strokes of the IRSSA—including a truth-sharing and reconciliation process—were taken from the recommendations of a 2004 report released by the Assembly of First Nations (Stanton 2011). Yet, for Jennifer Henderson and Pauline Wakeham (2009: 16), culturally mediated tropes such as "healing" that are repeated "on both sides of the settler-culture/ Indigenous community distinction might produce a certain reconciliation effect—a semblance of common ground or shared understanding. However, the iteration of the trope of healing might mean different things in different contexts of utterance." For residential school survivors, then, healing may be about healing—perhaps even a more holistic healing that encompasses larger processes of decolonization that are lost on government and settler society—while for the state it may be a subtle claim to political legitimacy. Indeed despite its apparent humanism, critics of transitional justice see in the therapeutic ethos a radical new form of state legitimation (Humphrey 2003;

Moon 2009), in that "the basis of the claim to govern made by some postconflict states, lies in their ability to lay national trauma to rest" (Moon 2009: 72).

But if some measure of healing takes place, does that alone make for reconciliation? Does reconciliation between the various parties occur, as the TRC's mandate seems to believe can happen, when residential school survivors do not necessarily find perpetrators, religious organizations, or governments present at the table? Or especially when they do not see the recognition of and a move to change the historical processes of dispossession, disempowerment, and marginalization that paved the way to the residential school in the first place? In this sense are they simply being reconciled to their own grief, suffering, and loss?

DEPOLITICIZATION: A RELATIONSHIP OF MANY WRONGS

Claire Moon (2009: 72) has observed that there is currently such power behind the notions of reconciliation and healing that they "appear, now, to be self-evidently right." Problematically, however, the notion of reconciliation is also quite *vague*. What reconciliation is, how it is achieved, and how we can know that it has been successfully achieved, are all unclear. For Richard Wilson (2003: 371), reconciliation is so abstracted that "'national reconciliation' is almost impossible to quantify or measure or assess in any meaningful way"—a quality, he suggests, that makes it suitable for nation-building projects. Such issues are not without mention in discussions of Canada's TRC. Matt James (2012: 196) writes that "the TRC's guidelines and funding criteria discuss the notion of reconciliation in quite general terms," while Courtney Jung (2011) has called the TRC's concept of reconciliation "underspecified." Keavy Martin (2009: 55) expresses concern "about the implications of reconciliation as an unproblematized objective."

As underspecified as it is, however, one observation seems warranted: the concept of reconciliation takes a *relationship* as its object. This is to say that violence, atrocity, and wrongdoing may be at the source of the rift between individuals or collectivities, and practices of repair for such wrongdoing may be deemed necessary to pave the way for some sort of reconciliation, but reconciliation itself speaks to *relationship*. This is reflected in the definitions of reconciliation offered up by proponents of transitional justice. At the center of any process of reconciliation, according to Andrew Rigby (2001: 12), is a "preparedness of people to anticipate a shared future." For Priscilla Hayner (2002: 161), reconciliation amounts to the "building or rebuilding of relationships today that are not haunted by the conflicts and hatreds of yesterday."

Yet if reconciliation has to do with relationship first and foremost, Hayner's (2002: 161) definition reminds us that "the conflicts and hatreds of yesterday" at the source of the estrangement can be, and often are, multiple. This is precisely the case with Canada's relationship with Aboriginal peoples. From this perspective we can accommodate a multiplicity of historical policies and processes effected upon Indigenous groups in Canada: dispossession of land, dishonoring treaties, removal of self-determination and traditional forms of government, assimilative residential schooling, loss of language and culture, forced relocations, and the proscription of traditional forms of subsistence as well as practices such as the potlatch and Sundance, to name a few. However, settler society's lack of concern for the unsettled controversies and infamies that form the historical foundation of the contemporary political landscape—what Roger Epp (2008: 126) describes as "an almost willful amnesia about whatever might be divisive"—seem to make it unreceptive, even hostile to any sense of unsettlement, to expressions of difference, and to alternative nationalities in its midst. Taiaiake Alfred (2009: 181) laments that "the complete ignorance of Canadian society about the facts of their relationship with Indigenous peoples and the wilful denial of historical reality by Canadians detracts from the possibility of any meaningful discussion on true reconciliation."

Thus if reconciliation is predicated primarily on relationship—on the *dyadic*, in Nicholas Tavuchis's (1991) terms—then this merits an interrogation not only of the TRC's one-sided approach to reconciliation but also the limited purview over those elements of rupture in the relationship. In short, if there is something depoliticizing about limiting a TRC to individual talk therapy without the other side present, there is also something profoundly depoliticizing about structuring the conversation so that it tends only toward the personal experience of one historical controversy. It becomes less surprising, then, to find Aboriginal authors such as Alfred (2009: 181) so unrestrained in their criticism of our current notion of reconciliation: "I see reconciliation as an emasculating concept, weak-kneed and easily accepting of half-hearted measures of a notion of justice that does nothing to help Indigenous peoples regain their dignity and strength. One of my concerns in any discussion of reconciliation is finding ways to break its hold upon our consciousness so that we can move towards a true and lasting foundation for justice that will result in meaningful changes in the lives of Indigenous peoples and in the return of their lands."

Troubling the Performance of Reconciliation

Many authors express discomfort with the temporality implied by truth commissions and the language of the therapeutic. Truth commissions conflate process with product, their very being performatively declaring the transition that they are meant to bring about, and seek to "constitute a foreclosure on the past" (Green 2012: 130). In effect "the new national self is one which is forged in the suffering and violence of the past, but no element of that political past has entered into the present" (Wilson 2003: 370). Henderson and Wakeham (2009: 7) suggest that the tendency toward prematurely invoking resolution and reconciliation in Canadian politics has become chronic:

> The temporality and teleology of mourning and closure are not necessarily orientations to the past that should be carried into politics: they do not necessarily favour justice-seeking and the kind of profound political changes that national "reconciliation" could be made to mean, in a different model of time where history was acknowledged as persisting in the present. The problem at the level of relations between Indigenous and non-Indigenous institutions in Canada is not one of inadequate closure, as statements like the prime minister's 2008 apology might suggest, but one of repeated, pre-emptive attempts at reaching closure and "cure."

Such an issue again goes to the heart of what reconciliation can and should mean. According to Joanna Quinn (2009: 5), some in the field of transitional justice see reconciliation as "a process, or a series of actions that eventually lead to a conclusion," while others see it as "an end-point, the stage at which the relationship in question has been repaired." Both claims, however, still seem to harbor the notion of some sort of end point at which no liberal settler state can rightly claim to have arrived. Using the legal politics of Australia as his point of examination, and perhaps sensitive to the tendency of settler states to prematurely invoke closure and end point, Andrew Schaap (2004: 538) proposes what he calls an "agonistic reconciliation"—namely, one that "would be predicated on an awareness that community is always not yet. The end of political reconciliation, then, would not be to arrive at a common identity that could encompass former enemies. Rather, it would be to make available a space for politics within which citizens divided by the memories of past wrongs could debate and contest the terms of their political association." In short, academic commentators express misgivings over the settler state's "emerging and compelling desire to put the events of the past behind us" (IRSSA 2006), precisely because of what it elides and occludes.

A proper sense of temporality, though, will recognize that there was a road of dispossession and disempowerment that led to the residential school and that cannot be dissociated from it. That road follows the changing contours of what the colonizer called "the Indian problem," and the journey needs to be retraced. While any form of healing that does happen for survivors through the TRC's activities would be most welcome, isolating residential school harm and imbuing it with a profoundly individualizing therapeutic ethos does not build the entire path to reconciliation between Canada and Aboriginal peoples. The reticence and the slow change concerning territory and self-government—and especially the utter dissociation of these issues from the history of residential schooling—is a far cry from the confessional and epiphanic catharsis sometimes associated with truth commissions. Indeed one of the ultimate lessons to be drawn from the history of residential schooling is that Aboriginal demands surrounding the restoration of land and self-determination are not just lofty, begrudging demands of principle. They are thoroughly and gravely entwined precisely because being subjected to genocidal institutional arrangements such as the Indian residential schools represents, par excellence, the disempowerment, dispossession, and loss of self-determination of a people. Consequently the restoration of self-government likely represents one of the most assured forms of inoculation against the possible repetition of paternalistic, destructive arrangements such as the residential schooling experience.

Notes

My thanks to Claire Moon at the London School of Economics and Political Science for her time and insight, as well as to the Social Sciences and Humanities Research Council of Canada for funding this research both in Canada and the United Kingdom.

1. As a caveat, one must be wary of excessively tidy forms of periodization. Because of the expanse of North America and the time necessary to colonize from shore to shore, dispossession, removal of self-determination, and residential schooling do not occupy distinct and exclusive moments in Canadian history but rather overlap significantly. One need only look to the fact that the historical treaties that the British Crown saw as extinguishing Aboriginal title to land throughout much of Canada were signed from 1764 to 1930. Nevertheless it still stands that the disempowerment and depredations of colonization served to create the conditions of possibility for the social engineering of residential schooling.

2. George R., Proclamation, October 7, 1763 (3 Geo. III), reprinted in Revised Statutes of Canada 1985, App. II, No. 1.

3. Confederation for Canada was in 1867, and in order to open up the West for agricultural settlement treaties 1 through 7 were signed in quick succession from 1871 to 1877. Treaties 8 through 10, in northern regions less suitable for agriculture, were signed from the turn of the twentieth century through the 1920s.

4. John Borrows (1997: 164) cites the superintendent of Indian Affairs at the time of the Royal Proclamation of 1763, Sir William Johnson, as expressing his own doubts about the terms of a treaty shortly after he had treated with the same group at Niagara: "By the present Treaty I find, they make expressions of subjection, which must either have arisen from the ignorance of the Interpreter or from

some mistake; for I am well convinced, they never mean or intend anything like it."

5. The chiefs of the Haudenosaunee (Iroquois) Confederacy, who had been vocal since the nineteenth century about their sovereignty and independent governmental status, created a certain amount of anxiety in the Canadian government in the 1920s by sending a delegation to London and Geneva in order to make their case before the international community. Although they were unsuccessful, Duncan Campbell Scott, the deputy superintendent general of Indian Affairs, removed the confederacy council and had it replaced by one elected under the Indian Act. "Without prior notice to the chiefs, they were removed from office by an order-in-council," and the Royal Canadian Mounted Police "seized the wampum used to sanction council proceedings, and posted a proclamation on the doors of the council house" (Borrows and Rotman 2007: 39).

6. Governments in Canada also discontinued the treaty process before it was complete. This left large portions of British Columbia and the North claimed by the Crown without the benefit of treaty—not to mention large portions of the eastern third of the country whose earlier treaties were not land surrender agreements.

7. Relatedly Chrisjohn, Young, and Maraun (1997) reference Erving Goffman's concept of the total institution to examine the use of residential schooling in Aboriginal assimilation.

8. In the first class action of *Blackwater v. Plint* (1998), 52 B.C.I.R. (3d) 18, commenced by victims of sexual and physical abuse committed by the dormitory supervisor Arthur Henry Plint at the Alberni Indian Residential School, both the federal government and the United Church claimed that the other held sole vicarious liability for the actions of Plint. The trial judge apportioned 75 percent fault to the federal government and 25 percent to the United Church. While the United Church convinced the B.C. Court of Appeal that it should have charitable immunity for its status as a nonprofit organization doing good works, thereby passing all fault for damages to the government, the original apportionment of the trial judge was later upheld and reinstated by the Supreme Court of Canada.

9. *Blackwater v. Plint* (1998), 52 B.C.I.R. (3d) 18.

10. *Baxter v. Canada (Attorney General)* (2006), 83 O.R. (3d) 481 (O.S.C.J.) at para. 13.

11. Note the specific criteria set out in the IRSSA: students of residential schools that were funded either provincially or solely by a church organization are not eligible, just as students who attended Aboriginal day schools are not eligible.

12. *Blackwater v. Plint* [2005] 3 S.C.R. 3, 2005 SCC at para. 9.

References

Alfred, Taiaiake. 2009. "Restitution Is the Real Pathway to Justice for Indigenous Peoples." In *Response, Responsibility, and Renewal: Canada's Truth and Reconciliation Journey*, edited by Gregory Younging, Jonathan Dewar, and Mike DeGagne, 179–87. Ottawa: Aboriginal Healing Foundation.

Bauman, Zygmunt. 1989. *Modernity and the Holocaust*. Ithaca, NY: Cornell University Press.

Bauman, Zygmunt. 1991. *Modernity and Ambivalence*. Ithaca, NY: Cornell University Press.

Borrows, John. 1997. "Wampum at Niagara: The Royal Proclamation, Canadian Legal History, and Self-Government." In *Aboriginal and Treaty Rights in Canada: Essays on Law, Equity, and Respect for Difference*, edited by Michael Asch, 155–72. Vancouver: UBC Press.

Borrows, John, and Leonard Rotman. 2007. *Aboriginal Legal Issues: Cases, Materials and Commentary*. 3rd ed. Markham, Canada: LexisNexis.

Chrisjohn, Roland David, Sherri Lynn Young, and Michael Maraun. 1997. *The Circle Game: Shadows and Substance in the Indian Residential School Experience in Canada*. Penticton, Canada: Theytus Books.

Corntassel, Jeff, Chaw-win-is, and T'lakwadzi. 2009. "Indigenous Storytelling, Truth-telling, and Community Approaches to Reconciliation." *ESC: English Studies in Canada* 35 (1): 137–59.

Corntassel, Jeff, and Cindy Holder. 2008. "Who's Sorry Now? Government Apologies, Truth Commissions, and Indigenous Self-Determination in Australia, Canada, Guatemala, and Peru." *Human Rights Review* 9: 465–89.

Epp, Roger. 2008. *We Are All Treaty People: Prairie Essays*. Edmonton: University of Alberta Press.

Green, Robyn. 2012. "Unsettling Cures: Exploring the Limits of the Indian Residential School Settlement Agreement." *Canadian Journal of Law and Society* 27 (1): 129–48.

Hayner, Priscilla. 2002. *Unspeakable Truths: Facing the Challenges of Truth Commissions*. New York: Routledge.

Henderson, Jennifer, and Pauline Wakeham. 2009. "Colonial Reckoning, National Reconciliation? Aboriginal Peoples and the Culture of Redress in Canada." *ESC: English Studies in Canada* 35 (1): 1–26.

Hughes, Jula. 2012. "Instructive Past: Lessons from the Royal Commission on Aboriginal Peoples for the Canadian Truth and Reconciliation Commission on Indian Residential Schools." *Canadian Journal of Law and Society* 27 (1): 101–27.

Humphrey, Michael. 2003. "From Victim to Victimhood: Truth Commissions and Trials as Rituals of Political Transition and Individual Healing." *Australian Journal of Anthropology* 14 (2): 171–87.

IRSSA. 2006. "Schedule N—Mandate for the Truth and Reconciliation Commission." In *Indian Residential Schools Class Action Settlement*. Accessed August 9, 2012. http://www.residentialschoolsettlement.ca/settlement.html.

James, Matt. 2012. "A Carnival of Truth? Knowledge, Ignorance and the Canadian Truth and Reconciliation Commission." *International Journal of Transitional Justice* 6: 182–204.

Jung, Courtney. 2011. "Canada and the Legacy of the Indian Residential Schools: Transitional Justice for Indigenous People in a Nontransitional Society." In *Identities in Transition*, edited by Paige Arthur, 217–50. Oxford: Oxford University Press.

Llewellyn, Jennifer J. 2002. "Dealing with the Legacy of Native Residential School Abuse in Canada: Litigation, ADR, and Restorative Justice." *University of Toronto Law Journal* 53 (3): 253–300.

Martin, Keavy. 2009. "Truth, Reconciliation, and Amnesia: Porcupines and China Dolls and the Canadian Conscience." *ESC: English Studies in Canada* 35 (1): 47–65.

Miller, James R. 1996. *Shingwauk's Vision: A History of Native Residential Schools.* Toronto: University of Toronto Press.

Miller, James R. 2000. *Skyscrapers Hide the Heavens: A History of Indian-White Relations in Canada.* 3rd ed. Toronto: University of Toronto Press.

Miller, James R. 2007. *Compact, Contract, Covenant: Canada's Treaty-Making Tradition.* Saskatoon: St. Thomas More College.

Milloy, John S. 1999. *A National Crime: The Canadian Government and the Residential School System, 1879–1986.* Winnipeg: University of Manitoba Press.

Moon, Claire. 2009. "Healing Past Violence: Traumatic Assumptions and Therapeutic Interventions in War and Reconciliation." *Journal of Human Rights* 8 (1): 71–91.

Neu, Dean, and Cameron Graham. 2004. "Accounting and the Holocausts of Modernity." *Accounting, Auditing and Accountability Journal* 17 (4): 578–603.

Quinn, Joanna. 2009. Introduction to *Reconciliation(s)*, edited by Joanna Quinn, 3–13. Montreal: McGill-Queen's University Press.

Rigby, Andrew. 2001. *Justice and Reconciliation: After the Violence.* Boulder, CO: Lynne Rienner.

Rotman, Leonard. 1996. *Parallel Paths: Fiduciary Doctrine and the Crown-Native Relationship in Canada.* Toronto: University of Toronto Press.

Royal Commission on Aboriginal Peoples. 1996. *Report of the Royal Commission on Aboriginal Peoples.* Vol. 1: *Looking Forward, Looking Back.* Ottawa: Canada Communication Group.

Schaap, Andrew. 2004. "Political Reconciliation through a Struggle for Recognition?" *Social Legal Studies* 13 (4): 523–40.

Scott, James C. 1998. *Seeing Like a State: How Certain Schemes to Improve the Human Condition Have Failed.* New Haven, CT: Yale University Press.

Sprague, D. N. 1995. "Canada's Treaties with Aboriginal Peoples." *Manitoba Law Journal* 23: 341–51.

Stanton, Kim. 2011. "Canada's Truth and Reconciliation Commission: Settling the Past?" *The International Indigenous Policy Journal* 2 (3).

Tavuchis, Nicholas. 1991. *Mea Culpa: A Sociology of Apology and Reconciliation.* Palo Alto, CA: Stanford University Press.

Titley, Brian. 2011. *A Narrow Vision: Duncan Campbell Scott and the Administration of Indian Affairs in Canada.* Vancouver: UBC Press.

Walker, Julian. 2009. *The Indian Residential Schools Truth and Reconciliation Commission.* Ottawa: Parliamentary Information and Research Service, Library of Parliament.

White, Richard. 2011. *The Middle Ground: Indians, Empires, and Republics in the Great Lakes Region, 1650–1815.* 20th anniversary ed. Cambridge: Cambridge University Press.

Wicken, William. 1994. "The Mi'kmaq and Wuastukwiuk Treaties." *University of New Brunswick Law Journal* 43: 241–53.

Wilson, Richard. 2003. "Anthropological Studies of National Reconciliation Processes." *Anthropological Theory* 3 (3): 367–87.

PART III

TRANSFORMATIONS

CHAPTER 8

THE HABIT OF ELIMINATION

Indigenous Child Removal in Settler Colonial Nations

in the Twentieth Century

Margaret D. Jacobs

David and Louisa Rendon, a White Earth Chippewa couple from Minnesota, had moved to Texas for David's employment in the oil fields. After Louisa had suffered several stillbirths, the couple were overjoyed when she delivered a premature but healthy baby boy, Jason, in a Texas hospital in April 1974. But the Rendons' elation was short-lived; while Jason was still in the hospital, the Texas Welfare Department obtained a court order giving the state temporary custody of Jason on the grounds that Louisa "had personal habits which keep her outside the home" and that she "was not prepared for such child" because she had not yet bought a crib or diapers. The Welfare Department also deemed the child to be in a potentially dangerous situation because David, a migrant worker, was "gone from the home for periods of time." For months the Rendons tried to regain custody of Jason ("AAIA Reunited" 1975). Finally, in January 1975, with the help of Bertram Hirsch, an attorney with the Association on American Indian Affairs (AAIA), the Rendons had their day in the Menard County District Court. Hirsch pointed out the unprecedented nature of removing a newborn child before it had even gone home from the hospital on the basis that his parents "would *probably* neglect this child." The judge decided in the Rendons' favor, but he astonished Hirsch when he told him during a court recess, "I'm going to give this child back to the Rendons but I'm not going to do it for another thirty days," adding, "I don't care what they do with this child; they can barbecue the child, for all I care" (Hirsch interview with author, September 30, 2011).

The Rendons were just one of thousands of Indian families from the late 1950s through the 1970s who found themselves at the mercy of non-Indian social workers and judges, many of whom seemed to assume that Indian people were inherently unfit to raise their children. This notion had become so taken for granted within American society that by the late twentieth century Indian children were grossly overrepresented in state child welfare systems, and many were increasingly fostered and adopted by non-Indigenous families. Unbeknownst to most of these Indian families, in the 1960s and 1970s the removal of Indigenous children reached equally epidemic proportions in Canada and Australia. Indigenous child removal had grown to be so naturalized in these three nations that it became a matter of common sense, a *habit* that was rarely challenged by state authorities, concerned non-Indigenous citizens, or even, initially, the Indigenous people who experienced child removal.[1] By comparing Indigenous child removal in the United States, Canada, and Australia—all settler colonial nations—and offering the United States as a case study, this essay seeks to understand how this "habit of elimination," to build off Patrick Wolfe's concept of the "logic of elimination," became ingrained in such nations in the twentieth century. Interestingly much of the impetus for Indigenous child removal derived from humanitarian efforts in the nineteenth century and liberalism in the late twentieth century. Increasingly complex bureaucracies in the late post–World War II era institutionalized the logic of elimination, turning it into a habit that was difficult to identify, let alone to break. Thus a practice linked to genocide could become accepted and even lionized as a gesture of liberal beneficence.

The Crisis in Indigenous Child Welfare, 1950s–1970s

By the late 1960s the numbers of Indian children removed from their homes had climbed so dramatically that a full-fledged Indian child welfare crisis had developed. In two state-by-state surveys conducted in 1968 and 1974, the AAIA found that in states with large Indian populations, an average of 25 to 35 percent of Indian children had been removed from their families and tribal communities and that Indian children were vastly overrepresented in the child welfare system. In South Dakota, for example, the per capita foster care rate for Indian children was twenty-two times higher than for non-Indian children (Association on American Indian Affairs 1977: 592–93).

At the same time, over the northern border of the United States and across the Pacific Ocean, Indigenous children in two other nations experienced a similar crisis. Although First Nations people made up just 3.5 percent of the population in Canada, they represented 20 percent of the total number of children in care in the late 1970s. In the western provinces the figures were much higher: 60 percent in Manitoba, for example (Hepworth 1980: 111–15). In Western Australia in 1963 Aboriginal children represented just 6 percent of the children in the care of the Child Welfare Department, but by 1972 they made up over 20 percent of departmental wards (Haebich 2008: 252).

What can we make of the fact that this became such a widespread phenomenon in these three nations in the second half of the twentieth century? Were these humanitarian interventions to uphold "the best interests of the child," as social workers asserted, or were these egregious human rights violations and acts of "cultural genocide," as many Indigenous activists claimed? A comparative historical approach may help to answer these troubling questions.

Indigenous Child Removal and the Logic of Elimination in Settler Colonial Societies

Each of these nations originated as a British settler colony, and all eventually turned to Indigenous child removal as a strategy of "elimination." In his now classic 2001 essay, Wolfe theorized that a "logic of elimination" governed the ideologies, racial categories, policies, and actions of settler colonial societies. Seeking to appropriate Indigenous land, such societies simultaneously aimed to dispossess and eradicate Indigenous people and to replace them with a settler population. Settler colonial authorities not only utilized violence and the imposition of new legal regimes and economic systems, but they also involuntarily removed Indigenous children as a means of erasing Indigenous identities and claims to land. As Wolfe and other settler colonial scholars have pointed out, settler colonialism differs substantively from other forms of colonialism, which by contrast have been interested in mobilizing the labor of, and thus maximizing, the local population to carry out extractive enterprises (Wolfe 2001; Veracini 2010).

The late twentieth-century removal of Indigenous children by these three nations was not new; agents of the state had been removing children since at least the late nineteenth century. Up to World War II, however, most removals had been to either boarding or residential schools (in the United States and Canada) or to "homes" and institutions set aside for Aboriginal children in Australia (Jacobs 2009). Increasingly, by the 1960s all three nations promoted the fostering and adoption of Indigenous children in non-Indigenous families instead of or in addition to institutionalization.

At the same time, in the 1950s and 1960s all three nations designed and sought to implement official policies to extinguish Indigenous land claims and to eradicate the distinctive status and identities of Indigenous peoples: termination and urban relocation in the United States, and assimilation and integration in Australia and Canada (Fixico 1990; Miller 2000: 325–35; Haebich 2008). Seen in this larger context, the widespread practice of Indigenous fostering and adoption appears to be another facet of an ongoing settler colonial policy bent on eliminating any vestiges of Indigenous sovereignty. Some Indigenous observers made such linkages between family destruction and Indigenous elimination explicit. Jeannette Goodhouse of the Devils Lake (now Spirit Lake) Sioux, for example, told a reporter that she feared the placing of Indian children in white homes was part of a plan for the "slow termination" of the tribe.[2]

Carried out over several generations and affecting about a quarter to a third of Indigenous children by the 1970s, child removal appears to qualify as an act of genocide according to the United Nations (1948) Convention on the Prevention and Punishment of the Crime of Genocide. Article II of the Convention includes in its definition of genocide "the forcible transfer of children" from one group to another if done with "a commitment to destroy, in whole or in part, a national, ethnical, racial, or religious group." Certainly many Indigenous activists believed these practices to be genocidal. In Australia attendees at the 1979 If Everyone Cared—Aboriginal Child Survival conference recommended that the Aboriginal Legal Services "put a case before the International Court of Justice seeking an injunction and conscionable damages against State Governments whose policies and practices in the past and at present amount to social, cultural and physical genocide of Aboriginal families, especially with regard to wholesale removal of Aboriginal children from their natural family and kin group."[3] American Indians in Minnesota similarly contended that "the entire practice of foster placement is a disguise for further humiliation, destruction of family life, assimilation of a people and the ultimate genocide of the American Indian."[4]

Scholars have been more divided on whether settler colonial societies possessed a genocidal intent, a "commitment to destroy," Indigenous peoples through child removal (Moses 2004; Regan 2010). Russell McGregor (2004: 290–311) argues that the removal of Aboriginal children for the purposes of "breeding out the colour" by some Australian states *prior* to World War II amounted to genocide in that it rested on intentionally "imposing measures intended to prevent births within the group," Article II(d) of the UN Genocide Convention. However, McGregor asserts that after World War II government officials removed children with the purpose of incorporating Aboriginal people into the nation through cultural assimilation, and he argues forcefully that this did not amount to genocide. Wolfe (2008) disagrees with McGregor that postwar Aboriginal assimilation was cultural as opposed to biological and therefore not genocidal. Regarding as "untenable" the assumption that culture and biology are discrete categories, Wolfe argues that child removal leads to both biological destruction—in preventing births to the group—and cultural devastation. Wolfe, however, is reluctant to use the term *genocide* to describe child removal. Instead he prefers to use settler colonialism, with its "logic of elimination," as a theoretical framework because it "is a specific social formation and it is desirable to retain that specificity" (119).

This essay follows and extends Wolfe's arguments. While acknowledging the productive intersection between settler colonialism and colonial genocide as theoretical models, I agree with Wolfe that settler colonialism offers a more precise framework for analyzing the policies and practices carried out against Indigenous peoples in the process of colonization. In particular I argue that by the second half of the twentieth century modern bureaucracies that expanded to manage Indigenous populations had become a defining feature of settler colonial nations, and it was these complex state organisms that transformed a logic into a habit of elimination (Shewell 2004).[5] Questions of intent become particularly difficult to trace in the byzantine state apparatuses that carried out Indigenous child removal. In the postwar era governments rarely designated one all-powerful individual or board to articulate an intended policy of elimination; more often they empowered numerous bureaucracies—divided among federal and state or provincial jurisdictions and sometimes between public and private agencies—that developed their own self-perpetuating logic of elimination. In a seemingly never-ending loop, this logic led to a habitual pattern of response, which in turn reinforced the commonsense set of assumptions that underlay policies and practices.

Thus rather than becoming entangled in definitional debates about genocide, this paper considers how such a detrimental practice with genocidal outcomes, if not conscious or stated intent, could have become so commonplace in these three settler colonial nations in the twentieth century. In fact just a few decades after the UN Convention was signed, authorities in these three nations did not recognize or acknowledge their practices regarding Indigenous children as genocidal in any way. Instead they touted them as compassionate gestures toward the benighted remnants of Indigenous peoples in their midst. By detailing the naturalization of Indian child removal in the United States, I offer a case study of how a settler colonial nation established and maintained a *habit* of elimination.

Developing the Habit of Elimination in the Late Nineteenth Century

Establishing the habit of elimination in these settler colonial societies required making the practice of Indigenous child removal seem to be a matter of common sense. At first, however, early efforts to remove and institutionalize Indigenous children appeared to be at odds with other social practices and required significant justification. Affluent members of British settler societies often sent their children to boarding schools as a means of training them for elite occupations. By contrast state officials designed institutions for Indigenous children for two main purposes: to break their ties of affiliation with their Indigenous communities so that they no longer could claim land or resources and to assimilate them into the colonial society just to the extent that they could fill unskilled labor needs and no longer require government assistance (Jacobs 2009: 25–86).

State authorities in Britain and its colonies had routinely removed and institutionalized one group of white children: those of poor parents, especially single mothers, who could not adequately support them. However, by the late nineteenth century two trends had reduced the numbers of poor children who were removed from their families in all of these nations. State agencies now required a court order to remove children deemed to be neglected, abused, or delinquent, and social reformers now regarded institutionalization as inhumane and agitated instead for the return of children to their families or their placement within family-like settings (Tiffin 1982: 18, 38–39, 66–69; Platt 1969; Swain and Hillel 2010; van Krieken 1991). However, just as these state entities were more carefully regulating the removal of poor white children, they now articulated and engaged in policies involving the widespread removal and institutionalization of Indigenous children, a policy that was not carried out against any other specific group of "minority" children (Haebich 2000; Miller 1996; Milloy 2001; Strong-Boag 2006: 22–23).

Furthermore removal was an unprecedented and draconian measure that sparked intense resistance from Indigenous peoples and incurred great expense on the part of states to build and maintain institutions as well as enforce the removal of Indigenous children. In the late nineteenth and early twentieth century, for example, the Bureau of Indian Affairs (BIA) expended untold efforts and funds to force both the Hopi and the Navajo to send their children to distant boarding schools (Jacobs 2004). Initially therefore Indigenous child removal represented a new and unprecedented colonial strategy.

Naturalizing Indigenous Child Removal—Part I

U.S. authorities justified such effort and expense in part by claiming that removal represented a humanitarian act of rescuing Indigenous children from a backward and deprived life. Commissioner of Indian Affairs Thomas Morgan (1896: 402–3) asserted, for example, that Indian babies, as compared to other American babies, were born as "alien[s], . . . shut off from opportunity, predetermined to degradation." While many nineteenth-century Americans shared Morgan's view of Indian reservations as backward and primitive places, few initially held his view that it was thus necessary to remove Indian children or to educate them. To further their case, reformers and authorities appealed not only to humanitarianism but to fears that if Indian children were not removed and reeducated, they would be "a perpetual menace to our western civilization" and a financial burden to boot (408). By 1902, in a well-organized campaign, reformers and their BIA allies had convinced Congress to fund Indian child removal and a system of 154 boarding schools (Adams 1995: 57–58; DeJong 1993: 107–9; Adams 1946: 57). Not until 1934 and the passage of the Indian Reorganization Act under John Collier's term as commissioner of Indian Affairs did the government question the wisdom of boarding schools and instead establish more day schools in Indian communities and give federal aid to states that enrolled Indians in public schools (Fuchs and Havighurst 1972: 12, 227; Philp 1977; Kelly 1983). Thus removal to and confinement within a boarding school became a common American Indian coming-of-age experience.

Indeed the practice became naturalized in many American Indian communities. For example, Navajo families, who initially were among the most resistant to the Indian boarding schools, by the mid-twentieth century were voluntarily sending thousands of children to these institutions. Some even opposed Collier's plans to open more day schools (Iverson 1981: 40–41; 2002: 172–76). This was due to several factors: opposition to Collier's heavy-handed sheep reduction policy; financial hardship that led to families using the schools as a form of economic relief; a belief that such schooling would lead to social mobility for their children; and the federal government's failure to establish enough day schools on the reservation. So "commonsense" had boarding schools become that many Navajo people in the postwar era came to prefer them to day schools. Dr. Robert Bergman, who in 1969 became the first director of Indian Health Services' Mental Health Branch, declared in 1974 that if a referendum were held on the Navajo reservation about whether to keep boarding schools open, 80 percent would be in favor. He explained, "Every parent today went to boarding school. . . . There are a lot of people among Navajo parents who think that being taught and putting up with all that was good for them." As a mental health professional, Bergman thought boarding schools were "a menace to the healthy development of children," but he realized that to Navajo parents, "to admit that it was bad for you is a little disconcerting. One doesn't want to be told that one's education was highly faulty."[6] The very act of removing children to boarding schools during the "latency period in child development, when behavior is internalized and a 'conscience' is developed," as one social scientist in the 1970s put it, ensured that as these children grew up and had children of their own they would regard removal and institutionalization as normal (Topper 1977: 49).

Just as intended, then, the practice of removal ruptured the intergenerational transmission of cultural knowledge in the United States and other settler colony nations. As Lavina White and Eva Jacobs (1992: 18–19), Indigenous members of a legislative review panel in British Columbia, explain, "The system of residential schools [in Canada] . . . resulted in large numbers of our children not being raised in situations where the traditional responsibilities could be passed down to them." Thus First Nations children did not learn basic parenting practices, and Indigenous "co-operative and supportive child care practices were replaced by authoritarian practices based on punishment and coercion" (22). Indigenous child removal thus became a self-perpetuating habit that would take enormous struggle to break.

The Government Crisis in Child Removal—The High Price of Institutional Care

Curiously, though, in the post–World War II era, as many American Indian people had become habituated to the boarding schools, they now fell out of favor with the U.S. government. As part of the new federal termination policy, the BIA sought to close many of the federal boarding schools and to transfer authority for the care of Indian children to the states. The states soon faced financial difficulties in paying for the costs of caring for Indian children who had been separated from their families. For example, when the federal government closed Pipestone Boarding School in Minnesota in 1953, the state suddenly had to pick up the cost of caring for many Indian children whose care had been provided by the BIA. Asking Congress to appropriate more funds, the Minnesota Department of Public Welfare argued that they were saving the government money; they calculated that the cost of supporting a child in the Pipestone Boarding School was about $750 per year per child, whereas the cost of supporting an Indian child in foster care was just $468.63 in 1956.[7] Later Minnesota and many other states contracted with the BIA to provide foster care for Indian children (Indian Child Welfare Program 1975: 195–203). However, federal efforts to transfer social services for Indian children to the states were never complete and resulted in additional layers of bureaucracy and complex jurisdictional disputes (Atwood 2010).

Even as they continued to follow the habit of elimination, then, state authorities denaturalized boarding schools for Indian children. Ironically they deflected attention away from the origins of the schools as a coercive state practice and transformed them into an Indigenous "tradition." In Minnesota the Department of Public Welfare recounted the story of "Chuck." After her husband insisted that Chuck was not his son, Chuck's mother allegedly asked the county welfare board to find a good home for her child. "Had Chuck been born several years earlier," department officials wrote, "his mother, *following what had been the long tradition of her people,* undoubtedly would have wanted Chuck to grow up in an Indian school."[8] Willfully ignorant of the origins of the boarding schools just a few generations before, department officials obscured their eliminating aims and turned them into an Indian "tradition."

Moreover just as they disparaged other Indian traditions, now many authorities condemned Indian boarding schools and extolled fostering and adoption as a more humane alternative for removed Indian children. If Chuck had been placed in an Indian boarding school, welfare authorities asserted, he "would have grown up with no experience in family living and no family to turn to in those moments when all of us . . . need to belong to someone." Institutional placement of children had long been out of favor for non-Indian children; now welfare workers argued that a home placement was also better for Indian children like Chuck. Thus the county welfare board initially placed Chuck with a foster family and then, supposedly with the consent of Chuck's mother, in a permanent adoptive home.[9]

The Indian Adoption Project: Privatizing the Care of Indigenous Children

If fostering Indian children proved cheaper than institutionalization, adoption provided the ultimate fiscal solution for states and the federal government, which now shared responsibility for Indian children. David Fanshel (1972: 340), who conducted a study of ninety-seven non-Indian families who adopted Indian children, characterized adoption as a money saver for the federal government: "From the perspective of society at large, the adoption of children who are destined to spend all of their childhood years in foster care or in Indian boarding schools provides a substantial financial saving. . . . The savings per [Indian] child would . . . come close to $100,000. . . . If one were to apply the approach of cost-benefit analysis to the adoption phenomenon, such data would be seen as highly significant."[10] As Fanshel's comments make clear, bureaucratic concerns often underlay the "best interests of the child." Moreover his remarks reveal that the separation of Indian children from their families had become so habitual that social scientists and bureaucrats considered only three options for their care—boarding schools, fostering, or adoption—not the cost of preventing Indian family breakups altogether.

Such cost-benefit analyses and bureaucratic logic came into play with the advent of the Indian Adoption Project (IAP), for which the BIA contracted with the premier children's welfare organization in the United States, the Child Welfare League of America, which served as an umbrella group for hundreds of child welfare and placement agencies around the country. From its inception in 1958 until it became subsumed into the Adoption Resource

Exchange of North America (ARENA) in 1968, the IAP placed 395 Indian children out of state in non-Indian homes.[11] Until the passage of the Indian Child Welfare Act in 1978, ARENA placed 323 more Indian children up for adoption, many of them from Canada, primarily with non-Indian families.[12]

Although these numbers seem small, the IAP additionally worked to increase the numbers of Indian children that state agencies placed with non-Indian families within their states.[13] Moreover IAP director Arnold Lyslo became involved in a number of bureaucratic maneuvers to make Indian children more readily available for adoption by decreasing tribal jurisdiction over child welfare, increasing state control over Indian children, and easing any legal obstacles to the free circulation of these children on the adoption market.[14] In 1968 Lyslo claimed that he had referred well over five thousand prospective adoptive families for Indian children to state agencies.[15] Other settler colonial nations made similar strenuous efforts to promote the adoption of Indian children. In Saskatchewan, for example, the provincial government launched the Adopt Indian Métis (AIM) program, apparently with no knowledge that a few hundred miles to the south, the American Indian Movement, using the same acronym, had quite a different connotation (Strong-Boag 2006: 152–53). Australia had no long-term programs, but many states made periodic efforts to place large numbers of Aboriginal children with white families, as for example in 1955, when the New South Wales Aborigines Welfare Board "launched a drive" to find homes for 150 Aboriginal children in its care, ranging from "babes in arms to boys and girls in their teens."[16]

Naturalizing Child Removal—Part II

Just as the removal and institutionalization of Indigenous children had once been unusual in the late nineteenth century, now, in the postwar era, the new emphasis on placing Indigenous children within non-Indigenous families was unprecedented and required a new round of naturalization. In the 1940s and early 1950s transracial fostering and adoption was neither common nor encouraged in any of these four nations. Adoption agencies practiced racial matching, trying their best to place children with adoptive families of the same racial background (Herman 2008: 121–54; Melosh 2002: 51–104; Strong-Boag 2006: 109; Balcom 2011: 196–97; Marshall and McDonald 2001; Briggs 2012).

Several factors emerged in the late 1950s and beyond to make the adoption of Indigenous children seem natural rather than aberrant. For one, more white families became interested in adopting transracially in the 1960s and 1970s due to the allegedly dwindling supply of "blue-ribbon babies," that is, white children, who were available for adoption. Between 1945 and the 1970s rates of unwed motherhood had risen in all four nations, as had social pressures on young single mothers to relinquish their babies for adoption. Between 1945 and 1973 unwed mothers in the United States, most of them white, middle-class teenagers, surrendered an estimated one and a half million babies for nonfamily adoptions. In the late 1960s and 1970s, however, as birth control options became more readily available, abortion was legalized, and women found more opportunities to financially support themselves, the stigma attached to unwed motherhood dissipated somewhat, and fewer young unwed white mothers were putting their babies up for adoption. Thus demand grew for "other" babies (Fessler 2006; Solinger 1994; Strong-Boag 2006: 86; Marshall and McDonald 2001: 11, 32, 39).[17]

In addition the fostering and adoption of Indigenous children may have become more popular due to the ascendancy of a liberal ideology that championed racial egalitarianism and colorblindness. In this climate social workers and many state agencies justified their increased removal of Indigenous children as a means of providing equitable services to Indigenous children. A Saskatchewan report in 1964–65 declared, for instance, that "The 32.3 per cent of children in care who are of Métis or Indian extraction have proven they are no different from the other 67.7 per cent, except for the colour of their skin. All children have one common denominator, they need secure homes. These children are being denied that basic human right" (quoted in Strong-Boag 2006: 152–53). In Australia Paul Hasluck, looking back on his term as minister for territories from 1951 to 1963, wrote, "We rejected the idea that race . . . made any difference between human beings. We tried to think of the Aborigines as we thought of ourselves, not as another race but as fellow Australians" (quoted in Haebich 2008: 195–96). In 1961 this led him to propose, paradoxically, that "half-caste children found living in camps of full-blood natives . . . should, if possible, be removed to better care so that they have a better opportunity for education" and an "opportunity to advance in status" (207).

A similar type of "color-blind liberalism" prevailed in the United States (Horton 2005; Bonilla-Silva 2003). Dorothy Buzawa, head of the IAP under ARENA in the 1970s, asserted that the project "is concerned in breaking down all the barriers that prevent children from being placed in a permanent home in the United States" (Indian Child Welfare Act 1981: 142). In this context the IAP and many state and private agencies portrayed the adoption of an Indigenous child by a white family as an act of liberal enlightenment. Thus they encouraged non-Indigenous families to become individual agents of racial integration, and many well-meaning progressive families took up the banner of racial equality. A defender of adoptive placements of Indian children in white families declared, "We *cannot* point with pride to the results of government policies during the past 150 years; in fact we should be ashamed of the way Indians have been treated. It seems to me that this present-day trend towards person-to-person assistance should be encouraged" (Indian Child Welfare Act 1977: 493). Thus Indigenous child removal became not only a habit but a liberal ideal.

Promoting the fostering and adoption of Indigenous children also rested on the creation of ubiquitous images of Indian communities as hopelessly mired in cycles of poverty and deprivation, as places unfit to raise children. Mary Davis (1961: 15) of the Children's Bureau of Delaware, one of the agencies that worked with the IAP, provided a typical comment: "I have the sense that for many Indians living on a reservation, there is a dead-end quality and a humdrumness to their existence which transcends any ability or wish to accomplish or achieve." Narratives of Indian deprivation—usually studded with grim statistics on infant mortality, low life expectancy, unemployment, suicide rates, and low income—had become dominant in the 1950s, overshadowing the popular representations of Indian life and culture prior to World War II that, while romantic, at least attempted to provide a holistic view of Indian societies and did not reduce Indians to passive victims (Jenkins 2004: 65–153; Jacobs 1999: 56–105).

To this increasingly dominant narrative Lyslo added a special twist, the notion that Indian children were "forgotten" children, abandoned and neglected by their dysfunctional families and in need of rescue by white middle-class families. "During the past decade there have been many programs designed to promote the adoption of all children—the handicapped child, the child in the older age group, children of other racial groups both within the United States and from foreign lands," Lyslo wrote in 1960. "But the Indian child has remained the 'forgotten child,' left unloved and uncared for on the reservation, without a home or parents he can call his own."[18] Interestingly Lyslo avoided a direct indictment of Indian families, instead relying on a passive voice sentence construction to more subtly convey the unfitness of Indian families (Jacobs 2013).

Although Lyslo portrayed the IAP as simply responding to public interest in filling a need to adopt Indian children, he carefully cultivated this demand by relentlessly promoting this message. He published a number of articles in *Child Welfare*, a journal primarily for social workers, to encourage them to inform prospective adoptive parents of the availability of Indian children (Lyslo 1960, 1961). Moreover he was successful in attaining national mainstream coverage of his program. In both 1965 and 1966 *Good Housekeeping*

ran articles on the fostering and adoption of Indian children, including Ar-
lene Silberman's "My 45 Indian Godchildren."[19] As a result of the publicity
he generated in 1966, Lyslo reported that he received 1,200 inquiries regarding
the adoption of Indian children in 1967.[20]

It was this type of publicity regarding Indian adoption that was most responsible for naturalizing Indian child removal. Lyslo was so effective that
he could convey this message and make Indian adoption seem commonsense
with minimal visual cues. In an article he wrote for *Catholic Charities*, Lyslo (1964: 13) included a photograph of an adorable Indian toddler, happily
frolicking on a stretch of sand, with the caption "Dead end—or a chance?"
So naturalized was the idea that Indian children were better off removed
from their families and raised among non-Indians that Lyslo and other state
officials could invoke the habit of elimination in such a brief, culturally coded
ad-like image.

The Shame of Indigenous Child Removal

Yet Indigenous child removal did not become a habit simply through the practices of non-Indigenous state agents. The nature of this practice also meant
that it became taken for granted among Indigenous people too. When she was
a child Valancia Thacker, chairwoman of the Campo Reservation in southern California, remembered the welfare worker "coming and taking some
of my cousins and friends. I didn't know why and I didn't question it. It was
just done and it had always been done" (Task Force Four 1976: 78). I raise
this issue not in any way to blame the victim but simply to inquire into the
painful ways Indigenous child removal became so habitual. To some extent
many Indian women who experienced the removal of their children believed
it to be their own personal failing. When he began his work defending Indian families against child removal, AAIA attorney Hirsch recalls, "[Indian]
people thought, 'This is my problem.' They didn't know that the family ... a
mile down the road or over the next butte ... was experiencing the same thing.
Everybody feeling shame about it and not talking about it. They thought it
was their own personal circumstance. ... So ... people kind of kept it to themselves and they did not seek out assistance from their own tribes" (Hirsch
interview 2011). In cultures where children were so revered and child raising
was carefully prescribed within each cosmology, the loss of one's children to
state authorities on charges of unfitness or neglect was not only a traumatic
event; it was a shameful stigma (Anderson 2000).

Moreover families who lost children doubted they could do anything
about it, believing the government all-powerful. This extended even to some

tribal officials. The AAIA commonly cited the case of an Indian tribal court judge on a reservation on the Great Plains who had approved the removal and foster or adoptive care placement of a large percentage of her reservation's children. When the AAIA appealed a case before her and pointed out that she could reverse her earlier decision, "she looked thunderstruck, broke into tears and said, 'I have signed papers for a hundred Indian children to be taken off this reservation. I did not know that I had the power to say no. I thought that my job was to certify the papers of the county welfare agency. I would not have placed one of those children off this reservation.'" The judge promptly quit ("'I Would Not'" 1974).[21] Because the habit of elimination was so entrenched even among Indigenous people, it would take enormous courage and effort to recognize and then break the habit of elimination.

In the late 1960s and early 1970s, in a climate of greater activism for Indigenous rights and movements for self-determination, Indigenous grassroots activists, many of them women who had been affected by these policies and who worked to provide social services to their communities, broke their silence and challenged the long habit of Indigenous child removal. By the late 1970s and early 1980s their efforts had come to fruition with the Indian Child Welfare Act in the United States, the application of the Aboriginal Child Placement Principle in many Australian states, and the negotiation of agreements between bands and provincial governments in Canada. Still, however, a century of child removal haunts each settler colonial nation, which has led both Canada and Australia to establish official inquiries into the residential schools and the Stolen Generations, respectively, to issue formal apologies, and to conduct an ongoing truth and reconciliation process in Canada.

A comparative approach enables us to see the overrepresentation of Indigenous children in the child welfare systems of these four nations in the late twentieth century not as a result of Indigenous failings or as a clash of cultures but as part of a series of concerted policies by state agents that were built on the logic of elimination. Justified as humanitarian and benevolent and institutionalized within modern, postwar bureaucracies, these policies became self-perpetuating, commonsense, and habitual. Thus a practice that has been identified as one means of carrying out genocide could be carried out with impunity for many decades and has only recently commanded serious soul-searching on the part of settler colonial nations.

Notes

1. I borrow the concept of common sense in part from Burke (1996: 9), who, following Antonio Gramsci, defines *common sense* as "a manufactured artifact consisting of dicta lodged in public memory of a given society that everyone 'knows' to be true, dicta that act to reproduce relations of domination as natural relations, thus serving the interests of ruling classes."

2. David Jordan, "Indians Battle to Keep Foster Children on Reservation," *Minneapolis Tribune*, July 28, 1968, clipping, Box 390, Folder 2, Association of American Indian Affairs (AAIA) Records.

3. "ACCA News, Views, Etc.," ca. 1979, Box 67, Folder 1, AAIA Records, 9.

4. "Indian Child Welfare Crisis," n.d., Box 248, Folder 4, AAIA Records, 10.

5. Shewell (2004: 23) argues that after World War II Canada developed an increasingly complex organization for its Branch of Indian Affairs, "which gradually mirrored the institutions of the modern state." Moreover "as professional expertise within the branch grew, holistic approaches to the Indian 'problem' became less and less possible as each area claimed its own special knowledge" (207).

6. Proceedings, Indian Child Welfare and Family Services Conference, AAIA, January 26, 1974, Biltmore Hotel, New York, Box 365, Folder 4, AAIA Records, 39, 40. For Bergman's "menace" quote, see Swenson, 1977: 62.

7. "Minnesota Legislative Interim Committee on Indian Affairs, Statement Prepared for Senate Committee on Organization for Department of Interior," March 1957, Box 120, Folder: "Indian Committee, 1957–1964, Child Welfare Services—Indian children," 3, United Way of Minnesota papers.

8. Department of Public Welfare, "Child Welfare Services—Indian Children," March 15, 1957, Box 120, Folder: "Indian Committee, 1957–1964, Child Welfare Services—Indian children," 3 (my emphasis), United Way of Minnesota papers.

9. Department of Public Welfare, "Child Welfare Services—Indian Children," 3.

10. For the use of such cost-benefit analysis as a "soft" technology of genocide, see Neu and Therrien 2003.

11. Arnold Lyslo, "The Indian Adoption Project, 1958–1967," Report, April 1, 1968, Box 17, Folder 4, Child Welfare League of America (CWLA) papers.

12. Barbara Lewis Roberts, "Indian Adoption Project Annual Report 1972," Box 17, Folder 4; Box 89, Folders: ARENA News, 1968–75 and ARENA News, 1977–79, CWLA papers. See also Balcom 2011: 212.

13. Arnold Lyslo, "Progress Report of the IAP," May 14, 1963, Box 17, Folder 4, CWLA papers.

14. Lyslo, "The Indian Adoption Project, 1958–1967," 9; Joseph Reid to Philleo Nash, CIA, May 7, 1963, Box 17, Folder 4, CWLA papers.

15. Lyslo, "The Indian Adoption Project, 1958–1967," 6, 7.

16. "Homes Wanted for 150 Young Aborigines: Policy to Assimilate," *Sun-Herald* (Sydney), November 20, 1955, Box 13/5, Press Cuttings, Children 1952–58, Council for Aboriginal Rights papers.

17. Briggs (2012) argues that there was always a shortage of "blue-ribbon babies" to adopt.

18. "Indian Adoption Project," April 1960, 1, Box 17, Folder 3, CWLA papers.
19. Arnold Lyslo, "1966 Year End Summary of the IAP," March 15, 1967, Box 17, Folder 4, CWLA papers.
20. Lyslo, "1966 Year End Summary of the IAP."
21. See also AAIA, "Indian Family Defense Legal Services Program," Proposal to the Lilly Endowment, n.d. (ca. 1975), Box 365, Folder 1, AAIA Records, 3.

References

UNPUBLISHED SOURCES

Association on American Indian Affairs Records. 1851–2010. Public Policy Papers, Department of Rare Books and Special Collections, Princeton University Library.
Child Welfare League of America papers, Social Welfare History Archives, Special Collections, University of Minnesota, Minneapolis.
Council for Aboriginal Rights papers. State Library of Victoria, Melbourne, Australia.
United Way of Minnesota papers. Social Welfare Archives, Special Collections, University of Minnesota, Minneapolis.

PUBLISHED SOURCES

"AAIA Reunited Five Indian Families." 1975. *Indian Family Defense* [bulletin of the Association on American Indian Affairs], no. 3 (May): 7.
Adams, David Wallace. 1995. *Education for Extinction: American Indians and the Boarding School Experience, 1875–1928*. Lawrence: University Press of Kansas.
Adams, Evelyn. 1946. *American Indian Education: Government Schools and Economic Progress*. Morningside Heights, NY: King's Crown Press.
Anderson, Kim. 2000. *A Recognition of Being: Reconstructing Native Womanhood*. Toronto: Second Story Press.
Association on American Indian Affairs. 1977. Indian Child Welfare Statistical Survey, July 1976. Appendix G in Indian Child Welfare Act of 1977, Hearing before the U.S. Senate Select Committee on Indian Affairs. 95th Congress, 1st Session, S. 1214. Washington, DC: Government Printing Office.
Atwood, Barbara Ann. 2010. *Children, Tribes, and States: Adoption and Custody Conflicts over American Indian Children*. Durham, NC: Carolina Academic Press.
Balcom, Karen. 2011. *The Traffic in Babies: Cross-Border Adoption and Baby-Selling between the United States and Canada, 1930–1972*. Toronto: University of Toronto Press.
Bonilla-Silva, Eduardo. 2003. *Racism without Racists: Color-Blind Racism and the Persistence of Racial Inequality in the United States*. New York: Rowman and Littlefield.
Briggs, Laura. 2012. *Somebody's Children: The Politics of Transracial and Transnational Adoption*. Durham, NC: Duke University Press.
Burke, Timothy. 1996. *Lifebuoy Men, Lux Women: Commodification, Consumption, and Cleanliness in Modern Zimbabwe*. Durham, NC: Duke University Press.
Davis, Mary. 1961. "One Agency's Approach to the Indian Adoption Project." *Child Welfare* (June): 12–15.

DeJong, David. 1993. *Promises of the Past: A History of Indian Education in the United States*. Golden, CO: Fulcrum Publishing.

Fanshel, David. 1972. *Far from the Reservation: The Transracial Adoption of American Indian Children*. Metuchen, NJ: Scarecrow Press.

Fessler, Ann. 2006. *The Girls Who Went Away: The Hidden History of Women Who Surrendered Children for Adoption in the Decades before* Roe v. Wade. New York: Penguin.

Fixico, Donald. 1990. *Termination and Relocation: Federal Indian Policy, 1945–1960*. Albuquerque: University of New Mexico Press.

Fuchs, Estelle, and Robert J. Havighurst. 1972. *To Live on This Earth: American Indian Education*. Albuquerque: University of New Mexico Press.

Haebich, Anna. 2000. *Broken Circles: Fragmenting Indigenous Families, 1800–2000*. Fremantle, Australia: Fremantle.

Haebich, Anna. 2008. *Spinning the Dream: Assimilation in Australia, 1950–1970*. Fremantle, Australia: Fremantle.

Hepworth, H. Philip. 1980. *Foster Care and Adoption in Canada*. Ottawa: Canadian Council on Social Development.

Herman, Ellen. 2008. *Kinship by Design: A History of Adoption in the Modern United States*. Chicago: University of Chicago Press.

Horton, Carol A. 2005. *Race and the Making of American Liberalism*. New York: Oxford University Press.

"I Would Not Have Placed One of Those Children off the Reservation." 1974. *Indian Family Defense* [bulletin of the Association on American Indian Affairs], no. 1 (winter): 3.

Indian Child Welfare Program. 1975. Hearings before the Subcommittee on Indian Affairs of the Committee on Interior and Insular Affairs. U.S. Senate, 93rd Congress, 2nd Session on "Problems that American Indian Families Face in Raising their Children and How these Problems are Affected by Federal Action of Inaction," April 8 and 9, 1974. Washington, DC: Government Printing Office.

Indian Child Welfare Act of 1977. 1977. Hearing before the U.S. Senate Select Committee on Indian Affairs, 95th Congress, 1st Session, S. 1214, August 4. Washington, DC: Government Printing Office.

Indian Child Welfare Act of 1978. 1981. Hearings before the Subcommittee on Indian Affairs and Public Lands of the Committee on Interior and Insular Affairs, House of Representatives, held February 9 and March 9, 1978. 95th Congress, 2nd Session, S. 1214, Serial No. 96–42. Washington, DC: Government Printing Office.

Iverson, Peter. 1981. *The Navajo Nation*. Westport, CT: Greenwood Press.

Iverson, Peter. 2002. *Diné: A History of the Navajos*. Albuquerque: University of New Mexico Press.

Jacobs, Margaret. 1999. *Engendered Encounters: Feminism and Pueblo Cultures, 1879–1934*. Lincoln: University of Nebraska Press.

Jacobs, Margaret. 2004. "A Battle for the Children: American Indian Child Removal in Arizona in the Era of Assimilation." *Journal of Arizona History* 45 (1): 31–62.

Jacobs, Margaret. 2009. *White Mother to a Dark Race: Settler Colonialism, Maternalism, and the Removal of Indigenous Children in the American West and Australia, 1880–1940*. Lincoln: University of Nebraska Press.

Jacobs, Margaret. 2013. "Remembering the 'Forgotten Child': The American Indian Child Welfare Crisis of the 1960s and 70s." *American Indian Quarterly* 37 (2): 136–59.

Jenkins, Philip. 2004. *Dream Catchers: How Mainstream America Discovered Native Spirituality*. New York: Oxford University Press.

Kelly, Lawrence C. 1983. *The Assault on Assimilation: John Collier and the Origins of Indian Policy Reform*. Albuquerque: University of New Mexico Press.

Lyslo, Arnold. 1960. "Adoption for American Indian Children." *Child Welfare* 39 (6): 32–33.

Lyslo, Arnold. 1961. "Adoptive Placement of American Indian Children with Non-Indian Families, Part I: The Indian Project." *Child Welfare* 40 (5): 4–6.

Lyslo, Arnold. 1964. "The Indian Adoption Project: An Appeal to Catholic Agencies to Participate." *Catholic Charities Review* 48 (5): 12–16.

Marshall, Audrey, and Margaret McDonald. 2001. *The Many-Sided Triangle: Adoption in Australia*. Carlton, Australia: Melbourne University Press.

McGregor, Russell. 2004. "Governance, Not Genocide: Aboriginal Assimilation in the Postwar Era." In *Genocide and Settler Society: Frontier Violence and Stolen Indigenous Children in Australian History*, edited by A. Dirk Moses. New York: Berghahn.

Melosh, Barbara. 2002. *Strangers and Kin: The American Way of Adoption*. Cambridge, MA: Harvard University Press.

Miller, J. R. 1996. *Shingwauk's Vision: A History of Native Residential Schools*. Toronto: University of Toronto Press.

Miller, J. R. 2000. *Skyscrapers Hide the Heavens: A History of Indian-White Relations in Canada*. 3rd ed. Toronto: University of Toronto Press.

Milloy, John S. 2001. *A National Crime: The Canadian Government and the Residential School System, 1879–1986*. 3rd ed. Winnipeg: University of Manitoba Press.

Morgan, T. J. 1896. "A Plea for the Papoose." *Baptist Home Mission Monthly* 18 (12).

Moses, A. Dirk, ed. 2004. *Genocide and Settler Society: Frontier Violence and Stolen Indigenous Children in Australian History*. New York: Berghahn.

Neu, Dean, and Richard Therrien. 2003. *Accounting for Genocide: Canada's Bureaucratic Assault on Aboriginal People*. Black Point, Canada: Fernwood.

Philp, Kenneth R. 1977. *John Collier's Crusade for Indian Reform, 1920–1954*. Tucson: University of Arizona Press.

Platt, Anthony M. 1969. *The Child Savers: The Invention of Delinquency*. Chicago: University of Chicago Press.

Regan, Paulette. 2010. *Unsettling the Settler Within: Indian Residential Schools, Truth Telling, and Reconciliation in Canada*. Vancouver: UBC Press.

Shewell, Hugh. 2004. *"Enough to Keep Them Alive": Indian Welfare in Canada, 1873–1965*. Toronto: University of Toronto Press.

Solinger, Rickie. 1994. *Wake Up Little Susie: Single Pregnancy and Race before* Roe v. Wade. New York: Routledge.

Strong-Boag, Veronica. 2006. *Finding Families, Finding Ourselves: English Canada Encounters Adoption from the Nineteenth Century to the 1990s*. Don Mills, Canada: Oxford University Press.

Swain, Shurlee, and Margot Hillel. 2010. *Child, Nation, Race and Empire: Child Rescue Discourse, England, Canada and Australia, 1850–1915*. Manchester, UK: Manchester University Press.

Swenson, Janet P., ed. 1977. *Supportive Care, Custody, Placement and Adoption of American Indian Children*. Report from a National Conference, April 19–22, Bottle Hollow, Utah. Washington, DC: American Academy of Child Psychiatry.

Task Force Four. 1976. *Report on Federal, State, and Tribal Jurisdiction*. Final report to the American Indian Policy Review Commission. Washington, DC: Government Printing Office.

Tiffin, Susan. 1982. *In Whose Best Interest? Child Welfare Reform in the Progressive Era*. Westport, CT: Greenwood Press.

Topper, Martin. 1977. "Mormon Placement." In *Supportive Care, Custody, Placement and Adoption of American Indian Children*. Report from a National Conference, April 19–22, Bottle Hollow, Utah, edited by Janet P. Swenson. Washington, DC: American Academy of Child Psychiatry.

United Nations. 1948. Convention on the Prevention and Punishment of the Crime of Genocide. Human Rights Web. Accessed August 8, 2012. http://www.hrweb.org/legal/genocide.html.

van Krieken, Robert. 1991. *Children and the State: Social Control and the Formation of Australian Child Welfare*. Sydney, Australia: Allen and Unwin.

Veracini, Lorenzo. 2010. *Settler Colonialism: A Theoretical Overview*. London: Palgrave Macmillan.

White, Lavina, and Eva Jacobs. 1992. *Liberating Our Children, Liberating Our Nations*. Report of the Aboriginal Committee. Victoria: Community Panel, Family and Children's Services Legislation Review in British Columbia.

Wolfe, Patrick. 2001. "Land, Labor, and Difference: Elementary Structures of Race." *American Historical Review* 106: 866–905.

Wolfe, Patrick. 2008. "Structure and Event: Settler Colonialism, Time, and the Question of Genocide." In *Empire, Colony, Genocide: Conquest, Occupation, and Subaltern Resistance in World History*, edited by A. Dirk Moses. New York: Berghahn.

CHAPTER 9

REVISITING CHOCTAW ETHNOCIDE
AND ETHNOGENESIS

The Creative Destruction of Colonial Genocide

Jeff Benvenuto

In the inaugural issue of *Holocaust and Genocide Studies* is an enterprising essay by the anthropologist Seena Kohl (1986) entitled "Ethnocide and Ethnogenesis: A Case Study of the Mississippi Band of Choctaw, a Genocide Avoided." This piece is interesting for a number of reasons, not the least of which is its conceptual framing of ethnocide and ethnogenesis. Kohl's argument is that the Mississippi band of Choctaw, the descendants of those Choctaw who resisted forcible removal by the United States in 1831, managed to narrowly avoid genocide and vitally regenerate their autochthonous society. This argument seems to be substantiated by contemporary data. According to the most recent census from 2010, the entire Choctaw diaspora, including not only the federally recognized tribes in Mississippi and Oklahoma but even smaller communities in Alabama, California, and elsewhere, boasts a total population of 195,764 people, making it one of the largest Indigenous groups in the United States (Norris, Vines, and Hoeffel 2010: 17). To put this into context, it is estimated that in 1850 the Choctaw population in their Mississippi homeland was as low as one thousand, a figure nearly twenty times smaller than it was only two decades earlier (Tolbert 1959: 88). This remarkable demographic seesaw reflects a larger trend in the decline and recovery of Native populations and poses a question about the theoretical relationship between group death and revitalization.

Of course numbers alone do not convey the loss or renewal of culture. As with other Indigenous communities, the preservation and practice of the Choctaw language is fundamental to their identity, and its potential demise is disconcerting. The anthropologist Tom Mould (2003: 198), who has done extensive fieldwork in Mississippi recording Choctaw oral traditions, reports that in 1997 only 3 percent of children age four to five were fluent in Choctaw, 11 percent spoke a mix of Choctaw and English, and a staggering 86 percent had little to no knowledge of the Choctaw language. At the same time, however, Choctaw traditions and ritual life have resurged, as is apparent to anyone attending the annual Choctaw Labor Day Festival in Tushka Homma, Oklahoma, or the Choctaw Indian Fair held every summer in Choctaw, Mississippi (Lambert 2001; Blanchard 1981). There seems to be an ongoing tension, then, between cultural loss and regeneration, or between social discontinuities and continuities.

Identities and cultural practices are in a constant state of historical flux and always subject to change over time, and yet they are also simultaneously able to provide ontological security by maintaining a certain degree of stability and perseverance. In confronting this dialectical tension between change and continuity, sociological ecologists have usefully adapted the concept of resilience, meaning "the capacity of a system to absorb disturbance and reorganize while undergoing change so as to still retain essentially the same function, structure, identity, and feedbacks" (Folke et al. 2010). Certainly this concept must be guarded against the impression that there is somehow a pure form of culture that is defiled only to return to homeostasis. Such a false impression would essentially reify a subject that is inherently dynamic. On the contrary there is no such thing as a purely unadulterated cultural form. Like a river, cultures are constantly evolving figurations (Powell and Peristerakis, this volume), periodically ebbing and flowing, always changing and adjusting according to circumstances. And like a dam on a river, cultural figurations are often radically diverted, upended, or altered by outside forces. Keeping with this analogy, colonial pressures have been like dams that force Indigenous peoples to modify their cultures. At the same time, however, the "flows" of Indigenous cultures have not altogether run dry, and while there is no homeostatic cultural essence that is restorable, they have nonetheless managed to keep vitally moving forward from their original sources.

The theoretical argument of this chapter is that there has been a dimension of "creative destruction" in the experiences of colonial genocide targets. This concept, creative destruction, was originally put forth by the economist Joseph Schumpeter ([1943] 2003: 81–86) to explain how the growth of capitalist economies is driven by the radical innovations of profit-driven entrepreneurs, resulting in the obsolescence and elimination of their competitors' products and ideas. The genealogy of this basic idea is arguably traceable to the Hindu deity Shiva, who is responsible for destroying the universe and planting the seeds for its regeneration (Reinert and Reinert 2006: 58). While not specifically cited in genocide studies, this general idea has been used to help explain the perpetration of genocide. For instance, Raphael Lemkin (1944: 79) pairs destruction and creation in his "two phases" of genocide, the first being the destruction of the victims, and the second being "the imposition of the national pattern of the oppressor." Patrick Wolfe (2006: 388) has elaborated this relationship in settler colonial contexts. However correct they may be, these propositions suggest that destruction and creation are distinct steps that occur sequentially and that the creative aspect primarily concerns the perpetrators. I suggest instead that creation and destruction can be complexly braided together in a simultaneous process that enables a positive response from the targets of genocide.[1]

I thus explore the process of creative destruction in the ethnogenesis of the Choctaw, an Indigenous people from the North American Southeast that historically developed out of the context of what Robbie Ethridge (this volume) has dubbed the Mississippian shatter zone. I begin with an overview of the processes and moments of group destruction that led to the collapse and radical transformation of proto-Choctaw groups from roughly 1450 to 1700. I briefly provide a conceptual clarification between ethnocide and genocide, arguing that they are actually synonyms, while also supporting the argument that genocide is mutable, both as a phenomenon and a concept, and should thus be understood in context-specific forms. Next I situate the process of Choctaw ethnogenesis in the larger context of the early modern Atlantic world, where patterns of group destruction and ethnic formation were prevalent. Finally, I conclude by meditating on what the concept of ethnogenesis, as well as the dialectic between group death and regeneration, has to offer the field of genocide studies. Referencing Gerald Vizenor's (2008) notion of "survivance," or the remarkable ability of Native American communities to maintain strong presences despite perennial pressures for erasure, I suggest that understanding the creative destruction of colonial genocide targets allows us to see beyond the false dichotomies between destruction and regeneration, victimization and agency, or domination and resistance in order to appreciate what was lost and gained in Indigenous responses to colonialism.

Death, Destruction, and Genocide in the Mississippian Shatter Zone

As described by Ethridge, both in this volume and elsewhere, from roughly 1540 to 1730 the human geography of the North American Southeast was radically transformed with the colonial integration of the region into the nascent modern world system (Ethridge and Shuck-Hall 2009; Ethridge 2010). The Mississippian shatter zone is a complex multicausal framework that explains how the dense networks of Indigenous chiefdoms across much of what is now the American South collapsed in this radical transformation. Although precise demographics are impossible to elucidate, the Native southern population during this era was probably cut in half, if not more (Ethridge 2009: 14). And yet the Native peoples of the South were not obliterated, as modern tribal nations such as the Choctaw were pieced together from the shattered remains of these precontact polities.

Given the scale of this cataclysm, one would think that genocide studies would be inclined to address the Mississippian shatter zone. However, when the field has considered the history of genocide in the Native South, it has generally focused on the Trail of Tears, the forced removal of nearly 100,000 Indigenous people during the 1830s (Thornton 1984; Chalk and Jonassohn 1990: 196–97; Stannard 1992: 121–24; Churchill 1997: 143–44, 160–62, 215–17; Levene 2005: 23–24, 86–88; Kiernan 2007: 330–34; Wolfe 2008). Perhaps this truncated perspective reflects the uncertainty of applying the concept of genocide to the earlier historical context of the Mississippian shatter zone. After all, the violence of the shatter zone was not simply a one-sided affair played out by homogeneous actors, in which Europeans were perpetrators and Natives were victims.[2] In fact many Native southern groups maintained a strategic potency and willingly contributed to the endemic violence of the era. Moreover the Mississippian shatter zone was as much about Indigenous revitalization as it was about destruction (Ethridge 2009: 42–43; Jennings 2010: xv–xxvii, 82, 207–8). Thus a certain degree of conceptual clarification is necessary in order to appreciate how genocide entails not only obliteration through various forms of destruction but even sociocultural regeneration.

While I cannot explore definitions of genocide in any great detail in this chapter, some conceptual clarification is necessary. To briefly return to Kohl (1986: 93), a fundamental premise of her essay is the categorical distinction between ethnocide ("forced change") and genocide ("annihilation"). However, Lemkin (1944: 79), who originally coined the word *genocide*, actually considered *ethnocide* to be its synonym. Since Lemkin, however, the term *ethnocide* has instead become another word for the concept of *cultural genocide*, which itself is generally but misleadingly understood as distinct from "real" genocide. As a matter of colloquial convention, then, ethnocide has come to mean cultural destruction, whereas genocide refers to a form of physical mass murder (Chalk and Jonassohn 1990: 23). As noted elsewhere in this volume (Powell and Peristerakis), such a distinction does not appreciate the group-oriented nature of genocide. Genocide is not merely the annihilation of individuals but is rather the attempted destruction of groups. As such, in this chapter I follow the emerging trend in genocide studies that conflates this distinction and instead sees cultural destruction as a fundamental aspect of genocide.[3]

With that said, genocide remains an "essentially contested concept" (Gallie 1955–56; Powell 2007: 529–30), but this should not be as serious a problem as it appears. While genocide is an inherently unstable concept that is difficult to define or delimit, this quality may also give it greater meaning and efficacy. Henry Theriault (2010) has thus recently argued that genocide as a phenomenon mutates over time. As such, scholars and jurists must respond appropriately by modifying and reconceptualizing genocide in response to emergent forms of group destruction. For example, Theriault notes that while rape was not originally considered, let alone included, in the United Nations Genocide Convention, it was effectively deployed in the Rwandan and Bosnian genocides and thus had to be considered by their respective International Criminal Tribunals. Likewise he argues that the spread of disease in Indigenous North America can be legitimately reconsidered as a mode of genocide. Accordingly we can attempt to understand forms of group destruction in the Mississippian shatter zone as a distinct variant of genocide.

Having at least partially clarified the terminology at stake, what were the experiences of the Choctaw during the two-centuries-long history of the Mississippian shatter zone? First, when in 1540–41 the Spanish *conquistador* Hernando de Soto became the first European to pass through what eventually became the Choctaw homeland in the present-day state of Mississippi, the Choctaw did not yet exist as *Choctaw* per se. Scholars have combined the limited documentary records of the Soto expedition with archaeological findings to begin piecing together a theoretical picture of the region's sociopolitical groupings at the time, thus making it possible to speculate on the experiences of possible proto-Choctaw peoples (Hudson and Tesser 1994). Of particular interest is Soto's violent confrontation with the Tascaluça (or Tuskaloosa) chiefdom at the fortified village of Mabila, probably somewhere near the confluence of the Coosa and Tallapoosa rivers in central present-day Alabama. In a ferocious pitched battle Tascaluça's warriors launched a devastating surprise attack on the belligerent conquistadors before they were eventually routed, as Soto's men razed the entire Mississippian village (Knight 2009; Ethridge 2010: 26–28; Jennings 2010: 48–50). Borrowing the words of Dirk Moses (2000: 92), this was arguably a "genocidal moment" that emerged from "a particular constellation of circumstances" arising from Native resistance to Soto's colonial project. About twenty years later the expeditions of Tristán de Luna and Juan Pardo passed through the same general area and made no mention of Mabila or the Tascaluça chiefdom, leaving one to suspect that this particular polity had recently collapsed due in no small part to its deliberate destruction by Soto. It is highly probable that at least some of the inhabitants of this Mississippian sociopolitical entity eventually moved westward and coalesced with other proto-Choctaw (Galloway 1995: 166, 263, 342).

Such violent military engagements were the first in a series of factors that added to the tumult of the shatter zone, as the Soto expedition and subsequent colonial incursions had considerable epidemiological effects. While the notion of "virgin soil epidemics" in Native America has been overgeneralized, it was undoubtedly a factor in the depopulation of the Native South, although its effects were unevenly distributed (Milner 1980; Blakely and Detweiler-Blakely 1989; Jones 2003). On the one hand, more densely populated areas with concentrated settlements of proto-Choctaw peoples, such as the Yazoo Basin and Natchez Bluffs regions in western present-day Mississippi, were significantly afflicted by disease. On the other hand, areas with more dispersed settlement patterns, such as parts of the upper Pearl River in east-central Mississippi and the western tributaries of the Tombigbee River in west-central Alabama, were less plagued. In either case most of these surviving populations later coalesced as an emerging Choctaw sociopolitical formation, a process described in greater detail below.

The role of disease in the context of colonial genocides has been hotly debated, as some have argued that microbes cannot be endowed with agency, let alone intentionality (Lewy 2007). Others have responded more convincingly that epidemics cannot be understood out of context, as political, economic, and strategic factors played major roles in structuring the degrees of vulnerability of affected populations (Briggs and Briggs 1997; McDonnell and Moses 2005: 517–20; Levene 2005: 10–11; Woolford 2009: 89–91). Likewise the multicausal framework of the Mississippian shatter zone situates the epidemiological history of the Native South in a broader context. In fact the spread of disease was closely related to the rise of the Indigenous slave trade, colonial market forces, and internecine warfare. The historian Paul Kelton (2002, 2007) has persuasively argued that there was no major regionwide epidemic in the Native South until 1696, when cases of smallpox were reported along the East Coast before spreading across the emerging slave-trading network that connected the Atlantic Ocean to the Mississippi River. And while epidemics such as this indeed caused great death and destruction, they were precipitated by slave raiding and endemic violence, both of which were stoked in large part by colonial economic pressures. As depicted by Ethridge (2010: 149–68), by the 1680s planter class interests out of Charles Town (present day Charleston, South Carolina) and its environs were instigating conflicts among various Indigenous militaristic slaving societies in order to supply forced labor markets for the emerging plantation complex. By then the commercial slaving network had reached the Mississippi River, where the Chickasaw were becoming integral trading partners with the English. As the most powerful, fire-armed militaristic slaving society in the area, the Chickasaw wreaked havoc on the emergent Choctaw and other neighboring groups.

It was in this context of intense warfare and slave raiding that the first face-to-face contact between Europeans and Choctaw occurred in 1699, when a Choctaw delegate met with French colonists at the newly established fort at Old Biloxi (Carson 1999: 11; Galloway 1994a: 406; 1995, 183–99). Three years later the French explorer and colonial administrator Pierre Le Moyne d'Iberville hosted an attempted peace conference between the Choctaw and Chickasaw, hoping to draw the latter away from the British realm of influence. According to records of the meeting, he laid bare the human costs of the shatter zone, indicating that the Chickasaw had taken over five hundred Choctaw prisoners and had killed more than 1,800 Choctaw in the span of a few years, while also losing eight hundred of their own warriors in the process. It has been suggested that Iberville probably inflated these figures (Ethridge 2010: 202–3; Atkinson 2004: 28), but they nonetheless indicate the drastic effects of colonial-induced warfare. Putting these casualties into context, it is estimated that the total Choctaw population in 1700 was roughly twenty-one thousand, whereas the Chickasaw numbered about five thousand. In fact from 1700 to 1715 the Choctaw alone lost approximately 4,200 people, or nearly a quarter of their population, due to warfare, disease, and enslavement (Wood 1989: 92–99; Galloway 1994b: 45).

By 1715, as Indigenous slave raiding gave way to the rise of the transatlantic slave complex, the Choctaw had managed to establish themselves as a formidable confederacy, although endemic violence persisted in the region for nearly a century. During the 1730s and 1740s the French spurred a series of wars between the Choctaw and the Chickasaw, attempting to use the former to do their dirty work for them. In the words of the French governor of Louisiana, the colonists' aim was to bring about "the entire destruction" of the Chickasaw, although they ultimately failed in this endeavor (Atkinson 2004: 40; Foret 1990).[4] This was followed in the late 1740s by a brutal civil war in the Choctaw Confederacy, where at least eight hundred Choctaw were killed, and another 1,000 to 1,200 died from a concurrent smallpox epidemic whose effects were undoubtedly exacerbated by the hostilities (Galloway 1982; O'Brien 2002: 10). And from 1765 to 1775 the Choctaw fought the Creek Confederacy in a war largely instigated by British colonial interests (O'Brien 2008). The transformations wrought by the colonial incorporation of the Native South into the early modern world-system were clearly tremendous, particularly with the intensification of Indigenous warfare patterns due to the introduction of new commercial motivations and weaponry, as well as the spread of disease (Ferguson and Whitehead 1992). A more detailed description of these upheavals is beyond the purview of this chapter. Rather the purpose of this section has been to briefly depict the prevalence of group destruction in the context from which the Choctaw developed. The crucial question now is how Choctaw ethnogenesis picked up some of the shattered pieces of the Mississippian shatter zone.

Choctaw Ethnogenesis in an Early Modern Atlantic Context

There is no way to precisely answer this question, as the absence of sufficient evidence creates formidable epistemological barriers. As noted, when Soto's expedition passed through what would become the Choctaw homeland of present-day east-central Mississippi in 1540–41, the Choctaw did not yet exist as Choctaw per se. They did not appear in European-written historical documents until the French began colonizing the region in the late seventeenth century. There is a dearth of evidence during this crucial interlude in which the Choctaw coalesced into a coherent entity, and whatever documentary records there are were constructed through the biased perspectives of Europeans. Patricia Galloway (2006), a preeminent expert on Choctaw ethnohistory, has long reflected on these challenges, and her magisterial study *Choctaw Genesis: 1500–1700* (1995) is an invaluable resource in piecing together the clues of this mystery.

In speculatively reconstructing the process of Choctaw ethnic formation, it is necessary to overcome the tendency to see 1492 as a radical disjuncture, a "Year Zero" marking an impermeable barrier between "history" and "prehistory." Such a temporal division may lead one to presume that, at the point of contact, Native peoples were frozen in time and stuck in a perpetual present, thereby essentializing Indigeneity into primitivism (Hill 1992: 16–17; Cobb 2005; Mitchell and Scheiber 2010: 11–15). This deep-seated caricature of a "people without history" fails to acknowledge the perennial patterns of cultural change and continuity in Native America. On the one hand, it is necessary to appreciate how the historical process of global political economic integration that began with European commercial expansion in the fifteenth century transformed the social figurations of those on the periphery of the modern world-system (Wallerstein 1976). On the other hand, following the work of Eric Wolf (1982), it is also necessary to see those on the periphery as agents of changes themselves, seriously involved in the dynamics of global history while remaining embedded in their autochthonous settings. Thus after briefly outlining the basis of Choctaw ethnogenesis, I will proceed to a contextualization of the Choctaw experience in the early modern Atlantic world, where such complexly entwined patterns of social death and regeneration were especially prevalent.

To begin with, much of the resiliency of the Choctaw and other Native southerners was hard-wired into them from their Mississippian heritages. Mississippian chiefdoms regularly cycled in and out of existence in recurring patterns of emergence, expansion, and fragmentation. When a particular chiefdom collapsed, whether because of political instabilities, excessive population growth, or ecological constraints, there were regional adjustments as kinship groups either integrated into other existing polities or began new ones altogether. These cycles ensured long-term stability, as the structural foundations of the Mississippian world remained intact despite periodic fluctuations (Anderson 1994: 1–52; Hally 2006). Native southerners of the Mississippian world were thus adept at reestablishing and reaffirming their sense of "place" (Cobb 2005: 566–69). In fact significant population movements of proto-Choctaw began just before the arrival of Europeans. By 1450 a large paramount chiefdom on the Moundville archaeological site in the western part of the present-day state of Alabama had collapsed (Peebles 1987; Galloway 1994a; 1995, 54–67). As per the cyclical dynamics of the Mississippian world, the constituent groups of Moundville proceeded to fission off into other areas. Many moved westward along the upper Tombigbee River into the relatively underpopulated area of present-day east-central Mississippi along the upper Pearl River (Galloway 2006: 231).

These proto-Choctaw formerly associated with Moundville eventually began mixing with groups later affected by colonial contact and who were likewise pulled toward this underpopulated area. From the southwest came peoples formerly inhabiting the lower Yazoo River basin and the Natchez Bluffs region, areas hard hit by postcontact epidemics. These were remnants of the Plaquemine culture of present-day western Mississippi and eastern Louisiana (Galloway 1994a: 402; 1995, 44–54; Ethridge 2010: 134). A third set of groups from the southeast, originally from the remnants of the Bottle Creek chiefdom on the Mobile-Tensaw Delta, were likewise heavily impacted by disease and fled westward to the lower Pearl River, where they transformed into what archaeologists have dubbed the Burial Urn people, before moving farther north to join other proto-Choctaw. These three incoming groups—the Moundville remnants, the Plaquemines, and the Bottle Creek–Burial Urn peoples—were welcomed to the proto-Choctaw homeland by a host group (the so-called prairie peoples) that had long settled the area, however sparsely. Clearly the long history of population movements in the Mississippian world constituted a deep sociocultural logic of transformation and resilience, survival skills that endured throughout the colonial era.

It is impossible to precisely reconstruct the processes by which this proto-Choctaw host population amalgamated with the incomers, but certain eth-nohistorical evidence leaves tantalizing clues. For instance, Choctaw origin stories include two seemingly contradictory but perhaps reconcilable themes, emphasizing migration on the one hand and earth emergence on the other, thereby suggesting that the proto-Choctaw were both newcomers to the area and aboriginal. The ancient burial mound of Nanih Waiya, the spiritual heart of the Choctaw that is geographically located along the upper Pearl River, is central to both narrative themes and constitutes a centripetal foundation of Choctaw ethnogenesis (Galloway 1995: 324–37; Mould 2004: 61–93). This cohesiveness was balanced by the centrifugal spatial organization of the Choctaw as a confederacy, with three to four distinct districts, all more or less politically independent from each other but still united as an alliance. The Western Division (known as Okla falaya in Choctaw) originally comprised the host population, the so-called prairie peoples. Migrants from Mound-ville and Bottle Creek mostly provided the basis for the Eastern Division (Okla tannap) as well as the Chickasawhay towns in the southern part of the Choctaw homeland, although the latter may be considered a distinct division. Finally, the peoples formerly from the Plaquemine culture were the core for the Six Towns Division (Okla hannali), located in the southwest (Carson 1999: 11; Galloway 1995: 338–60). While this political organization ensured divisional autonomy, the confederacy was tied together by a moiety (iska) system that dictated exogamy practices. There were two iskas, or groupings of clans, dispersed across the divisions, establishing a common bond by orga-nizing marriage alliances between different subgroups (Carson 1999: 15; Gal-loway 1994a: 407–9). These three features—origin stories, the sociopolitical organization of the confederacy, and kinship ties—all worked to create what would eventually be seen by the Europeans in the early eighteenth century as a cohesive sociopolitical entity.[5]

Of course much more could be said about the process of Choctaw eth-nogenesis, but the point here is to consider the general theoretical issues in-volved with the relationship between group death and social regeneration or between cultural changes and continuities. In order to describe the types of groups generated out of the remains of the Mississippian shatter zone, schol-ars of the Native South have proposed the concept of "coalescent societies" (Ethridge and Hudson 2002; Kowalewski 2006). Coalescence was effectively an institutionalized corporate strategy to cope with the severe pressures of colonialism and collapse. Institutions such as the Choctaw divisional organi-zation and the iska system were not simply "invented traditions" made from scratch, however. Instead, in the cauldron of the shatter zone these coalescent institutions and practices were reinterpreted and rearranged from preexisting cultural forms into bricolages. In other words, these "new" social institutions and cultural practices were reconfigured using the diverse materials of already existing traditions, strategies, and norms, as they were "less invented than transformed" (Spear 2003: 14). Certainly there were significant discontinuities, but despite all the tribulations, there were (and are) still deeper, long-term continuities.[6]

This discussion of cultural continuities and discontinuities parallels a long-standing debate among scholars of transatlantic slavery. On one side are those who argue for strong and sustained cultural survivals from Africa to the Western Hemisphere, that is, that enslaved Africans and their descendants were not as thoroughly deracinated as is commonly assumed, and that key institutions and practices survived the Middle Passage (Thornton [1992] 1998; Sweet 2003). On the other side are proponents of the creolization model who instead posit a significant rupture and discontinuity in the early modern African experience in the Atlantic world. Not only did the inherent violence of the transatlantic slave complex forcibly uproot Africans from their homelands, but the fragmented nature of plantation societies, in which slaves from different ethnic backgrounds were mixed together, all compelled African American communities to create new cultural forms. This position assumes that, while the "deep structure" and "grammatical principles" of African culture may have been unconsciously carried over, they were subsequently remixed into something entirely novel (Mintz and Price [1976] 1992; Price 2001). In either case it is clear that slave populations in the Americas forged syncretic cultures out of the diverse traditions and identities inherited from Africa. Core beliefs and practices were maintained, at least to some degree, in order to provide structure and meaning to the everyday demands of coping with enslavement and oppression, and holding onto these cultural legacies were ingenious sources of survivability.[7] As such the theoretical insights provided by this literature can usefully inform the study of not entirely dissimilar Native American experiences of ethnogenesis.

Affirming Survival and Revitalization in Genocide Studies

It is undoubtedly true that the longue durée of colonization since 1492 has caused enormous death and cultural loss. Millions of Indigenous peoples have unjustly died, and many social groups and cultural traditions have disappeared. And of course entire continents have been stolen. Indeed the analytical purpose of genocide is to describe this sort of destruction and elimination. However, there is a concern that by placing too much emphasis on comprehensive obliteration, the prospects of resistance, survival, and regeneration are overlooked. This oversight has been subtly yet problematically implied by some scholars attempting to distinguish between cultural genocide and "real" genocide. Berel Lang (1984–85: 8), for instance, contends that "where life itself remains, as in cultural genocide or ethnocide, there remains always the possibility of individual and then of group revival—but this surely is not the case with physical extermination." More recently Scott Straus (2001: 364) suggests that "ending life is an irreversible, direct, immediate, and unambiguous mode of annihilation. By contrast, cultural destruction does not necessarily bring about elimination." The implication here is that "real" genocide involves utter extinguishment, connoting the explicit finality of biological death, thereby precluding the possibility for sociocultural revitalization.

While Lemkin (2002: 393) was disappointed with the move to categorically separate cultural genocide from the concept as a whole, he did distinguish, in a manner not entirely dissimilar from the suggestions of Lang and Straus, the cultural techniques of genocide from what he called cultural "diffusion." The former "violently undermined" a group, and its abruptness was sharply differentiated from the "gradual changes a culture may undergo" in response to new circumstances. In fact he said that such "gradual changes" were necessary, lest the group become "static" and "disintegrate entirely when exposed to strong outside influences."[8] Lemkin's argument has a certain degree of logical appeal. The cultural changes wrought by genocide are clearly forced upon the victims, yet cultural diffusion is deliberately initiated on the part of the group itself in order to survive. In other words, this description of genocide implies powerless victimization, whereas diffusion connotes active transformation. However, does this distinction not also discount the agency and resistance of genocide targets? Why must destruction and regeneration be mutually exclusive possibilities? As Moses has argued, Lemkin appears to have been misguided. In analyzing his writings on the aftermath of the Spanish genocide against the Mayans, where Lemkin endorsed the conclusion that "the race is dead," Moses (2008: 30) suggests that Lemkin "does not seem to have considered the possibility that genocide could be attempted, that much destruction could take place, and that cultural adaptation occurred nonetheless" (compare Short 2010b: 840–43).

I suggest that it is necessary to overcome the problematic dichotomies between destruction and regeneration, victimization and agency, or domination and resistance. Rather than strict binaries, these conceptual pairings are often deeply relational and dialectical. The ideas of the Anishinaabe writer and literary scholar Gerald Vizenor reflect both sides of these pairings. For example, he has called on state universities in the United States to establish genocide tribunals to consider the crimes, both historical and contemporary, against Native Americans. Yet he also argues that Native epistemological traditions should be accepted in such tribunals as relevant forms of evidence. Such ways of knowing are exemplars of what he calls *survivance*, that is, an active sense of presence and continuity in the face of tragedy, nihility, and victimry (Vizenor 2009: 131–58).

As such it is important to acknowledge that the proto-Choctaw were indeed violently undermined, either through outright physical annihilation, disease, and enslavement, or profound socioeconomic and political changes wrought by the inauguration of the early modern world-system. These were external pressures that radically transformed their cultural figurations. While these destructive forces caused immense havoc, however, the proto-Choctaw directed their own social changes in response to evolving circumstances. Accordingly, to return to Kohl's (1986: 99) essay cited at the outset, apart from her conceptual confusion, her main point that the Choctaw represent "in one sense a success story" is entirely valid. In spite of the threats against them, the Choctaw were self-made products of the creative destruction of colonial genocide. Like so many other Indigenous peoples of North America, they have been adaptive and resilient in the face of colonizing pressures. However much they may have had to change courses, the flows of their cultural rivers have not run dry, and they continue to keep vitally moving forward from their autochthonous sources of existence.

Notes

1. My thanks to Andrew Woolford for this point.
2. Only some scholars maintain that genocide is necessarily "one-sided" (Chalk and Jonassohn 1990: 23–24), while others have a more refined interpretation that appreciates the relational conflicts underlying genocide, as well as how resistance factors into processes of group destruction (Shaw 2007: 129, 154).
3. Damien Short (2010a: 48–49) argues that cultural destruction is by itself a sufficient condition for genocide. Dirk Moses (2008: 13) offers a moderate position, in which cultural destruction must be accompanied by physical and biological attacks in order to conceptually qualify as genocide. Personally I find both arguments persuasive, and I am making the more general point that cultural destruction is nevertheless fundamental to the concept of genocide, which, again, is understood as a form of group destruction (Powell 2007: 538; Moshman 2008: 88–89; Moses 2010).
4. The quote is from the document "From Bienville to Maurepas (August 26, 1734)," cited in Rowland and Sanders 1927: 235.
5. The role of language in Choctaw ethnogenesis, however crucial, is difficult to discern. Galloway (1995: 320–21, 358) suggests that there was no homogeneous Choctaw language spoken even into the eighteenth century and that a common vernacular only eventually emerged as a tool of external diplomacy.

6. My argument here in regard to the Choctaw supports the general thrusts of Carson (1999) and O'Brien (2002). In contrast I find the narrative of cultural declension and degradation found in White (1983) lacking such nuance.

7. It should be noted that the "survival" and "creolization" theses among Atlantic historians are being reconciled (Miller 2003; Sidbury and Cañizares-Esguerra 2011).

8. Raphael Lemkin, "The Concept of Genocide in Anthropology," Reel 3, Box 2, Folder 3, n.p., Raphael Lemkin Papers, Manuscript Collection 1730, Manuscript and Archives Division, New York Public Library.

References

Anderson, David G. 1994. *The Savannah River Chiefdoms: Political Change in the Late Prehistoric Southeast*. Tuscaloosa: University of Alabama Press.

Atkinson, James R. 2004. *Splendid Land, Splendid People: The Chickasaw Indians to Removal*. Tuscaloosa: University of Alabama Press.

Blakely, Robert, and Bettina Detweiler-Blakely. 1989. "The Impact of European Diseases in the Sixteenth-Century Southeast: A Case Study." *Midcontinental Journal of Archaeology* 14 (1): 62–89.

Blanchard, Kendall. 1981. *The Mississippi Choctaws at Play: The Serious Side of Leisure*. Urbana: University of Illinois Press.

Briggs, Charles L., and Clara Mantini Briggs. 1997. "'The Indians Accept Death as a Normal, Natural Event': Institutional Authority, Cultural Reasoning, and Discourses of Genocide in a Venezuelan Cholera Epidemic." *Social Identities* 3 (3): 439–70.

Carson, James Taylor. 1999. *Searching for the Bright Path: The Mississippi Choctaws from Prehistory to Removal*. Lincoln: University of Nebraska Press.

Chalk, Frank, and Kurt Jonassohn. 1990. *The History and Sociology of Genocide: Analyses and Case Studies*. New Haven, CT: Yale University Press.

Churchill, Ward. 1997. *A Little Matter of Genocide: Holocaust and Denial in the Americas, 1492 to the Present*. San Francisco: City Lights.

Cobb, Charles R. 2005. "Archaeology and the 'Savage Slot': Displacement and Emplacement in the Premodern World." *American Anthropologist* 107 (4): 563–74.

Ethridge, Robbie. 2009. "Introduction: Mapping the Mississippian Shatter Zone." In *Mapping the Mississippian Shatter Zone: The Colonial Indian Slave Trade and Regional Instability in the American South*, edited by Robbie Ethridge and Sheri M. Shuck-Hall, 1–62. Lincoln: University of Nebraska Press.

Ethridge, Robbie. 2010. *From Chicaza to Chickasaw: The European Invasion and Transformation of the Mississippian Shatter Zone, 1540–1730*. Chapel Hill: University of North Carolina Press.

Ethridge, Robbie, and Charles Hudson. 2002. *The Transformation of the Southeastern Indians, 1540–1760*. Jackson: University of Mississippi Press.

Ethridge, Robbie, and Sheri M. Shuck-Hall, eds. 2009. *Mapping the Mississippian Shatter Zone: The Colonial Indian Slave Trade and Regional Instability in the American South*. Lincoln: University of Nebraska Press.

Ferguson, R. Brian, and Neil L. Whitehead, eds. 1992. *War in the Tribal Zone:*

Expanding States and Indigenous Warfare. Santa Fe, NM: School of American Research Press, 1992.

Folke, Carl, Stephen R. Carpenter, Brian Walker, Marten Scheffer, Terry Chapin, and Johan Rockström. 2010. "Resilience Thinking: Integrating Resilience, Adaptability and Transformability." *Ecology and Society* 15 (4). Accessed July 18, 2012. http://www.ecologyandsociety.org/vol15/iss4/art20/.

Foret, Michael J. 1990. "War or Peace? Louisiana, the Choctaws, and the Chickasaws, 1733–1735." *Louisiana History* 31: 273–92.

Gallie, W. B. 1955–56. "Essentially Contested Concepts." *Proceedings of the Aristotelian Society* 56: 167–98.

Galloway, Patricia. 1982. "Choctaw Factionalism and Civil War, 1746–1750." *Journal of Mississippi History* 44 (4): 289–327.

Galloway, Patricia. 1994a. "Confederacy as a Solution to Chiefdom Dissolution: Historical Evidence from the Choctaw Case." In *The Forgotten Centuries: Indians and Europeans in the American South, 1521–1704*, edited by Charles Hudson and Carmen Chaves Tesser, 393–420. Athens: University of Georgia Press.

Galloway, Patricia. 1994b. "Prehistoric Population of Mississippi: A First Approximation." *Mississippi Archaeology* 29 (2): 44–71.

Galloway, Patricia. 1995. *Choctaw Genesis: 1500–1700.* Lincoln: University of Nebraska Press.

Galloway, Patricia. 2002a. "Colonial Period Transformations in the Mississippi Valley: Dis-Integration, Alliance, Confederation, Playoff." In *The Transformation of the Southeastern Indians, 1540–1760*, edited by Robbie Ethridge and Charles Hudson, 225–48. Jackson: University of Mississippi Press.

Galloway, Patricia. 2002b. "The Great Southeastern Smallpox Epidemic." In *Transformation of the Southeastern Indians, 1540–1760*, edited by Robbie Ethridge and Charles Hudson, 21–37. Jackson: University of Mississippi Press.

Galloway, Patricia. 2006. *Practicing Ethnohistory: Mining Archives, Hearing Testimony, Constructing Narrative.* Lincoln: University of Nebraska Press.

Galloway, Patricia. 2007. *Epidemics and Enslavement: The Economic Origin of Biological Catastrophe in the Native Southeast, 1492–1715.* Lincoln: University of Nebraska Press.

Hally, David J. 2006. "The Nature of Mississippian Regional Systems." In *Light on the Path: The Anthropology and History of the Southeastern Indians*, edited by Thomas J. Pluckhahn and Robbie Ethridge, 26–42. Tuscaloosa: University of Alabama Press.

Hill, Jonathan D. 1992. "Introduction: Ethnogenesis in the Americas, 1492–1992." In *History, Power, and Identity: Ethnogenesis in the Americas, 1492–1992*, edited by Jonathan D. Hill, 1–19. Iowa City: University of Iowa Press.

Hudson, Charles, and Carmen Chaves Tesser, eds. 1994. *The Forgotten Centuries: Indians and Europeans in the American South, 1521–1704.* Athens: University of Georgia Press.

Jennings, Matthew H. 2010. *New Worlds of Violence: Cultures and Conquests in the Early American Southeast.* Knoxville: University of Tennessee Press.

Jones, David S. 2003. "Virgin Soils Revisited." *William and Mary Quarterly* 60 (4): 703–42.

Kelton, Paul. 2002. "The Great Southeastern Smallpox Epidemics." In *Transformation of the Southeastern Indians, 1540–1760*, edited by Robbie Ethridge and Charles Hudson, 21–37. Jackson: University of Mississippi Press.

Kelton, Paul. 2007. *Epidemics and Enslavement: The Economic Origin of Biological Catastrophe in the Native Southeast, 1492–1715*. Lincoln: University of Nebraska Press.

Kiernan, Ben. 2007. *Blood and Soil: A World History of Genocide and Extermination from Sparta to Darfur*. New Haven, CT: Yale University Press.

Knight, Vernon James, Jr. 2009. *The Search for Mabila: The Decisive Battle between Hernando de Soto and Chief Tascalusa*. Tuscaloosa: University of Alabama Press.

Kohl, Seena B. 1986. "Ethnocide and Ethnogenesis: A Case Study of the Mississippi Band of Choctaw, a Genocide Avoided." *Holocaust and Genocide Studies* 1 (1): 91–100.

Kowalewski, Stephen A. 2006. "Coalescent Societies." In *Light on the Path: The Anthropology and History of the Southeastern Indians*, edited by Thomas J. Pluckhahn and Robbie Ethridge, 94–122. Tuscaloosa: University of Alabama Press.

Lambert, Valerie Long. 2001. "Contemporary Ritual Life." In *Choctaw Language and Culture: Chahta Anumpa*, edited by Marcia Haag and Henry Willis, 317–21. Norman: University of Oklahoma Press.

Lang, Berel. 1984–85. "The Concept of Genocide." *Philosophical Forum* 16 (1–2): 1–18.

Lemkin, Raphael. 1944. *Axis Rule in Occupied Europe: Laws of Occupation, Analysis of Government, Proposals for Redress*. Washington, DC: Carnegie Endowment for International Peace.

Lemkin, Raphael. 2002. "Totally Unofficial Man." In *Pioneers of Genocide Studies*, edited by Samuel Totten and Steven L. Jacobs, 365–99. New Brunswick, NJ: Transaction.

Levene, Mark. 2005. *Genocide in the Age of the Nation State*. Vol. 2: *The Rise of the West and the Coming of Genocide*. New York: I. B. Tauris.

Lewy, Guenter. 2007. "Can There Be Genocide without the Intent to Commit Genocide?" *Journal of Genocide Research* 9 (4): 666–72.

McDonnell, Michael A., and A. Dirk Moses. 2005. "Raphael Lemkin as Historian of Genocide in the Americas." *Journal of Genocide Research* 7 (4): 501–29.

Miller, Joseph C. 2003. "Retention, Reinventing, and Remembering: Restoring Identities through Enslavement in Africa and under Slavery in Brazil." In *Enslaving Connections: Changing Cultures of Africa and Brazil during the Era of Slavery*, edited by José C. Curto and Paul E. Lovejoy, 81–121. Amherst, NY: Humanity Books.

Milner, George R. 1980. "Epidemic Disease in the Postcontact Southeast: A Reappraisal." *Midcontinental Journal of Archaeology* 5 (1): 39–56.

Mintz, Sidney W., and Richard Price. [1976] 1992. *The Birth of African-American Culture: An Anthropological Perspective*. Boston: Beacon.

Mitchell, Mark D., and Laura L. Scheiber. 2010. "Crossing Divides: Archaeology as Long-Term History." In *Across a Great Divide: Continuity and Change in Native North American Societies, 1400–1900*, edited by Laura L. Scheiber and Mark D. Mitchell, 1–22. Tucson: University of Arizona Press.

Moses, A. Dirk. 2000. "An Antipodean Genocide? The Origins of the Genocidal Moment in the Colonization of Australia." *Journal of Genocide Research* 2 (1): 194–219.

Moses, A. Dirk. 2008. "Empire, Colony, Genocide: Keywords and the Philosophy of History." In *Colony, Empire, Genocide: Conquest, Occupation, and Subaltern Resistance in World History*, edited by A. Dirk Moses, 3–54. New York: Berghahn.

Moses, A. Dirk. 2010. "Raphael Lemkin, Culture, and the Concept of Genocide." In *The Oxford Handbook of Genocide Studies*, edited by Donald Bloxham and A. Dirk Moses, 19–41. New York: Oxford University Press.

Moshman, David. 2008. "Conceptions of Genocide and Perceptions of History." In *The Historiography of Genocide*, edited by Dan Stone, 71–92. New York: Palgrave.

Mould, Tom. 2003. *Choctaw Prophecy: A Legacy of the Future*. Tuscaloosa: University of Alabama Press.

Mould, Tom. 2004. *Choctaw Tales*. Jackson: University of Mississippi Press.

Norris, Tina, Paula L. Vines, and Elizabeth M. Hoeffel. 2010. *The American Indian and Alaska Native Population: 2010*. Accessed October 13, 2012. http://www.census.gov/prod/cen2010/briefs/c2010br-10.pdf.

O'Brien, Greg. 2002. *Choctaws in a Revolutionary Age, 1750–1830*. Lincoln: University of Nebraska Press.

O'Brien, Greg. 2008. "Protecting Trade through War: Choctaw Elites and British Occupation of the Floridas." In *Pre-Removal Choctaw History: Exploring New Paths*, edited by Greg O'Brien, 103–22. Norman: University of Oklahoma Press.

Peebles, Christopher S. 1987. "The Rise and Fall of the Mississippian in Western Alabama: The Moundville and Summerville Phases, A.D. 1000 to 1600." *Mississippi Archaeology* 22 (1): 1–31.

Powell, Christopher. 2007. "What Do Genocides Kill? A Relational Conception of Genocide." *Journal of Genocide Research* 9 (4): 527–47.

Price, Richard. 2001. "The Miracle of Creolization: A Retrospective." *New West Indian Guide* 75 (1–2): 35–64.

Reinert, Hugo, and Erik S. Reinert. 2006. "Creative Destruction in Economics: Nietzsche, Sombart, Schumpeter." *European Heritage in Economics and the Social Sciences* 3: 55–85.

Rowland, Dunbar, and A. G. Sanders, eds. 1927. *Mississippi Provincial Archives, 1729–1740: French Dominion*. Vol. 1. Jackson: Press of the Mississippi Department of Archives and History.

Schumpeter, Joseph A. [1943] 2003. *Capitalism, Socialism and Democracy*. New York: Routledge.

Shaw, Martin. 2007. *What Is Genocide?* Cambridge: Polity.

Short, Damien. 2010a. "Australia: A Continuing Genocide?" *Journal of Genocide Research* 12 (1–2): 45–68.

Short, Damien. 2010b. "Cultural Genocide and Indigenous Peoples: A Sociological Approach." *International Journal of Human Rights* 14 (6): 831–46.

Sidbury, James, and Jorge Cañizares-Esguerra. 2011. "Mapping Ethnogenesis in the Early Modern Atlantic." *William and Mary Quarterly* 68 (2): 181–208.

Spear, Thomas. 2003. "Neo-Traditionalism and the Limits of Invention in British Colonial Africa." *Journal of African History* 44 (1): 3–27.

Stannard, David E. 1992. *American Holocaust: The Conquest of the New World*. New York: Oxford University Press.

Straus, Scott. 2001. "Contested Meanings and Conflicting Imperatives: A Conceptual Analysis of Genocide." *Journal of Genocide Research* 3 (3): 349–75.

Sweet, James H. 2003. *Recreating Africa: Culture, Kinship, and Religion in the*

African-Portuguese World, 1441–1770. Chapel Hill: University of North Carolina Press.

Theriault, Henry C. 2010. "Genocidal Mutation and the Challenge of Definition." *Metaphilosophy* 41 (4): 481–524.

Thornton, John. [1992] 1998. *Africa and Africans in the Making of the Atlantic World, 1400–1680.* 2nd ed. New York: Cambridge University Press.

Thornton, Russell. 1984. "Cherokee Population Losses during the Trail of Tears: A New Perspective and a New Estimate." *Ethnohistory* 31 (4): 289–300.

Tolbert, Charles. 1959. "A Sociological Study of the Choctaw Indians in Mississippi." Ph.D. dissertation, Louisiana State University.

Vizenor, Gerald, ed. 2008. *Survivance: Narratives of Native Presence.* Lincoln: University of Nebraska Press.

Vizenor, Gerald. 2009. *Native Liberty: Natural Reason and Cultural Survivance.* Lincoln: University of Nebraska Press.

Wallerstein, Immanuel. 1976. *The Modern World-System: Capitalist Agriculture and the Origins of the European World-Economy in the Sixteenth Century.* New York: Academic Press.

White, Richard. 1983. *The Roots of Dependency: Subsistence, Environment, and Social Change among the Choctaws, Pawnees, and Navajos.* Lincoln: University of Nebraska Press.

Wolf, Eric R. 1982. *Europe and the People without History.* Berkeley: University of California Press.

Wolfe, Patrick. 2006. "Settler Colonialism and the Elimination of the Native." *Journal of Genocide Research* 8 (4): 387–409.

Wolfe, Patrick. 2008. "Structure and Event: Settler Colonialism, Time, and the Question of Genocide." In *Colony, Empire, Genocide: Conquest, Occupation, and Subaltern Resistance in World History*, edited by A. Dirk Moses, 102–32. New York: Berghahn.

Wood, Peter H. 1989. "The Changing Population of the Colonial South: An Overview by Race and Region, 1685–1790." In *Powhatan's Mantle: Indians in the Colonial Southeast*, edited by Peter H. Wood, Gregory A. Waselkov, and M. Thomas Hatley, 57–132. Lincoln: University of Nebraska Press.

Woolford, Andrew. 2009. "Ontological Destruction: Genocide and Canadian Aboriginal Peoples." *Genocide Studies and Prevention* 4 (1): 81–97.

CHAPTER 10

POLITICAL GENOCIDE

Killing Nations through Legislation
and Slow-Moving Poison

Kiera L. Ladner

First Words

My family comes from an area well known in Canadian history. It is the place called Cypress Hills, Saskatchewan or, as it was known by some of my family, merry hills (a description that includes the rolling step to the north of the Hills that lead to the farm). This land has other names, though—names that resonate with the multiple histories of the Indigenous nations of the Americas. The Hills themselves are known in Cree as Manatakawikewin. As the name suggests, it is and has always been that sacred space that rises up out of the prairie, that serves as a sacred gathering place for economic, political, spiritual, and other purposes of subnational, national, and multinational concern. It was a shared space, reflecting the permeable nature of some territorial boundaries among and between Indigenous nations.

In the Canadian telling of history, it is a place known for the massacre of twenty-two Nakota men, women, and children in 1873, as it is this event that precipitated the creation of the North West Mounted Police (NWMP) in 1874 as the government of Canada quickly moved to protect "its sovereignty" and to establish "peace, order and good governance" north of the medicine line. The decapitation of Little Soldier and his extended family in the Cypress Hills massacre is not the only time that this sacred land has witnessed the spilling of the blood of Indigenous peoples at the hands of the invaders, colonizers, and settlers (both as individuals and nations). In fact in the 1880s the government of Canada engaged a multipronged approach to remove or extirpate Nehiyaw (the Plains Cree) from their territory. In the early 1880s, following the near extermination of the buffalo and their extirpation from Nehiyaw territory, the government ordered the NWMP to discontinue the provision of rations, despite their having been guaranteed to the Cree in the treaties. When Canada's efforts to starve Nehiyaw out of their territory (and the reserve lands promised in the treaties) were "unsuccessful," the government closed Fort Walsh (then the headquarters of the NWMP) in Cypress Hills in 1882, the removal of which served to threaten those who stayed in these borderlands with the possibility of armed incursions by American wolfers, militants, and whiskey traders. This, however, did not persuade the Nehiyaw to disperse, so government forces (the NWMP) rounded them up and physically forced them out of Cypress Hills. As reported in the *Regina Leader Post* at the time, the expulsion was heralded by settlers and their governments alike, especially since nothing was "wasted" on the Cree who walked from the Hills northward to the Battlefords or eastward into the Qu'Appelle Valley, many without horses or shoes and most without food or shelter.[1] As if this were not enough death on this sacred land, the government of Canada had pursued the same removal strategies with the Lakota people who sought refuge following their "wars" with the American government in the 1870s, culminating in the expulsion of Sitting Bull and his followers in 1881. Prior to these trails of tears out of these lands of peace and refuge, it is said that much life had been lost as it has been rumored by many that smallpox blankets made their way into the Hills, and many a person died from the diseases, poisons (strychnine), guns, and "whiskey" that invaders (and possibly invading nations) brought into the Hills.[2]

This is my history, and it is the point from which I enter this discussion. At the same time, this is everyone's history as it is the place from which the great myth of Canadian history and the great mantra of Canadian colonialism emerges. After all, the Hills are not only Manatakawikewin in Cree. Here language unifies two stories as the Hills are that place of peace and of responsibility that emerges out of the vast prairie landscape in Canadian mythology. The only problem is that these two narratives of Manatakawikewin explain very different histories and very different experiences of those shared histories. I say this because the story that emerges from this land and is told in history books throughout the country is that, following the American-led massacre in Cypress Hills, the government of Canada established the Mounties to bring peace, order, and good governance to the west, to lay the groundwork for the peaceful expansion of civilization as opposed to the American model of war, lawlessness, and conquest. It is this story of peaceful expansion that is said to differentiate Canada from its American cousin. In many ways it is the founding myth of Canada. It represents Canada's mythologized exceptionalism, which constructs Canada as the good colonizer, a peaceful nation that did not engage in Indian wars but has instead always dealt justly with Canada's Indigenous peoples.[3]

Despite the fact that there were no widespread Indian wars in western Canada, the history of Canada may not be so different. Canada's exceptionalism is indeed the creation of myth makers and historians. Sure, we did not have a Canadian army running roughshod into Wounded Knee and murdering everyone in sight. But there were other massacres on so-called Canadian soil. There were smallpox epidemics that were willingly spread by colonial nations and their occupiers. There was mass starvation, which was often aided by colonial occupiers who refused to assist (even where rations were a legal requirement under treaty) or even perpetrated the starvation by destroying crops or food sources such as the buffalo. While there were variations in the degree of atrocity or the means used to perpetrate atrocity, the history of Canada is not so different after all. Indigenous peoples were completely decimated; they were extirpated from their lands, and their territories were occupied by other nations. As David Stannard (1993) and Ward Churchill (1997) write, Indigenous nations that were occupied by Canada still endured their own genocide or, as Stannard suggests, their own Holocaust.

Though Canada may wish to present itself as a nation of peace, order, and good government, Canadians must remember that there is nothing peaceful about colonialism or good about near extermination of other human beings and the forced removal of those who survived. Colonialism did not establish peace, and it has not created good governance (or anything close to it) for Indigenous people. Canadians need to understand this. Foundational myths have to be dismantled and decolonized. As Indigenous peoples have been arguing for decades through movements such as the American Indian Movement and Idle No More, Canadians need to acknowledge and reconcile themselves with the true history of these lands. These were not unoccupied lands. These were not uncivilized peoples without spirituality, national territories, systems of governance, laws and science (Deloria 1994, 1995; Ladner 2003a). Peace did not define the mind of the colonizer (as nations or individuals), their colonial intentions, or their relationship with Indigenous peoples. We need to stop framing colonialism in Canada in terms that suggest that it was peaceful and righteous. We need to understand that disguising genocide by repackaging and re-presenting it in terms of civilization (a project intent on saving Indigenous peoples from their own supposed inhumanity, savagery, and inferiority) is not acceptable.

Along with other chapters in this book, my intention is to destabilize these great Canadian myths and to address the "little matter of genocide" (Churchill 1997). However, I will not address the matter of genocide as a substantive or theoretical whole. Instead, assuming that it is possible to take but a small slice of the history of genocide in Canada (and its perpetual legacies) and to examine it in some isolation from other parts of the larger whole, the scope of this paper is limited such that I seek to explore political genocide and in so doing to better ascertain the applicability of this label and the means of political genocide.

Political Genocide?

I first used the term *political genocide* in a chapter that I wrote for an introduction to a Canadian politics reader ten years ago to explain Canada's deliberate and systematic destruction of Indigenous nations as nations and its deliberate attempts to destroy Indigenous political systems (Ladner 2003b: 49).[4] I willingly admit that my choice of terms was political, with little thought given to prominent theoretical or legal constructions of genocide and the subsequent debates. It simply made sense and was a fast and simple means of conveying the history of colonialism and the spirit and intent of the Indian Act. I used it because, "with the Indian Act, the Canadian government committed an act of genocide—political and otherwise—by ignoring international law and the domestication of that law, thereby denouncing Indian sovereignty and nationhood. Instead, they 'legalized' and institutionalized practices aimed at the total destruction of Indigenous peoples, their political systems, and their ability to exercise sovereignty—or for that matter, even exist—within their own territory" (48–49). Simply put, using instruments such as the Indian Act, Indian residential schools, and even Indian day schools, Canada willfully engaged in acts best described as political genocide. Laying claim to a political genocide was contentious then, and to some extent it still is. Though some have agreed with my use of *genocide*, others have completely rejected this claim as historical falsehood. Still others have half-heartedly accepted the label to the extent that they acknowledge historical evidence but insist that this is not a real genocide, insisting instead that it should be understood in terms of a cultural genocide (something less than a "real" genocide or one characterized by the death of individuals). Needless to say, such reactions have led to some fascinating discussions and debates—several spanning ten years—and they have led me to dive deeper into genocide theoretically, legally, and substantively.

There is no debating the fact that Canada has long had a policy goal for the intentional destruction and eradication of Indigenous polities or nations. The literature makes this abundantly clear (Tobias 1991). Many have even gone so far as to argue that Canada continues to pursue these same goals of (or tantamount to) political genocide today (Ladner and Orsini 2003; Simpson 2011; Alfred 2005b). In the past the government of Canada employed the brute force of the state and legislatively destroyed and obliterated Indigenous sovereignty and Indigenous structures of governance. Today, acting as though its genocidal dreams had been realized and Indigenous institutions and sovereignty destroyed, the Canadian government refuses to acknowledge or to deal with any remnants of these structures or of sovereign Indigenous nations. They have been legislated out of existence, and in so doing they have been deliberately and systematically destroyed.

Though some may choose to call this colonization and assimilation, many have argued that its intent and effects are exactly the same as genocide (Stannard 1993; Churchill 1997). It is not as though Canada was an empty land just waiting to be discovered by European explorers, British or French sovereignty proclaimed, and settler nations established. Rather the true story is one of legal magic: the extirpation of Indigenous nations from their lands, the denial of nationhood (and sovereignty), and the destruction and attempted assimilation of Indigenous nations (collectively and individually). Nations were not only forcefully removed or extirpated from their territories; through various means these nations faced an arsenal of destructive forces armed with Canada's legislated intent of eradicating Indigenous nations as sovereign nations, destroying them as collectivities, and assimilating or absorbing the remnants into Canadian society. In many respects similar to the cultural genocide envisioned by Raphael Lemkin (1944), political genocide does not necessitate the extermination of individuals but rather the extermination or an attempted extermination of nations, their sovereignty, their institutions, and their collective or body politic. It is a collective genocide in which individuals not only physically survive the genocide but are to be assimilated into the offending nation.

As it has been defined by the UN, the mere idea of political genocide (understood as a collective form of genocide rather than one focused on the killing of individuals or the destruction of another nation's sovereignty and machinery of governance) does not fit the Canadian case as there is no mention of the destruction of a nation as a nation by bureaucratic and legislative means. Further, within international relations (and its coverage and analysis) the destruction and replacement of political systems and sovereignty is most often referred to as regime replacement and not political genocide. Thus my use of the term appears inconsistent and incongruent. But is this apparent incongruence inherent or necessarily so?

Sticking with the narrow, legalistic interpretation of genocide provided in the UN's 1948 Genocide Convention, it may be possible to understand political genocide as a form of genocide given both the Indian Act and residential schools. The primary policy goals of the Indian Act are, according to John Tobias (1991), the "protection, civilization and assimilation of the Indian." While these goals do not necessarily read as evidence of genocidal intent or action, they are. As policy objectives, civilization represents the intent to eradicate both the culture and the nationhood of every Indigenous person and collective, while assimilation represents the end goal of incorporating (without any accommodation of difference) Indigenous collectives as individuals (terminating nations) into the wider Canadian society. With this in mind, how are these not considered "acts committed with the intent to destroy a national group"? One can even go beyond this and look at how both day schools and residential schools represent the "forced transfer of children" to another culture and acted as a slow-moving poison (a genocide of sorts) within the political system, ultimately aiding in its destruction through the imposition of contradictory and oppositional cultural and political values.

While regime replacement and the introduction of cultural cancers might not fully comply with a legal or more conservative interpretation of genocide, I would argue that they do reflect the spirit and the intent with which Lemkin originally conceptualized genocide. In *Axis Rule in Occupied Europe*, Lemkin (1944: 79) conceived of genocide much more broadly, writing that genocide can include the "disintegration of the political and social institutions, of culture, language, national feelings, religion, and economic existence of national groups, and the destruction of personal security, liberty, health, dignity, and even the lives of individuals belonging to such groups. Genocide is directed against the national group as an entity, and the actions involved are directed against individuals, not in their individual capacity, but as members of the national group." Further, Lemkin writes that genocide can, and does, take multiple forms: political, social, cultural, economic, religious, moral, biological, and physical (chapter 9). Though Lemkin's writings are largely confined to occupied Europe (all occupied nations and not just the Jewish, Russian, Gypsy/Romani, disabled, and queer victims, whether individuals, identity groups, and nations of the Nazi Holocaust), his conceptualization of genocide and its multiple forms has broader applicability.

Lemkin's description of the political form of genocide is consistent with colonialism, such that the genocide can refer to an occupier's dismantling and systematic destruction of self-determination and the replacement of such national (and subnational) structures of government with their oppressor's puppet regime. As the work of Michael McDonnell and Dirk Moses demonstrates, Lemkin was actively engaged in researching colonialism and its global history as genocide (McDonnell and Moses 2005; Moses 2008). As these authors explain, it is in this unpublished work on colonialism that Lemkin clarifies his understanding of genocide, genocidal intent, and the relationship with colonialism. They argue that there are

> three significant features of Lemkin's thinking on genocide and colonialism. The first is that he regarded the extinction of the culture as genocide. It did not require the entire physical extermination of the victims, only the elimination of the culture-bearing strata. As he wrote elsewhere, the "permanent crippling" of a people was tantamount to genocide. The second feature is that he equated culture with high culture, because it is synonymous with national, as opposed to local, peasant, consciousness. Finally, Lemkin wanted to show that the conquerors not only destroyed the indigenous culture but replaced it with their own, just as he postulated in *Axis Rule* in relation to the German wartime occupation of Europe. There, we recall, he posited that "Genocide has two phases: one, destruction of the national pattern of the oppressed group; the other, the imposition of the national pattern of the oppressor." (McDonnell and Moses 2005: 514)

Clearly Lemkin would agree with my framing of political genocide as a form of genocide—one that is just as real and just as devastating to the victim or collective as the type of genocide perpetrated by Nazi Germany against gypsies, queer or LGBT people, and Jews (among others). From Lemkin forward many scholars have taken issue with the narrow interpretation of genocide that was taken up within the United Nations Convention. Some have posed their own inclusive definitions or suggested the use of parallel interpretive frameworks such as ecocide, linguicide, and cultural genocide.[5] Still others have gone further, and in an attempt to understand how and why genocides happen and issues of intent (societal and governmental) they have looked at genocide within a societal context or a bureaucratic context (Powell 2011; Neu and Therrien 2003). Despite these multiple and competing definitions and approaches to genocide and the ever-present confusion that more expansive nonlegal constructions of genocide cause, I have decided to forgo the urge to add my own to this quagmire of definitions. Instead I suggest that we take a broad, decolonizing approach to understanding political genocide as genocide (not categorized as some secondary form constituting something less than "real" genocide). Thus I will now turn to a discussion of political genocide in Canada and how it is that the systematic and intentional destruction of Indigenous political systems and nationhood was carried out and how it constitutes genocide. Prior to discussing the act of genocide, it is important to create at least some small semblance of understanding of the political systems or the national political cultures that were permanently crippled as the occupier, oppressor, or settler society attempted to impose its own political system and national political culture.

Governance without Power versus the Power to Govern

It is important to note that Indigenous political traditions, national political cultures, political systems, and prevailing political philosophies were (and are) extremely diverse, making it impossible to speak of an Indigenous political tradition in the singular. One can, however, make broad generalizations about Indigenous political traditions in the same manner that one can make broad generalizations about Western-Eurocentric political traditions. During the early colonial period Western-Eurocentric polities were generally monarchies and Christian, and commoners had few if any political, economic, or social rights. Ideas of constitutional monarchies, democracy, and liberalism were just that: ideas. Acknowledging the real limitations of such generalizations is important, for while I will proceed to discuss Indigenous political traditions generally, generalizations fail to address specificities and differences among Indigenous polities. Still, given that the point of this discussion of political traditions is to forge a general understanding of Indigenous political traditions and to lay a foundation for understanding the nature and scope of political genocide, such specificities are neither required nor possible.

Indigenous political systems were and are complex structures of governance designed and created to meet the specific needs of a nation to make, interpret, and enforce laws in a manner that was consensual and inclusive and was compatible with their territory, spiritual beliefs, and economy (Ladner 2003b). Indigenous political systems were created and are maintained by constitutional orders that set forth a system of government, provided a defined and limited ability to make, interpret, and enforce law within a territory, and set forth the rules of the political game and the roles and responsibilities of all members of the nation. Such constitutions were not written documents, and quite often—as is the case with the British Constitution—these constitutional orders consisted of myriad documents (albeit oral documents such as songs, stories, ceremonies, orations, and bundles). Such constitutional orders were not subject to the authority of another nation or another government, but they were subject to the people of the nation and the manner in which they decided to live together the best way possible. This idea truly captures the meaning of good governance within Indigenous thought (insofar as one can speak of Indigenous thought due to consistencies among nations such as the Mohawk, Nehiyaw, and Mikmaw), for it is quite simply about the way in which a people lives best together in (or as part of) their territory or the various complex, inclusive, community-building, consensus-based, adaptive, and transformative structures of governance that people created to live in a territory.

Governance is about finding and maintaining peace and good order or the way we live best together as a nation and among the rest of Creation. While this explains the relationship between Indigenous politics and territory and the common understanding that the land and one's relationship with the land define the nation and the parameters of sovereignty, it also explains the resulting differences between these two intellectual and political traditions. The Western-Eurocentric tradition is about power and its control and manipulation through institutional parameters or power as the legitimization of hierarchy, authority, and coercion, whereas Indigenous traditions stand in opposition to both this conceptualization and institutionalization of power while striving toward peace and good relations among the nation and between themselves and other beings.

This understanding of good governance as antidominium or as being grounded in a relationship with territory and as a purposeful facilitation of the way a people lives best together in said territory translates into very different political structures and institutional development. In *Society against the State*, Pierre Clastres (1989: 5) describes Indigenous polities as "A vast constellation of societies in which the holders of what would elsewhere be called power are actually without power, where the political is determined as a domain beyond coercion and violence, beyond hierarchical subordination; where, in a word, no relationship of command-obedience is in force." It is not that Indigenous polities are without power but rather that most Indigenous polities in the Americas conceptualized power as the essence of all beings—the life force within and the gifts (or responsibilities) that each holds. As individuals have the responsibility to find and realize their gifts or powers, it was generally believed that individuals are self-governing (often referred to as the doctrine of noninterference) so long as one is acting responsibly or within the accepted parameters of a nation's laws and sense of community or relations (Ross 1996: 84).[6] As a result of this doctrine of noninterference and the related conceptualization of power, hierarchical, coercive, and authoritative structures of governance did not exist (all of those that I am familiar with). Applying Clastres's analysis, Indigenous polities were societies against the state that intentionally denied the operationalization of one's power (understood within the Indigenous context) through coercive, hierarchical, and authoritative relationships (institutionalized or otherwise).

If Indigenous governance operates without power in a Western sense, then one must ask how governance within an Indigenous context works. Taiaiake

(Gerald) Alfred (2005a: 25) summarizes the characteristic attributes of the political traditions predominant within the Indigenous context:

> A crucial feature of the indigenous concept of governance is its respect for individual autonomy. This respect precludes the notion of "sovereignty"—the idea that there can be some permanent transference of power from the individual to an abstraction called "government." The indigenous tradition sees government as the collective power of the individual members of the nation; there is no separation between society and state. . . . In the indigenous tradition, the idea of self-determination truly starts with the self; political identity—with its inherent freedoms, powers and responsibilities—is not surrendered to any external entity. Individuals alone determine their interests and destinies. There is no coercion: only the compelling force of conscience based on those inherited and collectively refined principles that structure the society.

While there was no separation between government and the governed and no central or hierarchical coercive authority, there was governance, and though others may be read as suggesting otherwise, Indigenous political structures did not completely lack political power; they were simply devoid of hierarchical structures of authority and coercive power, or power and authority as they are conceived in the dominant Western-Eurocentric tradition. Instead they operationalized a collective understanding of power through processes of consensus decision making.

Collective power is both the decision-making process itself and the resulting decisions, for there was no authority greater than the autonomous individual, and leaders had no ability to forge or implement decisions other than coordinating the process of "coming to one mind." This is because authority was not defined as "power over" but the power that emanated from the collective in its entirety. Simply put, it was a collectively defined communitism (community activism) as it was both the process deciding how to act and acting as an entire community, or the continual process of a community horizontally and collectively governing itself.

Creating a Civilization: Legislation and Political Genocide

Though these political traditions, systems, and philosophies might today be understood as a kind of utopia given Canada's democratic deficit and lackluster political culture, this has not always been the case. Until the 1960s, Indigenous political traditions, like Indigenous cultures, institutions, and knowledge systems, generally were looked upon as the products of uncivilized

societies and vestiges of some prehistorical phase that demarcated predominant teleological constructions of social history and evolution. Such "uncivilized" ways stood in the path of progress, and the progress of both the
civilized and the uncivilized depended on destroying the old and making
way for the new—be that the new settler society or civilized and assimilat-
able Indigenous individuals. Making way for the new settler society and its
magical claims of sovereignty necessarily meant denying Indigenous sovereignty and replacing Indigenous political systems and therefore Indigenous
constructions of power with a new, "highly civilized" political system that
embraces power in the most violent, hierarchical, visceral, controlling, and
authoritative manner possible. This was largely achieved with the Indian Act.
Though the Indian Act is often understood in terms of regime replacement,
civilization, and assimilation, it is important to draw our attention away from
these pleasant descriptors of genocide and remember that the visceral power
of the Indian Act is nothing less than a legislated form of political genocide.

The Indian Act was introduced in 1876 and has remained relatively un-
changed since its inception. It represents the culmination of Indian policy
in Canada, for it served to amalgamate the existing Indian policies of British
North America and to establish what was to become Canada's Indian policy.
The Indian Act is perhaps the most comprehensive of all acts of the Canadian
Parliament, with the exception of the Canadian Constitution, for it touches
on nearly every aspect of an Indigenous person's life, from conception to
death (and arguably after death). At conception the Act determines whether
the child will be deemed eligible to be an Indian person; thus the Act grants
status (and with this the legal rights and privileges, both individual and collective) on the basis of one's paternity and whether one or both parents are
eligible to have status offspring. Throughout one's life the Act determines
one's eligibility to receive those rights negotiated by one's ancestors under
treaty (such as education and health care) as well as eligibility to live on reserve
(that which remains of Indigenous homelands). At death the Act determines
one's eligibility to be buried on reserve (this could be the place of birth given
that one could merely be ineligible for registration), and it can also provide
the federal government or its delegate the right to override the deceased's will.

As I have stated previously, for the purposes of this chapter it is important
to understand that the Indian Act was created by the federal government to
advance the policy goals of protection, civilization, and assimilation (Tobias
1991). Pursuing these goals the federal government set forth on a mission of
political genocide. By political genocide I am referring to the federal government's policies and practices that were designed to eliminate Indigenous
sovereignty, Indigenous governments, and Indigenous constitutional orders

(Ladner 2003b). The idea was that Indigenous forms of governance and Indigenous constitutional orders were to be eliminated by the federal government and replaced by "civilized" governance—in the form of the band council system and governed in accordance with the colonizers' oppressive authority.

According to the framers of the Indian Act, the band council system of government was designed as a temporary measure to provide Indigenous peoples with the opportunity to familiarize themselves with "civilized" government and to practice governing themselves (Ladner 2003b; Tobias 1991). The original plan was that once enough experience had been gained, Indigenous peoples would cease being Indians under the terms of the Indian Act and would be granted self-government by way of remodeling band councils as regular municipal governments (Ladner and Orsini 2003). In and of itself the Indian Act is designed to replace Indigenous systems of governance with municipal governance once communities gained enough experience in governing themselves using the institutions of the settler state, thus destroying Indigenous structures and sovereignty and imposing the colonizer's form of (subservient) government. Just as Lemkin suggests in *Axis Rule* and his unpublished works, both the destruction of Indigenous political traditions and the imposition of the oppressor's political traditions are tantamount to genocide, be that a cultural genocide or what I would term a political genocide (McDonnell and Moses 2005). In short it is a legislated genocide or a political genocide achieved by legislative means intended to both destroy the old and replicate the settler state, while also exterminating group consciousness and the group's political culture and agency.

Under the Indian Act band councils were not provided with the tools, jurisdictions, and structures of accountability that are typically associated with government. As a result few would disagree with the statement that the Indian Act did not and does not provide for a system of good governance. Rather the Indian Act's system of band council government was created to aid the federal government in administering Indian reserves. Functioning very much as puppet governments or subordinate administrators, Indian Act band councils have few responsibilities or abilities that are independent of federal oversight. Band councils have the ability under Section 81 of the Act to make by-laws in a variety of areas of interest to local governments, including traffic regulations (excluding speed), the establishment of dog pounds, the construction and maintenance of local infrastructure such as roads and ditches, and the regulation of beekeeping (Government of Canada 1985). It is true that band councils have been delegated much responsibility for administering federal policies and programs such as health care, education, and social services (Elias 1991). But the Department of Aboriginal Affairs is able to influence and interfere in a multiplicity of ways, including through its control of all band funds, departmental administrative and accountability requirements, the use of third-party management protocols, and its ability to override election results and thus call elections or appoint new band councils (Sections 74–79; Elias 1991).

The sheer magnitude of such powers and the federal ability to circumvent and administratively oppress local governments has most recently been demonstrated in Attawapiskat, a northern community that made national news in 2011–12 when its chief Theresa Spence declared a state of emergency due to the deteriorating conditions in the community following a sewage crisis caused by De Beers mining, which resulted in the contamination and condemnation of the majority of the community's houses and education and healthcare facilities. Following this declaration the community was placed in third-party management by the Department of Aboriginal Affairs due to issues of financial mismanagement. What is interesting here is that the so-called financial mismanagement resulted from the attempts of the band government to address the housing, education, and medical crises in the community by reallocating portions of its budget. Later the Federal Court found that the community has been devastated by Ottawa's bureaucratic oppression both with respect to the band council's inability to respond to community needs and Ottawa's attempts to reassert its control over the community through financial management and budgeting processes (*Attawapiskat v. Minister of Aboriginal Affairs* 2012).

As both the case of Attawapiskat and the actual scope and magnitude of the Indian Act itself demonstrate, it is the legislation in and of itself and the manner in which it has been institutionalized by the federal government that constitute a political genocide. It is more than simply a regime replacement, for its sole purpose was to destroy Indigenous forms of governance and to replace these with a system of government modeled after the settler state. To simply call this a regime replacement or an act of civilization or assimilation completely misses the fact that Lemkin is trying to make in addressing the multiple forms of genocide. Genocide need not be equated solely with the execution of individuals, as the obliteration of nations and "cessation of self-government and local rule, and their replacement by that of the occupier" (Moses 2008: 13) also counts as genocide. But as Attawapiskat and my discussion of the legislative framework for the Indian Act band council system of government surmise, it is not simply the act of replacement that constitutes the genocide; it is the manner in which power and oppression have been institutionalized to obfuscate and deny nationhood, the exercise of sovereignty, or for that matter even responsible government.

Obliterating Nations

When I used to teach about the Indian Act in my introduction to Canadian politics course at a southern Ontario university, I was typically horrified by the sheer ignorance of so many Canadians who managed to conceive of it as a pro-Indian piece of legislation that Indigenous people had created or at the very least consented to. Somewhere along the way Indigenous people learned to live with it, and some have accepted it as an inalienable state of reality, but this is far from a statement of consent. In fact, given the protracted fight for the recognition and implementation of the inherent right to self-determination that has been going on since the 1960s or the fight to protect and reinvigorate Indigenous sovereignty that dates back to the outset of the invasion, it is fairly clear that the Indian Act continues to represent an attempt to destroy Indigenous sovereignty and systems of government and to oppress Indigenous nations (as individuals and collectives). This reality is surprisingly similar to that which is described by Lemkin as constituting a political (and cultural) form of genocide. Thus it is not simply a matter of the Indian Act constituting a political genocide whereby the Act represents both legislated intent and the perpetuation of genocide through the destruction of nationhood, sovereignty, and Indigenous political systems. The Act itself also represents the destructive element or the first phase of genocide such that it was through the Act that Indigenous political systems were intentionally destroyed.

Across the country, in almost every community, Indigenous governments were either wiped out or ceased to exist as governments (thus the existence of "traditional chiefs" or "traditional governments" in many communities that are no longer recognized as constituting governments by colonial administrators and often even Indigenous members of those nations). As Lemkin suggests, Indigenous governments ceased to exist as governments wielding some semblance of collective power or sovereignty such that "every reminder of former national character was obliterated" (cited in Moses 2008: 13). Most often traditional governments ceased to be recognized as governments and were replaced through fairly peaceful administrative means whereby Canadian officials appointed (or had elected) individuals as puppet regimes (chief and council) that would serve to assist federal employees, church officials, and Indian agents. Quite often, traditional leadership constituted these early puppet regimes, in essence becoming leaders in name only as all power and all resources resided with state officials.

That many traditional governments were peacefully replaced is not a suggestion that political genocide did not exist or that such can be explained solely in terms of assimilation, progress, or a belief in Western-Eurocentric civilization. Regardless of how it was done, this was not destruction "by invitation." Destruction of nationhood, sovereignty, political culture, laws, and institutions is nonetheless necessarily political genocide. Moreover the "peaceful" nature of this genocide is largely due to the instruments that were used to force traditional leadership into compliance and to assume an outwardly subservient role to colonial authorities. Though historians have yet to pay attention to this question in any detail, it is commonplace in Cree and Blackfoot communities to hear elders (those who are community historians) speak of Indian agents bribing communities or political leaders with promises of food or better rations or promising to save a compliant leader's child from the horrors of residential school. While such tactics were used, it is also common to hear (from both professional historians and community historians) that traditional leaders continued in their roles within a new system despite the oppressive nature of the Indian Act simply because they were leaders and chose to live those responsibilities regardless. When this first generation of hybrid leaders (traditional and Indian Act band council) was no longer, their communities were wholeheartedly thrust into the band council system.

Regardless of who occupied these positions, as Lemkin writes, these situations still constitute a political form of genocide such that these nations lost the ability to govern themselves as nations in accordance with their own laws due to the oppressive regime of the colonizer. One should also note that regime replacement was not necessarily peaceful as there are instances of leaders being shot by government officials (police; such was the case in Akewasne in 1899), leaders being temporally imprisoned (as was the case at Six Nations in 1924), leaders being forced to move underground, and leaders being arrested and jailed for such offenses as hosting public gatherings, engaging in governance through ceremonies and activities such as potlatch, or even dancing (as was the case at multiple reserves, including Thunderchild). Though there was little blood shed, this was nevertheless a genocide perpetrated through violence, the threat of violence (including the real threat of starvation in the early period of reserve life), or the still-used threat of withholding of government funds (for health, education, social assistance, housing) for noncompliance, and the constantly present bureaucratic assault that Neu and Therrien (2003) call genocide.

It is interesting to note that Neu and Therrien see this genocide as continuing rather than letting up despite the outward appearance of violence subsiding. True band councils now operate within a rubric of delegated jurisdictions that provide an illusion of government—of governments that have the capacity to address the problems, needs, and aspirations of communities. For the most part, however, this is just an illusion, as band councils continue to operate within the same system that defined and confined them in the past. While a band council may now have the delegated authority to operate schools and to provide social services, their capacity to act and to respond to the needs of communities is still limited by the fact that they simply administer federal programs, lack financial resources and jurisdiction, and are both accountable to and financially dependent on the federal government. As I have argued elsewhere, this has little to do with decolonization and nothing to do with the lessoning of oppression or an acknowledgment of Indigenous nationhood or self-determination; it is a perpetual state of negotiation inferiority whereby Indigenous peoples are forced into continued submission under the colonial orders (Ladner 2001; Alfred 2005a). As Neu and Therrien (2003: 7) stress, they occupy these areas of policy delivery and delegated responsibilities only because to do so they have had to accept the subjugation of nationhood.

Final Words

As this chapter demonstrates, genocide in the Americas was not limited to physical acts of individualized destruction through instruments of death such as smallpox blankets or the cultural genocide perpetrated through the "civilizing" process of "killing the Indian, saving the child" in residential (and potentially day) schools. While it is important to understand that a political genocide occurred, it is equally important to understand that such genocides did not occur in isolation from each other; they were part of a wider plan of extirpation in the sense that Indigenous peoples were to be dispossessed of and removed from their territories and extermination in the sense that while Indigenous peoples failed to become the dying race, as had been widely predicted, the Canadian government explicitly engaged in practices of cultural, linguistic, and political extermination through both residential schools and the Indian Act itself.

The legislated political genocide and the cultural genocide perpetrated through residential and day schools are inextricably linked. The relationship between the two goes beyond their joint role in Canada's extermination policy (what is typically understood as civilization and assimilation), as residential schools also had a visceral secondary effect as an internal form of political genocide as opposed to the external legislative and bureaucratic sources of political genocide under the Indian Act. It is not only that Indigenous systems have been legislated out of existence or destroyed through the violence and domination of the Indian Act and the bureaucrats and church officials that oversaw the Indian Act. As if that were not enough, what remained of these systems and of Indigenous political philosophies and systems operationalized within the Indian Act system (or in the vestiges of old) has in large part become imbued with foreign ideas and values and the dysfunctional normalcy of residential school. Simply put, what we see is a political genocide from forces within (internal colonialism) and external oppressors (both the legislation and the bureaucracy; Neu and Therrien 2003; Goodwill and Sluman 1984).[7] As scholars such as Alfred and Smith have suggested, this form is insidious for it has become internalized within the very beings of people and is manifested in all forms of relations and the disfunctionality (read as residential school normalcy) that dominates power relations in many families, communities, and nations.

Though the relationship between residential schools and political genocide must be left to future research, it is important to draw the legacy of residential school into this discussion of political genocide to fully understand the magnitude of the genocide that occurred. While the Indian Act in and of itself is an act of political genocide such that it legislated the destruction and annihilation of Indigenous nationhood, sovereignty, and political systems while imposing the institutions of the oppressor (to use the language of Lemkin), residential schools (and arguably day schools) destroyed political culture, knowledge, and practices in individuals by means of an individualized attempt at cultural extermination.

This relationship is evident if we return to the discussion of Indigenous political traditions presented earlier and consider the manner in which power is understood and vested within Indigenous political traditions. Given the predominant conceptualization of individuals as autonomous entities, and the fact that authority was typically vested in the collective as a whole, it is fairly obvious that residential schools introduced people into this system that were not acculturated within it and conceived of power in the most violent, hierarchical, visceral, controlling, and authoritative manner possible. In so doing it is quite possible that residential school survivors ended up as agents of their own political genocide—devastating the political traditions, knowledge, and practices that survived under the Indian Act despite being legislated out of existence. After surviving the normalcy of power over others that dominated residential schools, many students came home wielding that same form of power in their families, communities, and nations. Communities became increasingly dominated by those who had foreign values and beliefs, and in turn Indigenous communities and their puppet governments became dominated by the same. There was less and less space (physical and otherwise) where that true sense of power remained unmitigated and unimpeded by foreign conceptualizations of power. Though the two have coexisted somewhat since, and though many individuals, families, and communities still hold to the cultural ethic of noninterference, the effect has nevertheless been that of a slow-moving poison within traditional political philosophies and the operationalization of those philosophies within government.

Notes

I wish to acknowledge the financial support of the Canada Research Chairs Program. I also wish to thank the editors of this volume, Myra Tait, Tasha Hubbard, Chad Cowie, and the reviewers for their assistance with this project.

1. Twenty some years ago Hugh Dempsey provided me with a copy of an article published by the *Leader Post* (possibly entitled "The Hegira of Indians"). While I misplaced this article many, many years ago, I have never forgotten the words that I read on that piece of paper and the zealousness with which one individual heralded both the removal of human beings from their home(land)s and the means of removal.

2. Over the years (in both my personal and professional life) I have heard countless stories of atrocities and tragedy in Cypress Hills recounted in Cree, Nakoda, Anishnaabe, and Blackfoot oral traditions. Much of this history was also recounted in the negotiation of Treaties Four and Six, as evidenced by both the written and oral traditions. Amazingly such tragedy also became embedded in Canadian popular culture through novels such as *Wolf Willow* (see Stegner 1955; Ray, Miller, and Tough 2000).

3. I use "Canada's Indigenous peoples" here to denote that sense of ownership.

4. As I stated in 2003 with reference to an instance of regime replacement, "What this amounted to was government-sanctioned murder of the political leader of a sovereign nation. Murder and the destruction of a political system were thus justified in the name of advancing 'civilization' and imposing the 'authority' of the Crown and the Indian Act system."

5. For quite an extensive list of such definitions, see Powell (2011).

6. What is meant by acting responsibly differs among nations, but essentially it means respecting the autonomy of others (i.e., not committing murder, not acting corrosively, and not stealing). In some cases, such as among the Siiksikaawa and Nehiyaw, this also means not interfering with the communal hunt. Failure to respect the autonomy of individuals and the community are dealt with in a variety of ways, all of which limit the autonomy of the individual to some degree or another. Failure to "live one's relationships" or act responsibly in a manner that does not impede the autonomy of others is typically dealt with through ridicule and noncoercive instruction.

7. *John Tootoosis* (Goodwill and Sluman 1984) is also important for this due to its description and discussion of the state that Indigenous children were in upon returning to their communities and the impact they would have.

References

Alfred, Taiaiake. 2005a. *Peace, Power, Righteousness: An Indigenous Manifesto*. Don Mills, Canada: Oxford University Press.

Alfred, Taiaiake. 2005b. *Wasase: Indigenous Pathways of Action and Freedom*. Peterborough, Canada: Broadview Press.

Attawapiskat First Nation v. Minister of Aboriginal Affairs and Northern Development Canada, 2012, T-2037-11.

Churchill, Ward. 1997. *A Little Matter of Genocide: Holocaust and Denial in the Americas, 1492 to the Present*. San Francisco: City Lights.

Clastres, Pierre. 1989. *Society against the State: The Leader as Servant and the Humane Use of Power among the Indians of the Americas*. New York: Zone Books.

Deloria, Vine, Jr. 1994. *God Is Red: A Native View of Religion*. Vancouver: Fulcrum.

Deloria, Vine, Jr. 1995. *Red Earth, White Lies: Native Americans and the Myth of Scientific Fact*. Vancouver: Fulcrum.

Elias, P. D. 1991. *Development of Aboriginal People's Communities*. North York, Canada: Captus Press.

Goodwill, Jean, and Norma Sluman. 1984. *John Tootoosis*. Winnipeg: Pemmican.

Government of Canada. 1985. Indian Act. Ottawa: Public Works and Government Services Canada.

Ladner, Kiera. 2001. "Negotiated Inferiority: The Royal Commission on Aboriginal People's Vision of a Renewed Relationship." *American Review of Canadian Studies*, 241–64.

Ladner, Kiera. 2003a. "Governing within an Ecological Context: Creating an Alter-Native Understanding of Blackfoot Governance." *Studies in Political Economy* 70 (spring): 125–52.

Ladner, Kiera. 2003b. "Rethinking the Past, Present, and Future of Aboriginal Governance." In *Reinventing Canada: Politics of the 21st Century*, edited by Janine Brodie and Linda Trimble, 43–60. Toronto: Prentice Hall.

Ladner, Kiera, and Michael Orsini. 2003. "The Persistence of Paradigm Paralysis." In *Canada: State of the Federation*, edited by M. Murphy, 185–203. Kingston, Canada: Queens Institute of Intergovernmental Relations.

Lemkin, Raphael. 1944. *Axis Rule in Occupied Europe: Laws of Occupation, Analysis of Government, Proposals for Redress*. Washington, DC: Carnegie Endowment for International Peace.

McDonnell, Michael, and Dirk Moses. 2005. "Raphael Lemkin as Historian of Genocide in the Americas." *Journal of Genocide Research* 7 (4): 501–29.

Moses, A. Dirk. 2008. "Empire, Colony, Genocide: Key Words and the Philosophy of History." In *Empire, Colony, and Genocide: Conquest, Occupation and Subaltern Resistance in World History*, edited by A. Dirk Moses, 3–54. New York: Berghahn Books.

Neu, Dean, and Richard Therrien. 2003. *Accounting for Genocide: Canada's Assault on Aboriginal Peoples*. Winnipeg: Fernwood.

Powell, Chris. 2011. *Barbaric Civilizations: A Critical Sociology of Genocide*. Montreal: McGill-Queen's University Press.

Ray, Arthur J., Jim Miller, and Frank Tough. 2000. *Bounty and Benevolence: A History of Saskatchewan Treaties*. Montreal: McGill-Queens University Press.

Ross, Rupert. 1996. *Returning to the Teachings: Exploring Aboriginal Justice*. Toronto: Penguin Books.

Simpson, Leanne. 2011. *Dancing on Our Turtle's Back: Stories of Nishnaabeg Re-Creation, Resurgence and a New Emergence*. Winnipeg: Arbeiter Ring.

Stannard, David. 1993. *American Holocaust: The Conquest of the New World*. Don Mills, Canada: Oxford University Press.

Stegner, Wallace. 1955. *Wolf Willow: A History, a Story, and a Memory of the Last Plains Frontier*. New York: Viking Press.

Tobias, John. 1991. "Protection, Civilization, and Assimilation: An Outline History of Canada's Indian Policy." In *Sweet Promises*, edited by J. R. Miller, 127–44. Toronto: University of Toronto Press.

CHAPTER 11

DISPOSSESSION AND CANADIAN
LAND CLAIMS

Genocidal Implications of the
Innu Nation Land Claim

Colin Samson

> *Some will rob you with a six-gun,*
> *and some with a fountain pen.*
> —Woody Guthrie, 1939

In 1994 Innu leaders in northern Labrador first told me about "land claims" as a way of stopping the industrial projects appearing on their lands and in the skies over them. This was made real to me when I went to the land with them and spent three weeks in a camp along the shores of a lake called Utshisk-nipi, hunting and fishing while military jets soared above the trees at supersonic speeds (Wadden 1991). I could see the disturbing effect of these jets on the hunting families, and with it the need to do something to allow the cultural survival of the Innu.

Seeing the deep attachments Innu people had to the land made me wonder about the curious words *land claims*. At one level, *land claims* implies a virtuous and compassionate gesture on the part of a government wishing only to give recognition to the rights of the people living at Utshisk-nipi and elsewhere before the arrival of Europeans. Indeed the language of the process as enunciated by the Canadian government is remarkably similar to that of liberal theorists of multiculturalism and human rights who generously conjoin *recognition* in the abstract with concrete *claims*. These claims are at the center of what is largely depicted as a benign process of decolonization, the crowning achievement of which is recognition within a multicultural state (Kymlicka 2002; Anaya 2004). To claim is often conceived as an act of petitioning or reaching out for something that is one's own or should be one's by right. But conversely there is no person, group, or organization within or outside the state to which the state itself needs to make claims. Rather the state simply extends its authority over "its" populations, hears claims, and, according to the liberal vision, "recognizes" them by attending to various measures of justice, fairness, and equality, which, as Agamben (2005) has argued, it is free to ignore or suspend. James Anaya (2004: 61), the United Nations special rapporteur, sees this process as a "challenge" for the state, but he and other liberals fall short of any sociohistorical analysis of how state power is created and asserted. Equally far from the attention of current-day liberalism in general is, as James Tully (1995: 34–36) has observed, that the language and protocol used in assessing claims to recognition suffocates cultural differences. I would like to go further and interpret the Canadian land claims process as a policy designed to formalize land dispossession and transform Indigenous lands and ways of life to such an extent that it destroys a unique culture, and therefore can be considered a form of genocide.

In formal land claims negotiations, we must ask, Who claims from whom? Who is being recognized by the claim, and what kind of recognition is it? Once we start asking such questions, it becomes obvious that peoples whose land has been occupied and over which an external sovereignty has been asserted are themselves the petitioners. As petitioners, they are "recognized" only insofar as they concede to the state that they are its subjects. In the liberal mind this is an element of citizenship, but as citizens, Indigenous peoples' independence, sovereignty, and cultural integrity are not being recognized. Through their signatures on a land claim, they simply affirm *their* recognition of the state and, although it scarcely needs it, grants legitimacy to the state by making a "claim" on it. In exchange the state then gives them monies and accords them specific kinds of rights that are of a completely different and vastly diminished order than the rights they formerly had as autonomous peoples. In the process the state determines how Innu, in this case, will be able to orient themselves to their lands and how they will be governed. In its powers to accord these new rights, which are in Orwellian fashion termed *self-determination*, Canada formalizes a process of radical cultural disintegration and restructuring of Aboriginal society.

As Damien Short (2010) and Andrew Woolford (2011) have argued in relation to land dispossession processes involving Indigenous peoples, if we consider the intent of Raphael Lemkin, the author of the concept of genocide, it is clear that the destruction of culture, and in this case the destruction of the distinctly Indigenous relationships to lands and to each other, is genocide. While settlers transplanted themselves to North America in order to create a new society, Indigenous societies, based on hunting, agriculture, and movement, exist on the lands upon which settler society is built. The meanings and identities that were fashioned over millennia on these lands were largely incompatible with what settlers wished to create. In order to realize the settler society, formalized means of dispossession and ultimately genocide were employed. The Canadian Land Claims process is merely a recent incarnation of this.

This may seem far-fetched, but in order to understand how land claims specifically might be genocidal, it is important to examine the social and political contexts within which a people can be extricated from their lands and their rights curtailed. In this chapter I read the Innu Nation Tshash Petapen agreement as part of the architecture of dispossession and, ultimately, the destruction of culture.

Social Suffering

Land claims negotiations are entirely post hoc, taking place *after* the state has already asserted authority over Indigenous peoples' lands. In the Labrador-Quebec peninsula, the assertion of this authority corresponded most visibly with the sedentarization process, by which Innu who had been living in mobile multifamily groups across the tundra and forests were settled in government-built villages on the Labrador coast, on the North Shore of the St. Lawrence, and in north-central Quebec. What happened afterward was not pretty. From the 1960s onward many Innu descended into alcoholic oblivion, families broke up, suicide became commonplace, and social workers removed children and dispatched them to Euro-Canadian families in Ontario and Newfoundland. Beginning with white priests and teachers, sexual abuse also became common, and, fueled by alcohol and torpor, it spread within Innu families themselves (Samson 2003a). Those who continued to pursue hunting and fishing were sometimes arrested under Newfoundland game laws, amounting to a criminalization of their way of life. There was, and still is, social suffering, and the land claims negotiations have taken place with this as an essential backdrop. Children in the village of Davis Inlet (relocated to Natuashish in 2003) have persistently engaged in mass gas sniffing, and this continues to the present (CBC News 2012b). This situation is mirrored across Canada, where in many Indigenous communities social suffering accompanies land claims negotiations (Irlbacher-Fox 2009: 27–31).

Hence the Innu were collectively traumatized by the state's maneuvering them off the land and, while in this condition, were put in the position of having to make a bureaucratic case for some measure of recognition of their occupancy of it. This echoes the North American treaty process, a system that was put into effect when Indigenous peoples had either been removed from their lands, were under threat from forcible removal, or were deprived of the means to live on their lands, especially during westward expansion in the nineteenth century. Treaty negotiations in North America frequently were undertaken when Indigenous groups had already been severely weakened by European contact. The commercial slaughters of the bison, the transmission of fatal infectious diseases, and forced assimilation policies were to the imposition of reservations on the Plains Indians in Canada and the United States (Isenberg 2000: 151–52; Lux 2001: 32–70) what sedentarization is to the negotiation of the land claims of the Innu. Indeed Tasha Hubbard (this volume) powerfully makes the case that the purposeful slaughter of bison was a means of killing Native Americans in vast numbers, and with that the deep associations between the bison and the peoples of the Great Plains. While it is difficult to say that Canadian authorities "knew" that sedentarization would precipitate catastrophic sufferings across the Far North, they surely would have been aware of historical antecedents in the United States.

Leadership Structures

The social suffering that coincides with land claims is exacerbated by the loss of traditional forms of social organization that in the past might have been a source of collective healing and solidarity. In the Labrador-Quebec peninsula, as elsewhere claimed by Canada, Indigenous peoples' lands were simply commandeered before any treaty or land claim agreement was concluded with any Indigenous person or group. A small list of the unconsented violations in the Innu territories would include (a) the building of the Goose Bay airbase on Innu lands by and for the U.S. Air Force during World War II, then handed over to the Royal Canadian Air Force, which leased it to NATO; (b) the Upper Churchill hydroelectric complex, built in the late 1960s on one of the most important rivers to the Innu, and which flooded the beloved Meshikamau area, turned it into a wasteland incapable of use for hunting or fishing, and reduced the massive waterfalls Patshetshunau to a trickle; and (c) the Voisey's Bay mine, discovered by prospectors in the early 1990s, which now turns a massive profit from the mining of nickel for the Brazilian company Vale Inco. The area where the mine is located was a place favored by the Innu for generations; many were born there—for example, Kaniuekutat, the celebrated Innu hunter of Georg Henriksen's (2009: 32, 242) biography. There are also burial sites around Voisey's Bay and it is close to breeding grounds for geese and ducks and on the migration route of caribou.

Seeing their lands gradually stolen from them, the Innu filed for a land claim in 1977 under the Naskapi-Montagnais Innu Association, an organization that initiated formalized leadership structures among them. Canada was satisfied that Innu could make a claim in Labrador only in 1990, and the process started in earnest then. When the state started to make more demands on the Innu to prove their claim, the Innu Nation was formed, and the elected leaders called upon a number of non-Innu professionals to help them; through these intermediaries the Innu began to negotiate with the state. The Innu were not recognized as "status Indians" until 2002, and their land claim, the "Tshash Petapen" or "New Dawn" Agreement in Principle (AIP), was finalized in 2008 and approved in 2011 by a decisive ratification vote in the two villages Innu Nation represents, Natuashish and Sheshatshiu. It has yet to reach a final ratification.

Innu Nation is funded by Canada, which is effectively the adversary of the Innu in the land claims negotiations. In its institutionalization of permanent political authority and hierarchical decision making, Innu Nation incorporates many values that the Innu had hitherto regarded as offensive. In fact their relatively recent pre-sedentarization lives were organized around small and flexible family groupings, in which sharing was valued and the assumption of status was sometimes ridiculed because it was dysfunctional to the social cohesion needed to survive on the land. Nonetheless, under the AIP, the Innu Nation must "warrant" Canada that it represents Innu and has the authority to enter into the agreement on behalf of Innu who hold preexisting rights such as Aboriginal title (Aboriginal Affairs and Northern Development Canada 2011: 2.25.1).

The Innu Nation contains elected officials in various departments structured to contest the land claim. Operating according to Canadian rules for elections, officials such as the president and vice president are elected by popular vote. To indicate the enhanced importance of the positions, the leaders recently altered their titles to grand chief and deputy grand chief, forms of aggrandizement that would have been seen as vulgar and divisive not so long ago. It is well known that elections operate within a patronage system whereby candidates receive donations from local non-Innu businesses, distribute goods, often alcohol, and make promises to voters to attend to their needs (see CBC News 2012a). Once they are elected, those who aligned themselves with the successful candidates benefit in one way or another, and some of these perks can be life-changing. Through their interconnections with the leaders of the band councils who are also participants in the land claims negotiations, Innu Nation leaders, for example, influence the allocation of housing, so vital to communities with extremely high birth rates. It is a rare day when people in Natuashish and Sheshatshiu do not visit their officials to urge that they make good on campaign promises. In return the local donors also expect some pay-off from various business contracts involving the Innu. These leaders are servants to several different masters. As well as pacifying those who voted for them and funded them, their primary role is to negotiate the land claim, a sizable portion of which they outsource to Canadian advisors who deal with the technical details required by the Canadian government. These advisors often have little personal interest in the process beyond financial and professional stakes and this encourages compromises. Irlbacher-Fox (2009: 166) notes the "constant tension between the white technocrats and the beneficiaries they served" in regard to Inuvialut and Gwich'in land claims. At the same time, many leaders, anticipating the vast numbers of companies that will be hungry to develop Innu land, have enlisted the technocrats' assistance in making deals for extractive industrial and other projects before the agreement has even been concluded.

This all makes for an unbalanced negotiating platform, in which one party demands that its forms of leadership and political authority be employed by the other party. It is not surprising, then, that Innu politics leads to bitterness, jealousies, fractiousness, and even violence, all of which Innu hunting society was organized to avoid. This is multiplied further by the fact that land claims are applied to discrete groups of people rather than a people as a whole. The Innu-aimun–speaking peoples are spread across two provinces. The Innu who happen to be domiciled in Labrador are misleadingly called the Innu Nation, but several other groups in Quebec are configured into separate organizations. Each can claim only a defined territory that recognizes not Indigenous land use patterns but colonial borders, in this case the 1927 border drawn by the British to separate French and British colonists' access to fishing and trapping areas. The very fact of making a land claim for one group of Innu such as the Innu Nation means extinguishing the rights of other Innu to whom they are related and from whom they are separated by the arbitrary fact that they were subject to sedentarization in different places.

In that case, why do they collaborate with a procedure that will dismantle the unity and cultural coherence and distinctiveness of the Innu people?

No Alternatives to the Agreement

They say that necessity is the mother of invention, and indeed necessity forced the hand of the Innu people to seek some means to abate the plunder of their lands. The only remedy that Canada held out to them was the land claims process. Had they tried to take Canada to court, they would probably have been unsuccessful. Other Aboriginal groups, including the Nisga'a in the original 1973 *Calder* decision that affirmed the existence of preexisting Aboriginal title, were denied a land claim, and such denials persisted up until the 1990s. From the *Baker Lake* case onward denial of land claims was often based on Canadian courts embracing the cultural evolutionism contained in the British Privy Council decision of 1919 *Re Southern Rhodesia*. This was "the leading precedent with respect to tests for Aboriginal Title" (Bell and Asch 1997: 59), holding that Indigenous peoples were not entitled to land rights because they did not constitute an "organized society."

Aboriginal groups could pursue, and many have pursued, international remedies, such as conducting international media campaigns via NGOs, taking the state to the Inter-American Court of Human Rights, lodging complaints at the UN, and participating in the process that led to the 2007 UN Declaration on the Rights of Indigenous Peoples. The UN Permanent Forum on Indigenous Issues also offers opportunities to influence implementation of the Declaration. While engagement in the international arena can lead to the visible questioning of state policies, international institutions do not and cannot challenge state sovereignty, which is at the heart of the land claims conflicts. International human rights institutions can embarrass states into action, and much can be achieved by internationalizing Indigenous grievances with states, but regarding land conflicts, Canada proceeds as if these international standards were no impediment to its own policies.

One effect of the limitations of such remedies is to make people in Aboriginal communities feel as if there is only one path to the recognition of rights to their lands: the one mapped out by the Canadian state and to which the land claims technocrats are principally oriented. Speaking of the Kluane people in his study *Hunters and Bureaucrats*, Paul Nadasdy (2003: 224) states, "They forge ahead [with land claims] because they see it as the only viable option to their survival as a people." This leads to fatalistic attitudes among many Aboriginal people. Paul Pone, a young hunter I got to know in 1995, told me in 2012, "What else can we do? We need jobs and money and security for the future. Other Aboriginals have only small reserves. We are going to get a much bigger area." He is just one who, perhaps through necessity, has embraced the land claims process and believes that it will bring many benefits to the Innu. In doing so he uses the language of claims, an acknowledgment, perhaps grudging, of the magnanimity of the state. It is not land relinquished that is highlighted, but land granted to the Innu, along with jobs, business opportunities, and cash compensation that will form the basis of this security. This might be a form of cognitive dissonance. When people are confronted with a situation in which opposition appears to them hopeless, they may invest credence in ideas that they originally rejected and start to articulate a corresponding logic. This may not be durable without some kind of incentive, and here the incentives are quite plentiful for those who are positioned to take advantage of the financial packages that are attached to the agreement.

Yet even those Innu who are in or close to the leadership are aware that some parts of the agreement mean huge sacrifices, and indeed they have made these known to their Canadian advisors. The general reaction of the advisors in the recent past was similar to the reaction of Canada to any group that has challenged the logic and the mechanics of land claims: "Take it or leave it" (Samson 2003b: 57–86). The Innu are thus under extreme pressure to take it because if they do not the state simply assumes sovereignty, checked only by legal mandates to consult, such as those emanating from the 1998 *Delgamuukw* Supreme Court decision.

Manufacturing Consent

The Canadian government used several techniques to elicit consent to the land claims agreement. One was to insulate the Innu public from the contents of the agreement itself and thus circumvent cognitive dissonance. During my trips in 2009 and 2012 virtually everyone I asked in Sheshatshiu and Natuashish told me that they knew very little about Tshiash Petapen. There were several versions of it published, most prominently an eighty-page document of what would be a 436-page agreement. This and other precursors to the draft AIP were shrouded in secrecy, with large notices plastered on almost every summary indicating that only "Labrador Innu" could see it, that they were not to show it to others, and that the information in it was "commercially sensitive." The summary was available to community leaders in English, but there was no opportunity for all those who were called on to ratify this life-changing agreement to read the summary, let alone the AIP. The full agreement could not have been communicated in all its technical detail to the voters in Innu-aimun, a language that has no equivalent terms for the majority of the phrases, words, concepts, and provisions in the agreement (Samson and Cassell 2013). As far as I am aware there were only a small number of sparsely attended community meetings in which some parts of the AIP were summarized in Innu-aimun.

Although some of the AIP is translated, most Innu find the written version of their language more cumbersome than English, and many do not know how to read it. Older Innu who would have the most knowledge about the land are largely illiterate in both English and Innu-aimun. This, however, may be a moot point, since the only authoritative versions of the AIP are the English and French ones. It is a moot point, however, for a more basic reason. The AIP weighs in at about 132,000 words and is set out in numbered paragraphs, many of which contain the most mind-numbingly perplexing clauses, subclauses, and qualifications that one must have a high tedium threshold to want to read it carefully. This is one of the reasons there exists an entire class of professionals who command large sums both for creating and deciphering such verbiage to those on whose behalf they allegedly act. The complexity of the text itself, in addition to the arrangements for self-government, mineral exploration, economic development, and the convoluted "resource management board," ought to guarantee work for lawyers for centuries. For the Innu, few of whom have any higher education or legal training, the deciphering falls to a team of lawyers, Olthuis, Kleer, and Townsend (OKT), based in Toronto. In an effusive statement on the firm's website, the lead lawyer, John Olthuis (2011), writes, "I am deeply honoured to have worked with the Innu of Labrador for 28 yrs (the last 15 hand in hand with my partner Nancy Kleer) to achieve these reconciling agreements that will ensure self determination for this and many future generations of Innu." On the whole, the Innu must take Olthuis's word for it that the agreement is almost exclusively positive. The entire text of OKT's feature on the New Dawn is phrased in the affirmative: "Innu will get . . . ," and so on. However, the Innu rely not merely on Olthuis but also on other Canadian technocrats whose handsome fees are paid by the state, then deducted by Canada at the signing of the Final Agreement. This total is rumored by people in Natuashish to be about $60 million and this pattern is mirrored across Canada. The auditor-general in British Columbia estimated that the fees for lawyers and bureaucrats for land claims negotiations in that province amounted to $1 billion over a thirteen-year period (*Vancouver Sun* 2006).

Working in favor of the proponents of land claims is the fact that the agreement flatters the Innu, depicting them as if they are at least semi-autonomous. Even though the political body representing the Innu domiciled in Labrador has little or no relationship to Innu forms of social and political organization, it is referred to as the "Innu Government," and the laws that this "government" is able to enforce on Labrador Innu lands regarding access, fees, permits, and the like are termed "Innu Law." If readers persevere to chapter 20, however, they will see that this "government" is "subject to the appropriation of funds" by Canada (20.1.5), making it analogous to a small municipal authority.

One further aid to the process of eliciting consent is the rules on voting. The AIP required only 51 percent of voters to assent to it, regardless of the turnout. Shortly before the AIP vote in November 2011, the Innu leadership reduced the voting age to sixteen for the initial vote. The future ratification for the Final Agreement, however, will require a voting age of eighteen (4.1.1) and 60 percent approval (31.3.2). This means that a huge swath of voters with potentially even less knowledge of the contents of the agreement was added to the numbers of those who could pass it forward for ratification. At the other extreme are older Innu such as Shushep Mark, who has on several occasions taken me out onto the land for fishing trips. Shushep could not read the agreement; he told me that he didn't know much about it, except that it was "all about money." He thought that he would lose a lot of freedom. He said that the elders didn't understand it and had given up. "No one knows anything about it," Dominic Pokue, my host all those years ago at Utshisk-nipi, told me in conversation in 2009. With his brother-in-law George Gregoire translating, Dominic said, "It's all about business deals. When they take the elders to the meetings they just choose two people who don't understand anything, and they just say 'yes.'"

For these Innu, the land claims are about business deals. OKT does not deny this, and in fact highlights it as a positive feature of the agreement. For example:

> The Upper Churchill Redress Agreement and the Lower Churchill Innu Impacts and Benefits Agreement will provide:
>
> Compensation to the Innu (worth about $100 million over 30 years) for the flooding of hunting grounds that occurred when the Upper Churchill hydroelectric project was built in the 1960s
>
> Innu rights to a 3% share of the future Upper Churchill project revenues when Newfoundland and Labrador's contract with Quebec expires in 2041
>
> Innu rights to 5 million dollars a year (indexed) during construction and during operation 5% of the cash flow from the Muskrat Falls hydro project (a $6.2-billion project which will export 825 megawatts of power to Newfoundland and Nova Scotia) and the larger Gull Island hydro project when it proceeds
>
> Training, employment and business opportunities and a role in environmental permitting for these hydro projects. (Olthuis 2011)

While the meaning, adequacy, and distribution of monies could be the subjects of an entire study, what is not said here is that the "benefits" come with considerable costs. These costs are inflicted upon the Innu way of life, independence, and sovereignty. The end result of the land claims agreement is to engineer new lifestyles that will displace key elements of the Innu way of life and the values upon which it is based. In the process the Innu move to a position in which they become one among many groups who have various recognized rights and claims within the state, but no meaningful independence from it.

Certainty

Leading up to the AIP, the Innu public was provided with various selectively abbreviated versions of the full text. In one summary, entitled "Tshash Petapen Agreements: Summaries of the Following Agreements Prepared Exclusively and only for the Innu of Labrador," distributed to Innu leaders in 2010, the extinguishment of preexisting Innu rights including Aboriginal title is mentioned only under "Other Provisions" at the end of the document. The mention of it as a "release that the Innu will give to Newfoundland and Labrador and Canada" could easily be interpreted as innocuous, slipping the attention of even the most alert reader. In the AIP itself extinguishment is dealt with only in a footnote stating the province's preferred model, which is that "Innu hereby cede and release to Canada and the province all the aboriginal rights which Innu ever had, now have or may in future have within Canada" (2.12.2 fn). Extinguishment is contrary to both the UN Indigenous rights protocol and Canada's own Royal Commission on Aboriginal Peoples (1996). The AIP simply indicates that this issue will be negotiated and that Innu disagree.

Under the Certainty provisions, however, disagreement itself is rendered invalid. This and many other totalizing provisions are not subject to negotiation. For example, the agreement is said to "constitute the full and final settlement of the aboriginal rights of the Innu in Canada" and to "*exhaustively* set out the rights of the Innu in Canada" (my emphasis). This means that the Innu have no other rights than what the text stipulates. Their former rights as Indigenous peoples with Aboriginal title no longer apply, since their Aboriginal title is effectively extinguished on the ratification of the Final Agreement. The title they obtain in return is a subsidiary state-issued title over a vastly diminished land base. The "release," for which a sexual interpretation is most inviting, is of course the release of Canada's obligation to treat the land and rights of the Innu as preexisting, making it analogous to how a client might regard a prostitute after negotiating the payment.

The "release" the Innu give to Canada and other third parties is articulated in a highly significant addendum to the Certainty section of the AIP: "If the Parties reach the Agreement, Innu will release Canada, the Province and all other Persons from all claims, demands, actions or proceedings, of whatever kind, whether known or unknown, that Innu ever had, now have, or may have in the future, relating to or arising from, any act or omission occurring before the Effective Date that may have interfered with, affected or infringed any aboriginal rights of Innu in Canada" (2.13.1). This ungainly prose containing repeated additions of stipulations that are so all-embracing as to cover every eventuality in perpetuity requires repeated readings. Its totalitarian meaning is that the Innu agree that they have no legal claims other than those mentioned in the AIP for any violations of their Aboriginal rights "known or unknown" *ever*! The next section informs the Innu that if any lawsuit is brought for any "claims"—and here the message turns decidedly illiberal—those who bring the action must indemnify the Canadian government, while the succeeding section, "Invalidity," prohibits any party from challenging the validity of any provision in the agreement. Certainty locks the Innu into the agreement as surely as it locks them into small Bantustan-like parcels of land. In this respect Aboriginal Affairs and Northern Development Canada (AANDC), the latest incarnation of the government agency that negotiates land claims, is far more direct about the aims of land claims agreements to benefit business than are OKT, who frame almost all the benefits in terms of financial payoffs to the Innu. AANDC indicates that land claims are negotiated for two primary reasons: "greater certainty over rights to land and resources therefore contributing to a positive investment climate and creating greater potential for economic development and growth; greater control for Aboriginal people and Northerners over the decisions that affect their lives" (Aboriginal Affairs and Northern Development Canada 2010). The first point underscores the importance of the commercial imperative driving land claims. The second remains an assertion that is true only if one understands that the kind of control Aboriginal people are gaining is minuscule compared to that which they had in the recent past.

Ever-Diminishing Lands

The land that the Innu can claim is misleadingly titled "Labrador Innu Settlement Area." This is misleading because it makes the state entity of "Labrador" a component of Innu identity when it is merely an artifact of a colonial border. They are in fact people of Nitassinan, an area stretching across the Labrador-Quebec peninsula, as far north as Kujjuaq and south to the North Shore of the St. Lawrence, with a western periphery that could extend to Hudson's Bay. The Atlantic Ocean forms the eastern boundary. Sedentarization in villages in two provinces now delimits their "claims," meaning that those domiciled in the two Labrador villages have in theory most of Labrador to claim, the only exception being the far northern coastal areas occupied by Inuit. The "settlement area" has been negotiated to consist of fourteen thousand square miles of mostly north-central Labrador. Other areas in western and southern Labrador extensively used by Innu, even today, are off the map and simply become "Crown Land." The same applies to about nine thousand square miles within this settlement area. The "Labrador Innu Lands" under which the "Innu Government" will have specified types of jurisdiction covers a patchwork of only five thousand square miles of land, which they will receive in fee simple (5.8.2, 5.11). Maps 11.1 and 11.2, adapted from the AIP, show the extent of the new administrative land categories.

Third parties that are already encamped on Innu lands, from Vale Inco mining company at Voisey's Bay to operators of sports fishing and hunting operations within Labrador Innu Lands, are not required to give any kind of release equivalent to that which Certainty demands of the Innu. Their squatters' rights remain untouched, and in the case of Voisey's Bay are considered "for greater certainty" (22.2.4) to be outside both the Labrador Innu Settlement Area and Labrador Innu Lands. Although they cannot be enlarged and if they are put up for sale the "Innu Government" has the right of first refusal (7.8.3, Schedule 7-D), "third-party" lands such as those at Voisey's Bay are not obliged to be returned to the Innu when extraction possibilities have been exhausted (22.4.6). Lands available to Innu are again reduced by "major developments" such as the Lower Churchill Hydroelectric complex, areas that "third parties" such as settlers or sports hunting businesses have already seized and lands otherwise occupied by Canada.

The lands that Innu have lived on for centuries are further reduced by the stipulation that Canada or the province administers and has jurisdiction over "subsurface resources" (5.14). Although bound by a complex system of state, provincial, and "Innu Government" jurisdiction, explorers and prospectors seeking resources such as minerals, waters, or forests in Labrador Innu Lands need only "notify the Innu Government" (5.14.4), which must allow access (5.14.13). Under section 5.3.5 the province will "endeavour to locate and agree upon replacement lands . . . if such lands are reasonably available." The risk is, of course, that lands available to Innu to hunt, fish, travel, and practice *their* way of life will be continuously infringed upon and diminished. Except for a new national park and a few protected areas, the claiming of the smaller land base as Labrador Innu Land is not a conservation of the land or a return of the land to Indigenous control. In fact, ecological damage from developers is a real possibility in these lands, and this is indicated by the inclusion of provisions in chapter 10 of the AIP for making a claim for compensation and liability for loss or damage to "Innu Domestic Harvest" and the wildlife,

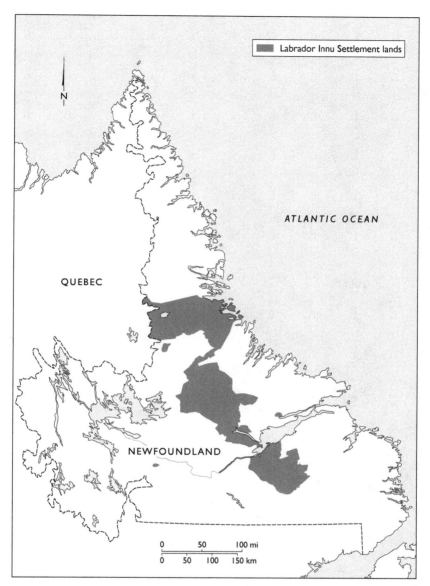

Map 11.1. Labrador Innu Settlement Area, as depicted in the Tshash Petapen Labrador Innu Land Claims Agreement-in-Principle, comprising fourteen thousand square miles and demarcating lands within the purview of the Agreement. The vast bulk of historical and contemporary Innu lands are unmarked and handed over as "Crown Land," including lands used by Innu domiciled in Quebec villages. These lands are areas within which there will be limited "Innu Government" jurisdiction, but Innu will need hunting permits on these lands, which are also exempt from the Impact and Benefits Agreement should resource extraction companies wish to establish operations. *Source:* Adapted from Labrador Innu Land Claims Agreement-in-Principle, ccl_farim_nl_labinnu_caip_1331749872252_eng by Bill Nelson.

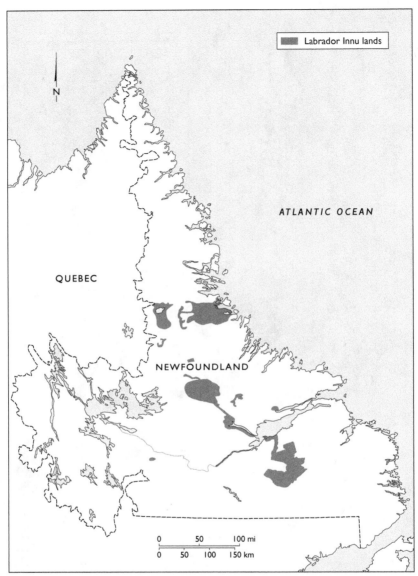

ATLANTIC OCEAN

QUEBEC

NEWFOUNDLAND

J

| 0 | 50 | 100 mi |
| 0 | 50 | 100 | 150 km |

Map 11.2. Labrador Innu Settlement Lands, as depicted in the Tshash Petapen Labrador Innu Land Claims Agreement-in-Principle, comprising five thousand square miles, over which the "Innu Government" will also have limited jurisdiction and Innu people will have hunting rights. However, these survive with most of the exemptions for resource extraction companies of the Labrador Settlement Areas intact. *Source:* Adapted from Labrador Innu Land Claims Agreement-in-Principle, ccl_farim_nl_labinnu_caip_1331749872252_eng by Bill Nelson.

migratory birds, and fish. Chapter 11 continues with statements affirming the need for state land use planning policies to consult with—and, significantly, not obtain consent from—the "Innu Government" for developments within the Labrador Innu Settlement Areas.

The fact that the economic exploitation of natural resources on Innu land is the major motive behind the land claims agreement is indicated by the way discussion of the rules and regulations concerning these issues dominate the text of the AIP. In chapter 5, titled "Land and Non-Renewable Resources," for example, only six of the thirty-one pages deal with hunting and related issues. The rest of it deals with mineral and other kinds of exploration. It details how, on some "Crown Land," the Innu Nation will be able to share in "major developments," but only through an Impact Benefit Agreement (IBA). They will have no right to prevent such developments on what was historically their land (part 5.5, 5.15). The wording used to describe the process of obtaining these Labrador Innu Lands for mineral development are framed in terms of consultation rather than consent, meaning that the Innu do not in any sense "own" such lands. They are owned by the state, and the state requires only that those corporations that wish to turn a profit from the lands consult with the "Innu Government." Under the AIP what was collective Innu land becomes fee simple; this means that the "Innu Government" may transfer or sell land to Canada and the province, which then presumably has the right to transfer it to third parties (5.8.5).

The reduction of lands continues as one reads through the agreement. Canada may expropriate Labrador Innu Lands under a compulsory purchase order by Canada's Expropriation Authority. Although it "shall endeavour to avoid Expropriating Labrador Innu Lands" (16.2.2), the state may confiscate 12 percent of it at any one time. This is expressed in conveniently convoluted language: "If at any time twelve (12) percent of the quantum of Labrador Innu Lands set out in 5.3.1 have been and remain Expropriated, no further Expropriation of Labrador Innu Lands shall occur unless the Expropriation Authority provides compensation that includes an amount of previously Expropriated Labrador Innu Lands equivalent in significance and value to the Labrador Innu Lands proposed for Expropriation" (16.2.22). In addition to expropriation, lands in the settlement area can be "alienated" by Canada for rights of access to developers and utility providers (17.2.5), and non-Innu can access Labrador Innu Lands for the "harvesting of small game and Migratory Birds" and eco-tours of up to eleven participants (17A.2.1). Additionally the Canadian military and foreign military under them "may enter, cross or remain on Labrador Innu Lands to carry out activities related to national defense and security" (17A.5.3).

Finally, although this has to be negotiated for the Final Agreement, the AIP mentions in a footnote that if by some chance "a court of last resort" in the future determines that Innu have an aboriginal right in lands other than those set out in the Agreement, they must extinguish the right immediately in favor of Canada. The vertiginous text shows the *intent* of the state to reduce the land rights of the Innu to the minimum. It indicates how every possible eventuality, including a judgment in favor of the Innu from the state's highest court, will be rendered void if Innu rights to their lands are recognized in the future. This makes any appeal the Innu may have to reclaim their lands effectively futile: "If, despite the Agreement and the Federal and Provincial Legislation referred to in Part 4.5, it is determined by a court of last resort that Innu have an aboriginal right in and to Labrador Innu Lands that is other than, or that is different in attributes or geographical extent from, the rights of Innu as set out in the Agreement, Innu, from the Effective Date, cede and release that aboriginal right to Canada and the Province to the extent that the aboriginal right is other than, or different in attributes or geographical extent from, the rights of Innu as set out in the Agreement" (2.12.5 fn).

What to Do with the People Whose Title Is Extinguished?

It is well documented that Indigenous peoples across North America were often not aware that by signing the treaty papers thrust in front of them, they were agreeing to have no further claim or rights to their lands (Fumoleau 1974; Brody 1981: 68; Treaty 7 Elders and Tribal Council et al. 1996; Bussidor and Bilgen-Reinart 1997: 25–28). This is not surprising because the colonists often identified, organized, or appointed the leaders who did the negotiating. Sometimes the signatories were opportunists seeking quick and immediate favor from those wanting to appropriate Indigenous lands. This process occurred in the United States with "the well-established policy of appealing to the avarice of . . . corruptible chiefs" (Foreman 1932: 19). Even where there was more genuine representation by leaders, there were numerous details lost in translation or not fully grasped by the Indigenous negotiators. This was especially so with the notion that boundaries were to be permanent and rights to collective occupancy forever extinguished. These points are well documented in regard to several treaties, including the Treaty of Luguna Negra involving the Navajo, who lost two-thirds of their traditional homeland (Utley 1984: 51). However, even the duplicity in the negotiations was not enough to give settlers all they wanted: every one of the 370 treaties entered into by the United States was violated (Wilson 1998: 279).

Today's land claims process is based on this treaty system. It contains within it every inducement for Indigenous peoples to be unaware of the costs of the settlement they are reaching. This is especially so in relation to their unique ways of life, which, while not always abandoned after a treaty, often become difficult to sustain on a much smaller land base. The treaty or land claims agreement affects a kind of break with the past by which more communal and egalitarian ways of doing things give way to individualism and commerce. As in all neoliberal capitalist societies, the system works to assist individuals and groups that are better placed to procure business deals and to sell collectively owned lands and other resources. In contemporary Indigenous communities in Canada these individuals are often those who have occupied top posts in the political bodies. For example, community members in Sheshatshiu were incensed to discover that former chief Paul Rich was paid $1 million in salary over two years as CEO of a company called Innu Development Partnerships Limited, set up to establish joint venture businesses with corporations seeking to exploit Innu land or provide goods and services to residents of Labrador. It was subsequently revealed that large proportions of the revenue received by the company went to Rich and other community leaders. Protests in Sheshatshiu closed down the Innu Nation office in August 2012 (CBC News 2012a, 2012d). This is merely one example of a process that occurs around the world with the introduction of vast sums of money into small communities. Apart from the sluicing of monetary advances into Aboriginal villages that have signed land claims, there is little of the "trickle down" that advocates of corporate development often claim. If the local Indigenous labor force is not educated to the levels required by these businesses, or if the businesses choose to bring in another labor force, as is often the case, large numbers of local Indigenous people remain unemployed. Many people in Sheshatshiu and Natuashish, for example, are living on very little income compared to other, extremely wealthy Innu who only a generation ago would have been their equals. Indeed the promise of rapid cash injections is a prime lever for the operation of Canadian land claims. As Stephanie Irlbacher-Fox (2009: 165) maintains, "Anyone working in the Indigenous rights industry in the North is familiar with the stories about how support in favour of land claims was gained. Some people believed that once a claim was signed there would be a new truck in every driveway. . . . That did not happen. The implementation of some agreements . . . floundered for years. People lived much as they had before the claim."

The historian Robert Utley (1984: 42) points out that in the nineteenth century the Bureau of Indian Affairs (BIA) had two main purposes: "to extinguish Indian land titles and to grapple with the vexing problem with what to do with the people whose title had been extinguished." The AANDC is today what the BIA was to the American frontier. Like the BIA it is concerned with both extinguishment and this "vexing problem," and like the BIA it has developed only crude ideas about what to do with those whose titles are extinguished. Just as the treaties concluded during westward expansion were often intended to permit the settlement and industrialization of Native American lands (Hoxie 1984: 147–49), the Canadian land claims creates "certainty" for commercial interests, especially in resource extraction.

Violability, Money, and Debt

As we have seen, companies and individuals that have preexisting "interests" on Innu land are not subject to the Certainty release in the AIP. Hence non-Aboriginal interests are largely nonviolable, while all those interests that would help sustain Innu identity, prosperity, and way of life on the land are violable. Even though there are "permit-free hunting areas" for Innu, the violability of the Innu way of life will be a permanent possibility.

Violability is the consequence of the release to Canada and third parties; in exchange the Innu receive largely monetary compensation. But the disbursing of such funds is complex, qualified, and riddled with payments going back to the state. Under the benign label of "revenue sharing," in addition to an IBA, the "Innu Government" is entitled to receive 25 percent of the revenue from subsurface resource in Labrador Innu Lands, 50 percent of the first $2 million in revenue (21.3), and 5 percent of the revenue from Voisey's Bay (22.3.1). Although the "Innu Government" has little power to prevent mining on Innu lands, it now has financial incentives to accept it with open arms. Most of chapter 21 of the AIP outlines the complex financial transfers that this revenue sharing will entail, but reading on, it becomes clear that if corporations do not generate certain proportions of revenue, payments will be deferred. What's more, revenue is of course a tiny fraction of profits, being defined as Royalty Tax received from companies to the province (p. 19). It is impossible to know what the balance sheet will be, but these revenues will be offset against the repayment of the loans that Canada forwarded to the Innu to negotiate their land claim. This is described thus: "A provisional schedule of payments for the repayment of negotiation loans shall be negotiated prior to the signing of the Agreement" (23.3.1). We have here a dizzying round of negotiations over payments for the repayment of loans for negotiating the release of Innu lands. In this crucial sequence of what can only be formalized dispossession, Canada establishes itself as a creditor by creating a need for the Innu to incur a debt by issuing a credit for them to pay Canadian advisors to negotiate the handover of their assets to Canada. If they incur further difficulties in repaying this, provision is made for "the potential for loans from Canada to the Innu Government against the then unpaid balance of the payments" (23.5.1), thus incurring another cycle of debt.

There is of course an exchange, but what precisely that involves is bound up in more revenues and IBAs, which are calculated as hypothetical proportions. To offset the ambiguity, some funds are straightforwardly transferred to the Innu government: $10.3 million each for economic development, training and capacity, and heritage (23.4). These funds complement others that are attached also in the AIP in a most complex manner to what is called the Lower Churchill Project, a massive hydroelectric power project to be sited at Muskrat Falls and Gull Island on the vast Mista-shipu River in the heart of Innu territory. This project will be run by Nalcor, a Newfoundland provincial energy corporation. At the outset of chapter 28, where this component of the AIP is articulated, the area, including all the water, sequestered for the project is stated "for greater certainty" not to be either in Labrador Innu Lands or the Labrador Innu Settlement Area—*ever*. It is by fiat Crown Land. The chapter proceeds with numerous release clauses for Nalcor from many responsibilities and liabilities for injuries and loss of property, as well as various types of "inundation" commonly caused by building dams. The text mentions that an IBA is not included in the Lower Churchill deal but would be applicable if a "subsequent" developer took over the project from Nalcor.

The IBA is currently not available for public scrutiny, but advisors to the Innu Nation have circulated a summary with dire confidentiality and commercial sensitivity warnings on it. These warnings have been overtaken by events because construction has begun *before* the signing of the final draft of the agreement, and CBC News (2013) has already reported that Innu workers are alleging that they are being treated in a racist manner at the site. Inside the draft IBA are stipulations for the training and education of Innu workers. Most of these are quite vague and conditional, and the employment itself will be mostly available only during the construction phase. There are some specific undertakings that resemble a highly qualified affirmative action policy. These include training opportunities for Innu workers during the construction phase, but these workers will be offered jobs only if they are available (p. 4). There will also be a hiring preference for Innu and 20 percent of permanent positions set aside for them, but only if they attain the qualifications necessary for the vacant positions. Nalcor will donate $25,000 per year to education in the Innu communities (p. 5)—enough for, say, one or two university students.

The real meat of the summary IBA comes in what will be chapter 4 on business opportunities. According to the preliminary version of the IBA,

Nalcor will have to use Innu businesses for $400 million in contracts for the planning and construction phases of the project (p. 10). However, these are only targets, and if they are not met, Nalcor will have to pay 5 percent of the difference between the actual amount of the contracts and the target. There are other unspecified and vague conditions noted in the text. If, for example, one of the generating stations does not get built—a distinct possibility with legal challenges already being prepared against the project—no penalty is payable and no contracts need be signed with Innu businesses.

Another set of "implementation payments" will amount to $5 million per year for the Innu Nation as long as construction goes ahead and several other favorable business conditions obtain (pp. 20–21), but this will last for only ten years. Nalcor will also pay $5 million or 5 percent of "after debt net cash flow," which is defined by reference to numerous forms of income and expenses, to a trust set up by the Innu Nation (p. 21). These funds are understood in the IBA as means of indemnifying Nalcor against any claims against it for any adverse environmental or other effects of the hydroelectric project. Again this is referred to as a "release" and used in conjunction with indemnity. Readers are told boldly that "the purpose of the indemnity is to discourage individual Innu and the Innu of Labrador from bringing any Claims about Adverse Effects, except for Remaining Claims" (p. 25). These "remaining claims" are of a far less serious nature than all the possible claims that could arise from indemnification. In a parallel kind of indemnification, the "Labrador Innu" will receive compensation amounting to about $2 million per year for the sequestering of their lands in the late 1960s for the Upper Churchill hydro-electric development. This compensation, while releasing the corporation running the hydroelectric plant from responsibility for damages incurred by their theft of Innu lands, will last until 2041, and the Innu will receive dividends thereafter. However, as with almost all forms of compensation, there are amounts that will be clawed back by either the state or companies. In this case, and in what amounts to collective punishment, 50 percent of the unpaid hydroelectric bills of individual Innu families will be deducted from IBA payments. The rest will be "absolved," but beginning in January 2012 Innu customers were expected to pay their electric bills.

Apart from its secrecy, the mock IBA shares with the main AIP a certain totalitarian quality. For example, "the Parties cannot challenge the validity of the IBA." They may challenge its interpretation, but should an argument arise in the future that would question the IBA itself—for example, that the land is simply sequestered by fiat and not considered a constituent part of Innu lands without any kind of agreed release—it will have no force, since validity is unchallengeable (p. 27). Copies of the IBA are available only to certain parties subject to numerous tightly regulated conditions, and within the Innu communities only Innu (and presumably their non-Innu advisors) are technically allowed to read the IBA (p. 34). This rules out non-Innu spouses, for instance, who may have lived most of their lives in Natuashish or Sheshatshiu.

Closing Observations

The technical details of land claims are important to know, but we should not necessarily dignify the documents that result from them with the name *agreements* since they are undertaken under conditions that are largely created and imposed by the state, thus eliminating the sovereignty of the Indigenous party (Lyons 2000: 453). Equally important is to understand what the wider personal and sociological implications of this process might be, especially for the survival of the unique ways of thinking and being.

This is by no means the only factor, but the process of negotiating a land claim itself encourages amnesia about historical experiences and identities. This has been witnessed in Indigenous leaders in Quebec (Ross Tremblay 2012: 225–28). There are concrete inducements for many people involved in land claims to embrace inequality and individualism since money lubricates the whole process from beginning to end, in the form of cash, travel, and luxuries that would ordinarily have been out of the reach of most Indigenous people. It is, of course, not only Indigenous peoples for whom such induced amnesia may occur. Many people experience cognitive dissonance, abandon various principles over time, and, especially when money, power, and coercion are brought to bear, change their views. For example, the young John Olthuis, the same lawyer who enthusiastically paraded the economic benefits of resource extraction and other forms of industry on the OKT website in 2012, in 1977 coauthored a book titled *Justice, Energy, the North and Native People* in which it is written, "We say optimizing economic growth has not been good for southern Canadians and it will not be good for the North. Besides, we believe that the majority of Canadians are searching for new values and would not wish to impose discredited economic growth values on the North. . . . This is why we call for a moratorium: so that fundamental social change can be discussed, so that people can once again participate in planning their future. Just as the Dene, the Nisga'a, the Yukon Indians, and the Inuit are calling for justice, self-determination, and an end to colonialism in all our lives" (McCallum, McCallum, and Olthuis 1977: 194, 195). The experience of working on a land claims agreement that demands extinguishment, the release of rights, the acceptance of violability, and the construction of one of the world's largest dam projects must mean that Olthuis started to believe that economic growth was *not* a discredited value. More cynically, perhaps it was a simple irony to bear in doing one's job and driving through the land claim.

More profound is the social transformation of the Innu. The agreement makes many external structural changes that will have an impact on their circumstances and how they will be encouraged to see the world. Over time they will have much less land for hunting. Since hunting is at the heart of their way of life, the effects of this will eradicate much of the land-based culture. Many areas that will become "Crown Land" are where they would meet their relatives domiciled in Quebec and are part of travel routes between Labrador villages and those in Quebec. But more crucial will be the fact that the land is to be violable, privatizable, and a commodity. To paraphrase Olthuis et al., the land is the main source of "economic growth."

Because it is a source of *capitalist* economic growth, it will likely be the site of relentless expansion. The process will also open up vast inequalities among the Innu, intensifying the already deep rifts that obtain between Innu families and factions. There may be parallels with the industrialization process in nineteenth-century Britain, where the Enclosure Acts drove rural laborers off common lands. Their penury forced them to migrate to cities, where they lived as an industrial proletariat in overcrowded, unhealthy, and depressing conditions. Despite some of the assurances in the A I P, one can envision many Innu filling the manual labor vacancies in the resource extraction industry, and since jobs on such projects will be short term, many Innu might become a kind of migratory subproletariat that one finds among some Indigenous peoples in urban areas in Canada and elsewhere.

Innu from now on will be identified by the administrative categories of the state. There will be no concept of a people across the whole Labrador-Quebec peninsula, but small Indigenous municipalities within the larger governing structure of the Canadian state—a state that has finally achieved "release" through the social death of others.

References

Aboriginal Affairs and Northern Development Canada. 2010. *Acts, Agreements, Treaties and Land Claims.* http://www.aadnc-aandc.gc.ca/eng/1100100028568/110010000 28572.

Aboriginal Affairs and Northern Development Canada. 2011. *Labrador Innu Land Claims Agreement-in-Principle.* http://www.aadnc-aandc.gc.ca/eng/1331657507074.

Agamben, Giorgio. 2005. *State of Exception.* Chicago: University of Chicago Press.

Anaya, James. 2004. "International Human Rights and the Rights of Indigenous Peoples: The Move toward the Multicultural State." *Arizona Journal of International and Comparative Law* 21 (1): 13–61.

Bell, Catherine, and Michael Asch. 1997. "Challenging Assumptions: The Impact of Precedent in Aboriginal Rights Litigation." In *Aboriginal and Treaty Rights in Canada: Essays on Law, Equity, and Respect for Difference*, edited by Michael Asch, 38–74. Vancouver: UBC Press.

Body, Hugh. 1981. *Maps and Dreams*. New York: Pantheon.

Bussidor, Ila, and Üstun Bilgen-Reinart. 1997. *Night Spirits: The Story of the Relocation of the Sayisi Dene*. Winnipeg: University of Manitoba Press.

CBC News. 2012a. "Innu Angry over Development Company Salaries: Now-departed CEO Made $1 Million over the Past Two Years." July 12. http://www.cbc.ca/news/canada/newfoundland-labrador/story/2012/07/11/nl-711-innu-development-salaries.html.

CBC News. 2012b. "Labrador Innu Kids Sniffing Gas Again to Fight Boredom: Davis Inlet All Over Again as Natuashish Parents Say They've Seen Lives Destroyed." June 18. http://www.cbc.ca/news/canada/newfoundland-labrador/story/2012/06/18/nl-natuashish-sniffing-618.html.

CBC News. 2012c. "Natuashish Ordered to Hold New Vote by Federal Court: 'Substantial Problems' in 2010 Election, Judge Says." January 5. http://www.cbc.ca/news/canada/newfoundland-labrador/natuashish-ordered-to-hold-new-vote-by-federal-court-1.1131930.

CBC News. 2012d. "Protesters Shut Down Sheshatshiu Innu Nation Office: Looking for Answers about Innu Development Limited Partnership Spending." August 13. http://www.cbc.ca/news/canada/newfoundland-labrador/story/2012/08/13/nl-innu-spending-protest-813.html.

CBC News. 2013. "Racism Common at Muskrat Falls Site, Say Innu Workers: Nalcor Energy Says It Strictly Prohibits Discrimination and Will Not Tolerate Workplace Harassment." August 23. http://www.cbc.ca/news/canada/newfoundland-labrador/story/2013/08/23/nl-innu-muskrat-823.html.

Foreman, Grant. 1932. *Indian Removal*. Norman: University of Oklahoma Press.

Fumoleau, René. 1974. *As Long as This Land Shall Last: A History of Treaty 8 and Treaty 11, 1870–1939*. Toronto: McClelland and Stewart.

Henriksen, Georg. 2009. *I Dreamed the Animals: Kaniuekutat. The Life of an Innu Hunter*. Oxford: Berghahn.

Hoxie, Frederick. 1984. *A Final Promise: The Campaign to Assimilate the Indians, 1820–1920*. Lincoln: University of Nebraska Press.

Irlbacher-Fox, Stephanie. 2009. *Finding Dahshaa: Self-Government, Social Suffering, and Aboriginal Policy in Canada*. Vancouver: UBC Press.

Isenberg, Andrew. 2000. *The Destruction of the Bison: An Environmental History, 1750–1920*. Cambridge: Cambridge University Press.

Kymlicka, Will. 2002. "Multiculturalism and Minority Rights: West and East." *Journal of Ethnopolitics and Minority Politics in Europe* 4: 1–27.

Lux, Maureen. 2001. *Medicine That Walks: Disease Medicine and Canadian Plains Native People, 1880–1940*. Toronto: University of Toronto Press.

Lyons, Scott Richard. 2000. "Rhetorical Sovereignty: What Do American Indians Want from Writing?" *College Composition and Communication* 51 (3): 447–68.

McCallum, Hugh, Karmel McCallum, and John Olthuis. 1977. *Moratorium: Justice, Energy, the North and the Native People*. Toronto: Anglican Book Centre.

Nadasdy, Paul. 2003. *Hunters and Bureaucrats: Power, Knowledge and Aboriginal-State Relations in the Southwest Yukon*. Vancouver: UBC Press.

Olthuis, John. 2011. "Labrador Innu Sign Historic Land Claim, Self-Government and Hydro Agreement."Olthuis Kleer Townshend LLP. November 22. http://www.oktlaw.com/blog/labrador-innu-sign-historic-land-claim-self-government-and-hydro-agreement/.

Ross Tremblay, Pierrot. 2012. "A Genealogy of Amnesia: Memory and Forgetfulness in Essipinnuat's Narratives of the Salmon War (1980–81)." PhD dissertation, University of Essex.

Royal Commission on Aboriginal Peoples. 1996. *Looking Forward, Looking Backward*. Ottawa: Minister of Supply and Services Canada.

Samson, Colin. 2003a. "Sexual Abuse and Assimilation: Oblates, Teachers and the Innu of Labrador." *Sexualities* 6 (1): 47–54.

Samson, Colin. 2003b. *A Way of Life That Does Not Exist: Canada and the Extinguishment of the Innu*. London: Verso Press.

Samson, Colin, and Elizabeth Cassell. 2013. "The Long Reach of Frontier Justice: Canadian Land Claims 'Negotiation' Strategies as Human Rights Violations." *International Journal of Human Rights* 17 (1): 35–55.

Short, Damien. 2010. "Cultural Genocide and Indigenous Peoples: A Sociological Approach." *International Journal of Human Rights* 14 (6): 831–46.

Treaty 7 Elders and Tribal Council with Walter Hildebrandt, Sarah Carter, and Dorothy First Rider. 1996. *The True Spirit and Original Intent of Treaty 7*. Montreal: McGill-Queen's University Press.

Tully, James. 1995. *Strange Multiplicity: Constitutionalism in the Age of Diversity*. Cambridge: Cambridge University Press.

Utley, Robert. 1984. *The Indian Frontier of the American West 1846–1890*. Albuquerque: University of New Mexico Press.

Vancouver Sun. 2006. "$1 Billion Fails to Land One Treaty." November 30. http://www.canada.com/vancouversun/news/story.html?id=bded643e-422e-4947-9a0a-e074 20e31eaa.

Wadden, Marie. 1991. *Nitassinan: The Innu Struggle to Reclaim Their Homeland*. Vancouver: Douglas and MacIntyre.

Wilson, James. 1998. *The Earth Shall Weep: A History of Native America*. New York: Grove Press.

Woolford, Andrew. 2011. "Transition and Transposition: Genocide, Land and the British Columbia Treaty Process." *New Proposals: Journal of Marxism and Interdisciplinary Inquiry* 4 (2): 67–76.

PART IV

(RE)IMAGININGS

CHAPTER 12

COLONIAL GENOCIDE AND HISTORICAL TRAUMA IN NATIVE NORTH AMERICA

Complicating Contemporary Attributions

Joseph P. Gone

My research, situated in clinical, community, and cultural psychology, grapples with the ideological implications of providing mainstream mental health services in (post)colonial American Indian settings (Gone 2007, 2008; Gone and Kirmayer 2010; Gone and Trimble 2012). Few doubt that the remnant indigenous communities of the United States and Canada continue to suffer from behavioral health disparities that affect nearly every extended family throughout Native North America. The most salient response to these problems has been the state-sponsored application and extension of various forms of human services for a burgeoning Indigenous clientele. But culturally distinctive clients can require novel kinds of institutional knowledge for guiding professional assessment, referral, and rehabilitation. One important source of this new knowledge relative to Indigenous community behavioral health is the expanding cadre of formally trained researchers in the psy- disciplines and health sciences who themselves identify as Native or Indigenous. In the second decade of the new millennium, such individuals are no longer fringe exotics in the fields of psychology, social work, public health, and nursing. Instead they are producing novel and influential knowledge that impacts the discourses and practices of human services professionals in tangible fashion. Most of these researchers remain dedicated to advancing Indigenous well-being through their professional contributions by challenging the injustices of the status quo and by engaging the lived experiences and shared ambitions of their own kin and communities.

As a consequence Indigenous researchers in the "psy-ences" (Raikhel 2012) have sought to account for contemporary tribal disparities in behavioral health problems by contextualizing these disorders within historical experiences of

European colonization. In this regard contemporary psychosocial distress in Indigenous communities has increasingly been attributed to *historical trauma* (HT). The concept of HT (and the synonymous term *soul wound*) entered the mental health literature in the 1990s as an explanatory frame for rampant substance abuse, trauma, violence, depression, pathological grief, and suicide in present-day American Indian communities (Braveheart-Jordan and De-Bruyn 1995; Duran 1990; Duran and Duran 1995; Terry 1995). HT has been theorized as a form of embodied vulnerability to mental health problems stemming from ancestral suffering that has accrued across generations into formidable legacies of disability for contemporary descendants. In tracing the origins of current problems to collective experiences of European colonization, the advocates of HT seek to counter paralyzing self-blame within Native communities and foster collective empowerment toward healing and recovery from overwhelming distress (Duran et al. 1998; Evans-Campbell 2008; Gone 2009, 2013; Sotero 2006; Walters et al. 2011; Wesley-Esquimaux and Smolewski 2004; Whitbeck et al. 2004). Nevertheless by wedding *psychological trauma* to *historical oppression* in this fashion, proponents of HT inadvertently promote a discourse that misrepresents the true range of Native subject positions in response to colonization and that pathologizes Indigenous identities as essentially wounded or damaged by history (Gone 2014; Maxwell 2014; Waldram 2004).

In this chapter, however, I am concerned less with the prospects and pitfalls of embracing and promoting the discourse of indigenous HT (instead see Gone 2014) than with the routine references to colonial genocide that so frequently accompany discussions of HT. Specifically this literature regularly advances the sweeping assertion that Indigenous HT originates from tribal experiences of *genocide* as historically perpetrated against Native peoples by European settler populations: "What was done to indigenous people in the Americas had all the characteristics of genocide and . . . evoked similar responses to trauma that researchers observe not only in people who survived genocide, but also in their children and grandchildren" (Wesley-Esquimaux and Smolewski 2004: 7). According to Evans-Campbell (2008: 321), "These [predisposing] events are not only human initiated and intentional but also fall under the category of genocide (e.g., physical, cultural, or ethnocide), making them particularly devastating." Whitbeck et al. (2004: 119) invoked "more than 400 years of genocide, 'ethnic cleansing,' and forced acculturation," yielding what Duran and Duran (1995: 152) identified as "post-traumatic stress disorder as a consequence of the devastating effects of genocide perpetrated by the U.S. government." Brave Heart and DeBruyn (1998: 62) wrote, "Like the transfer of trauma to descendants from Holocaust survivors, the genocide of American Indians reverberates across generations," all as a result of colonial "policies of genocide and ethnocide," according to Walters and Simoni (2002: 520). In sum almost anyone who promotes HT in the academic literature makes explicit reference to genocide, by which they intend to signify in the North American context the violent subjugation of Indigenous peoples by European colonizers.

And yet, from its origins as a neologism some seven decades ago (Lemkin 1944), the term *genocide* as taken up by scholars and circulated through popular discourse has come to reference the most extreme forms of group-based violence. Thus, for a host of rhetorical, political, and ethical reasons, sweeping attributions of genocide remain a controversial business. In this chapter I critically consider the general applicability of the term to the colonization of Native North America. Allow me to acknowledge at the outset, however, that *genocides (plural) against Indigenous peoples did indeed occur during the European settlement of North America* (for examples, see Madley, this volume; Whaley, this volume). Therefore my concern in this chapter is *not* whether genocide actually happened during European colonization (because it did) but rather whether genocide can be appropriately claimed *to characterize the overarching pattern* of European dispossession of Indigenous peoples throughout the history of North American contact. I thus consider the problem of defining genocide prior to engaging the question of what is at stake in generalizing the attribution of genocide to the colonization of North America. Specifically, in keeping with ideas promoted by earlier generations of scholars in genocide studies, I propose that the concept of genocide is best reserved for instances of *group-based mass murder*. On this basis I observe that genocide was only one among several patterns of colonial dispossession that therefore warrants more restrained attribution than is typical of routine overgeneralizations by some Indigenous scholars, activists, and their allies. Finally, I argue that such restraint is more ethically, politically, and rhetorically conducive to productive developments in intergroup exchanges relative to the future of Native and non-Native relations.

Defining Genocide in the Context of European Colonization

Any determination of the applicability of the term *genocide* to widespread forms of Indigenous suffering in the wake of European colonization substantively turns on questions of definition. Unfortunately academic consideration of abstract definitional issues in the face of the incomprehensible loss of Indigenous life—not to mention associated forms of colonial agony and anguish—can seem a pitiless endeavor. And yet it is this very regard for the ultimate sanctity of each human life that would seem to require a well-elucidated means for differentiating and distinguishing human culpability in the deaths of others (akin to common conceptual distinctions between murder, voluntary manslaughter, and involuntary manslaughter). Unsurprisingly questions of definition are not new to the field of genocide studies. In his seminal textbook on genocide, Jones (2011) constructed a table of some twenty-two scholarly definitions of genocide proposed during the past fifty years. In reviewing these definitions Jones highlighted six key domains that most definitions of genocide appear to address in various fashion: "agents, victims, goals, scale, strategies, and intent" (21). For example, according to Jones, *agents* are often identified as state authorities and the *victims* as social minorities. The *goals* typically include the destruction of the targeted group; the *scale* varies as to whether total or partial eradication is attempted; and the *strategies* refer to either direct or indirect actions in all of their specificity. Finally, Jones cited a virtual consensus among scholars that such actions must be undertaken with purposeful and deliberate *intent*. Obviously variations across these domains are what lead to different definitions of the concept. For example, in his recent review of second-generation scholarship exploring various historical examples of genocide, Straus (2007) found that independent researchers actually selected in common very few historical cases for comparative analysis. This fact led him to conclude that "genocide is a complex, contested, and ambiguous concept, and comparative research on the topic suffers as a result" (495).

One possibility for explaining this conceptual ambiguity is inspired by classic research in cognitive psychology about how humans categorize objects in nature (Medin 1989). One approach to formulating categories is *criterial*, in which necessary and sufficient features (e.g., capacity for flight) for membership in a category (e.g., "birds") are applied to the objects in question. In this regard Fein (1990: 25) proposed five "necessary and sufficient conditions for a finding of genocide": attempted physical destruction, organized perpetration, targeting based on group membership, victim vulnerability, and murderous intent. The classification task that follows from such definitions is merely a logical assessment of whether a proposed instance of genocide does or does not meet all of the criteria. In other words, criterial categories possess sharp boundaries, leading perhaps inevitably to debates about defining features and the validity of resultant lines of demarcation (e.g., in biology, how to classify flightless birds). An alternative to the criterial approach to formulating categories is the *prototypical* approach. This kind of classification centers on representative exemplars that manifest all the attributes of the category (e.g., a robin), while additional instances of the phenomenon in question possess some but not all of the attributes of these prototypes (e.g., an ostrich). Whether an object is classified as a category member depends on the *degree to which it resembles exemplary instances*. In other words, prototypical categories possess fuzzy boundaries, leading to debates about inclusion, particularly at the category margins, where much fewer of the prototypical attributes are shared. Thus in genocide studies the Holocaust is virtually always classed as an exemplary instance of the phenomenon (though scholars in this field increasingly seek to destabilize the hegemony of this particular case); in contrast the devastation of European colonization for Indigenous peoples has long been conceptually positioned near the fuzzy margins of category membership.

Unlike constructions of classifications about the natural world, however, constructions of genocide are free to expand and contract on the basis of discourse alone. Nevertheless the key contribution of viewing genocide as a prototypical category rather than a criterial category is the recognition that *development of a consensual definition of the concept is simply not possible*; rather ambiguity and contestation at the margins of category membership are intrinsic to the conceptual problem at hand. Moreover conceptual expansion and contraction have been readily visible throughout the history of genocide studies. For example, Lemkin's (1944) original formulation of the concept construed genocide as not only or always in reference to the extinguishing of group lives but also or alternatively in reference to the destruction of a group's collective way of life (see Benvenuto, this volume; Powell and Peristerakis, this volume). In the subsequent formulation of the Convention on the Prevention and Punishment of the Crime of Genocide as ratified by the United Nations General Assembly in 1948, Lemkin's proposed conception was substantially curtailed, reflecting what some have argued is a "methodologically individualist ontology of the social" (Powell and Peristerakis, chapter 3). More specifically such critics contest the politically liberalist assumption that individual lives are more fundamental and essential than collective social existence and affiliation, and therefore urge reconsideration of what precisely genocide is assumed to kill. Nevertheless even the United Nations Convention on Genocide reflects a construal of the term that remains more expansive than early scholarly delineations (and resulting dictionary definitions) of the concept, defining this crime as the "intent to destroy" a group as such, inclusive of practices such as "forcibly transferring children of the group to another group" (Jones 2011: 13). Such qualifiers afford interpretation well beyond customary references to mass killing and death (which persist even among recent scholars who, despite their conceptualization of colonial genocide as a "dynamic process," nevertheless continue to reference "murder, or attempted murder, of groups" [Moses 2000: 90]).

My point here thus far is that a definition of genocide is (1) necessary for an assessment of claims about the colonization of Native North America, (2) contestable in light of arbitrary or fuzzy boundaries that circumscribe the concept, and (3) contingent on historical factors that can be recognized as influencing various constructions of the concept since its initial formulation. As a consequence, in searching for a working definition I am particularly interested in what the term has come to signify since Lemkin's (1944) initial introduction of the word. More specifically I believe that important lessons may follow from briefly considering what genocide now means in everyday discourse as a result not only of Lemkin's initial formulation but also of the analyses and arguments of earlier generations of genocide scholars. After all, once a neologism finally arrives at the vernacular stage, there is perhaps good reason to attend to its colloquial usage as one analytic lens for appreciating its referential, aesthetic, and pragmatic functions (which, of course, is not to argue that scholars cannot or should not attempt to contest or disrupt such popular definitions when warranted). In this regard Google Dictionary defines genocide as "the deliberate killing of a large group of people, especially those of a particular ethnic group or nation." That is, genocide in colloquial usage refers to instances of attempted or enacted *mass murder*. Furthermore, when not used in this conventional sense, such invocations are frequently qualified (as in *cultural* genocide) in order to differentiate what is denoted from common parlance. I see this as important because the term *genocide* has come to serve both *descriptive* and *evaluative* purposes in everyday usage, and its evaluative function of indexing the most extreme form of morally reprehensible intergroup violence would appear to *simultaneously constrain* its descriptive function. More specifically the appeal of the word is based on the fact that it occupies the extreme end of a continuum of moral evaluation relative to group-based violence that would be effectively undermined by expanding its descriptive function to instances beyond mass murder proper.

By way of example, consider the following vignette from the workshop on colonial genocide that gave rise to the edited collection in which this chapter appears. In his keynote presentation that inaugurated the workshop, Justice Murray Sinclair addressed the question of genocide relative to the residential school experiences of Aboriginal Canadians. As chairman of the Truth and Reconciliation Commission of Canada—which was tasked with reporting on the impacts of assimilative education for Aboriginal children (see Patzer, this volume)—Sinclair recounted that in their testimonies before the Commission many survivors of these repressive institutions had characterized their mandatory schooling as genocidal. He conveyed as much to the media several months prior to the workshop, setting in motion a fierce national controversy about the applicability of the term to the Canadian residential school system. During his keynote address Sinclair set forth a cogent argument for ascribing genocide to residential schooling on the basis of the section of the United Nations Genocide Convention that references the forcible transfer of children as one of the indicators of genocide. Sinclair's logic was unassailable: if one privileges the reference to forcible transfer of children from the Convention, then one can conclude that the residential schools were genocidal. But what most caught my attention in his address was his reported reaction to the media frenzy surrounding this public characterization. During his address Sinclair recounted his subsequent outreach to a Jewish survivor of the Nazi concentration camp at Buchenwald to "apologize" for perhaps offending those who had experienced "true genocide." The Holocaust survivor was apparently respectful of Sinclair's attribution, but it was Sinclair's instinctive move to offer an apology that I believe is most telling: it indexed the common understanding that genocide most properly applies to the most extreme form of group-based violence, namely, physical extermination (as opposed to coercive assimilation, no matter how reprehensible the latter might be).

Thus Sinclair's instinct reflects the deep contradiction between the descriptive and evaluative functions of the term *genocide*. On one hand, following a particular interpretation of the United Nations Genocide Convention, he sought to trace the descriptive contours of the genocide concept well beyond mass murder to coercive cultural assimilation; on the other hand, in deference to commonplace understandings of the term, he sought to qualify the evaluative contours of the genocide concept by apologizing for his application of the term to residential schooling rather than to "true" instances such as the Holocaust. In itself, of course, this vignette does not preclude the extension of the concept of genocide beyond instances of group-based mass murder, but in doing so it reveals a *necessary trade-off* between the term's descriptive and evaluative functions. That is, once the concept is expanded to accommodate phenomena beyond mass murder, the moral force of the attribution is attenuated. As a result the term's ready reference to the extreme end of the moral continuum relative to group-based violence is diminished. Moreover there already exists a host of concepts for describing related forms of group-based violence that occupy a less extreme, more encompassing segment of the evaluative continuum: "crimes against humanity," "human rights violations," "ethnic cleansing," "colonization," "massacres," "forced assimilation," and so forth. Thus what seems to be distinctive about the term *genocide* is its reference to the "crime of all crimes," namely, group-based mass murder. Nevertheless some will continue to argue for expansion of the concept in service to some purpose or another. If so, then it strikes me that we will still require (and will therefore need to designate) some new term—another neologism?—to occupy the extreme end of the continuum of moral evaluation with reference to group-based violence. Why then abandon the term *genocide* in this regard when it has already (finally) come to occupy precisely this evaluative location in common parlance?

Attributing Genocide in the Context of European Colonization

Based on this reasoning I believe that the term *genocide* is best reserved for references to attempted or enacted group-based mass murder. It is my purpose in this section to consider to what degree genocide in this sense characterizes the colonial dispossession of Indigenous peoples of North America. In reviewing a handful of discussions about the case of Indigenous peoples by genocide studies scholars, I was most struck by the degree of ambivalence and qualification expressed in these analyses. For example, in glaring contrast to the titles of other essays in the collection, Hitchcock and Twedt (2009: 420) titled their chapter "Physical and *Cultural* Genocide of Indigenous Peoples" (italics added), demonstrating how "most writers" of the scholarly literature on Indigenous peoples "use a fairly broad definition of the concept of genocide." Similarly in Fein's (1990: 80) consideration of "*Ethnocide*, Genocide and *Mass Death* of Indigenous Peoples" (italics added), she allowed that, "although many studying genocide refer to the genocide of the American Indians . . . , no one has documented an over-all pattern of genocide by the government of the United States in the post-colonial period." In this regard she favorably cited Chalk and Jonassohn (1990: 195): "The case of the American Indian in the nineteenth century is one of the most complex in the history of genocide. . . . Very few American leaders wanted to annihilate the American Indian; the government-organized murder of peaceable Indians with the intention of destroying tribes in whole or in part rarely occurred." Interestingly in the most authoritative reference work about Native peoples in the United States, the Smithsonian Institution's definitive fifteen-volume *Handbook of North American Indians*, the 838-page volume dedicated to "Indian-White relations" (Washburn 1988) contains only one reference to genocide, which appears in the chapter dedicated to representations of American Indians in English literature.

Given this trend, one might wonder how genocide ever came to be generically associated with the European colonization of Native North America. Certainly few would dispute the overwhelming degree of colonial suffering experienced by Indigenous communities in the wake of contact and dispossession. For example, no one doubts the fact that Native North Americans experienced catastrophic loss of life on a truly massive scale in the wake of European colonization, primarily from disease (Thornton 1987). Furthermore colonial policies in the United States were expressed through sustained campaigns of brutal dispossession, removal, and containment, including the deployment of military force that at various times erupted in the wanton slaughter of Indigenous noncombatants (as examples, Hitchcock and Twedt [2009] cited massacres of Cheyennes and Arapahos at Sand Creek in 1864 and of Lakotas at Wounded Knee in 1890). Indeed a subset of these violent campaigns—including well-documented examples from the settlement of California and Oregon (Madley 2008, this volume; Whaley, this volume)—involved coordinated actions by settlers with governmental support that qualify as genocides by almost any definition. Finally, once Native peoples were settled on reservations, deep ambivalence about federal expenditures for meeting basic community needs, combined with systematic graft by personnel in the Indian service, resulted in inadequate support, yielding starvation and other forms of desperate suffering (Hagan 1988). None of these facts—or the appraisals of them as gross injustices—appears to be in dispute. Rather the question is whether such experiences together constitute an overarching pattern that might properly warrant the sweeping assertion that the colonial settlement of North America was genocidal.

Perhaps the most influential scholar to advance this claim is Stannard (1992), who consistently asserted in his book *American Holocaust: Columbus and the Conquest of the New World* that European settlement not just of North America but in fact of the entire "new world" was genocidal. Beginning with the arrival of Columbus to Hispaniola in the late fifteenth century, Stannard recounted in grueling detail the wide range of horrors visited upon the Indigenous inhabitants of the Western Hemisphere across the centuries in the wake of contact. Although he acknowledged the primary role of disease in Indigenous depopulation (responsible for the deaths of over 90 percent of these communities), Stannard emphasized the wanton slaughter of Native peoples by, first, the Spanish conquistadors and, later, English traders and settlers. He attributed these depredations to Old World formations grounded at the intersection of Christianity, empire, and racism, and on this basis characterized the overarching pattern of European conquest over time and across regions as genocidal. In response to this argument, some distinguished historians cried foul; both Elliott (1993) and White (1993) dismissed Stannard's sweeping attribution of genocide as overheated polemic. For example, White (1993: 33) countered that Stannard "takes the horrible and seeks to make it worse." Citing virgin soil epidemics of disease as the primary source of Indigenous decline, White questioned Stannard's precontact Indigenous population estimates and chided him for conflating unintentional exposure to deadly pathogens with intentional killing of Indigenous peoples by Europeans. Furthermore White noted the shifting and complex history of white-Indian alliances that furthered Indigenous dispossession, complicating contemporary assessments of moral culpability. In sum White faulted Stannard for his oversimplified pursuit of a "verdict of mass murder" in the colonization of North America when "manslaughter" is perhaps the more appropriate judgment (34).

Critiques of such sweeping attributions of genocide with reference to European colonization seem as relevant today as they did two decades ago because scholars in Indigenous and ethnic studies have increasingly invoked the term with broad reference to Native North America (Churchill 1998, 2002, 2004; Jaimes 1992; Smith 2005). But White's (1993) and Elliott's (1993) counterclaim is simply that this multicentury history is so nuanced and complicated that it does not lend itself particularly well to breezy moral dichotomies inspired by contemporary racial politics. If genocide was one pattern of violent dispossession in the colonization of North America, other patterns were evident as well. Nongenocidal warfare was a common occurrence, even when this erupted in appalling massacres perpetrated either by intrusive settlers or besieged Natives. (Indeed Rensink [2009] has drawn on the complex historical record to complicate the question of genocide even with reference to prototypical colonial massacres such as at Sand Creek.) Warfare by allied Natives and Europeans against other Natives and/or Europeans was an additional pattern, as was true of the French and Indian War during the mid-eighteenth century. Ethridge (this volume) illustrated still another pattern in which English traders centered in Carolina enlisted and equipped nearby Indigenous peoples to raid and enslave other Indigenous peoples deep inside the southern colonial "shatter zone" (i.e., a region of "widespread internecine warfare resulting in dislocations, migrations, amalgamations, and, in some cases, extinctions of Native peoples"). According to Ethridge, this expression of European commercial interests—fueled by English orchestration of the Indian slave trade primarily to the West Indies—was responsible for the demise of the mound-building chiefdoms of this region and the resultant rise of new remnant peoples such as the Choctaw, Cherokee, and Chickasaw.

A final pattern involved catastrophic disruptions to Indigenous ways of life resulting from contact that were not necessarily intended or attended by colonizing Europeans. For illustrative purposes, consider briefly the historical context of one region of Native North America, namely, the high northern Plains during the nineteenth century. My own people, the Gros Ventre, were very significantly affected by colonial disruptions in what later became Alberta, Saskatchewan, and Montana during the 1800s (Flannery 1953; Fowler 1987; Gone 2014). During this period our population catastrophically declined from perhaps three thousand individuals to 595 in total. And yet we never engaged the U.S. Army in combat or suffered concentrated killings of our people by Euro-Americans; in fact our most salient experiences of mass violence resembling anything like genocide occurred at the hands of allied Crees and Assiniboines in the Sweetgrass Hills during 1834 and by the Piegans in the Cypress Hills during 1867. Instead colonial impacts during this century resulted from dramatic economic shifts that gave rise to grave power asymmetries between rival Indigenous groups that were competing for control of the regional trade in horses and guns (both originally introduced by Europeans). Indeed Euro-Americans did not exercise military strength adequate for violent subjugation of this region until the bison were finally decimated in 1884. Rather the dominant military powers of the high northern Plains throughout the nineteenth century were the Blackfoot Confederacy, the Cree and Assiniboine alliance, and the Teton Sioux. The last were especially influential during the post–Civil War era, when they effectively outmaneuvered U.S. troops to close the Bozeman Trail and later routed Custer at the Little Bighorn (Utley 1988). Owing in part to their occupation of territories that afforded ideal ecological resources for maintaining large horse herds, the Lakota's westward expansion toward the dwindling bison herds during the latter half of the nineteenth century signaled their emergence as a "hegemonic power" in this region (Hamalainen 2003: 860).

This was the context for military engagement of Native peoples by the U.S. Army throughout this period, during which national policy was consistently and primarily concerned with confiscation of Indigenous lands and settlement of Indigenous groups on reservations, by military force when necessary. In other words, the principal Euro-American commitment throughout most of this history was *dispossession* (centered on *land*) rather than *extermination* (centered on *life*). Generally speaking U.S. troops were strikingly ineffective at achieving these objectives until subsistence hunting in the region was no longer possible. These soldiers did, however, perpetrate intermittent colonial massacres, such as Colonel Baker's slaughter of Heavy Runner's band of Piegans on the Marias River in 1870 and Colonel Forsyth's murder of Lakota noncombatants at Wounded Knee in 1890. (Note that the defeat of the Nez Perce leader Joseph in 1877 within forty miles of the Canadian border is usually not described as a massacre.) But these incidents were not typical of military engagements during this period (and most were not authorized by higher authorities beyond the commanders who took to the field). Instead it may be that the full force of colonial suffering for these Indigenous groups commenced prior to confrontations with Euro-American military forces when disease and intertribal violence took their toll. Or perhaps such suffering peaked during the reservation era, when human agency, expectation, hope, and purpose were most severely challenged (Lear 2006), a period marked by government policies resulting in community poverty, Christian proselytization, cultural suppression, and boarding and residential school matriculation that advocates of Indigenous HT have consistently identified as "cultural genocide." But cultural genocide is not genocide (absent qualification and full stop). Instead cultural genocide embodies an odd contradiction; it is akin to murder without death. And yet murder means death. As in *extinguished*—and finally, irreversibly so.

Surmounting Genocide in the Context of European Colonization

Beyond exploring the substance of sweeping attributions of genocide in the history of European colonization of North America, I wish now to consider the contemporary significance of these attributions. Before proceeding, however, summary presentation of two points is in order. First, scholarly skepticism toward such sweeping attributions is concerned with the appropriateness of the generic claim that the colonization of Native North America was *fundamentally genocidal* as opposed to the more moderate claim that the colonization of Native North America was *intermittently genocidal* in this or that specific instance. Thus far I have contested the assertion that such genocides—which did in fact occur in various settings—were at all *typical* or *representative* of the European project of colonization, or that colonization can be casually equated with genocide. Rather the historical record has documented that European colonization occurred through a variety of patterned processes, with perpetrations of genocide by European settlers against Indigenous peoples seeming (if anything) the exception rather than the rule. Second, it seems apparent that Indigenous and scholarly promoters of the term themselves harbor implicit reservations about the global applicability of genocide to Native experiences of colonization, leading to evident equivocation in their use of the term (i.e., by alternately or additionally referencing "cultural genocide," "ethnocide," "ethnic cleansing," "forced acculturation," and the like). This is important because it reveals a *glossing of terms* that invokes other aspects of Indigenous colonization experience beyond mass murder proper. Recognition of such glossing is important for understanding the observations that follow. The point here is that casual overgeneralization of the term *genocide* to the case of colonial dispossession of North America's

Indigenous peoples—beyond distorting the historical record and perhaps diminishing the ethical enormity of group-based mass murder—threatens to undermine the possibility for Native and non-Native reconciliation.

Given that the European colonization of North America was largely completed by the end of the nineteenth century, commonplace claims about genocide relative to Indigenous experiences of colonization appear to serve *contemporary* rhetorical and political functions. Revisiting the Sinclair vignette described earlier, it seems clear that genocide is frequently invoked in discussions of historical U.S. and Canadian policies that attempted to assimilate Indigenous children into the mainstreams of their respective societies through compulsory attendance at industrial boarding or residential schools (Adams 1995; Churchill 2004; Fontaine 2010; Miller 1996). And yet the application of the term to these educational practices—no matter how misguided and destructive they were—strikes me as particularly discordant given that genocide is so typically characterized by efforts to achieve *physical eradication or extermination* as opposed to *national assimilation or incorporation*. So why do Indigenous critics invoke genocide at all in such discussions? I believe they do so principally to harness the evaluative functions rather than the descriptive functions of the concept; indeed during the workshop that gave rise to this volume, Aboriginal Canadian participants defended their use of the term in the context of residential schooling on the grounds that words such as *colonization* and *racism* were inadequate for capturing the ethical enormity of systematic and coercive cultural assimilation. Yet is it not also the case that expansive overgeneralization of the term risks attenuating the ethical enormity of actual instances of mass murder—some of which occurred during the colonization of Native North America—that were authorized, organized, and directed toward the physical eradication of Indigenous peoples? Is it morally credible or persuasive to class the Indian killer, the buffalo hunter (Hubbard, this volume), and the schoolteacher all together as perpetrators of genocide?

Regardless of how one answers these questions, the increasingly common practice of ascribing genocide to assimilative schooling reveals two additional and interrelated purposes served by such overgeneralized attributions. The first is concerned with expressions of grief and subsequent idealizations of the past, and the second is concerned with expressions of resentment and subsequent assignations of blame for ongoing suffering. Proponents of Indigenous HT have associated "impaired" or "unresolved" grief with this concept since its initial formulation (Brave Heart 1998; Brave Heart and DeBruyn 1998; Duran and Duran 1995; Wesley-Esquimaux and Smolewski 2004). In essence their observation is that Indigenous peoples have endured such swift,

sweeping, and catastrophic changes during the period of European colonization that there have not been adequate opportunities or means for mourning
these stunning losses (especially when many ceremonial mourning practices
have been deliberately suppressed). With reference to these group emotional
dynamics, proponents have claimed that the end result of unexpressed grief
includes widespread psychosocial dysfunction and disability that continue to
afflict Native communities today. Zembylas (2011) has traced the important
connections between *aporetic mourning* and *restorative nostalgia*. Drawing on
Derrida, he described aporetic mourning as "the struggle to deal effectively
with a loss of the past" that contains "an impossible-to-resolve contradiction"
in the sense that "no memory or mourning can retrieve what was lost" (650).
Instead such mourning lends itself to a restorative form of nostalgia that
creates "images of an idealized yesterday" in the homogenization of a remembered past that happens to serve distinctive ideological purposes (643). One
aspect of the ideological work undertaken by restorative nostalgia is the notion that recollections of history are "connected with 'traditional' memories
and narratives focusing on claims about ancient bonds of blood, continuity,
and fixed categorizations of 'us' and 'them'" (648).

Thus aporetic mourning and restorative nostalgia lend themselves to dichotomous polarizations—say, between Indigene and colonizer—that enable
overgeneralized expressions of resentment and oversimplified assignations of
blame for Native circumstances. Certainly overly extensive claims of genocide, when extrapolated to actions and occurrences not involving mass murder, appear to express relational antipathy and to reinforce fixed categorizations of "us" versus "them." Indeed contemporary expressions of resentment
by some Indigenous critics appear to shade into what Nietzsche ([1887] 1997)
described as *ressentiment*, and yet Zembylas (2011) advocated for a different
kind of nostalgia that may allow for a more promising path forward in the
face of aporetic mourning. For Zembylas, *reflective nostalgia* cultivates an
awareness that problematizes coherent and convenient accounts of the past
with the goal of adopting "critical rather than static views of memory and
loss" (645). Most important, these concepts herald the possibility "for a renewed politics of relationality":

> The notion of aporetic mourning suggests that social transformation can
> take place within a context in which sufferers endure pain but are ethically
> generous in wanting to build an inclusive society. . . . Without refusing to
> acknowledge the extent of past injustice, subsequent responsibilities are not
> locked into static identities of *oppressor* and *victim*, *repentant* and *forgiver*.
> This ethics of otherness constitutes an engagement with history that aims

to interrupt all totalities . . . through one's infinite ethical responsibility to the other. Such an ethical responsibility is not tied to restorative notions of nostalgia . . . but poses instead a reflective nostalgia that provides space for solidarity with others. (651)

This renewed politics of *relationality*—based on ethical generosity and the allowance of space for solidarity with others—is just one obvious responsibility of the *non*-Indigenous citizens of the United States and Canada, but Indigenous peoples (for our part) would likewise appear to fall under and to benefit from this sweeping ethical mandate as well.

Such a mandate seems incompatible with the casual and overgeneralized attributions of genocide as currently circulated by many Indigenous scholars, including behavioral health researchers who promote the concept of HT. Thus, irrespective of whether HT endures as a compelling explanatory model for rampant psychosocial distress in contemporary Native communities, I have argued that its advocates must attend more closely to the concrete and specific historical events that have shaped the emergence of any contemporary Indigenous community (Gone 2014). In short, my claim in this chapter is that there can be no productive references to "Generokee" Indigenous experiences of colonial genocide in the North American context. Indeed the rhetorical and political efficacy of the overgeneralized attribution of this term remains in serious question, for, as Conley-Zilkic and Totten (2009: 610) observed, "Once the specter of 'genocide' looms, debates and discussion about . . . the phenomenon are sidetracked by the single issue of whether or not 'genocide' is indeed [the appropriate description]." As a result, beyond those actual instances of group-based mass murder that intermittently occurred during the colonization of Native North America, it may be that understatement will serve Indigenous interests more effectively than hyperbole. Moreover the terms *colonization* and *colonial subjugation* would appear to serve readily enough for general characterizations of the postcontact historical experiences of Indigenous North Americans *without* sacrificing either historical accuracy or scholarly integrity. Most important, neither risks trivializing the intermittent occurrences of murderous settler campaigns undertaken for outright extermination of Indigenous peoples that even today threaten to rend the very fabric of human communality in the United States and Canada.

References

Adams, David W. 1995. *Education for Extinction: American Indians and the Boarding School Experience*. Lawrence: University Press of Kansas.

Brave Heart, Maria Yellow Horse. 1998. "The Return to the Sacred Path: Healing the Historical Trauma and Historical Unresolved Grief Response among the Lakota through a Psychoeducational Group Intervention." *Smith College Studies in Social Work* 68 (3): 287–305.

Brave Heart, Maria Yellow Horse, and Lemyra M. DeBruyn. 1998. "The American Indian Holocaust: Healing Historical Unresolved Grief." *American Indian and Alaska Native Mental Health Research* 8: 56–78.

Braveheart-Jordan, Maria, and Lemyra DeBruyn. 1995. "So She May Walk in Balance: Integrating the Impact of Historical Trauma in the Treatment of Native American Indian Women." In *Racism in the Lives of Women: Testimony Theory and Guides to Anti-racist Practice*, edited by Jeanne Adelman and Gloria Enguidanos, 345–68. New York: Haworth.

Chalk, Frank, and Kurt Jonassohn. 1990. *The History and Sociology of Genocide: Analyses and Case Studies*. New Haven, CT: Yale University Press.

Churchill, Ward. 1998. *A Little Matter of Genocide: Holocaust and Denial in the Americas, 1492 to the Present*. San Francisco: City Lights.

Churchill, Ward. 2002. *Struggle for the Land: Native North American Resistance to Genocide, Ecocide and Colonization*. San Francisco: City Lights.

Churchill, Ward. 2004. *Kill the Indian, Save the Man: The Genocidal Impact of American Indian Residential Schools*. San Francisco: City Lights.

Conley-Zilkic, Bridget, and Samuel Totten. 2009. "Easier Said than Done: The Challenges of Preventing and Responding to Genocide." In *Century of Genocide: Critical Essays and Eyewitness Accounts*, edited by Samuel Totten and William S. Parsons, 609–36. 3rd ed. New York: Routledge.

Duran, Eduardo. 1990. *Transforming the Soul Wound: A Theoretical/Clinical Approach to American Indian Psychology*. Berkeley, CA: Folklore Institute.

Duran, Eduardo, and Bonnie Duran. 1995. *Native American Postcolonial Psychology*. Albany: State University of New York Press.

Duran, Eduardo, Bonnie Duran, Maria Yellow Horse Brave Heart, and Susan Yellow Horse-Davis. 1998. "Healing the American Indian Soul Wound." In *International Handbook of Multigenerational Legacies of Trauma*, edited by Yael Danieli, 341–54. New York: Plenum.

Elliott, J. H. 1993. "The Rediscovery of America." *New York Review of Books*, June 24, 36–41.

Evans-Campbell, Teresa. 2008. "Historical Trauma in American Indian/Native Alaska Communities: A Multilevel Framework for Exploring Impacts on Individuals, Families, and Communities." *Journal of Interpersonal Violence* 23 (3): 316–38.

Fein, Helen. 1990. "Defining Genocide as a Sociological Concept." *Current Sociology* 38 (8): 1–126.

Flannery, Regina. 1953. *The Gros Ventres of Montana: Part I—Social life*. Washington, DC: Catholic University of America Press.

Fontaine, Theodore. 2010. *Broken Circle: The Dark Legacy of Indian Residential Schools.* Victoria, Canada: Heritage House.

Fowler, Loretta. 1987. *Shared Symbols, Contested Meanings: Gros Ventre Culture and History, 1778–1984.* Ithaca, NY: Cornell University Press.

Gone, Joseph P. 2007. "'We Never Was Happy Living Like a Whiteman': Mental Health Disparities and the Postcolonial Predicament in American Indian Communities." *American Journal of Community Psychology* 40 (3–4): 290–300.

Gone, Joseph P. 2008. "Introduction: Mental Health Discourse as Western Cultural Proselytization." *Ethos* 36 (3): 310–15.

Gone, Joseph P. 2009. "A Community-Based Treatment for Native American Historical Trauma: Prospects for Evidence-Based Practice." *Journal of Consulting and Clinical Psychology* 77 (4): 751–62.

Gone, Joseph P. 2013. "Redressing First Nations Historical Trauma: Theorizing Mechanisms for Indigenous Culture as Mental Health Treatment." *Transcultural Psychiatry* 50 (5): 683–706.

Gone, Joseph P. 2014. "Reconsidering American Indian Historical Trauma: Lessons from an Early Gros Ventre War Narrative." *Transcultural Psychiatry* 51 (3): 387–406.

Gone, Joseph P., and Laurence J. Kirmayer. 2010. "On the Wisdom of Considering Culture and Context in Psychopathology." In *Contemporary Directions in Psychopathology: Scientific Foundations of the DSM-V and ICD-11*, edited by Theodore Millon, Robert F. Krueger, and Erik Simonsen, 72–96. New York: Guilford.

Gone, Joseph P., and Joseph E. Trimble. 2012. "American Indian and Alaska Native Mental Health: Diverse Perspectives on Enduring Disparities." *Annual Review of Clinical Psychology* 8: 131–60.

Hagan, William T. 1988. "United States Indian Policies, 1860–1900." In *Handbook of North American Indians.* Vol. 4: *History of Indian-White Relations*, edited by Wilcomb E. Washburn, 51–65. Washington, DC: Smithsonian Institution.

Hamalainen, Pekka. 2003. "The Rise and Fall of Plains Indian Horse Cultures." *Journal of American History* 90 (3): 833–62.

Hitchcock, Robert K., and Tara M. Twedt. 2009. "Physical and Cultural Genocide of Indigenous Peoples." In *Century of Genocide: Critical Essays and Eyewitness Accounts*, edited by Samuel Totten and William S. Parsons, 413–58. 3rd ed. New York: Routledge.

Jaimes, M. Annette. 1992. *The State of Native America: Genocide, Colonization, and Resistance.* Boston: South End Press.

Jones, Adam. 2011. *Genocide: A Comprehensive Introduction.* 2nd ed. New York: Routledge.

Lear, Jonathan. 2006. *Radical Hope: Ethics in the Face of Cultural Devastation.* Cambridge, MA: Harvard University Press.

Lemkin, Raphael. 1944. *Axis Rule in Occupied Europe: Laws of Occupation, Analysis of Government, Proposals for Redress.* Washington, DC: Carnegie Endowment for International Peace.

Madley, Benjamin. 2008. "California's Yuki Indians: Defining Genocide in Native American History." *Western Historical Quarterly* 39: 303–32.

Maxwell, Krista. 2014. "Historicizing Historical Trauma Theory: Troubling the

Trans-Generational Transmission Paradigm." *Transcultural Psychiatry* 51 (3): 407–435.

Medin, Douglas L. 1989. "Concepts and Conceptual Structure." *American Psychologist* 44 (12): 1469–81.

Miller, James R. 1996. *Shingwauk's Vision: A History of Native Residential Schools*. Toronto: University of Toronto Press.

Moses, A. Dirk. 2000. "An Antipodean Genocide? The Origins of the Genocidal Moment in the Colonization of Australia." *Journal of Genocide Research* 2 (1): 89–106.

Nietzsche, Friedrich. [1887] 1997. *On the Genealogy of Morality*. Cambridge: Cambridge University Press.

Raikhel, Eugene. 2012. "Call for Papers: The Psy-ences and Mental Health in East Central Europe and Eurasia, April 26–27, 2013." Somatosphere, October 5. Accessed October 8, 2012. http://somatosphere.net/?p=4149.

Rensink, Brenden. 2009. "The Sand Creek Phenomenon: The Complexity and Difficulty of Undertaking a Comparative Study of Genocide vis-à-vis the North American West." *Genocide Studies and Prevention* 4 (1): 9–27.

Smith, Andrea. 2005. *Conquest: Sexual Violence and American Indian Genocide*. Boston: South End Press.

Sotero, Michelle M. 2006. "A Conceptual Model of Historical Trauma: Implications for Public Health Practice and Research." *Journal of Health Disparities Research and Practice* 1 (1): 93–108.

Stannard, David E. 1992. *American Holocaust: Columbus and the Conquest of the New World*. New York: Oxford University Press.

Straus, Scott. 2007. "Second-Generation Comparative Research on Genocide." *World Politics* 59 (3): 476–501.

Terry, Michael J. 1995. "Kelengakutelleghpat: An Arctic Community-Based Approach to Trauma." In *Secondary Traumatic Stress: Self-care Issues for Clinicians, Researchers, and Educators*, edited by B. H. Stamm, 149–78. Baltimore: Sidron Press.

Thornton, Russell. 1987. *American Indian Holocaust and Survival: A Population History since 1492*. Norman: University of Oklahoma Press.

Utley, Robert M. 1988. "Indian–United States Military Situation, 1848–1891." In *Handbook of North American Indians*, Vol. 4: *History of Indian-White Relations*, edited by Wilcomb E. Washburn, 163–83. Washington, DC: Smithsonian Institution.

Waldram, James B. 2004. *Revenge of the Windigo: The Construction of the Mind and Mental Health of North American Aboriginal Peoples*. Toronto: University of Toronto Press.

Walters, Karina L., Selina A. Mohammed, Teresa Evans-Campbell, Ramona E. Beltran, David H. Chae, and Bonnie Duran. 2011. "Bodies Don't Just Tell Stories, They Tell Histories: Embodiment of Historical Trauma among American Indians and Alaska Natives." *Du Bois Review* 8 (1): 179–89.

Walters, Karina L., and Jane M. Simoni. 2002. "Reconceptualizing Native Women's Health: An 'Indigenist' Stress-Coping Model." *American Journal of Public Health* 92 (4): 520–24.

Washburn, Wilcomb E., ed. 1988. *Handbook of North American Indians*. Vol. 4: *History of Indian-White Relations*. Washington, DC: Smithsonian Institution.

Wesley-Esquimaux, Cynthia C., and Magdalena Smolewski. 2004. *Historic Trauma and Aboriginal Healing*. Ottawa: Aboriginal Healing Foundation.

Whitbeck, Les B., Gary W. Adams, Dan R. Hoyt, and Xiaojin Chen. 2004. "Conceptualizing and Measuring Historical Trauma among American Indian People." *American Journal of Community Psychology* 33 (3–4): 119–30.

White, Richard. 1993. "Morality and Mortality." *New Republic*, January 18, 33–36.

Zembylas, Michalinos. 2011. "Reclaiming Nostalgia in Educational Politics and Practice: Counter-Memory, Aporetic Mourning, and Critical Pedagogy." *Discourse: Studies in the Cultural Politics of Education* 32 (5): 641–55.

CHAPTER 13

BUFFALO GENOCIDE IN NINETEENTH-CENTURY NORTH AMERICA

"Kill, Skin, and Sell"

Tasha Hubbard

The Buffalo are very numerous on the ne side the Red Deers river &
near . . . the ground is entirely covered by them & appears quite black.
I never saw such amazing numbers together before. I am sure there
was some millions in sight as no ground could be seen for them in that
complete semicircle & extending at least 10 miles.
　　　　　　　　　　　—Peter Fidler (1792), quoted in Brink,
　　　　　　　　　　　　　　　　　　Imagining Head-Smashed-In

Peter Fidler and other eighteenth- and early nineteenth-century Euro-Western observers could not help but be overwhelmed by the numbers of buffalo on the Great Plains. Scholars debate the exact number of buffalo that ranged from what is now central Saskatchewan and Alberta down to Mexico, but a generally accepted number falls between 30 and 60 million. Their sheer numbers made them a keystone species, influencing almost every other living being that inhabited the Plains, humans included. Winona Laduke (1999: 143) explains their impact in the following way: "Buffalo determine landscape. By their sheer numbers, weight, and behavior, they cultivated the prairie, which is the single largest ecosystem in North America."

When Euro-Westerners began to eye the Great Plains as part of the imperialist project, they identified two major obstacles to claiming the land: Indigenous peoples and the buffalo. Through philosophers and thinkers of the day the foundation was laid for colonial genocide, couched in the language of progress. Charles Lyell, one of Darwin's mentors, said the following in *Principles of Geology*: "We human beings . . . have no reason to feel guilty because our progress exterminates animals and plants. In our defense, we can state that when we conquer the earth and defend our occupations by force, we are only doing what all species in nature do" (quoted in Lindqvist 1992: 117). By positioning extermination of entire species as a "natural" process, Lyell and his followers were able to mitigate their guilt. After all, why say one does not have to feel guilty, unless one is guilty?

Following Lyell, Herbert Spencer, in his 1850 treatise, *Social Statistics*, says that imperialism is "the great scheme of perfect happiness" and the Indigenous peoples were obstacles to achieving said happiness. Thus "be he human or be he brute—the hindrance must be got rid of" (quoted in Lindqvist 1992: 8). Spencer is equating Indigenous peoples with animals in an attempt to relegate them to the status of "savage" in the colonial mind, thereby absolving the perpetrators of the colonial project. For Spencer, "savagery itself was often, by definition, a sufficient explanation for the extinction of some, if not all, savage races" (Brantlinger 2003: 18). The explanation is easily transformed into justification of action toward that end.

In the language of imperialism, Indigenous peoples and buffalo became conflated, both categorized as brutes that needed to be erased. Colonel Nelson A. Miles wrote the following of the buffalo slaughter: "This might seem like cruelty and wasteful extravagance but the buffalo, like the Indian, stood in the way of civilization and in the path of progress" (quoted in Smits 1994: 333). Savagery, represented by the Indian and the buffalo, must give way to civilization, represented by the Euro-Western man and his agrarian ideal. Daniel Heath Justice (2010: 66) posits that erasure "provides the philosophical and legal justification for land and resource theft, cultural and spiritual appropriation, subversion of social and political sovereignty, degradation, dehumanization, abuse, misrecognition, and slaughter." A few of the authors in this collection have outlined the physical genocide of Indigenous peoples in the Americas, but it is the specific act of slaughter that I grapple with in this chapter. I wish to make the argument that the slaughter of the buffalo constitutes an act of genocide.

Obviously the loss of the buffalo was catastrophic for Plains Indigenous peoples and, alongside actual massacres of Indigenous peoples, is often characterized as part of the colonial genocide of Indigenous people: "Starvation tactics, the destruction of homes and shelters during the freezing winter, and the killing of horses and buffalo herds ensured the submission or deportation of the survivors of the various tribes" (Travis 2010: 129). By removing the means of survival, the perpetrators of genocide succeed in removing Indigenous peoples. Raphael Lemkin agreed, including Indigenous experience in the Americas as part of his writings on genocide, arguing, "Colonial genocide involved the destruction of the foundations of the collective life of hunter-gatherers and their subsequent extermination" (quoted in Breen 2011: 73). In other words, destroy the buffalo, and one destroys the foundation of Plains Indigenous collectivity and their very lives.

I do not disagree with this idea. My traditional teachers describe the loss of the buffalo as the second major wave of trauma for Plains Indigenous peoples (epidemic disease is the first). Many people starved to death after the herds were extinguished. However, I endeavor to apply the concept of genocide to the buffalo slaughter of the late nineteenth century within an Indigenous epistemological framework, while not excluding the impact of the near-extinction of the buffalo on the Indigenous peoples and the land itself.

Solidifying a definition of genocide is the subject of numerous scholarly and ideological positions. Christopher Powell (2007: 530) reminds us of the following: "Different definitions of 'genocide,' different conceptions of what 'genos' could refer to, presume different theories about the nature of social life." An Indigenous paradigm expands the conception of *people* to include other-than-human animals. George Tinker (1996: 165), an Osage theologian, explains this: "In one of the polyvalent layers of meaning, those four directions hold together in the same egalitarian balance the four nations of two-leggeds, four-leggeds, wingeds, and living-moving things. In this rendition human beings lose their status of 'primacy' and 'dominion.' Implicitly and explicitly American Indians are driven by their culture and spirituality to recognize the personhood of all 'things' in creation." In other words, being "a people" is not a domain exclusive to humans. Animals-as-people is found throughout Indigenous epistemologies. Linda Hogan (1998: 12), in her essay "First People," echoes Tinker's statement: "For us, the animals are understood to be our equals. They are still our teachers. They are our helpers and healers. They have been our guardians and we have been theirs."

For some Plains Indigenous peoples, buffalo are known as the first people. Arvol Looking Horse, keeper of the Sacred White Buffalo Calf pipe, explains this to Laduke (1999: 162): "With the teaching of our way of life from the time of being, the First People were the Buffalo people, our ancestors which came from the sacred Black Hills, the heart of everything that is." My own teachings tell me that the buffalo people take care of us and teach us how to live, much like a benevolent grandparent.

Many Euro-Western viewpoints disregard this knowledge or relegate it to the category of folk tales. However, Griffan Huggan and Helen Tiffin (2010: 11), in their *Postcolonial Ecocriticism: Literature, Animals, Environment*, remind us that colonial domination over Indigenous peoples "was effected over the ensuing centuries through environmental—and hence cultural—derangement on a vast scale, such destructive changes were premised on *ontological* and *epistemological* differences between European and Indian ideas of human and animal being-in-the-world." According to Indigenous ways of knowing, humans do not hold exclusive title to personhood, and therefore neither to genocide.[1]

Specific genocidal practices and their theoretical underpinnings can be applied to the buffalo slaughter. As Andrew Woolford reminds us in this volume, "Study of colonial genocide should help decolonize genocide studies by challenging Eurocentric biases within the field." I maintain that this entails, among other things, challenging human-centric and territorially shallow conceptualizations of group life. It is specifically the "human-centric" bias that I wish to dispute by arguing that Euro-Western governments and their representatives undertook buffalo genocide in order to consolidate political power in the Great Plains.

Recent research on the late nineteenth-century western United States draws a firmer line between the army and the slaughter of the buffalo. Sarah Carter (1999: 96) explains this recent development in scholarship, which suggests that the army's involvement in the buffalo extermination was part "of a well-calculated policy to subdue Native Americans and drive them onto reserves . . . by employing and providing assistance to non-Aboriginal buffalo hunters, by routinely sponsoring and outfitting civilian hunting expeditions that slaughtered on a massive scale, and by encouraging troops to kill large numbers of buffalo using artillery and cannon." The army, representing the colonial U.S. interest in erasing buffalo in order to clear Indigenous peoples from the land, engaged in the genocidal process through policy and action, and at the same time "allowed," according to Israel Charny's (1994) definition, genocide to happen by encouraging civilian sport hunters and hide hunters to indiscriminately slaughter the buffalo.

David Smits (1994: 333), in his article "The Frontier Army and the Destruction of the Buffalo: 1865–1883," not only outlines the details of the slaughter but posits that the slaughter was unwritten official army policy, whereby "the decree had gone forth that they must both give way," referring to Indigenous peoples and the buffalo. This includes orders from General Phillip Sheridan, appointed in 1867 to lead the U.S. military during the Indian Wars, the campaign to pacify Indigenous Nations in the west. Because of Sheridan's past practice of issuing kill orders without written documentation, Smits says, "it is probable that Sheridan deliberately refused to issue the relevant written orders knowing that orally conveyed orders could be more easily concealed or more plausibly denied. . . . Why subject himself and the army to avoidable Indian enmity and humanitarian disapproval?" (333).

Sheridan can be understood as one of the engineers of buffalo genocide. His biographer refers to his "pragmatism and elastic ethics," which made him "the perfect frontier soldier" (Hutton 2009: 180). Thus, willing to undertake gruesome tasks in order to fulfill his frontier goals, "Sheridan authorized an conscious extermination of the remaining bison (and, where appropriate, horses too) to starve intractable tribes into submission" (Levene 2005: 96). Sheridan and other military leaders fostered an atmosphere in which killing buffalo was a patriotic practice. When one officer admitted that he had indiscriminately killed buffalo while out on a hunting party, his superior responded, "Kill every buffalo you can! Every buffalo dead is an Indian gone" (quoted in Smits 1994: 328). The infamous 7th Cavalry general George Armstrong Custer is known to have used buffalo as target practice for his new recruits.

Much has been written about the period in U.S. history known as the Indian Wars and its inclusion within the category of genocide. However, there were periods when the army was hampered in its efforts for various reasons. Smits (1994: 318) elaborates:

> Frustrated bluecoats, unable to deliver a punishing blow to the so-called "Hostiles," unless they were immobilized in their winter camps, could, however, strike at a more accessible target, namely, the buffalo. That tactic also made curious sense, for in soldiers' minds the buffalo and the Plains Indian were virtually inseparable. When Captain Robert G. Carter of the Fourth Cavalry referred to the "nomadic red Indian and his migratory companion, the bison," he linked the two together in a manner typical of military men. Soldiers who associated the buffalo with the Indian so inseparably could even occasionally pretend that slaughtering buffalo was actually killing Indians.

Again Custer provides the best example of this, as he is known to have described the tactics of a buffalo hunt in the same terms as a military action against Indigenous peoples.

There was also collusion between official U.S. government representatives and the army to decimate buffalo in order to decimate Indigenous peoples. In the Fort Laramie Treaty the "government agreed to abandon the Bozeman Trail and its guardian forts and to look upon the Powder River country as 'unceded Indian territory' in which the Sioux might continue to roam" (Utley and Washburn 2002: 233). However, wording was included in the treaty to ensure the right to this territory existed only "so long as the buffalo may range thereon in such numbers as to justify the chase" (Rinella 2008: 81). As soon as the treaty was concluded, the military looked the other way as the hide hunters went in and began slaughtering buffalo. With their food sources depleted, the Lakota were forced to ask for provisions, suggesting the buffalo numbers no longer justified the chase. "That effectively undid the treaty and opened the door for more hide hunters to go down there with military protection and kill whatever buffalo were left" (81).

Collusion between the army and the government had a third party with which to enact buffalo genocide: hide hunters themselves. Records exist of a speech Sheridan delivered before the Texas legislature, which was contemplating a bill to protect the buffalo in 1875: "[The buffalo hunters] have done in the last two years and will do more in the next year to settle the vexed Indian question, than the entire regular army has done in the last thirty years. They are destroying the Indian's commissary, and it is a well-known fact that an army losing its base of supplies is placed at a great disadvantage. Send them powder and lead, if you will; for the sake of a lasting peace, let them kill, skin, and sell until the buffaloes are exterminated" (quoted in Dary 1989: 129). The words "kill, skin, and sell" are an appropriate mantra for the hide hunters, whose efforts had begun in earnest in 1871. According to William Hornaday (2002: 494), a former hunter turned conservationist, "The buffalo country fairly swarmed with hunters, each party putting forth its utmost efforts to destroy more buffaloes than its rivals." While buffalo had been hunted in significant numbers prior to 1871, what focused the efforts was the development of an industrial tanning process in that year. "Buffalo leather suddenly became part of the world economy, prized for machinery belts and army boots. The United States government realized it could subdue the Plains tribes by letting freelance hunters (many of whom were Civil War veterans) kill off their food supply" (Wright 2008: 164). Ironically the genocide of the buffalo and the subsequent use of their hides became fuel for the overall genocidal project of colonizing the entire western territory.

The numbers are stunning: "Colonel Dodge once counted one hundred and twelve carcasses of buffalo 'inside a semicircle of 200 yards radius, all of which were killed by the one man from the same spot, and in less than three-quarters of an hour'" (Hornaday 2002: 469–70). Dodge went on to describe the slaughter: "Where there were myriads of buffalo the year before, there were now myriads of carcasses. The air was foul with a sickening stench, and the vast plain, which only a short twelvemonth before teemed with animal life, was a dead, solitary, putrid desert" (quoted in Smits 1994: 327). By 1883 the buffalo were effectively removed from the Great Plains, relegated to remnant herds of orphan calves, a few animals in captivity, and a refugee herd in Yellowstone. Estimates put their numbers as low as a few hundred animals by 1889.

Patrick Wolfe's (2006: 387) discussion about the "logic of elimination" and the ways "settler colonialism destroys to replace" is especially relevant for this period. The buffalo were now essentially destroyed, facilitated in part by their replacement with cattle: "Only the smaller northern herd [of buffalo] remained by 1879. Its destruction by 1883 resulted from a combination of hide-market (and 'sport') hunting, drought, and the arrival of nearly a half million head of cattle in Wyoming alone, whose appetite for grass and water competed with that of the diminishing bison" (Magoc 2006: 92). In fact, as Andrew Isenberg (2000: 130) observes, "the belief that domestic livestock were destined to replace the bison sustained the hide hunter's destructive harvest." Remove the existing species and replace it with one of European origins in order to solidify ownership of the land.

I should pause here to note that there is considerable dissent about the primary cause of the buffalo's near extinction. There are those, including Shepherd Krech (1999), Dan Flores (2001), and even Andrew Isenberg (2000), who posit that Indigenous peoples share equal (or more) responsibility for the destruction of the buffalo herds, thereby minimizing the actions of the government, the army, and hide hunters. The most commonly cited example is Indigenous overhunting by the use of buffalo pounds or Indigenous participation in the hide trade. There is some good Indigenous (and non-Indigenous) scholarship about the breakdown of the intricate relationship between the buffalo and Indigenous people due to colonization and some accounts of over-hunting as part of participation in the hide trade.[2] However, the evidence of Euro-Western culpability is overwhelming: "Still, even with some profligate hunting, estimates are that all Indian tribes on the Great Plains killed no more than half a million bison annually" (Magoc 2006: 90).

Furthermore Krech, Flores, and Isenberg rely on such evidence as comparing cattle's impact on the land in 1910 to buffalo's use of the land over millennium, manipulate numbers of the buffalo to minimize the destruction, and conflate European and Indigenous peoples' actions, such as in the following passage from Isenberg (2000: 197): "From the perspective of the bison, there were striking similarities between the nomads and the Euroamericans. Both were newcomers to the plains in the eighteenth century. Both employed new technologies and adopted new modes of production to hunt the bison. Both sacrificed bison to meet social demands of integration, prestige, or conquest. Both increasingly adapted to capitalism in the eighteenth and nineteenth centuries. In the end, that adaptation was fatal to millions of bison." This statement not only fails to take into account the oral history of Indigenous existence and interrelatedness with other inhabitants of the land over thousands of years but also completely disregards the uneven power dynamics that were occurring during the time of the buffalo slaughter. Sebastian Braun (2007: 195) explains Isenberg's reasoning this way: "Following his own agenda . . . he in turn does not contextualize relations between Indians and Euro-Americans, which makes him ignore any notions of distribution of power, and ultimately any notion of cultural difference."

Genocide and denial of genocide work in conjunction, and the buffalo genocide is no exception. After all, "the battle is not only about history and the authenticity of the records of past events in our civilization, it is about the extent to which we today hold our governments responsible for their actions" (Charny 1994: 74). Isenberg and the others attempt to render the government, army, and hide hunters inculpable by reinforcing notions of Indigenous culpability in their own destruction.

Returning now to the Indigenous epistemology that applies "peoplehood" to the buffalo, the actions of the trinity of destruction (government, army, and hide hunters) can be viewed through the lens of genocide. For example, it has been established, in this volume and elsewhere, that colonial genocide includes the removal of children, which is destructive to the future of a people. "The sportsmen adventurer John Mortimer Murphy claimed to have seen a troop of cavalry lasso one hundred buffalo calves and bring them to a corral near the post barracks. Although the little ones had sufficient room to run about and an abundance of hay and grass, 'few of them lived more than a week'" (Smits 1994: 320). Other accounts abound of the removal of calves from the herds for both sport and curiosity. In exploring the parameters of the concept of genocide, Powell (2007: 538) writes, "Given that a genos is a network of practical social relationships, destruction of a genos means the forcible breaking down of those relationships." The army in effect broke down the family relationships of the buffalo by removing the calves, contributing to the genocidal project. The destruction of the buffalo's social relationships did not stop with the removal of calves from the herd. Even Isenberg (2000: 136) discusses the impact on the buffalo's ability to reproduce, which depended on the ability to gather together: "Reproductive success likely declined with group size in the 1870s, as unceasing predation (by hide hunters) prevented the congregation of the herds in the rutting season, upsetting the bison's patterns of migration and reproduction and thus inhibiting a recovery of the bison's population."

Hide hunter accounts also provide a perspective on the impact of the genocide on the buffalo themselves, albeit through a Euro-Western filter. John Cook (1938: 249) wrote his memoirs of his days as a hide skinner, following the hunters:

When Charlie and Jimmie drove out the next morning to get the hides, there was a young calf standing by one of the carcasses, its mother being one of the victims of yesterday's work. It still had the reddish color that all buffalo calves have in their infancy, not obtaining their regular blackish brown until in the fall of the year, when they are very fat, plump and stocky, and take on a glossy look. I have watched buffaloes many times during my three years' hunt, not with a covetous eye at the time, but to study the characteristics of the animal, and I do not remember ever seeing buffalo calves frisky, gamboling, and cavorting around in playful glee like domestic calves. Perhaps their doom has been transmitted to them! Yes, this was the pathetic side of the question. And thousands of these little creatures literally starved to death, their mothers being killed from the time they were a day old on up to the time they could rustle their own living on the range.

Buffalo feel grief for their dead, according to both my traditional teachers and the longtime buffalo warden at the Grasslands National Park, Wes Olsen. He has observed the behavior of the wild herd and their reaction to a death. Rather than abandon the body, buffalo will stay with the deceased, attempt to revive their family member, and make audible sounds of grief. The hide hunters' practice of shooting from a hidden location with a high-powered rifle did not give warning to the buffalo of the coming danger. Hide hunter accounts of what happened after they shot their first victims intersect with Olsen's observations: "When one of their number was killed the rest of the herd, smelling the blood, would become excited, but instead of stampeding would gather around the dead buffalo, pawing, bellowing and hooking it viciously. Taking advantage of this well-known habit of the creature, the hunter would kill one animal and then wipe out almost the entire herd" (quoted in Magoc 2006: 95). Hornaday's (2002: 469) accounts also support the buffalo's expression of grief: "They cluster around the fallen ones, sniff at the warm blood, bawl aloud in wonderment, and do everything but run away."

In the latter days of the buffalo slaughter, many of the buffalo's social relationships broke down. Cook describes the hunters' practice of surrounding available waterways, forcing the buffalo to approach anyway, and gunning them down. Those buffalo who managed to find a water source that was free from hunters "would rush and crowd in pell-mell, crowding, jamming, and trampling down both the weak and the strong, to quench a burning thirst. Many of them were rendered insane from their intolerable, unbearable thirst" (Cook 1938: 198). Instead of living cooperatively in their herd society, the buffalo were tortured prior to their death at the hands of the hide hunters.

It is not surprising that Indigenous accounts describe buffalo genocide as a war on buffalo. Note the account told by Old Lady Horse (1968: 170) in "The Last Buffalo Herd":

> There was a war between the buffalo and the white men. The white men built forts in the Kiowa country, and the wooly-headed buffalo soldiers [the 10th Calvary, made up of Negro troops] shot the buffalo as fast as they could, but the buffalo kept coming on, coming on, even into the post cemetery at Fort Sill. Soldiers were not enough to hold them back. . . . But then the whites came and built the railroad, cutting the people's land in half. The buffalo fought for the people, tearing up the tracks and chasing away the whites' cattle. So the army was sent to kill the buffalo. The army brought in hunters, who killed until the bones of the buffalo covered the land and the buffalo saw they could no longer fight.

Indigenous peoples saw the buffalo as their protector, who took a position on the front line in the genocidal war against Indigenous peoples. Laduke (1999: 154), in her exploration of buffalo genocide, discovered that "many native people view the historic buffalo slaughter as the time when the buffalo relatives, the older brothers, stood up and took the killing intended for the younger brothers, the Native peoples." Laduke contextualizes buffalo genocide as an example of a colonial war on nature, "a war on the psyche, a war on the soul" (149). Others have characterized the destruction of nature with similar terminology. The Indigenous psychologist Eduardo Duran (2006) describes it as a "soul wound." He remarks that elders understand such circumstances as the erasure of the buffalo from the land as an earth wounding: "When the earth is wounded, the people who are caretakers of the earth are also wounded at a very deep soul level" (16).

Pretty Shield describes her reaction to witnessing the aftermath of buffalo genocide: "Ahh, my heart fell down when I began to see dead buffalo scattered all over our beautiful country, killed and skinned, and left to rot by white men, many, many hundreds of buffalo. The first I saw of this was in the Judith basin. The whole country there smelled of rotting meat. Even the flowers could not put down the bad smell. Our hearts were like stones. And yet nobody believed, even then, that the white man could kill *all* the buffalo. Since the beginning of things there had always been so many!" (quoted in Calloway 1996: 131). Her being as an Indigenous person was profoundly impacted by the loss. Crow Plenty-Coups describes his grief in the same terms: "But when the buffalo went away the hearts of my people fell to the ground, and they could not lift them up again. After this nothing happened. There was little singing anywhere" (quoted in Lindemann 1930: 169). Both Indigenous individuals are expressing what Justice (2010: 63) categorizes as "an understanding of nationhood that's fully rooted in broadly ecosystemic concepts of Indigenous kinship" with the buffalo, which intertwines their respective and interrelated genocides. The buffalo gone from the land meant the Plains Indigenous peoples who had been holding out to negotiate better treaties and claims to their land were forced to submit and relocate to small reservations scattered across the newly forming states and provinces. The destruction of the interrelated bond between buffalo, Indigenous people, and the land reminds me of Waldau's claim that cultural imperialism affects both human and nonhuman animals (2006: 636). The stories of genocide need to be told and accepted as truth in order to clear space for Indigenous stories, many of which lay out ways to live on the land in healthy and non-destructive ways.

In her work outlining what she terms the "pillars of white supremacy," the Cherokee scholar Andrea Smith (2006: 68) lists the logic of genocide as the second pillar: "This logic holds that indigenous peoples must disappear. In fact, they must *always* be disappearing, in order to allow non-indigenous peoples rightful claim over this land." Through a complex and interrelated policy of buffalo genocide, enacted by the state, military, and hide hunters, the buffalo disappeared from the land, forcing the disappearance of Indigenous people at the same time. Both Indigenous peoples and buffalo were the subjects of colonial elegies, which lamented their loss with a pen held in one hand and a gun in the other. "Extinction discourse often takes the form of proleptic elegy, sentimentally or mournfully expressing, even in its most humane versions, the confidence of self-fulfilling prophecy, according to which new, white colonies and nations arise as savagery and wilderness recede" (Brantlinger 2003: 3).

These tropes remain with us still. As we examine the current realities facing the Great Plains, including widespread drought, continued animal genocides (wolves come to mind), and the relentless extraction of what is termed "resources," it would be wise to revisit the historic buffalo genocide in order to consider the repercussions of applying a Euro-Western ideology to the land, propped up by the continued hierarchy in which humans occupy an exalted place at the top.[3] Huggan and Tiffin (2010: 6) put it this way: "In assuming a natural prioritization of humans and human interests over those of other species on earth, we are both generating and repeating the racist ideologies of imperialism on a planetary scale." How can the past lessons of buffalo genocide speak to us now?

I wish to conclude by returning to my own teachings as a Nehiyaw human person. I am reminded that the buffalo remains with us. I am reminded that everything comes back to our spiritual understandings. Their bodies were destroyed; their spirits were not. Our stories, still told and still understood, tell us the buffalo will return one day.

Notes

1. These kinds of discussions are also happening in recent animal studies scholarship. David Sztybel (2008: 252) discusses the limitations in both language and understanding: "'Person' is interchangeable with humans in most dictionaries but we need to update our lexicon in order to overcome speciesist thinking."
2. The Blackfoot scholar Betty Bastien (2004) is the best example.
3. Buffalo genocide continues into the present time, with the systemic slaughter of buffalo that leave the confines of Yellowstone National Park, a genocide sanctioned by the state government of Montana until a Montana Supreme Court ruling in March 2014. For the first time in centuries, buffalo in Yellowstone are free from genocidal practices.

References

Bastien, Betty. 2004. *Blackfoot Ways of Knowing: The Worldview of the Siksikaitsitapi.* Calgary: University of Calgary Press.

Brantlinger, Patrick. 2003. *Dark Vanishings: Discourse on the Extinction of Primitive Races, 1830–1900.* Ithaca, NY: Cornell University Press.

Braun, Sebastian F. 2007. "Ecological and Un-Ecological Indians: The (Non)portrayal of Plains Indians in the 'Buffalo Commons' Literature." In *Native Americans and the Environment: Perspectives on the Ecological Indian*, edited by Michael E. Harkin and David Rich Lewis, 192–210. Lincoln: University of Nebraska Press.

Breen, Shayne. 2011. "Extermination, Extinction, Genocide, British Colonialism and Tasmanian Aborigines." In *Forgotten Genocides: Oblivion, Denial, and Memory*, edited by Rene Lemarchand, 71–90. Philadelphia: University of Pennsylvania Press.

Brink, Jack W. 2008. *Imagining Head-Smashed-In: Aboriginal Buffalo Hunting on the Northern Plains.* Edmonton: Athabaska University Press.

Calloway, Colin G. 1996. *Our Hearts Fell to the Ground: Plains Indian Views of How the West Was Lost.* Boston: Bedford/St. Martin's.

Carter, Sarah. 1999. *Aboriginal People and Colonizers of Western Canada to 1900.* Toronto: University of Toronto Press.

Charny, Israel W. 1994. "Toward a Generic Definition of Genocide." In *Genocide: Conceptual and Historical Dimensions*, edited by George J. Andreopoulos, 64–94. Philadelphia: University of Pennsylvania Press.

Cook, John R. 1938. *The Border and the Buffalo: An Untold Story of the Southwest Plains.* Chicago: Lakeside Press.

Dary, David A. 1989. *The Buffalo Book.* Athens, OH: Swallow Press.

Duran, Eduardo. 2006. *Healing the Soul Wound: Counseling with American Indians and Other Native Peoples.* New York: Teacher's College Press.

Flores, Dan. 2001. *The Natural West: Environmental History in the Great Plains and Rocky Mountains*. Norman: University of Oklahoma Press.

Hogan, Linda. 1998. "First People." In *Intimate Nature: The Bond between Women and Animals,* edited by Linda Hogan, Deena Metzger, and Brenda Paterson, 6–19. New York: Fawcett Columbine.

Hornaday, William Temple. 2002. *The Extermination of the American Bison*. Washington, DC: Smithsonian Institution.

Huggan, Griffan, and Helen Tiffin. 2010. *Postcolonial Ecocriticism: Literature, Animals, Environment*. New York: Routledge.

Hutton, Paul Andrew. 2009. "Philip H. Sheridan." In *Soldiers West: Biographies from the Military Frontier*, edited by Paul Andrew Hutton and Durwood Ball, 174–200. Norman: University of Oklahoma Press.

Isenberg, Andrew C. 2000. *The Destruction of the Bison: An Environmental History, 1750–1920*. New York: Cambridge University Press.

Justice, Daniel Heath. 2010. "A Relevant Resonance: Considering the Study of Indigenous National Literatures." In *Across Cultures across Borders: Canadian Aboriginal and Native American Literatures,* edited by Paul DePasquale, Renate Eigenbrod, and Emma LaRocque, 61–76. Peterborough, Canada: Broadview Press.

Krech, Shepherd, III. 1999. *The Ecological Indian: Myth and History*. New York: Norton.

Laduke, Winona. 1999. *All Our Relations: Native Struggles for Land and Life*. Cambridge, MA: South End.

Levene, Mark. 2005. *The Rise of the West and the Coming of Genocide*. New York: Palgrave Macmillan.

Lindemann, Frank B. 1930. *Plenty Coups: Chief of the Crows*. Lincoln: University of Nebraska Press.

Lindqvist, Sven. 1992. *"Exterminate All the Brutes."* New York: New Press.

Magoc, Chris J. 2006. *Environmental Issues in American History: A Reference Guide with Primary Documents*. Westport, CT: Greenwood Press.

Old Lady Horse (Spear Woman). 1968. "The Last Buffalo Herd." In *American Indian Mythology*, edited by Alice Lee Marriott and Carol K. Rachlin. New York: New American Library.

Powell, Christopher. 2007. "What Do Genocides Kill? A Relational Conception of Genocide." *Journal of Genocide Research* 9 (4): 527–47.

Rinella, Steve. 2008. *American Buffalo: In Search of a Lost Icon*. New York: Spiegel and Grau.

Smith, Andrea. 2006. "Heteropatriarchy and the Three Pillars of White Supremacy: Rethinking Women of Color Organizing." In *Color of Violence: The Incite! Anthology*, edited by Andrea Smith, Beth E. Richie, and Julia Sudbury, 66–73. Cambridge, MA: South End.

Smits, David D. 1994. "The Frontier Army and the Destruction of the Buffalo: 1865–1883." *Western Historical Quarterly* 25 (3): 312–38.

Sztybel, David. 2008. "Animals as Persons." In *Animal Subjects: An Ethical Reader in a Posthuman World*, edited by Jodey Castricano, 241–58. Waterloo, Canada: Wilfred Laurier University Press.

Tinker, George E. 1996. "An American Indian Theological Response to Ecojustice." In

Defending Mother Earth: Native American Perspectives on Environmental Justice, edited by Jace Weaver, 163–76. New York: Orbis Books.

Travis, Hannibal. 2010. *Genocide in the Middle East: The Ottoman Empire, Iraq, and Sudan*. Durham, NC: Carolina Academic Press.

Utley, Robert M., and Wilcomb E. Washburn. 2002. *Indian Wars*. New York: American Heritage.

Waldau, Paul. 2006. "Pushing Environmental Justice to a Natural Limit." In *A Communion of Subjects: Animals in Religion, Science and Ethics*, edited by Paul Waldau and Kimberley Patton, 629–642. New York: Columbia University Press.

Wolfe, Patrick. 2006. "Settler Colonialism and the Elimination of the Native." *Journal of Genocide Research* 8 (4): 387–409.

Wright, Roland. 2008. *What Is America? A Short History of the New World Order*. Toronto: Knopf Canada.

CHAPTER 14

GENOCIDE IN THE INDIAN
RESIDENTIAL SCHOOLS

Canadian History through the Lens of
the UN Genocide Convention

David B. MacDonald

> *I don't see why a German who eats a piece of bread should torment*
> *himself with the idea that the soil which produced this bread has been*
> *won by the sword. When we eat wheat from Canada, we don't think*
> *about the despoiled Indians.*
>
> —Adolf Hitler, discussing German
> expansionism in *Table Talk*

For too long we Canadians have portrayed ourselves as morally superior to our neighbors to the south. Our mythology includes Canada avoiding military misadventures like Vietnam, ending slavery early, more peacefully settling the west, and generally treating Aboriginal peoples better (Granatstein 1996: chapter 1). Yet our tendency to engage in "chosen amnesia" (Buckley-Zistel 2006: 132–34) has been thrown into question by two decades of revelations about the horrific treatment of Aboriginal children in Canada's network of Indian residential schools (IRS). More contentious than the facts of systemic abuse and intergenerational trauma have been claims of genocide and cultural genocide, with both terms enjoying widespread use in public discourse. In 2011, for example, the chief commissioner of Canada's Truth and Reconciliation Commission (TRC), Justice Murray Sinclair, argued on the CBC documentary series *8th Fire* that genocide had been committed ("Q & A" 2012). Assembly of First Nations National chief Shawn Atleo made a similar argument around the same time ("Residential Schools Fit Definition of Genocide" 2011). They are hardly alone. Since the 1970s a number of academics have asserted that the United Nations Genocide Convention (UNGC) does indeed apply to Aboriginal experiences (Davis and Zannis 1973: 175–76; Chrisjohn and Young 1994: 2–6, 33–35; Neu and Therrien 2003; Cardinal 1999; Grant 1996: 69, 270–71; Haig-Brown 1988: 11; Woolford 2009: 81–97; Powell 2011; Ladner 2009; Nicholas 2001: 10–13). My goals in this chapter are, first, to explore whether the IRS system was genocidal and, second, to suggest ways we might move forward with reconciliation if we accept that genocide was a goal of the system's architects.

I begin with a brief background of the IRS system before plunging into my main discussion as to whether the system can be deemed genocide. I focus primarily on Article 2(e) of the UNGC, "forcibly transferring children of the group to another group." Space prohibits me from engaging in any detail with the other four elements of Article 2. Death in the schools is not a major focus of this chapter, although it is clear that large numbers of children died as a result of their experiences in the IRS system (TRC 2012b: 31). I also do not engage with recent studies of nutrition experiments in several residential schools from 1942 to 1952 (Mosby 2013).[1] I conclude with a brief discussion of what we are to do now, in Canada, if we recognize that the IRS system was genocidal. What sort of restitution and reconciliation needs to occur between Aboriginal and settler peoples, and how much will this change Canada as it is now politically constituted?

Having worked with Anishinaabeg IRS survivors and elders, I use the term *Shognosh* to refer to Canada's European settler populations as well as multicultural people like me who are assimilated into European ways of thinking and acting. This is consistent with the use of *Pākehā* in New Zealand to designate those of European ancestry and others who are not Māori (King 1985; Mulgan 1989).[2] Since it is reasonable in political science to refer to *Aboriginal* or *Indigenous* people, we should, in the interests of fairness, be willing to categorize ourselves using Anishinaabeg, Cree, Haida, and other languages of this country. The use of *Shognosh* is a crucial signifier in the interests of academic rigor, since it can act to discursively de-neutralize terms like *settler*, *mainstream*, *authorities*, *government*, and *Canadian*.

Why Was the IRS System Created?

The IRS system should be contextualized as one aspect of a much larger colonial project that began with early Shognosh colonizers in the sixteenth century and continues to this day. The system marked a deliberate attempt to destroy many aspects of Aboriginal distinctiveness over several generations to facilitate Shognosh colonization. It began in an era when the economic benefits of partnership with Aboriginal peoples through the fur trade were largely irrelevant; rather than being economic assets, Aboriginal peoples were perceived as an impediment to further colonization (Miller 1996: 62–63). If we use Wolfe's (2010: 103) analysis of settler colonialism, Shognosh expansion should be framed as a territorial project, whereby Aboriginal peoples were to be alienated from their lands and subdued, as what was formerly theirs became ours.

The IRS system was developed in the context of Aboriginal uprisings in the late nineteenth century. It also acknowledged the English-French conflicts that had divided the fledgling country for a considerable time, conflicts that were expressed in political, cultural, linguistic, and religious terms (Haig-Brown 1988: 31–32). The system was also an answer to the decimation of Aboriginal populations during the nineteenth century due to starvation (a result of the decimation of food like the bison), disease (smallpox, malaria, whooping cough, tuberculosis), and other conditions (Carter 1999: 37–39, 100). Indeed of the 2 million Aboriginal people estimated to have been in what is now Canada at the end of the fifteenth century, the population had been reduced by some 95 percent by the end of the nineteenth century, leaving about 100,000 to 125,000 people remaining (Saul 2008: 22–23; for British Columbia statistics, see Manuel and Posluns 1974: 27).

Although the first experiments in residential schools go back to the seventeenth century in Canada, no systematized effort was undertaken until the nineteenth century. Various Shognosh initiatives to deal with the "Indian problem" included the 1842 Bagot Commission, which proposed a system of rural boarding schools. Legislation like the Gradual Civilization Act (1857) and the Act for the Gradual Enfranchisement of the Indian (1869) laid the foundations for the IRS system that was to follow (Aboriginal Healing Foundation 2002: 2). In 1879 a residential school was established at a former military barracks in Carlisle, Pennsylvania, which served as a model for the network of boarding schools established in the United States (Milloy 1999: 13). Strongly influenced by the United States, our IRS system was established in the mid-1880s and was conceived in partially benign terms: to help Aboriginal people better adapt to life in a Shognosh-dominated country. Many treaties contained provisions for government-funded on-reserve schools, and Aboriginal leaders like Chief Shingwauk intended for "teaching wigwams" to educate his people and prepare them for a better life. The early balance between Shognosh and Aboriginal worldviews gave way to a far more coercive system that entailed forced assimilation and cultural destruction.

The federal government worked closely with mainline Canadian churches, which initiated the creation of many schools and were responsible for running most of them until the 1950s. The Catholic Church entities ran approximately 60 percent, the Anglicans about 30 percent, with the Presbyterian, Methodist, and United Churches running most of the remainder. Until the 1950s attendance for children age five to sixteen was compulsory (Milloy 1999; Miller 2004: 84). An early distinction was drawn between boarding and industrial schools. Boarding schools were located on or near reserves and were designed to attract local Aboriginal children. Industrial schools, by contrast, were located farther from Aboriginal reserves and closer to settler towns and cities (Furniss 1995: 27). After 1923 the distinctions between these types of schools mattered little, and in government parlance all were known as residential schools (Miller 1996: 141–42). At least 150,000 children passed through 125 schools, the last of which closed only in 1996 (Barkan 2003: 130–31). Of these there are approximately seventy-five thousand Survivors alive today, and many face myriad social, economic, and other problems as a result of their experiences.

What Is Genocide in Canada?

The UN Genocide Convention is hardly a perfect document. While it marked a milestone in international law, the final document was nevertheless a compromise among states, many of whom had committed atrocities against their own populations, some of these ongoing at the time the UNGC was being negotiated. Certainly Canada's role in the UNGC process was not benign; indeed our contribution, as outlined in the *Travaux Preparatoires*, was to actively exclude cultural genocide, while at the same time (and not without irony) stressing the English and French heritage of the country (Abtahi and Webb 2008: 2:1509). When Canada did ratify the UNGC in 1952, we did so highly selectively. Portions of the Convention were excluded from the Criminal Code, such that genocide still means only Article 2 (a) and (b) (Criminal Code Canada 1985). The official reasons given to Parliament by the *Report of the Special Committee on Hate Crimes in Canada* was that portions of the UNGC "intended to cover certain historical incidents in Europe that have little essential relevance to Canada" could safely be omitted. They even asserted that "mass transfers of children to another group are unknown . . . in Canada" (Churchill 2004: 9, 86).

Despite problems of how genocide is defined under the Criminal Code, the argument can be made that forced transfer is clearly a form of biological genocide. This was Raphael Lemkin's conclusion in 1951, when he posited that "genocide can be committed either by destroying the group now or by preventing it from bearing children or keeping its offspring." He further responded to the question "Can genocide be committed by kidnapping children?" by stating emphatically, "The answer is yes!" (Lemkin 1951). Kidnapping, he argued, was certainly a form of biological genocide: "From the point of view of genocide or the destruction of a human group, there is little difference between direct killings and such techniques which, like a time-bomb, destroy by delayed action" (Lemkin n.d.). Kurt Mundorff (2009: 117) has articulated the same view, seeing forcible transfer as both physical and biological: "It does so biologically, by preventing children from reproducing within the group, and physically, by discouraging children from returning to their group." He continues, "Childrearing is the quintessential process that racial, ethnic, religious, or national groups perform as these groups perpetuate themselves primarily through childrearing. Any instrument protecting these human groups should recognize the central role of children" (125).

TARGETED PROPORTION OF THE GROUP

How large a part of the group must be targeted to invoke the UNGC? Jim Miller (1996: 141–42) is correct that no more than one-third of Aboriginal children were targeted with compulsory attendance in residential schools. Indeed it is clear from Miller's work that off-reserve schools were always in the minority, with the majority of Indian children enrolled in day schools located on the reserves. Further, there were few residential schools in eastern Canada and only one in Atlantic Canada, the majority being in British Columbia, James Bay, and the prairies (Miller 2004: 245; 1996: 141–42). In part these regional differences can be explained by the territorial expansionist motives of the government. Settling and pacifying the West were nineteenth- and twentieth-century objectives. Any putative threat posed by First Nations in Atlantic Canada had been subdued much earlier. This reality does not, however, invalidate arguments in favor of calling the behavior genocide.

In determining what percentage is sufficient, most international case law is vague on this matter, relying primarily on judicial intuition. The UN special rapporteur Benjamin Whitaker put it that "in part" should imply "a reasonably significant number, relative to the total of the group as a whole, or else a significant section of a group such as its leadership" (quoted in Mundorff 2009: 88). This was revisited by the International Criminal Tribunal for the former Yugoslavia in *Prosecutor v. Radislav Krstić*, wherein the Trial Chambers recognized that "'in part' . . . must be a substantial part of that group" (United Nations 2004: 2). In my view the UNGC would still apply to one-third. First, even if one unceremoniously lumps all Aboriginal people together, one-third of a group by any standard would still count as significant enough to invoke the UNGC. Certainly in Srebrenica eight thousand of forty thousand Muslims killed amounted to roughly the same percentage (see MacDonald 2009).

Yet, second, if one accepts the point that we are dealing with multiple victim groups, then there may be dozens of groups that have been victims of genocide. It would be grossly inaccurate to look at Aboriginal peoples as only three groups (First Nations, Métis, and Inuit). Even now we have some fifty-three distinct Aboriginal languages divided into eleven families (Spielmann 2009: 30). We would not talk about one undifferentiated genocidal era stretching from the late nineteenth to the mid-twentieth century, but genocidal episodes, time periods when genocidal action was more concentrated, when, for example, more children were taken than in other periods.

TO TRANSFER

The elements subsumed in the verb *transfer* are as follows:

1. Shognosh governments create departments such as Indian Affairs and enact discriminatory legislation (such as the Indian Act) that allows for large-scale policies of transfer. At the federal level, government officials, bureaucrats, and others in positions of influence express a desire for transfer to take place.
2. Shognosh organizations such as the Royal Canadian Mounted Police (RCMP) and individual Indian agents and other interested Shognosh persons (priests, ministers, and their proxies) carry out what is ostensibly the kidnapping of children from their families.
3. Shognosh church administrators receive children and then, in the guise of altruism, seek to destroy those elements of the children's identity that tie them to their group of origin, elements that enable the group to perpetuate its existence into future generations. The suppressed aspects of the children's identity are then forcibly replaced with loosely cognate Shognosh religious, cultural, and linguistic elements.
4. Arrangements are made through Shognosh government, churches, and other supporting organizations to ensure that the transfer "sticks"; that is, impediments to Aboriginal cultural "backsliding" are introduced to make return to the group problematic.

These four elements constitute transfer and are consistent with the Royal Commission on Aboriginal Peoples' "three-part vision of education in the service of assimilation" (Hurley and Wherrett 1999: 312). The fourth step is the proverbial icing, because by the time stage 3 was successful, the child's worldview was irrevocably damaged. We can acknowledge Kress's argument, discussed in Munsdorff (2009: 91), that transfer should be understood to have occurred when the children are in the control of another group. They do not necessarily have to be integrated into the mainstream of the perpetrator group, just taken from their group of origin. As such, even if children are held in residential schools or orphanages, transfer for the purposes of the UNGC can be judged to have taken place.

ELEMENTS OF TRANSFER: LEGISLATIVE INTENT

What did the founders of the IRS system intend? Nicholas Flood Davin and other Shognosh political leaders later in the century were keenly interested in using the schools as a vehicle for the destruction of Aboriginal identity. Davin, an early influence on the IRS system, took forty-five days to research and write a report, which he submitted in 1879. Davin recommended (in contradistinction to the American system) forging a partnership between government and churches, partly for cost savings but, more important, to effect a more thorough level of assimilation. He concluded that since the IRS "would undermine existing spiritual and cultural beliefs," it would be important not to destroy a child's faith "without supplying a better" one: Christianity (quoted in TRC 2012b: 10). Davin was clear that residential schools were preferable to day schools on reserve since "the influence of the wigwam was stronger than the influence of the school" (Haig-Brown 1988: 29).

Davin's report found support in Ottawa. Superintendent General of Indian Affairs Hector Langevin made it clear to Parliament in 1883 that residential schooling would enable Aboriginal children to "acquire the habits and tastes . . . of civilized people" (quoted in Grant 1996: 64). The intention of ending the separate existence of Aboriginal peoples as Aboriginal peoples was expressed in 1887 by John A. MacDonald when he argued, "The great aim of our legislation has been to do away with the tribal system and assimilate the Indian people in all respects with the inhabitants of the Dominion, as speedily as they are fit for the change" (quoted in Miller 2004: 191). To this senior Indian Affairs official Hayter Reed expressed his department's perspective in the 1890s; the IRS system should make "every effort . . . against anything calculated to keep fresh in the memories of the children habits and associations which it is one of the main objects of industrial education to obliterate" (quoted in Hurley and Wherrett 1999: 312).

Then we move to Duncan Campbell Scott, the now infamous deputy minister of Indian Affairs, who opined similar sentiments about ending the separate existence of Aboriginal peoples. In 1915 Scott described his vision for the department: "The happiest future for the Indian Race is absorption into the general population, and this is the object of the policy of our government. The great forces of intermarriage and education will finally overcome the lingering traces of native custom and tradition" (quoted in Neu and Therrien 2003: 102). Scott later gave his famous speech in 1920: "I want to get rid of the Indian problem. . . . Our object is to continue until there is not a single Indian in Canada that has not been absorbed into the body politic and there is no Indian question, and no Indian Department" (quoted in Miller 2004: 35).

One could amass a large collection of these statements and musings that would provide, in anecdotal form, snapshots of the zeitgeist of the IRS founders and their intentions. Such snapshots are useful in demonstrating several recurring elements:

1. A discourse motivated by a desire to destroy Aboriginal peoples *as* Aboriginal peoples, or in other words, to destroy the group *as such* in whole or in part.
2. A belief that destruction was *creative* in that it would save individual Aboriginal people with the genetic capacity to excel once they had been freed from the shackles of their inferior cultural background.
3. A belief that no matter how difficult the process of removal and assimilation might be in the short term, in the long term the visionary goals of Shognosh IRS boosters would be vindicated.

The Process of Removals

In terms of legislation, two dates stand out. In 1894 an amendment to the Indian Act, in force by 1895, made residential schooling compulsory, although this was not rigorously or universally applied (Milloy 1999: 70–71; Miller 1996: 129; Furniss 1995: 108). The more significant date is 1920, when attendance was made compulsory for all Aboriginal children age seven to fifteen ("Residential Schools—A Chronology" 2008). Truant officers, including RCMP officers, priests, ministers, and Indian agents, could prescribe fines or imprisonment to those who did not comply. Stricter legislation greatly increased the numbers of children attending residential schools (Milloy 1999: 71; Miller 1996: 169–70; Assembly of First Nations [AFN] 1994: 16–17). The Indian Act, sections 114–22, dealt with schools for Aboriginal children; section 119 covered "truant officers," who were empowered to "take into custody a child whom [they believe] on reasonable grounds to be absent from school contrary to this Act and may convey the child to school, using as much force as the circumstances require" (Aboriginal Affairs Canada 2010). It is worth mentioning that force for the purposes of the UNGC can include the threat of force, or, as the International Criminal Tribunal for Rwanda put it in

Akayesu, "threats or trauma which would lead to the forcible transfer of children from one group to another" (quoted in Mundorff 2009: 96).

A larger climate of legal suppression and what we could call cultural genocide made it exceedingly difficult for Aboriginal parents to resist the coercive nature of the system. Forms of cultural genocide were intertwined with overt policies of forced removal. One recalls here the outlawing of the potlatches in 1884, give-away ceremonies among Prairie First Nations, the Thirst Dance of the Saulteaux and Cree, and the Blackfoot Sun Dance. Such laws were rescinded only in 1951 (Furniss 1995: 24; Carter 1999: 164). Miller (2004: 184–85) notes that despite sporadic enforcement, a number of high-profile arrests "created a climate of fear and resentment." In 1885 the pass system was introduced; individuals wishing to leave the reserve were required to receive written consent from the Indian agent or their employer stating the duration of their absence and its purpose. Selling cattle, farm produce, or any goods required written permission (Carter 1999: 162–63). Carter observes, "Oral and written testimony from reserve residents indicated that it was both enforced and resented as a result" (163–64). In 1927 an amendment to the Indian Act made it illegal for Aboriginal people to hire lawyers in pursuit of land claims or other matters (Miller 2004: 17), and until 1960 Aboriginal peoples did not have the right to vote. These and other impediments thwarted Aboriginal desires to seek justice within Shognosh legal and legislative systems.

The Schools

In understanding the high level of coercion in the IRS system, the AFN (1994: 3–4) described the schools as "total institutions," wherein "all activities of the children—eating, sleeping, playing, working, speaking—were subject to set time tables and to regulations determined by staff comprised of supervisors and teachers who, for the most part, belonged to a variety of Christian denominations." Comparing the IRS to penitentiaries, the AFN highlighted the divergence between the almost complete control wielded by adult staff and the almost total powerlessness of their young charges. Chrisjohn and Young's (1997: 91) exploration of total institutions describes a process of "'unmak[ing]' the people over whom they gain control." The use of corporal punishment was widespread, as was verbal, emotional, physical, and sexual abuse (Milloy 1999: chapters 5, 6, 7; Miller 1996: chapter 11). These too should be seen as means of facilitating the forced transfer of children, while promoting the totalizing influence of the institution. Survivor testimony recounts that sexual abuse rates at some schools reached 75 percent, and physical abuse rates were even higher. It is difficult to generalize from these findings, but clearly abuse was an endemic and recurring feature (Rice 2011).

Implicit in the Indian Act is the condoning of forced conversion as a concomitant to the transfer process. Section 118 reads as follows: "No child whose parent is a Protestant shall be assigned to a school conducted under Roman Catholic auspices and no child whose parent is a Roman Catholic shall be assigned to a school conducted under Protestant auspices, except by written direction of the parent" (Aboriginal Affairs Canada 2010). Such legislation was meant to safeguard the rights of Catholics and Protestants to avoid their own transfer but also gave the schools carte blanche to forcibly convert non-Christian peoples.

Forced linguistic change was one of the hardest elements of transfer for many Survivors, because it not only detached them from their own pre-IRS identity but also deracinated them from their siblings, parents, and other family members if they returned home. While some schools were more lenient than others, a central goal of Shognosh administrators was to deprive children of their ability to communicate in their own language, while adopting either English or French (TRC 2012a: 24–25). Brutal penalties were often meted out for infractions (AFN 1994: 16–17). Certainly language was crucial to the ontology of the child, and destroying it was a key means by which the child's cultural inheritance could be broken. The obverse was also true: changing the child's language could help the transfer of the child from one group to another. Cuthand (2007: 62) ably conveys the implications of language loss, which is "a major blow to a culture" because "in many cases the culture ceases to exist. The oral history in the mother tongue disappears, the grandparents can no longer speak to their grandchildren, and the descriptive nuances and sense of humour change."

The fear of "backsliding" was a pressing one, since the permanence of any transfer depended on continuing the process of assimilation after the children had left the IRS. It was clear to some officials that every effort had to be made to prevent familial or tribal influences during the process of "reorientation." For this reason former superintendent general Dewdney supported keeping Aboriginal visitors off the grounds of residential schools, even if this involved using the police. He favored restricting student vacations, especially if this involved a return to the reserve: "Taking children in for short terms and letting them go again is regarded perhaps as worse than useless" (quoted in Milloy 1999: 30).

The same held true once students had left the system; concerted efforts were made to prevent what Indian Affairs called "retrogression"—a return to the reserve and the resumption of old ways. Overly optimistic about the prospects for racial and social harmony, Indian Affairs argued in its 1887 *Annual Report* that efforts should be directed "to prevent those whose education at an industrial institution . . . has been completed from returning to the reserves." Instead Aboriginal students were to integrate into the Shognosh world, "to reside in towns, or, in the case of farmers, in settlements of white people, and thus become amalgamated with the general community" (Hurley and Wherrett 1999: 317–18).

Ultimately transfer never meant full transfer, akin to Himmler's *Lebensborn* program. Due to Shognosh racism, the IRS could never have created an egalitarian society or a truly level playing field. Rather it was designed to ensure that Aboriginal peoples would be subservient and no longer, as Scott once put it, "an undesirable and often dangerous element in society" (quoted in Neu and Therrien 2003: 103). Training Aboriginal people to compete with Shognosh was never the intention of the system. Rather they were to enter mainstream society primarily as workers and servants, at the lower rungs of the economic ladder (Friesen and Friesen 2002: 110; Deiter 1999: 15–16). While the IRS system failed to completely assimilate Aboriginal peoples, it certainly created a halfway house—a cultural, spiritual, and linguistic limbo land for large numbers of Survivors. A considerable body of evidence has been gathered on this topic, particularly on the problems of intergeneration trauma and the many social problems that have resulted from IRS experiences (Woolford 2009: 85).

When did the genocide end? In 1947, in part due to the atrocities witnessed in World War II and to the decreasing popularity of segregation south of the border, the Canadian government visibly switched its approach from forced assimilation to integration. Aboriginal education would now fall to the provinces and would become secular. The rationale remained deliberately coercive: children would be integrated by attending Shognosh day schools, absorbing dominant social values in the process (Friesen and Friesen 2002: 108). Indian Affairs closed down residential schools in areas where integration into the provincial system was possible (Hamilton 1986: 19). In areas where day schools were not available, the IRS system continued. In the late 1960s there were still some sixty residential schools with approximately ten thousand students in attendance. These were under secular administration by this stage, and by 1954 all IRS teachers were federal government employees (AFN 1994: 18–19).

Despite the denouement of the IRS system, the violation of Article 2(e) continued in other forms. Beginning in the 1930s and 1940s, thousands of Aboriginal children were taken from their parents and sent for adoption or to foster homes, the majority sent to Shognosh homes. Many were shipped to the United States. At its height, one in four status Indian children were removed from their parents. Emily Alston-O'Connor's (2010: 4) reading of this period suggests that genocide occurred here as well. The process, known as the "60s scoop," demonstrates a consistent desire to effect forced removals, although by different means. As one system of transfer wound down, another coercive system increased in significance. This makes intuitive sense when one engages with the early history of the IRS in the United States and the two tracks that were advocated at the time: residential schools and "planting out." Pioneered in Pennsylvania, the idea was to remove children and send them to white foster homes in an effort to remove their "Indianism" (Milloy 1999: 28).

Genocide and the Clash of Collective Memories

While Shognosh Canadians are beginning to learn about the IRS system and other aspects of Aboriginal inequality, there are fundamental differences between how our two peoples approach our national experiment. Sharene Razack (2002: 2) has termed our history a "fantasy" insofar as we tend to disavow notions of conquest, invasion, and genocide, promoting instead myths of peaceful settlement and colonization. Ervin Staub (2008: 5), a major theorist of ethnic conflict, observed recently, "Anyone who has worked with Survivors of genocide, or engaged with groups that have survived genocide . . . will know that Survivors desperately want to have the truth of what was done to them be established and their suffering acknowledged. Acknowledgement, especially when it is empathic, is healing." If there is dissonance in understanding between the victimized group and the perpetrator group, this makes it "difficult for Survivors to heal, look into the future, and move on psychologically" (6).

Certainly we are at an early stage of the reconciliation process; healing is taking priority over other considerations. But collective memory is crucial; how Shognosh and Aboriginal peoples choose to remember and reflect on the collective memories of colonization and the IRS system will determine the way forward. Obfuscation will be a constant temptation—blaming selected priests or administrators, who may become scapegoats in much the same way *Historikerstreit* historians blamed Nazi leaders to exculpate Germany (Hillgruber 1986). A full engagement with IRS history must mean not isolating this era as an aberration in Canadian history but understanding its formative nature in the creation of our Shognosh society and contextualizing this within the current relationships Shognosh and Aboriginal peoples maintain, including power and status differentials.

Institutional and Cultural Change

Most Canadians supported Prime Minister Stephen Harper's apology for the IRS system in 2008, but without real change the apology amounts to little. Chrisjohn and Wasacase (2009: 219) are rightly frustrated by the fact that while the government admits wrong, the institutions that committed the crimes, from the mainline churches to the RCMP to the Department of Aboriginal Affairs, retain their power.[3]

Central to any genuine reconciliation must be the adoption of a new form of binationalism, one that is properly between Aboriginal peoples and Shognosh peoples, not between two very similar white European Christian colonizing peoples, as it has been for centuries. The ideal of a nation-to-nation partnership, embedded in treaties, affirmed through Royal Commission on Aboriginal Peoples, and reiterated in the Idle No More movement, is a crucial step forward. As Maaka and Fleras (2005: 275–76) point out, a binational relationship will inevitably imply a reworking of dominant institutions and narratives, since binationalism seeks to "restructure the constitutional core to foster power sharing," "provides a constitutional framework for engaging indigeneity as a majority-to-majority partnership," and "is concerned with the sharing of sovereignty between two dominant cultures in complementary co-existence." Binationalism might contribute to a process of "reframing," that is, changing the symbols, terms, and narratives used to interpret the past and to chart a course for the future (James and Bonner 2011).

One crucial way in which reconciliation might proceed is in the official recognition and promotion of Aboriginal languages. A genuine focus on reconciliation would direct resources to reinvigorating Aboriginal languages, not just for Aboriginal peoples but for all Canadians. Such languages could be made official languages in provinces, and Shognosh children would learn Aboriginal languages that were indigenous to their region. Unfortunately, little has been done to preserve First Nations languages, many of which are on the brink of collapse (Galley 2009: 243).

A central means of protecting and asserting Aboriginal rights is naturally through self-government, not Indian Act colonialism but a return to more traditional forms of governance and away from chief and council and the Department of Aboriginal Affairs. Self-government could include forms of dual citizenship and passports, as well as other measures for Aboriginal entities seeking to assert their right to be recognized as self-governing nations. I share Taiaiake Alfred's (2009: 43) conclusion that the best way to decolonize is for Aboriginal people to reestablish their ties to the land, which will allow them to connect "to land-based cultural practices and the reestablishment of authentic indigenous community life."

However, any model of Aboriginal sovereignty will first have to contend with the fact that the structures of tribal government are determined by the Indian Act, which also determines who does and does not have status

(Furniss 1995: 22–23). We can see changes taking place in this so-called era of reconciliation. Idle No More signals a new, more assertive and self-aware form of Aboriginal consciousness. Further, the *Daniels* case in January 2013 has dramatically increased the number of people now considered to be "Indians," extending recognition to some 600,000 urban-based First Nations and Métis people ("Court Rules Métis, Off-reserve Aboriginals Qualify as 'Indians'" 2012). Things are moving forward, hopefully in a good way.

Alongside self-determination, increased representation and changes to existing institutions constitute a *complementary* process of empowering Aboriginal peoples using multiple channels. While autonomous self-government would help some Aboriginal peoples empower themselves, Michael Murphy (2008: 197–200) argues persuasively that "indigenous representatives may also need an effective voice in local, regional, and national institutions that have the capacity to influence their individual and collective futures." Institutional changes could include, first, adopting a form of proportional representation, a system that has functioned well in New Zealand, where Māori have achieved parliamentary representation higher than their percentage of the overall population, with Māori in the cabinet and in other positions of national leadership. Second, recent studies demonstrate that Māori and Pākehā are equally committed to common New Zealand symbols and national culture, a unique situation relative to other Western settler societies (Sibley and Liu 2007).

Yet we need to go further than simply ensure that Aboriginal peoples are represented in our primarily Shognosh colonial institutions. Local, provincial, and federal institutions have to be reinvented to promote forms of nation-to-nation power sharing and mutual respect. The Royal Commission on Aboriginal Peoples outlined a blueprint for a "House of First Peoples" that would comprise Aboriginal representatives, but this is only one idea among many (Schmidt 2003: 5–6). I don't feel it incumbent on me to describe what sort of "traditional" governance institutions should be established, since this is a discussion that is ongoing between Aboriginal communities and Shognosh governments.

Conclusions

Article 2(e) constitutes a useful ground floor from where we can begin to think creatively about how to reframe our understandings of Canadian history, moving from dominant Shognosh views to a more binational framework that grounds Canadian history, politics, languages, and cultures in a power-sharing arrangement with Aboriginal peoples. Recognition of genocide is crucial to ensuring that the losses suffered by Aboriginal peoples are not taken for granted. Reconciliation is unlikely to be something any of us will see in our lifetimes, but this should not deter us from initiating the process by, at the least, identifying the problems and actively deliberating over potential solutions. Morally we need to work together to ensure that a genuine binationalism between Aboriginal and Shognosh peoples recognizes the inherent rights of Aboriginal people. This is only just. Many Aboriginal people know well that right conduct consists of ensuring that elders are able to eat first before the younger members of the community proceed, or else those with the most to offer are left only with the scraps. We would do well to keep this custom in mind.

Notes

My thanks to the SSHRCC and the University of Guelph for funding this research. Thanks to Kim Murray for her kind editorial comments, as well as Justice Murray Sinclair, Paulette Regan, Mike Cachagee, Harvey Trudeau, Jim Miller, Mike DeGagne, Jon Dewar, Rupert Ross, Kiera Ladner, Andrew Woolford, Jeff Benvenuto, and Alex Hinton. I dedicate this chapter to the Survivors.

1. Mosby (2013: 172) does not use the term *genocide* but describes the experiments as "one among many examples of a larger institutionalized and, ultimately, dehumanizing colonialist racial ideology that has governed Canada's policies towards and treatment of Aboriginal peoples throughout the twentieth century."
2. Another option would be the Cree word *Moonia*, which means the same thing.
3. The arguments in this section are more fully developed in MacDonald 2013.

References

Aboriginal Affairs and Northern Development Canada "Backgrounder—Changes to the Indian Act Affecting Indian Residential Schools" News Releases. 2010. http//www.aadnc-aandc.gc.ca/eng/1100100015573.

Aboriginal Healing Foundation. 2002. *The Healing Has Begun*. Ottawa: Aboriginal Healing Foundation.

Abtahi, Hirad, and Philippa Webb, eds. 2008. *The Genocide Convention: The Travaux Préparatoires*. Vol. 2. The Hague: Martinus Nijhoff.

Alfred, Taiaiake. 2009. "Restitution Is the Real Pathway to Justice for Indigenous Peoples." In *Response, Responsibility, and Renewal: Canada's Truth and Reconciliation Journey*, edited by Gregory Younging, Jonathan Dewar, and Mike DeGagné, 181–87. Ottawa: AHF Research Series.

Alston-O'Connor, Emily. 2010. "The Sixties Scoop: Implications for Social Workers and Social Work Education." *Critical Social Work* 11 (1): 53–61.

Assembly of First Nations. 1994. *Breaking the Silence*. Ottawa: AFN.

Barkan, Elazar. 2003. "Genocides of Indigenous Peoples: Rhetoric of Human Rights." In *The Specter of Genocide: Mass Murder in Historical Perspective*, edited by Robert Gellately and Ben Kiernan, 117–40. New York: Cambridge University Press.

Buckley-Zistel, Susan. 2006. "Remembering to Forget: Chosen Amnesia as a Strategy for Local Coexistence in Post-Genocide Rwanda." *Africa* 76 (2): 131–50.

Cardinal, Harold. 1999. *The Unjust Society: The Tragedy of Canada's Indians.* Vancouver: Douglas and McIntyre.

Carter, S. 1999. *Aboriginal People and Colonizers of Western Canada to 1900.* Toronto: University of Toronto Press.

Chrisjohn, Ronald, and Sherri Young. 1994. *The Circle Game: Shadows and Substance in the Indian Residential School Experience in Canada.* Self-published.

Chrisjohn, Ronald, and Sherri Young. 1997. *The Circle Game: Shadows and Substance in the Indian Residential School Experience in Canada.* Penticton, Canada: Theytus.

Chrisjohn, Roland, and Tanya Wasacase. 2009. "Half-Truths and Whole Lies: Rhetoric in the 'Apology' and the Truth and Reconciliation Commission." In *Response, Responsibility, and Renewal: Canada's Truth and Reconciliation Journey*, edited by Gregory Younging, Jonathan Dewar, and Mike DeGagné, 217–232. Ottawa: AHF Research Series.

Churchill, Ward. 2004. *Kill the Indian, Save the Man: The Genocidal Impact of American Indian Residential Schools.* San Francisco: City Lights.

"Court Rules Métis, Off-reserve Aboriginals Qualify as 'Indians.'" 2012. CTV News, January 8. Accessed June 15, 2013. http://www.ctvnews.ca/canada/court-rules-metis-off-reserve-aboriginals-qualify-as-indians-1.1105186#ixzz2Hav21ajo.

Criminal Code Canada. 1985. Part VIII: Offences against the Person and Reputation. Hate Propaganda. R.S. 1985 c. C-46 s. 318; 2004 c. 14 s. 1.

Cuthand, Doug. 2007. *Askiwina: A Cree World.* Regina, Canada: Coteau, 2007.

Davis, Robert, and Mark Zannis. 1973. *The Genocide Machine in Canada.* Montreal: Black Rose.

Deiter, Constance. 1999. *From Our Mothers' Arms: The Intergenerational Impact of Residential Schools in Saskatchewan.* Toronto: United Church Publishing House.

Friesen, John, and Virginia Friesen. 2002. *Aboriginal Education in Canada: A Plea for Integration.* Calgary: Detselig.

Furniss, Elizabeth. 1995. *Victims of Benevolence: The Dark Legacy of the Williams Lake Residential School.* Vancouver: Arsenal Pulp Press.

Furniss, Elizabeth. 1999. *The Burden of History: Colonialism and the Frontier Myth in a Rural Canadian Community.* Vancouver: UBC Press.

Galley, Valerie. 2009. "Reconciliation and the Revitalization of Indigenous Languages." In *Response, Responsibility, and Renewal: Canada's Truth and Reconciliation Journey*, edited by Gregory Younging, Jonathan Dewar, and Mike DeGagné, 241–60. Ottawa: AHF Research Series.

Granatstein, J. L. 1996. *Yankee Go Home? Canadians and Anti-Americanism.* Toronto: HarperCollins.

Grant, Agnes. 1996. *No End of Grief: Indian Residential Schools in Canada.* Winnipeg: Pemmican.

Haig-Brown, Celia. 1988. *Resistance and Renewal: Surviving the Indian Residential School*. Vancouver: Arsenal.

Hamilton, William. 1986. *The Federal Indian Day Schools of the Maritimes*. Fredericton, Canada: Micmac–Moliseet Institute.

Hillgruber, Andreas. 1986. *Zweierlei Untergang: Die Zerschlagung des Deutschen Reichs und das Ende des europäischen Judentums*. Berlin: Siedler.

Hitler, Adolf. 2000. *Hitler's Table Talk, 1941–1944*. Translated by N. Cameron and R. H. Stevens. New York: Enigma.

Hurley, Mary C., and Jill Wherrett. 1999. *Report of the Royal Commission on Aboriginal Peoples*. Ottawa: Library of Parliament.

James, M., and M. Bonner. 2011. "The Three R's of Seeking Transitional Justice." *International Indigenous Policy Journal* 2 (3): 1–29.

"Judge Calls Residential Schools a Form of Genocide." 2012. CTV News, February 18. Accessed June 15, 2013. http://www.ctv.ca/CTVNews/Canada/20120218/commission-chairman-residential-schools-120218/#ixzz1uIFEOMTf.

King, Michael. 1985. *Being Pakeha*. Auckland: Hodder and Stoughton.

Ladner, Kiera. 2009. "Take 35: Reconciling Constitutional Orders." In *First Nations, First Thoughts: The Impact of Indigenous Thought in Canada,* edited by A. M. Timpson, 279–300. Vancouver: UBC Press.

Lemkin, Raphael. 1951. Manuscript on genocide. February 2. Box 7, Folder 3, Raphael Lemkin Collection, American Jewish Archives. The Jacob Rader Marcus Center of the American Jewish Archives, Cincinnati.

Lemkin, Raphael. n.d. Paper on genocide 2. Statements and Memoranda Box 6, Folder 2, 1948–51, Raphael Lemkin Collection, American Jewish Archives. The Jacob Rader Marcus Center of the American Jewish Archives, Cincinnati.

Maaka, Roger, and Augie Fleras. 2005. *The Politics of Indigeneity: Challenging the State in Canada and Aotearoa New Zealand*. Dunedin, New Zealand: University of Otago Press.

MacDonald, David. 2007. "First Nations, Residential Schools, and the Americanization of the Holocaust." *Canadian Journal of Political Science* 40 (4): 995–1015.

MacDonald, David. 2008. *Identity Politics in the Age of Genocide: The Holocaust and Historical Representation*. London: Routledge.

MacDonald, David. 2009. "Subaltern Discourse and Genocide: Serbian Victimization and Historical Justifications for War: 1980–2000." In *Genocides by the Oppressed: Subaltern Movements and Retributive Genocide,* edited by Nicholas Robins and Adam Jones, 103–21. Indianapolis: University of Indiana Press.

MacDonald, David. 2013. "Reconciliation after Genocide in Canada: Towards a Syncretic Model of Democracy." *AlterNative: An International Journal of Indigenous People* 9 (1): 60–73.

MacDonald, David, and Graham Hudson. 2012. "The Genocide Question and Indian Residential Schools in Canada." *Canadian Journal of Political Science* 45 (2): 427–49.

Manuel, George, and Michael Posluns. 1974. *The Fourth World: An Indian Reality*. Don Mills, Canada: Collier Macmillan Canada.

Miller, James R. 1996. *Shingwauk's Vision: A History of Native Residential Schools*. Toronto: University of Toronto Press.

Miller, James R. 2004. *Lethal Legacy: Current Native Controversies in Canada.* Toronto: University of Toronto Press.

Milloy, John. 1999. *A National Crime: The Canadian Government and the Residential School System, 1879 to 1986.* Winnipeg: University of Manitoba Press.

Mosby, Ian. 2013. "Administering Colonial Science: Nutrition Research and Human Biomedical Experimentation in Aboriginal Communities and Residential Schools, 1942–1952." *Histoire Sociale/Social History* 46 (91): 146–72.

Mulgan, R. G. 1989. *Māori, Pākehā, and Democracy.* Auckland: Oxford University Press.

Mundorff, Kurt. 2009. "Other Peoples' Children: A Textual and Contextual Interpretation of the Genocide Convention, Article 2(e)." *Harvard International Law Journal* 50 (1): 61–127.

Murphy, Michael. 2008. "Representing Indigenous Self-Determination." *University of Toronto Law Journal* 58 (2): 185–216.

Neu, Dean, and Richard Therrien. 2003. *Accounting for Genocide: Canada's Bureaucratic Assault on Aboriginal People.* Blackpoint, Canada: Fernwood.

Nicholas, A. B. 2001. "Canada's Colonial Mission: The Great White Bird." In *Aboriginal Education in Canada: A Study in Decolonization*, edited by K. Binda and S. Calliou. Mississauga: Canadian Educators' Press.

Powell, Christopher. 2011. *Barbaric Civilization: A Critical Sociology of Genocide.* Montreal: McGill-Queen's University Press.

"Q & A: The Honourable Justice Murray Sinclair." 2012. *8th Fire.* CBC. Accessed June 15, 2013. http://www.cbc.ca/doczone/8thfire/2011/12/justice-murray-sinclair.html.

Razack, Sharene. 2002. "Introduction: When Place Becomes Race." In *Race, Space, and the Law: Unmapping a White Settler Society*, edited by Sherene Razack, 1–20. Toronto: Between the Lines.

"Residential Schools—A Chronology." 2008. Remembering the Children: An Aboriginal and Church Leaders' Tour to Prepare for Truth and Reconciliation. Accessed June 15, 2013. http://www.rememberingthechildren.ca/history/.

"Residential Schools Fit Definition of Genocide: Atleo." 2011. APTN National News, November 8. Accessed June 15, 2013. http://aptn.ca/pages/news/2011/11/08/residential-schools-fit-definition-of-genocide-atleo/.

Rice, Brian, and Anna Snyder. 2008. "Reconciliation in the Context of a Settler Society: Healing the Legacy of Colonialism in Canada." In *From Truth to Reconciliation: Transforming the Legacy of Residential Schools*, edited by Marlene Brant-Castellano, Linda Archibald, and Mike DeGagne, 43–63. Ottawa: AHF Research Series.

Rice, Joanna. 2011. "Indian Residential School Truth and Reconciliation Commission of Canada." *CSQ* 35 (1). Accessed January 10, 2012. http://www.culturalsurvival.org/publications/cultural-survival-quarterly/canada/indian-residential-school-truth-and-reconciliation-c.

Saul, John Ralston. 2008. *A Fair Country: Telling Truths About Canada.* Toronto: Viking.

Schmidt, Jennifer. 2003. "Aboriginal Representation in Government: A Comparative Examination." Paper prepared for the Law Commission of Canada, December.

Sibley, C., and J. Liu. 2007. "New Zealand = Bicultural?" *European Journal of Social Psychology* 37 (6): 1222–43.

Spielmann, R. 2009. *Anishnaabe World: A Survival Guide for Building Bridges between Canada and First Nations*. Sudbury, Canada: Scrivener Press.

Staub, Ervin. 2008. "Promoting Reconciliation after Genocide and Mass Killing in Rwanda." In *The Social Psychology of Intergroup Reconciliation*, edited by Arie Nadler, Thomas E. Malloy, and Jeffrey D. Fisher. Oxford: Oxford University Press.

Truth and Reconciliation Commission of Canada. 2012a. *Interim Report*. Winnipeg: TRC.

Truth and Reconciliation Commission of Canada. 2012b. *They Came for the Children: Canada, Aboriginal Peoples, and Residential Schools*. Winnipeg: TRC.

United Nations. 2004. ICTY Appeals Chamber, *Prosecutor v. Radislav Krstić*, United Nations Case IT-98-33-A. April 19. Accessed March 2, 2008. http://www.un.org/icty/krstic/Appeal/judgement/krs-aj040419e.pdf.

UN Secretariat. 1947. Convention on the Prevention and Punishment of the Crime of Genocide. The Secretariat and Ad Hoc Committee Drafts. First Draft of the Genocide Convention. May. UN Doc. E/447.

Wolfe, Patrick. 2010. "Structure and Event: Settler Colonialism, Time, and the Question of Genocide." In *Empire, Colony, Genocide*, edited by A. Dirk Moses. New York: Berghahn.

Woolford, Andrew. 2009. "Ontological Destruction: Genocide and Canadian Aboriginal Peoples." *Genocide Studies and Prevention* 4 (1): 81–97.

COLONIAL GENOCIDE IN
INDIGENOUS NORTH AMERICA

A View from Critical Genocide Studies

Alexander Laban Hinton

On the second day of the conference from which this volume emerged, Tamara Starblanket intervened in a panel to reprimand certain conference partici- pants who, she suggested, were effectively denying that the destruction of the Indigenous peoples of North America was a genocide. "I'm not going away," she promised. "I'm going to sit here and listen to the very end."

At the start of the conference, Starblanket herself had presented an essay entitled "Genocide: Indigenous Nations and the State of Canada." An Indig- enous scholar and graduate student in the College of Law at the University of Saskatchewan, Starblanket focused her presentation on two key aspects of colonial genocide: land and language. Citing Raphael Lemkin's work on genocide and territorial occupation, Starblanket noted that the genocide of Indigenous peoples was all about territorial expansion and the occupation of Indigenous lands.

She also stated that this process of deterritorialization had been masked by language that was deployed to minimize and conceal the effects of genocide. Even the use of a term like *cultural genocide* acted in this manner, misdirecting us, for example, from what had happened in the residential schools. The word *colonization*, she stated, suggests consumption, domination, and eradication. While pointing out that the term *genocide* didn't exist before the European invasion, she suggested that it was important insofar as it provided a tool to be used. She also informed the audience that she was the last surviving member of her family.

Starblanket's remarks appeared in part to be directed at another Indige- nous participant, Joseph Gone, a clinician and psychology professor at the University of Michigan as well as a member of the Gros Ventre Tribal Nation.

Gone's presentation had made a two-pronged argument. Gone noted the growing use of the concept of "historical trauma" among mental health providers and patients. This notion centers around the idea of intergenerational transmission of trauma, one that originated with the massive destruction of Native Americans in the past. Gone suggested that this notion misdirects us, individualizing pathology through a group identity. Instead of focusing on how mental health problems are linked to social injustice and structural violence, Gone argued, those who employ the notion of historical trauma suggest that the problems of today are linked to the extremities of past violence.

From the very start of the conference, Gone had expressed an unease with the framing of the Native American experience in terms of genocide. The term, he noted, is strongly linked to the Holocaust, which provides a prototype denoting the extremes of human behavior. To apply it to a wide range of other cases, he suggested, would dilute its meaning and reduce its potential power and impact. "Genocide without killing," he stated, "is like murder without death." Further, he suggested that Native American experience might be better characterized by other concepts, such as racism. To frame Native American experience in terms of genocide, and related notions like historical trauma, may divert us from an understanding of key issues impacting Native Americans today, including the Indigenous patients he sees in the clinic.

Starblanket's and Gone's remarks destabilize the concept of genocide in a number of ways, ones that emerged during the course of the conference. On the one hand, Starblanket's focus on land and long-term process contrasts with the common concern of genocide studies with bursts of mass murder. Gone, on the other hand, invoked what at first seemed like a frequently heard uniqueness argument about the overuse of the term *genocide*, but did so in part because the very use of this term has the potential to mask or divert attention from the critical contemporary issues, including racism and structural violence, which contribute to mental health problems faced by his patients.

These sorts of destabilizations took place throughout the conference and are evident in this volume, which emerged from the proceedings. They are also in the spirit of what has been called critical genocide studies (Hinton 2012; Moses 2008), which is one way of characterizing a recent turn in the field. In particular, critical genocide studies asks us to explore the presuppositions of genocide studies and its key concepts, an exercise that may be undertaken in a variety of ways. The conference itself had been partly formulated along these lines, to see what dialogues might be possible between genocide studies and Indigenous studies, whose genealogies have only infrequently intersected until the present, as discussed in detail in the introduction to this volume.

Exploring "hidden genocides" (Hinton, LaPointe, and Irvin-Erickson 2013), or cases that have been pushed to the background or out of sight, provides one example of a critical genocide studies approach. The chapters in this book make the case over and over again that genocides in Indigenous North America have been hidden in precisely this way, a masking that is linked to the ways histories have been written, who has had the voice to write them, and how the very acknowledgment of the violent past has much at stake, such as material wealth ranging from land to natural resources, including water and oil. The backgrounding and foregrounding of given cases of genocide have also contributed to the emergence of a canon of cases (see Hinton 2012 on one ideal typical representation of the genocide studies canon), which creates a sort of hierarchy of victimization and suffering.

Another way to consider the implications of this volume from a critical genocide studies approach is to put them in conversation with what might be called the "genocide studies imaginary." The notion of the imaginary draws on work of scholars like Benedict Anderson (2006) and Charles Taylor (2004), who have written of the ways communities, through technologies, practices, and identifications, imagine themselves. Elsewhere I have argued that transitional justice is characterized by such an imaginary (Hinton 2013), which involves given temporal, spatial, productive, performative, normative, and aesthetic assumptions and helps generate an imagined sense of belonging to a transitional justice community. An analogous imaginary is operative in genocide studies, which shares some features with the transitional justice imaginary, including an enmeshment with activism and a normativity linked to the "new world order" and human rights regime.

While a full exploration of the genocide studies imaginary is beyond the purview of this short afterword, I'd like to sketch some of the outlines of this imaginary, which has its own temporalities, spatialities, performativities, productivities, normativities, and aesthetics. I should note that there is, clearly, diversity within the field and practice of genocide studies. And, particularly after the first decade of this century, new countercurrents, including renewed interest in Lemkin, an exploration of colonial and other "hidden" or "forgotten" genocides, and the turn to a critical genocide studies began to emerge (e.g., Hinton 2012; Jones [2005] 2010; Moses 2002, 2008; Strauss 2007). Nevertheless there are foci and sets of understandings that are fairly widespread, even if by no means monolithic and homogeneous, and help generate an imagined sense of shared belonging to a community concerned with the study of genocide.

Several of these dimensions of the genocide studies imaginary are placed in relief by the chapters in this volume. The term *genocide*, for example, was coined in the wake of Nazi Germany, an event that catalyzed the widely used definition in the 1948 United Nations Convention on the Prevention and Punishment of the Crime of Genocide ("acts committed with the intent to destroy, in whole or in part, a national, ethnical, racial or religious group, as such," first and foremost including "killing members of the group"). Over time, and particularly after the Eichmann trial, the Holocaust came to be seen as prototypic of genocide, with the industrial mass murder at Auschwitz serving as a key metonym. Among a set of associations bound up with the Holocaust prototype are the notions that genocides are a sort of eruption, set in a delimited time period, characterized by a clear beginning and end that, if emerging from a historical context, involve the mass murder of large numbers of the members of specific groups residing within given localities.

Like some of the recent work on Lemkin and colonial genocide, many of the essays in this volume highlight the shortcomings of the Holocaust prototype and related spatiotemporalities. In the section "Intersections and Trajectories," for example, different authors illustrate the unevenness of colonial genocides in Indigenous North America. Thus Robbie Ethridge illustrates the spatiotemporal fluidity with "shatter zones" and Andrew Woolford notes how genocidal dynamics ebb and flow and vary across time and space, a process for which he uses the metaphor of a "colonial mesh."

Tasha Hubbard's essay further unsettles the spatial assumptions of genocide studies, in which the destruction of groups is linked to place, by noting that, within Indigenous conceptions, the land, group, and animals are interlinked, so that destruction of the land (e.g., by pollution and other environmental damage and resource exploitation) and animals living upon the land (she uses the example of the destruction of buffalo) cannot be separated from the destruction of Indigenous groups. To destroy the land and the animals that live upon it is to destroy the group. From this conception the destruction of the group continues to take place long after any episodic flare-up of physical killing occurs, a point highlighted in different ways by Jeff Benvenuto and other contributors.

Hubbard's essay also speaks to the normativity of the genocide studies imaginary, which privileges specific types of group belonging (race, nation, religion, ethnicity). How, her essay asks us, might we rethink our definitions of genocide to take account of different notions of group belonging that fall outside of this quaternity of protected groups? But it raises other questions about the normative assumptions implicit within the genocide studies imaginary, ones also noted by Joseph Gone. How and why are group identities delimited by the UN Genocide Convention? What sorts of alternative understandings of genocide exist, and how might seriously grappling with such alternative conceptions push the field? What does it mean that such local forms of knowledge are subordinated or pushed out of sight in the field of genocide studies? How are power and knowledge, ranging from the decisions of policy makers to the academic production of knowledge, interwoven in making such decisions? Such questions lead us back to the notion of "hidden genocide" and to the importance of critical genocide studies, which asks us to explore such issues, unpack our commonsense understandings, and remain open to conceptualizing the field in new ways.

Yet another implicit thread in the genocide studies imaginary is the binary of the savage and the civilized. These operate in different ways. For example, genocide studies scholarship has examined the ways perpetrators devalue target groups by deploying the language of savagery, a notion that, as these chapters illustrate, was frequently applied to Indigenous populations in North America. But the term *genocide* itself often connotes another binary of savagery and civilization, which suggests that the perpetrator is a savage who commits an offense against the civilized world. This idea was evident at the Nuremberg trials in the depiction of Nazis as atavistic, a throwback to the barbaric past that led to acts that began to be called "crimes against humanity" (see Douglas 2001). The UN Genocide Convention includes similar language, noting that genocide is "contrary to the spirit and aims of the United Nations and condemned by the civilized world" and that the Convention was needed "in order to liberate mankind from such an odious scourge."

This rhetoric of emancipation, which dovetails with humanitarian currents dating back to the emancipation movement and beyond, persists as a key undercurrent of the genocide studies imaginary, albeit most directly expressed in the genocide prevention movement. Implicit is the notion that the "civilized world" has a responsibility to prevent a "barbaric" and "savage" recurrence of genocide. Such prevention may connote a sort of paternalistic protection, the helping of those innocents unable to help themselves, an idea epitomized by essentialized notions of the victim. In the context of colonial genocides in Indigenous North America, this notion sometimes played out through the image of the "Noble Savage," whose innocent and pristine existence in a state of nature was threatened by the predations of genocidaires, sometimes "civilization" itself. Here a paradoxical doubleness comes into sharp relief, as the Noble Savage is supposedly subject to genocide by "civilization" even as the Noble Savage needs to be saved by "civilization." The very act of "saving," however, might itself involve genocide as the Noble Savages are confined in "safe" spaces (reservations) or "helped" by being "educated," actions that, as a number of essays in this volume illustrate, became part of the genocidal process.

This normative dimension of the genocide studies imaginary also suggests another potentially paradoxical aspect of the field, as it may be complicit with subjugations and logics of genocide, not just masking but providing a potential legitimation for genocide itself. This claim is a strong one. It does not mean that genocide scholars are genocidaires. But it does mean that the assumptions of the field may be linked to genocidal logics and potentially, in the extreme, genocidal practice. In my own discipline, anthropology, this sort of potentiality was illustrated by revelations that Nazi anthropologists had, among other things, helped make identifications for Nazi racial courts (Schafft 2004). Such a claim about genocide studies will no doubt be controversial, but it at least needs consideration since it is a potentiality that is almost completely obscured within the genocide studies imaginary.

Relatedly, and in keeping with the Holocaust prototype, much genocide studies research, at least until the more recent critical turn, has directly or implicitly assumed that genocide involves physical killings. Article II(a) in the Genocide Convention includes a designation of primacy—"a"—that is not coincidental. In keeping with this notion—as well as the mobilization and advocacy of interested parties (see, e.g., Moses 2013 and Logan, this volume, on the contestations involved in the Canadian Museum of Human Rights, in which different groups have advocated for "space" while others, such as the Canadian Cambodian population, have not)—certain cases have been foregrounded and others backgrounded. In the genocide studies imaginary there is, this suggests, a normative hierarchy of cases comprising the genocide studies canon (Hinton 2012).

However, there is no a priori reason why cases should be ranked in terms of their prototypicality, since it would ostensibly be possible to focus on other dimensions of genocide that are nonphysical or long term (rather than episodic bursts) and reframe the hierarchy of cases in the genocide studies imaginary. This is the case even if one takes the UN Genocide Convention as the starting point but focuses on different subarticles (Article II (b–e); see, e.g., Rosenberg 2012). As illustrated throughout this book, the experience of Indigenous groups in colonial North America involves not just short-term, episodic bursts of genocidal murder but also longer term physical destruction as well as many other acts that fall within the purview of the other subarticles. David MacDonald's chapter takes up this issue directly in relation to Article II(e) and genocidal violence in the Canadian residential schools.

To return to the issue of complicity, the genocide studies imaginary directs our sight in certain sorts of ways, potentially helping to background or even removing from sight cases of genocide both past and present, particularly if full consideration is given to long-term, nonphysical forms of destruction, including "structural genocide" (Jones [2005] 2010). Such misdirection, the provenance of "hidden genocide," may also be done with full awareness and intention, such as when the notion of cultural genocide was written out of the Convention, in part because colonial powers feared having their destructive colonial policies, past and present, labeled genocide.

A similar sort of argument could be made about the groups we study, as exemplified by the UN Genocide Convention group quaternity to which protective status is given and which become largely the focus of attention. Like Hubbard's essay, Kiera Ladner's chapter argues for the importance of acknowledging political genocide even though political groups were excluded from the Convention, an exclusion that was in part related to Soviet concerns that their policies toward political groups might be labeled genocide. (Such limitations were no doubt part of the reason that a number of scholars in this volume discuss Lemkin, whose broader conceptualization of genocide appears to better fit the dynamics of genocide in Indigenous North America.) In other words, the genocide studies imaginary may contribute to maskings, as the spatiotemporal and normative understandings it foregrounds focus our attention on certain topics and away from others, including the dynamics of genocide in Indigenous North America. In this manner, this imaginary may become bound up with political agendas and projects such as colonialism. The way genocide studies is imagined, in other words, involves normativities and other assumptions that are enmeshed with power and knowledge and have consequences.

A critical genocide studies requires attention to these presuppositions and their consequences, including a focus on what is obscured or hidden from sight, or, once again, hidden genocide. This book clearly challenges us in this regard, illustrating the biases and shortcomings of an array of assumptions underlying genocide studies. In this afterword I have sought to provide one way of considering such challenges by juxtaposing some of the insights about genocide in Indigenous North America that emerge in this volume against the genocide studies imaginary.

As noted earlier, this imaginary is not monolithic. And there is substantial variation within the field. Nevertheless the notion provides a way of fore-grounding and bringing into question key assumptions that help generate a sense of shared belonging for those working on the topic. Another way to think of it might be as a genocide studies "sensibility" that is characteristic of much work in the field. For work on genocide studies to deepen, scholars and practitioners need to attend to the erasures, backgroundings, and misdirections that lead us to focus on certain things and not others. This book illustrates the importance of attending to our ways of knowing and disciplinary optics, taking a critical genocide studies approach that opens the door to new conversations, such as the one that took place between Tamara Starblanket and Joseph Gone and that emerges as one reads and rereads the chapters in this book.

References

Anderson, Benedict. 2006. *Imagined Communities: Reflections on the Origin and Spread of Nationalism*. New York: Verso.

Castoriadis, Cornelius. 1987. *The Imaginary Institution of Society*. Cambridge, MA: MIT Press.

Douglas, Lawrence. 2001. *The Memory of Judgment: Making Law and History in the Trials of the Holocaust*. New Haven, CT: Yale University Press.

Hayden, Robert M. 1996. "Imagined Communities and Real Victims: Self-determination and Ethnic Cleansing in Yugoslavia." *American Ethnologist* 23 (4): 783–801.

Hinton, Alexander Laban, ed., 2010. *Transitional Justice: Global Mechanisms and Local Realities after Genocide and Mass Violence*. New Brunswick, NJ: Rutgers University Press.

Hinton, Alexander Laban. 2012. "Critical Genocide Studies." *Genocide Studies and Prevention* 7 (1): 4–15.

Hinton, Alexander Laban. 2013. "Transitional Justice Time: Uncle San, Aunty Yan, and Outreach at the Khmer Rouge Tribunal." In *Genocide and Mass Atrocities in Asia: Legacies and Prevention*, edited by Deborah Mayersen and Annie Pohlman, 86–98. London: Routledge.

Hinton, Alexander Laban, Thomas La Pointe, and Douglas Irvin-Erickson, eds. 2013. *Hidden Genocides: Power, Knowledge, Memory*. New Brunswick, NJ: Rutgers University Press.

Jones, Adam. (2005) 2010. *Genocide: A Comprehensive Introduction*. 2nd ed. New York: Routledge.

Moses, A. Dirk. 2002. "Conceptual Blockages and Definitional Dilemmas in the 'Racial Century': Genocides of Indigenous Peoples and the Holocaust." *Patterns of Prejudice* 36 (4): 7–36.

Moses, A. Dirk. 2008. "Toward a Theory of Critical Genocide Studies." In *Online Encyclopedia of Mass Violence*. http://massviolence.org/Toward-a-Theory-of-Critical-Genocide-Studies.

Rosenberg, Sheri P. 2012. "Genocide Is a Process, Not an Event." *Genocide Studies and Prevention* 7 (1): 16–23.

Strauss, Scott. 2007. "Second-Generation Comparative Research on Genocide." *World Politics* 59: 476–501.

Schafft, Gretchen E. 2004. *From Racism to Genocide: Anthropology in the Third Reich*. Champaign: University of Illinois Press.

Taylor, Charles. 2004. *Modern Social Imaginaries*. Durham, NC: Duke University Press.

CONTRIBUTORS

Jeff Benvenuto is currently a PhD student at Rutgers University, Newark in the Division of Global Affairs. He is working on a dissertation that analyzes the contestation of Indigenous rights in settler colonial countries. In 2008 he earned an MA in History from the University of North Carolina, Greensboro, where he focused on Holocaust studies and Atlantic history. In 2010 he completed a second MA in transatlantic studies from Jagiellonian University in Krakow, Poland, where he completed a thesis on cultural genocide and the legacy of Raphael Lemkin.

Robbie Ethridge is a professor of anthropology at the University of Mississippi. In addition to writing several articles and book chapters, and compiling three edited volumes on the ethnohistory of the Indians of the American South, she is the author of *Creek Country: The Creek Country and Their World, 1796–1816* (2003) and *From Chicaza to Chickasaw: The European Invasion and the Transformation of the Mississippian World, 1540–1715* (2010). She is a founding editor of the journal *Native South*, published by the University of Nebraska Press and currently North American editor of the journal *Ethnohistory*. Her current research is on the rise and fall of the Mississippian world, which examines the rise of the world of the pre-Columbian Mississippian chiefdoms, the seven-hundred-year history of this world, and the collapse of this world with European contact.

Theodore (Ted) Fontaine is a member of the Sagkeeng Anishinaabe First Nation in Canada and the author of a national best-seller, *Broken Circle: The Dark Legacy of Indian Residential Schools, a Memoir*. He is a regular speaker and media commentator on Indian residential schools. He has been called a survivor but sees himself more as a victor.

Joseph P. Gone (Gros Ventre) is an associate professor of Psychology (Clinical Area) and American Culture (Native American Studies) at the University of Michigan in Ann Arbor. He has published more than forty articles and chapters exploring the cultural psychology of self, identity, personhood, and social relations in indigenous community settings vis-à-vis the mental health professions, with particular attention to therapeutic interventions such as psychotherapy and traditional healing. A Fellow of the American Psychological Association, he has served on the editorial boards of six scientific journals and reviewed manuscripts for an additional forty-five journals in the behavioral and health sciences. In addition to two early career awards for emerging leadership in ethnic minority psychology, Gone most recently received the Stanley Sue Award for Distinguished Contributions to Diversity in Clinical Psychology from the Society for Clinical Psychology within the American Psychological Association.

Alexander Laban Hinton is the founder and director of the Center for the Study of Genocide, Conflict Resolution, and Human Rights, a professor of anthropology and global affairs, and the UNESCO Chair on Genocide Prevention at Rutgers University, Newark. He is the author of the award-winning *Why Did They Kill? Cambodia in the Shadow of Genocide* (2005) and seven edited or coedited collections: *Mass Violence: Memory, Symptom, and Response* (2014); *Hidden Genocides: Power, Knowledge, Memory* (2013); *Transitional Justice: Global Mechanisms and Local Realities after Genocide and Mass Violence* (2010); *Genocide: Truth, Memory, and Representation* (Duke University Press, 2009); *Night of the Khmer Rouge: Genocide and Democracy in Cambodia* (2007); *Annihilating Difference: The Anthropology of Genocide* (2002); *Genocide: An Anthropological Reader* (2002); and *Biocultural Approaches to the Emotions* (1999). Hinton is currently working on several other book projects, including a book on the Khmer Rouge Tribunal. In recognition of his work on genocide, the American Anthropological Association selected Hinton as the recipient of the 2009 Robert B. Textor and Family Prize for Excellence in Anticipatory Anthropology. He was recently listed in *Fifty Key Thinkers on the Holocaust and Genocide* (2011) and is also the immediate past president of the International Association of Genocide Scholars (2011–13). In 2011–13 Hinton was a member and visitor at the Institute for Advanced Study at Princeton University.

Tasha Hubbard (Cree/Nakota/Anishinaabe/Métis) comes from Treaty Six and Treaty Four territories, from a family of writers, artists, performers, and storytellers. She is the mother of a seven-year-old son. She is an assistant professor in the Department of English at the University of Saskatchewan. Her solo writing and directing documentary project, *Two Worlds Colliding*, won a Gemini and a Golden Sheaf in 2005. Her current film and academic work focuses on Indigenous creative representation of the buffalo and representing historic Indigenous stories. She is also expanding her film practice to include drama and experimental documentary.

Margaret D. Jacobs is the Chancellor's Professor of History at the University of Nebraska-Lincoln, where she teaches courses on U.S. women's and gender history, the history of the American West, and women, gender, and empire. She conducts comparative historical research on settler colonies, including the United States, Canada, and Australia. Her book *White Mother to a Dark Race: Settler Colonialism, Maternalism, and the Removal of Indigenous Children in the American West and Australia, 1880–1940* (2009) won three awards, including the 2010 Bancroft Prize from Columbia University. She published *A Generation Removed: The Fostering and Adoption of Indigenous Children in the Postwar World* in 2014.

Kiera L. Ladner is Associate Professor in Political Science at the University of Manitoba and holds the Canada Research Chair in Indigenous Politics and Governance in the Department of Political Studies. At present, she is working on two distinct SSHRC (Insight) funded projects. The first is creating several digital archives and examining the potential for community based knowledge mobilization and decolonization with Dr. Shawna Ferris. The other examines current efforts in constitutional reconciliation, renewal and 'recognition' in Australia and New Zealand. The project examines the potential for political reconciliation between Indigenous nations and settler states, given the long history of injustice, discrimination, oppression, domination, regime replacement and the (attempted) destruction of nations. Beyond this research, she is developing an Indigenous Leadership Initiative and building Mamawipawin (the Indigenous Governance and Community Based Research Space) at the University of Manitoba.

Tricia E. Logan (Métis) is a PhD student in the Department of History at Royal Holloway, University of London. Her dissertation topic focuses on the memory and legacy of residential schools in Canada and the history of the schools as a segment of settler colonial genocide in Canada. She holds an MA in Native studies from the University of Manitoba, for which her thesis was "Métis Experiences at Residential School." She also obtained her BA in Native studies at the University of Manitoba. Logan has spent the past decade working primarily in the areas of residential school history in Canada, Indigenous history in Canada, and Métis research. In that time she has worked with Métis, First Nations, and Inuit elders and residential school Survivors from across Canada, sharing in the transmission of countless stories and oral histories over the years. She has worked with the Aboriginal Healing Foundation, National Aboriginal Health Organization, Legacy of Hope, and the Manitoba Métis Federation. She also has an interest in Aboriginal language revitalization and spent time in a Michif language immersion course, living with Michif elders in Camperville, Manitoba. She is a member of the Aboriginal Curatorial Collective and of the International Network of Genocide Scholars and a former curator and researcher at the Canadian Museum for Human Rights.

David B. MacDonald is a professor of political science at the University of Guelph, Ontario, and formerly a senior lecturer in political studies at the University of Otago. He has a PhD in international relations from the London School of Economics. His work is focused on comparative Indigenous politics, international relations, and comparative foreign policy. His recent publications include *Identity Politics in the Age of Genocide* (2008), *Thinking History, Fighting Evil* (2009), and articles in *AlterNative*, the *Canadian Journal of Sociology*, the *Canadian Journal of Political Science*, *Journal of Human Rights*, *Third World Quarterly*, *International Politics*, *Raisons Politiques*, and *Journal of Genocide Research*. He also has a coauthored textbook entitled *Introduction to Politics* (2012), as well as three coedited works. He currently holds two SSHRC Grants: principal investigator on a four-year Insight Grant comparing indigenous-settler relations and debates about multiculturalism in Canada and Aotearoa New Zealand, and a co-investigator on a Partnership Develop Grant exploring visual/virtual representations of Canada's Indian Residential Schools. The research for this chapter was funded by a three-year SSHRC Standard Grant.

Benjamin Madley is an assistant professor of history at the University of California, Los Angeles. Educated at Yale and Oxford, he is a historian of Native America, the United States, and genocide in world history. Born in Redding, California, Madley spent much of his childhood in Karuk Country near the Oregon border, where he became interested in the relationship between colonizers and Indigenous peoples. He has written about California and Oregon Indians as well as colonial genocides in Africa, Australia, and Europe, often applying a transnational and comparative approach. His work has appeared in *European History Quarterly*, *Journal of British Studies*, *Journal of Genocide Research*, and *The Western Historical Quarterly* as well as five edited volumes. His first book, *An American Genocide: The California Indian Catastrophe, 1846–1873*, is forthcoming.

Jeremy Patzer (Métis) is a PhD candidate in sociology at Carleton University, Ottawa. His research interests lie in examining the contemporary practices of justice that are meant to resolve those outstanding issues of the past that hold an enormous (yet sometimes unspoken) moral purchase on the legitimacy of the contemporary political landscape. Having concentrated in the past on Aboriginal rights and title jurisprudence, he recently made use of the Joseph-Armand Bombardier CGS Doctoral Scholarship and the CGS Michael Smith Foreign Studies Supplement to take up a research study opportunity with the Department of Sociology and the Atrocity, Suffering, and Human Rights Research Group at the London School of Economics and Political Science.

Julia Peristerakis is a Master of Arts student in the Department of Sociology at Ryerson University. Her research investigates interconnections between the residential school system and the child welfare system in Canada, with a focus on assessing the degree to which post–residential school child welfare and relocation policies threaten the survival of Indigenous communities. She completed her BA in sociology at the University of Winnipeg, where her honors thesis examined sexual violence as a form of genocide.

Christopher Powell is an assistant professor in the Department of Sociology at the University of Manitoba. His recent book, *Barbaric Civilization: A Critical Sociology of Genocide* (2011), examines how Western civilization produces genocidal violence through the normal functioning of its institutions. He is also the author of "What Do Genocides Kill? A Relational Conception of Genocide" (2007), "Genocidal Moralities: A Critique" (in Adam Jones, ed., *New Directions in Genocide Research*, 2011), and "How Epistemology Matters to Public Sociology: Five Positions on Emergence" (*Critical Sociology*, 2012). Powell's work uses relational theory to examine the social distribution of violence, conflicts over ways of knowing, and the prospects for radical social change.

Colin Samson is a professor of sociology and the director of the BA Liberal Arts Program at the University of Essex. He has been working with the Innu of the Labrador-Quebec peninsula since 1994. His associations with them led to his coauthoring the widely cited human rights report *Canada's Tibet: The Killing of the Innu*, which won the Italian PioManzo Peace Prize in 2000. His book *A Way of Life That Does Not Exist: Canada and the Extinguishment of the Innu* won the Pierre Savard Award given by the International Council for Canadian Studies in 2006. His 2013 book *A World You Do Not Know: Settler Societies, Indigenous Peoples and the Attack on Cultural Diversity* examines the effects of willful ignorance in the establishment of settler societies. Samson has also worked in creative partnerships with the filmmaker Sarah Sandring who has made two documentaries about the Innu—*Nutshimit*, 2010, *Nutak*, 2013 for Nirgun Films.

Gray H. Whaley has a PhD in history from the University of Oregon and is an associate professor of history and an advisor for the Native American Studies Minor Field at Southern Illinois University, Carbondale. His research and teaching interests focus on the histories of the United States (West and Pacific Northwest) and American Indians. His first book is *Oregon, Illahee, and the Empire Republic: Colonialism, Race, and Native Sovereignty in Western Oregon, 1792–1859* (2010).

Andrew Woolford is a professor of sociology and the social justice and criminology research coordinator at the University of Manitoba. He is the author of *The Politics of Restorative Justice: A Critical Introduction* (2009) and *Between Justice and Certainty: Treaty-Making in British Columbia* (2005). He is also the coauthor of *Informal Reckonings: Conflict Resolution in Mediation, Restorative Justice and Reparations* (with R. S. Ratner, 2007). His most recent book, *This Benevolent Experiment: Indigenous Boarding Schools, Genocide, and Redress in Canada and the United States* is to be published in 2015. In addition, he is coediting (with Adam Muller and Karen Busby) a volume titled *The Idea of a Human Rights Museum* (2015) as well as a special issue of the *Journal of Genocide Research* on "Genocide in Canada" (coedited with Jeff Benvenuto, 2015).

INDEX

Canadian Museum for Human Rights (CMHR), 154, 156–59, 162
Canadian Museum of Civilization (CMC), 156
Canby, E. R. S., 95, 112–13
capitalism, 49, 62–63, 76–77, 213–14
Captain Jack's father, 105–6
Carolina, 57, 59–61
Cart, Superintendent, 37
Carter, Robert G., 296
cattle farming, 298
Chetco, 136
Chickasaw, 57, 58, 62, 214, 217, 282
child removal: by adoption, 197–202, 316–17; as genocide, 192–93, 309–10; history of, 191–92, 193–96; Indian shame over, 201–2; as liberal ideal, 198–201; in 1960s and 1970s, 189, 190; and percentage of Indigenous children in welfare system, 190–91; of residential schools, 309–13; and U.S. boarding schools, 195–97
Choctaw: changes in population of, 208; history of in Mississippian shatter zone, 57, 61, 62, 212–15; loss of culture within, 208–9; origins of, 215–17; revitalization of, 217–18, 220, 220n5
Chrétien, Jean, 5
churches, 308–9, 315
coalescent societies, 56–57, 59, 217
Collier, John, 195
colonial genocide: attempts to address in Canada, 4–5, 6–7; attempts to address in United States, 4, 7–9, 173; Australian studies on, 11–12; conceptual blockages to, 152–53; examples of, 161–62, 173; included in Canadian narrative, 151–52; and Mississippian shatter zone, 50; seen as ongoing process, 13; set apart from genocide, 10–11
colonial mesh, 31–33, 36, 44
corporations, 258, 263, 264–67, 268
Cosby, J. D., 105, 107–10
creative destruction, 209–10
Cree, 80, 173, 226–27, 240, 283
Creek Confederacy, 57, 59, 214
Crook, George, 111
Crow Plenty-Coups, 301

cultural genocide, 74–75, 219, 220n3, 231–32, 284, 330
culture, destruction of, 79–81, 195–96, 208–9, 314, 315
Culver, Samuel, 139
Curley Headed Jack (Modoc), 114
Curry, George, 138
Custer, George A., 283, 296
Cypress Hills, Saskatchewan, 85, 226–27, 243n2

Dakota Wokiksuye Memorial Ride, 20n3
Davin, Nicholas F., 35–36, 166, 312
Davis, Jefferson, 115, 116
Davis, John, 106, 135
Davis, Mary, 200
decolonization: of Canadian history, 152, 153, 155; and genocide studies, 44, 45n3; and land claims, 246; as ongoing process, 13; and reconciliation, 167; and residential school healing, 178; and self-government, 241
Dewdney, Edgar, 315
discipline, 37–38, 39
disease: effect on Canadian Natives, 227; effect on Choctaw, 212, 214; effect on European-Indigenous relations, 169; effect on natives of U.S. south, 51–52, 57; and genocide, 212, 281–82; and Modocs, 96, 118; and Oregon Indians, 137, 139
donation land laws, 141–42
Dowell, Benjamin, 135–36, 144n18
Drew, Charles S., 135, 140
Durieu, Paul, 38
Dyar, L. S., 113

Ellen's Man George (Modoc), 115
erasure, 149, 160–61
ethnocide, 211–12
ethnogenesis, 74
eugenics programs, 83
Evanoff, Lottie, 146n38

Fanning, William, 99
figurations, 73
Fitzgerald, E. H., 100, 102
folk imperialism: and clashes with federal

authorities, 134–35; conditions for in Oregon, 131–32; and conflict resolution, 133–34; intervention of federal authority in, 140–42; and support for genocide, 135–40, 142–43

Fontaine, Phil, 7

Fontaine, Theodore, 43

forgotten children, 200

Gage, Thomas, 169

gender relations, 81–82, 85

genocide: and belief in white supremacy, 141–42; of buffalo, 295–302, 303n3; Canadian Museum for Human Rights view of, 158–59; the case for in Canada, 75–86, 152–54, 162, 228, 240–41, 248; the case for land dispossession as, 247–48, 280–84; the case for not applying too broadly, 133, 192–93, 275, 284–85, 287, 326; child removal as, 192–93, 309–10; concocting excuses for, 132, 136–37, 139, 140; and critical genocide studies, 326–31; decolonization of, 155; definition of, 2, 9–10, 20n3, 211–12; denial of, 150, 159–61, 162; describing a relational view of, 70–75; evaluating the definition of, 275–80; hidden, 327, 329, 330; and historical trauma, 274–75; imperialist rationale for, 292–93; and inadequate mourning, 285–86; in Mississippian shatter zone, 50, 211, 212–15; and Modocs, 95, 96, 100, 104–6, 107, 109, 114, 117–20; and Oregon folk imperialism, 132, 135–40; and reconciliation, 317–20; and residential schools, 1, 2–3, 80, 159–61, 241–43, 278–79, 285, 306–7, 309–14; and revitalization, 86–87, 218–20, 286–87; role of disease in, 212, 281–82; sanitized as war, 103, 118–19; settler colonial, 152–53, 161–62, 173; studies of, 10–11; and theory of creative destruction, 209–10. *See also* colonial genocide; political genocide

genocide studies imaginary, 327–31

Gillem, Alvan, 114–15

Gone, Joseph, 325–26

Goodhouse, Jeannette, 192

Gover, Kevin, 7

Gradual Civilization Act, 308

Gradual Enfranchisement Act, 172, 308

Grant, Ulysses S., 114, 116, 166

Gregoire, George, 255

grief, 285–87, 300

Gros Ventre, 282–83

Harper, Stephen, 1

Hasluck, Paul, 199

Hirsch, Bertram, 189, 201

historical narratives, 155–57, 159–60, 161–62, 227–28, 306, 317

historical trauma (HT), 274–75, 285–86, 287, 326

Hitchcock, Ethan, 100, 102, 103

Holocaust, 6, 11, 119, 153, 158, 328

Holodomor, 156, 159

Huston, A. C., 40

Iberville, Pierre Le Moyne d', 214

identity, 72–73, 79, 81–82, 149

Idle No More movement, 5, 228, 312, 319

Indian Act (Canada): and residential schools, 313, 314, 315; and social engineering, 172, 174; as tool of political genocide, 229, 231, 236–39

Indian Adoption Project (IAP), 197–98, 199–200

Indian Residential Schools Settlement Agreement (IRSSA), 6, 167, 176, 177, 178

industrial schools, 309

Innu: and draft version of land claim, 253–56; and land claims process, 246, 250–53; politics of, 250–51; relocation of, 77; and social ills, 248–49; and Tshiash Petapen, 253–62, 264–68

Iroquois, 54–55, 61, 183n5

Jackson, James, 111

Johnson, J. Neeley, 108, 109

Johnson, William, 182n4

Jojola, Ted, 38

Judy, Captain, 107

Kaniuekutat, 249

Kershaw, William, 99, 101, 103